Study Guide
David W. Findlay

Macroeconomics

5th edition

Olivier Blanchard

Prentice Hall

Upper Saddle River, New Jersey

Editor-in-Chief: Eric Svendsen
Executive Editor: Chris Rogers
Editorial Project Manager: Susie Abraham
Managing Editor: Judy Leale
Operations Specialist: Arnold Vila

Pearson Education Ltd., London
Pearson Education Singapore, Pte. Ltd
Pearson Education, Canada, Inc.
Pearson Education–Japan
Pearson Education Australia PTY, Limited
Pearson Education North Asia, Ltd., Hong Kong
Pearson Educación de Mexico, S.A. de C.V.
Pearson Education Malaysia, Pte. Ltd
Pearson Education Upper Saddle River, New Jersey

Prentice Hall
is an imprint of

PEARSON

www.pearsonhighered.com

6 7 8 9 10 11 12 V036 12 11

ISBN-13: 978-0-13-207833-7
ISBN-10: 0-13-207833-3

Contents

Preface

This study guide has been developed to accompany *Macroeconomics*, by Olivier Blanchard. My primary objectives in the Study Guide and Tutorial are to help you learn the concepts that are presented in the textbook and to help you obtain a strong understanding of macroeconomics.

Success in your course depends on your ability to explain and apply the concepts presented in class. Specifically, you <u>must</u> be able to explain intuitively the underlying factors that determine the economic relationships included in the models. Simply memorizing the material is most likely an inefficient allocation of your time. You should, therefore, read the material carefully (and several times!), constantly review your lecture notes, and work through the material included in the Study Guide and Tutorial.

I have developed a study guide that gives you an opportunity to work through problems, to reinforce the concepts, and to apply the concepts. I have constructed the questions in such a way as to take you step by step through the models and their applications. The Study Guide and Tutorial includes approximately: 500 self-test questions; 400 review problems (many of which include multiple parts); and 600 multiple choice questions. While time constraints may prevent you from completing all of the questions, you should complete as many as possible.

DESCRIPTION OF CONTENTS

Each chapter of the Study Guide and Tutorial is divided into five sections.

- Objectives, Review, and Tutorial

This section includes a list of the objectives for each chapter. You might want to review this list prior to and/or after reading the chapters in the textbook. The objectives are followed by a summary of the key concepts in each chapter. These discussions will help reinforce the material presented. These sections also include highlighted Learning Tips. I have used the Learning Tips: (1) to emphasize particularly important concepts, (2) to offer an alternative presentation of a concept, and (3) to offer advice about how to study, learn, and apply the material.

- Self-Test Questions

This section includes questions about the basic concepts presented in each chapter. The answers to these questions are found in the corresponding section of each chapter included at the end of each question.

- Review Problems

These problems provide opportunities to practice the skills presented in each chapter. I have included a significant number of numerical problems to give you an opportunity to reinforce (and test) your understanding of the material presented in the textbook. I have also included questions that require you to use the graphs presented in the textbook. It is crucial that you become comfortable with the graphical presentation of the material. These questions will help you achieve this goal.

• Multiple Choice Questions

The multiple choice questions range in level of difficulty. Like the review problems, these questions require numerical and graphical analysis.

• Solutions and Answers

This section (located at the end of the Study Guide and Tutorial) includes the solutions to all problems and answers to all multiple choice questions.

USING THE STUDY GUIDE AND TUTORIAL

There are many ways to study in this course and to use this Study Guide and Tutorial. You should use the one that works best for you. Having noted that, let me offer you one possible approach.

1. After reading the chapter in the textbook and attending class (there are NO perfect substitutes for these activities!), you can review the list of objectives included in the Study Guide and Tutorial. Make sure you completely understand each of them.

2. If, after reviewing your lecture notes, you still are not comfortable with a particular topic, read through the relevant section of the Objectives, Review, and Tutorial section.

3. Now that you are familiar with the material, you can quickly test your understanding of the concepts by answering the Self-Test Questions. I recommend that you jot down your answers to these questions on a separate piece of paper. Check your answers by referring to the relevant section of the chapter (included, for your convenience, at the end of each question). If you cannot answer these questions, you should review the textbook material as soon as possible.

4. The best way to learn the material and reinforce your understanding of the concepts is to work through the review problems. I have included a mix of problems that give you an opportunity to apply the material. After you complete a problem, check your solution with that found in the Solution section. Once again, if you have difficulty with the problem, you should review: (1) the relevant section of the Study Guide and Tutorial, (2) your lecture notes, and (3) the chapter in the textbook.

5. In addition to the review problems, you should work through the multiple choice questions. However, be careful! While several of these questions are relatively easy (asking you, for example, to determine the components of the money supply), other questions will ask you to apply the concepts and conduct your own analysis of an example.

FINAL THOUGHTS AND ADVICE

I have several final suggestions for you. First, when examples are presented in class, make sure you can explain the opposite example (e.g. the output effects of a reduction versus increase in the money supply). Second, you should constantly ask yourself the following types of questions during the course. What does this curve (or equation) represent? Why does it have its particular shape? What causes the curve to shift? What causes the curve's shape/slope to change? If you can answer all of these questions, you will not only completely understand the mechanics of the model, but will also be able to examine the implications of the model.

In short, you should constantly practice your new skills. The more actively you participate in the learning process, the better will be your understanding of the important and exciting material presented in the textbook.

If you have any specific comments or suggestions about the Study Guide and Tutorial, please send them to me at Colby College, Department of Economics, Waterville, ME 04901, or you can send them to me via e-mail: dwfindla@colby.edu.

CHAPTER 1.
A TOUR OF THE WORLD

OBJECTIVES, REVIEW, AND TUTORIAL

After working through the chapter and the following material, you should be able to:

(1) Know the distinction between macroeconomics and microeconomics.

(2) Recognize the need for simplifying assumptions and the use of models in macroeconomics.

(3) Understand why macroeconomists sometimes disagree.

(4) Know the variables economists focus on when examining an economy.

(5) Know the two main issues concerning the United States economy.

(6) Know the two main issues concerning the European Union.

(7) Know the two main issues concerning the Chinese economy.

1. DISTINCTION BETWEEN MACROECONOMICS AND MICROECONOMICS

- Macroeconomics is the study of aggregate economic variables. Examples of aggregate economic variables are:
    (1) aggregate production (aggregate output);
    (2) the average price of all goods and services (the aggregate price level); and
    (3) unemployment rate.

- Microeconomics is the study of production and prices in specific markets.

2. THE SIMPLIFICATION OF MACROECONOMICS

The goal of macroeconomics is to explain the behavior of aggregate variables. To do so, macroeconomists:
(1) make assumptions to simplify the analysis; and
(2) construct simple structures (called models) to examine and interpret the economy.

Learning Tip

As you read through the text, pay particular attention to the assumptions (i.e., simplifications). Make sure you can explain how changes in assumptions can alter the ability of a model to illustrate economic behavior.

3. WHY MACROECONOMISTS DISAGREE

You should be aware that macroeconomists sometimes disagree. This can occur for two reasons.

(1) Different Objectives

Economists will place different weights on different objectives. These different objectives (or goals) include:

(1) to reduce wage inequality;
(2) to maintain (or increase) economic activity;
(3) to reduce the inflation rate; and
(4) to reduce the unemployment rate.

(2) Absence of controlled experiments

Actual economies are highly complex, consisting of many individuals, firms and markets. Because of this, it is difficult for macroeconomists to conduct controlled experiments. These controlled experiments could be used to study, for example, the effects of monetary policy on the economy. As a result, different macroeconomists can look at the same event and reach different conclusions.

4. FOCUS OF MACROECONOMICS

Macroeconomists focus on three measures of an economy:

- Aggregate output and its rate of growth.
- The unemployment rate: the proportion of the labor force that is unemployed.
- The inflation rate: the rate of change in the aggregate price level.

Learning Tip

The above variables can be used to describe several states of the economy.
- The economy is said to be in a recession when aggregate output falls (a decline in output which generally lasts at least two consecutive quarters (i.e., six months)). In the United States, the timing of recessions is determined by the Business Cycle Dating committee of the National Bureau of Economic Research (NBER).
- A period of stagflation occurs when the inflation rate and the unemployment rate are both high.

5. TWO ISSUES CONFRONTING UNITED STATES POLICY MAKERS

- A New Economy? Between 1970 and 1995, productivity growth in the United States was lower than it had been in previous decades. This situation had been described as the productivity slowdown. The increase in productivity growth between 1996 and 2006 caused some to claim that the United States had entered a period of faster technological progress and, hence, a New Economy. While the amount of evidence so far is somewhat limited, there are different views about whether the U.S. economy has entered a period of permanently faster productivity growth.

• Trade deficits. Since the early 1980s, the United States has consistently experienced trade deficits. That is, the United States has bought more goods and services from abroad than it has sold abroad. When a country buys more goods and services from abroad than it sells, its spending exceeds its income. To finance this trade deficit, a country must borrow from the rest of the world. While foreigners have been willing to finance this U.S. borrowing (by buying U.S. bonds and shares of U.S. stock), some are concerned that it cannot occur indefinitely. To reduce U.S. borrowing, some combination of a reduction in the size of the U.S. budget deficit or increase in the private (i.e., household) U.S. saving rate would have to occur.

6. TWO ISSUES CONFRONTING POLICY MAKERS IN THE EUROPEAN UNION

• High unemployment. The relatively high unemployment in Europe has a number of possible explanations ranging from labor market rigidities (e.g. high levels of worker protection) to misguided macroeconomic policy.

• Introduction of common currency. In 1999, the European Union started the process of adopting a common currency, the euro. In 2002, the euro was used as currency in eleven nations (that number as of 2005 is twelve). There are a number of issues surrounding the adoption of the euro:

(1) supporters of it believe it is of significant symbolic importance;
(2) it increases efficiency because of reduced need to convert currencies and because of it eliminates changes in relative prices caused by changes in exchange rates; and
(3) it may impose some costs because all of the nations that have adopted the euro now have a common (i.e., one) monetary policy – a policy set by the European Central bank.

7. ECONOMIC ISSUES CONCERNING CHINA

• Why the attention focused on China? First, a simple comparison of the level of economic activity or the amount of output per person in China with other developed countries suggests that the focus may not be justified. For example, using purchasing power parity numbers, output per person in China in 2006 was about $8,000, approximately one quarter of what it was in the United States. Second, despite these statistics, the Chinese economy has experienced tremendous growth for more than two decades.

• What are the sources of the high Chinese growth rates?. There have been two causes of this growth. First, there has been a high accumulation of capital. The investment rate in China (i.e., the ratio of investment to output) is between 40% and 45% of output. By comparison, the investment rate in the United States is approximately 17%. Second, China has experienced fast technological progress. For example, the Chinese government has encouraged foreign firms to move to China and to encourage joint ventures between Chinese firms and foreign firms. These developments have led to increases in technological progress.

Learning Tip

The issues confronting the United States, the European Union, and China have a number of possible explanations/interpretations. Not surprisingly, macroeconomists and policy makers differ on what policies should be implemented to address each issue. As you read through the text, think about these issues (and other issues) and about the policies that could be implemented. By thinking about such issues, you will apply the concepts learned in your course and will, therefore, assume a more active role in the learning process. As a result, you will increase your understanding of macroeconomics and of macroeconomic policy.

REVIEW PROBLEMS

1. Define macroeconomics.

2. Provide a list of six variables you think would be studied in a macroeconomics course.

3. Briefly explain why it is difficult for macroeconomists to conduct controlled experiments.

4. Why is the unemployment rate relatively high in Europe?

5. What are the benefits of a common currency for the twelve Euro-countries?

6. Why are individuals concerned about the persistent trade deficits in the United States?

7. What are some of the sources of economic growth in China?

MULTIPLE CHOICE QUESTIONS

1. Which of the following economic variables would most likely be studied in microeconomics?

a. the unemployment rate
b. automobile production
c. aggregate output
d. the aggregate price level

2. Which of the following economic variables would most likely be studied in macroeconomics?

a. the price of personal computers
b. the production of macroeconomic textbooks
c. aggregate output
d. the price of college tuition

3. Based on your understanding of the chapter, macroeconomists sometimes disagree because:

a. they dislike each other
b. they assign different weights to different objectives
c. they cannot conduct controlled experiments
d. both b and c
e. none of the above

4. The average (annual) output growth rate in the United States between 1960 and 1970 was:

a. higher than the average output growth rate in the United States between 1970 and 1996
b. lower than the average output growth rate in the United States between 1970 and 1996
c. the same as the average output growth rate in the United States between 1970 and 1996
d. none of the above

5. A comparison of the unemployment rates in the United States and in the European Union between 1970 and 2006 suggests that:

a. they are generally the same
b. the United States unemployment rate has been higher since the early 1980s
c. prior to the early 1980's, the unemployment rate in the United States was lower
d. the unemployment rate in the European Union since the early 1980s has exceeded the unemployment rate in the United States

6. Stagflation is a situation that occurs when:

a. the unemployment rate is high and the inflation rate is low
b. the unemployment rate and the inflation rate are both high
c. the unemployment rate and the inflation rate are both low
d. the unemployment rate is low and the inflation rate is high
e. aggregate output declines for two consecutive quarters

7. Which of the following is NOT viewed as a possible cause of the rapid economic growth in China?

a. accumulation of capital
b. technological progress
c. large Chinese trade deficits
d. joint ventures between Chinese and foreign firms

8. The level of Chinese output on a per person basis using purchasing power parity measures indicates that output per person in China is approximately equal to what percentage of U.S. output per person?

a. 10%
b. 20%
c. 50%
d. 90%

CHAPTER 2.
A TOUR OF THE BOOK

OBJECTIVES, REVIEW, AND TUTORIAL

After working through the chapter and the following material, you should be able to:

(1) Define gross domestic product (GDP).

(2) Understand the three different approaches to measuring GDP.

(3) Know the distinction between nominal GDP and real GDP.

(4) Understand what role hedonic pricing plays in the construction of estimates of real GDP.

(5) Know the definition and construction of the unemployment rate (u).

(6) Explain the definition and construction of the GDP deflator and the consumer price index.

(7) Discuss why economists care about the unemployment rate and the inflation rate.

(8) Recognize what role demand and supply factors play in affecting output in the: (1) short run; (2) medium run; and (3) long run.

(9) Understand the construction of real GDP and chain-type indexes.

1. DEFINITION AND MEASUREMENT OF GROSS DOMESTIC PRODUCT (GDP)

GDP is the value of the final goods and services produced in the economy during a given period. There are three approaches to measuring GDP. You should understand that all three will yield the same value of GDP.

- Approach 1: GDP is the sum of the value of the final goods and services produced in a given period. In the example found in Chapter 2, cars represented the only final good or service. The $210 of revenues from car sales represents GDP.

- Approach 2: GDP is the sum of value added in the economy. The value added of a certain stage of the production of a good is defined as the value of its product minus the value of the intermediate inputs (excluding labor) used in the production process.

- Approach 3: GDP is equal to the sum of incomes in the economy during a given period. To see why this is so, you must understand that the value of a firm's production and the value of its intermediate inputs must go towards:
  (1) workers as income (labor income)
  (2) the government in the form of indirect taxes (e.g. sales taxes)
  (3) the rent to the firm as capital income (profit).

In the example in Chapter 2, there are no indirect taxes; therefore, GDP is equal to the sum of labor income and firm profits.

Learning Tip

If we simply added the value of all goods and services (both intermediate and final) exchanged in an economy during a given period, we would overestimate the value of GDP for two reasons:
(1) Some of the transactions that occur in year t represent the value of intermediate goods. If we added, for example, both the value of a new 2005 Ford Mustang and the value of the Goodyear tires Ford purchased from Goodyear, we would "double count" the value of the tires; and
(2) Some final goods sold in 2005 were produced in a previous period and, therefore, were already included in the previous period's measure of GDP (e.g. the sale of a used car, used personal computer, ... etc.).

2. NOMINAL AND REAL GDP

(1) Nominal GDP

Nominal GDP in year t ($\$Y_t$) is the sum of the quantities of final goods and services produced in year t times their current prices. $\$Y_t$ measures the value of GDP in year t at year t prices. Nominal GDP is also called GDP in current dollars and dollar GDP.

Learning Tip

Be careful when interpreting changes in nominal GDP (or changes in the value of any variable measured in nominal terms, that is, measured in current dollars). Suppose $\$Y_t$ increases by 6% in 2005 (above its 2004 level). This increase in $\$Y_t$ can occur for two reasons:

(1) The actual amount of final goods and services produced can increase; and/or
(2) The prices of these final goods and services can increase.

(2) Real GDP

Real GDP in year t (Y_t) is the sum of the quantities of goods and services produced in year t times the prices of the same goods and services in some particular year. This "particular year" is called the base year. To calculate Y_t, we must first choose a base year. Once chosen (say, 2000), Real GDP in any year is the value of that year's final goods and services measured at 2000 prices. Real GDP is also called GDP in terms of goods, GDP in constant dollars, GDP adjusted for inflation, and GDP in 2000 dollars.

Learning Tip

Economists focus on real GDP since it eliminates the effects of changing prices on the measure of output. For example, if real GDP in 2005 (measured at 2000 prices) increased by 3% over the level of real GDP in 2004, we know that total output increased. When we receive information about nominal GDP, we do not know whether nominal GDP is changing because of changes in the amount of goods and services produced or because of changes in prices.

Economists use real GDP (Y_t) to calculate GDP growth in year t.

- GDP growth in year t is defined as $(Y_t - Y_{t-1})/Y_{t-1}$. This measures the percent change in real GDP between years t and t-1.

- Expansions are periods of positive GDP growth.

- Recessions are periods of two or more consecutive quarters of negative GDP growth. In the United States, the timing of recessions is determined by the Business Cycle Dating committee of the National Bureau of Economic Research (NBER).

3. TECHNOLOGICAL PROGRESS AND HEDONIC PRICING

Two developments in an economy complicate the calculation of GDP:

(1) the emergence of new goods; and
(2) goods (e.g. personal computers) whose characteristics change from year to year.

When the characteristics of a good changes from year to year, the price of that good might change to reflect these changes in characteristics. Economists will use an approach (called hedonic pricing) to adjust actual prices to changes in the products' characteristics.

Learning Tip

- You should review the discussion of hedonic pricing in Chapter 2.
- Review problem #7 will also focus on hedonic pricing.

4. DEFINITION AND CONSTRUCTION OF THE UNEMPLOYMENT RATE (u_t)

The unemployment rate represents the percent of the labor force that is unemployed. Specifically, $u_t = U/L$ where

- U is the number of individuals unemployed;
- L is the number of individuals in the labor force;
- L is equal to the number of individuals unemployed plus the number of individuals employed (N); and
- Therefore, L = U + N.

To be counted as unemployed, an individual:
(1) must not have a job; AND
(2) must have been looking for work in the past four weeks.

Learning Tip

You must understand that to be part of the labor force, an individual must either be: (1) employed; or (2) unemployed and actively searching for a job. Unemployed individuals who stop searching will no longer be counted as part of the labor force. These individuals are called discouraged workers. The exit or entry of discouraged workers from or into the labor force can cause the unemployment rate to change without any change in the number of employed workers. Review problem #8 will focus on this.

The participation rate is defined as the ratio of the labor force to the working age population. A high unemployment rate is typically associated with a low participation rate. Why? Because a larger number of unemployed individuals will drop out of the labor force (i.e., become discouraged workers) when the unemployment rate is high.

5. PRICE INDEXES: THE GDP DEFLATOR AND THE CONSUMER PRICE INDEX (CPI)

The GDP deflator in year t (P_t) is defined as the ratio of nominal GDP to real GDP in year t: $P_t = \$Y_t/Y_t$. The GDP deflator gives the average price of all goods and services included in GDP.

Learning Tip

- $P_t = 1$ in the base year. Why? In the base year (say, 2000), $\$Y_{00} = Y_{00}$. In other words, in the base year, the real and nominal value of GDP will be the same since, when obtaining real GDP, we will use the current prices to calculate this inflation-adjusted measure of output. Review problems #1 and #2 will allow you to verify this.
- How do you interpret the size of P_t? Suppose $P_t = 1.37$. This suggests that the average price of goods and services in year t is 37% higher than in the base year.
- We can rearrange the definition of P_t to illustrate why changes in nominal GDP can occur for two reasons. Multiply both sides by Y_t so that $\$Y_t = P_tY_t$. An increase in P_t and/or an increase in Y_t will cause increases in $\$Y_t$.

The Consumer Price Index (CPI) measures the price of a given "basket" of goods and services consumed by households. The current basket of goods and services is based on 1982-84 spending behavior; therefore, 1982-84 represents the base period.

Learning Tip

- Suppose the CPI in 2005 equals 1.97. This suggests that the average price of goods and services in 2005 is 97% higher than the average price of the same basket of goods and services in the base period (i.e., 1982-84).
- Be aware that, while both the GDP deflator and the CPI are price indexes and generally move together over time, there can be periods when the change in the CPI is different from the change in the GDP deflator. This is because:

  (1) The CPI includes the price of some goods NOT included in GDP and, therefore, not taken into account in the GDP deflator (e.g. the price of imported goods).

  (2) The GDP deflator includes the price of all final goods and services produced in the economy. Some of these goods are NOT consumed by households and, therefore, not included in the CPI (e.g. some expenditures by the government and by firms).

The GDP deflator and the CPI can be used to calculate the inflation rate. The inflation rate between year t and t-1 (using the GDP deflator) equals $(P_t - P_{t-1})/P_{t-1}$.

Learning Tip

Be careful when interpreting price indexes and the rate of inflation. If the CPI in 2005 equals 1.97, this does NOT mean that there has been a 97% ANNUAL rate of inflation between the 1982-84 and 2005 periods. This number DOES indicate that the average price of the basket of goods and services has increased 97% over the ENTIRE period. The inflation rate almost always is calculated on an annual basis indicating, for example, the percent change in the average price level from one year to the next.

6. WHY DO WE STUDY INFLATION AND UNEMPLOYMENT?

We study the unemployment rate because:

(1) The unemployment rate tells us something about the current state of the economy relative to some normal level (when the unemployment rate increases, GDP growth tends to fall); and
(2) The unemployment rate tells us something about the possible effects on the well being of the unemployed.

We study inflation because:

(1) Inflation can affect the distribution of income (e.g. an increase in inflation can cause a reduction in the real value of the income of individuals who receive fixed, nominal incomes);
(2) Inflation can cause changes in relative prices and, therefore, cause distortions;
(3) If tax brackets are not adjusted for inflation, inflation can cause distortions by moving individuals into higher tax brackets; and
(4) As a result of (2) and (3), inflation can cause uncertainty. This increased uncertainty can have negative effects on economic activity.

7. DETERMINANTS OF CHANGES IN OUTPUT

- Over short periods of time (i.e., the short run), changes in output depend primarily on changes in the demand for goods and services.

- Over long periods of time (i.e., the long run), changes in output depend on supply factors such as the capital stock, the size and skills of the labor force, and technology.

- For periods of time in between the short run and long run (i.e., the medium run), both demand and supply factors cause changes in output.

8. CONSTRUCTION OF REAL GDP AND CHAIN-TYPE INDEXES

The construction of real GDP described above uses the same set of prices for a particular year; this year is called the base year. There are several concerns associated with using such an approach to calculating real GDP:

(1) the choice of a particular base year fixes the weights (i.e., prices) associated with each good (and service), we know that relative prices change over time;
(2) because relative prices change over time, the calculated rates of growth of real GDP will depend on the base year chosen; and
(3) when the base year is changed, the calculated rates of growth of real GDP will change.

To avoid these problems, economists now use chain-type indexes to calculate rates of growth in real GDP. This involves several steps:

• The rate of growth of real GDP between 2005 and 2004 is based on using the average of prices in 2004 and 2005. The rate of growth of real GDP between 2006 and 2005 would be based on using the average of prices in 2006 and 2005.

• An index of real GDP is obtained by linking/chaining the calculated rates of change for each year.

• The index is set equal to one in some arbitrary year (say, 2000).

• By multiplying this index by nominal GDP in 2000 (the year in which the index equals 1), we can obtain a measure of real GDP in chained, 2000 dollars.

Learning Tip

Some instructors will emphasize the material contained in Appendix 1 of the text. I have included a short review of the material in Appendix 1 in the next section. This review contains a summary of this material and some questions. You should look at this material and work through the problems if you cover this in your course.

SELF-TEST QUESTIONS

1. Define Gross Domestic Product (1).

2. Explain the difference between nominal GDP and real GDP (1).

3. Why is hedonic pricing used when calculating GDP? Explain (1).

4. What does the unemployment rate measure, and briefly explain how it is calculated (2)?

5. What is the GDP deflator, and how is it calculated (2)?

6. What is the consumer price index (CPI), and how is it calculated (2)?

7. Why should we be concerned about an <u>increase</u> in the unemployment rate? Briefly explain (2).

8. Increases in the rate of inflation can have a number of negative effects on the economy. Briefly explain two (2) of them (2).

9. How is real GDP calculated using chain-type indexes (1)?

REVIEW PROBLEMS

1. Consider an imaginary economy that produces only three goods - steaks, eggs and wine. Information on the quantities and prices of each good sold for two years is given below.

	1995	2005
Output		
Steak (pounds)	10	7
Eggs (dozens)	10	13
Wine (bottles)	8	11
Price		
Steak (per pound)	\$2.80	\$3.10
Eggs (per dozen)	\$.70	\$.85
Wine (per bottle)	\$4.00	\$4.50

For this hypothetical economy, calculate each of the following for both years:

a. nominal GDP
b. real GDP in constant 1995 dollars (i.e., 1995 is the base year)
c. GDP deflator
d. the percentage change in real GDP and the GDP deflator between 1995 and 2005.

2. Based on your analysis in #1, was nominal GDP in 1995 greater than, less than, or equal to real GDP in 1995? If the values for nominal and real GDP in 1995 are different, explain why this is so.

3. Suppose you are provided with the following information about an economy that consists of just three firms.

STEEL COMPANY

Revenues from sales		\$400
Expenses (wages)		\$340
Profits		\$60

LOBSTER COMPANY

Revenues from sales		\$200
Expenses (wages)		\$160
Profits		\$40

CAR COMPANY

Revenues from sales		\$1000
Expenses		
wages	\$500	
steel purchases		\$400
Profits		\$100

a. Using the final goods approach, what is GDP?
b. Calculate the value added for each of the three firms. Based on your calculations, what is GDP using the value added approach?
c. What are the total wages (i.e., labor income) in this economy? What are total profits in this economy? Given your calculations and using the incomes approach, what is GDP?
d. Compare the levels of GDP obtained in parts (a), (b) and (c). Which of these approaches yields the highest and smallest level of GDP? Explain.
e. Based on your analysis, what percentage of GDP is allocated to: (1) labor income; and (2) profits?

4. Suppose nominal GDP in 2005 increased by 7% (over its level in 2004). Based on this information, what happened to the rate of inflation (as measured by the GDP deflator) and real GDP growth between 2005 and 2004? Explain.

5. Use the information provided below to answer the following questions.

Year	Nominal GDP (billions of dollars)	GDP Deflator (1987 = 1.0)	Real GDP (in 1987 dollars)
1984	3777.2	.91	
1985		.94	4296.5
1986	4268.6	.969	
1987	4539.9	1.00	
1988	4900.4	1.039	
1989	5250.8	1.085	
1990	5546.1	1.133	
1991	5724.8	1.176	
1992	6020.2		4979.5
1993	6343.3	1.235	

Source: *Survey of Current Business*, September, 1994.

a. What was nominal GDP in 1985? What was the GDP deflator in 1992?
b. Using the GDP deflator (where 1987 = 1), calculate real GDP for the remaining years. In what years, if any, did real GDP fall? If reductions in real GDP did occur, what does this tell us about the level of economic activity during those years?
c. Based on your calculations in part (b), compare the levels of real GDP with the levels of nominal GDP for each year. What does this comparison suggest about prices (in that year relative to 1987)?
d. Explain why economists focus on real rather than nominal GDP when analyzing the level of economic activity.

6. Briefly explain how nominal GDP can increase and real GDP can decrease during the same period.

7. Suppose an economy produces only three goods: potatoes, automobiles, and personal computers. Further suppose that over the past 10 years, the actual price of potatoes increased by 20%, the actual price of automobiles increased by 50%, and the actual price of personal computers did not change. If a hedonic price index were calculated for each of the three goods over this period, how would the hedonic pricing affect the change in the good's price during the period (when compared to the change in the actual price, would it be higher, lower, or the same)? Explain.

8. Suppose you are provided with the following information about an economy. There are 100 million working age individuals in the economy. Of these 100 million, 50 million are currently working, 10 million are looking for work, 10 million stopped looking for work 2 months ago, and the remaining 30 million do not want to work.

a. Calculate the number of unemployed individuals, the size of the labor force, the unemployment rate, and the participation rate.
b. Now suppose that of the 10 million individuals looking for work, 5 million stop looking for work. Given this change, calculate what will happen to the size of the labor force, the unemployment rate, and the participation rate. Did the unemployment rate and participation rate move in the same direction? Explain.
c. Use the original numbers to answer part (c). Suppose firms experience an increase in the demand for their products and they respond by increasing employment. Specifically, 2 million of the previously unemployed individuals now have jobs. Given this change, calculate what will happen to the size of the labor force, the unemployment rate, and the participation rate.
d. If discouraged workers were officially counted as unemployed, explain what would happen to: (1) the size of the labor force; (2) the number of employed individuals; (3) the number of unemployed individuals; (4) the unemployment rate; and (5) the participation rate.

MULTIPLE CHOICE QUESTIONS

1. Suppose nominal GDP decreased during a given year. Based on this information, it is always true that:

a. real GDP fell during the year
b. the GDP deflator fell during the year
c. real GDP and/or the GDP deflator fell during the year
d. both real GDP and the GDP deflator fell during the year

2. Suppose <u>nominal</u> GDP increased by 5% in 2006 (over its previous level in 2005). Given this information, we know with certainty that:

a. the aggregate price level (i.e., the GDP deflator) increased in 2006
b. real GDP increased in 2006
c. both the aggregate price level and real GDP increased in 2006
d. more information is needed to answer this question

3. Suppose nominal GDP in 1990 was <u>less</u> than real GDP in 1990. Given this information, we know with certainty that:

a. the price level (i.e., the GDP deflator) in 1990 was greater than the price level in the base year
b. the price level in 1990 was less than the price level in the base year
c. real GDP in 1990 was less than real GDP in the base year
d. real GDP in 1990 was greater than real GDP in the base year

Use the information provided below to answer questions 4, 5, and 6. Suppose this economy consists of just three firms.

STEEL COMPANY

Revenues from sales	$600
Expenses (wages)	$440
Profits	$160

POTATO COMPANY

Revenues from sales	$400
Expenses (wages)	$260
Profits	$140

CAR COMPANY

Revenues from sales		$2000
Expenses		
wages	$1200	
steel purchases		$600
Profits		$200

4. The value added created by the car company is:

a. $1400
b. $200
c. $800
d. $1200

5. The value added created by the potato company is:

a. $140
b. $260
c. $400
d. $120

6. GDP for this economy is:

a. $3000
b. $500
c. $2400
d. $2000

7. Hedonic pricing is used:

a. to convert nominal values to real values
b. to calculate the difference between nominal GDP and real GDP
c. to measure the rate of change in the GDP deflator
d. to adjust the price of goods for changes in their characteristics

Use the information provided below to answer questions 8 - 11. Suppose you are provided with the following information about an economy. There are 200 million working age individuals in the economy. Of these 200 million, 100 million are currently working, 20 million are looking for work, 20 million stopped looking for work 2 months ago, and the remaining 60 million do not want to work.

8. The size of the labor force for this economy is:

a. 200 million individuals
b. 100 million individuals
c. 120 million individuals
d. 140 million individuals

9. Given the current definitions used to classify the labor force in the United States, the number of unemployed individuals in this economy is:

a. 20 million individuals
b. 40 million individuals
c. 60 million individuals
d. 100 million individuals

10. Given the current definitions used to classify the labor force in the United States, the unemployment rate is:

a. 10%
b. 16.7%
c. 20%
d. 14.3%

11. Given the current definitions used to classify the labor force in the United States, the labor force participation rate in this economy is:

a. 86%
b. 83%
c. 70%
d. 60%

12. Suppose a recent report indicates that the number of individuals who fall into the "discouraged worker" category has increased. Based on the definitions used to determine the size and composition of the labor force and assuming that all other factors are constant, this report would indicate that:

a. the number of employed individuals has fallen
b. the unemployment rate has decreased
c. the percent of the labor force that is unemployed has increased
d. the number of unemployed individuals has increased

13. Given the current definitions used to classify the labor force in the United States, which of the following individuals would be considered to be unemployed:

a. an individual who does not have a job and stopped searching for work 6 weeks ago
b. an individual who does not have a job and stopped searching for work 5 weeks ago
c. an individual who has a job but is working less than 40 hours a week (i.e., part-time)
d. an individual who does not have a job and is currently searching for work
e. an individual who does not have a job and never searches for a job

14. Suppose the GDP deflator in year t equals 1.2 and equals 1.35 in year t+1. The rate of inflation between year t and year t+1 is:

a. .15%
b. 15%
c. 12.5%
d. 1.125%

15. Prices for which of the following are included in the GDP deflator, but not included in the Consumer Price Index?

a. intermediate goods and services
b. firms' purchases of new plants and machinery
c. imports
d. consumption goods and services

16. In the medium run, changes in GDP are caused by changes in:

a. demand factors
b. supply factors
c. demand and supply factors
d. only monetary policy

17. The calculated rate of growth of real GDP between the years 2001 and 2002 will be based on which of the following years using the current methodology (i.e., chain-type indexes)?

a. the average of prices in 2001 and 2002
b. the prices in the base year, 1992
c. the average of prices in 2002 and 2003
d. prices in 2002

APPENDIX 1.
AN INTRODUCTION TO NATIONAL INCOME AND PRODUCT ACCOUNTS

OBJECTIVES, REVIEW, AND TUTORIAL

Some instructors spend a considerable amount of time on the material included in this appendix. If your instructor emphasizes this material, you should review the material included below (even if this material is not emphasized, you should review it!). After working through this appendix (and taking notes!) and the following material, you should be able to:

(1) Recognize that there is an income side and product side to the National Income and Product Accounts.

(2) Know the distinction between gross domestic product (GDP) and gross national product (GNP).

(3) Understand the components of national income.

(4) Understand the relation among national income, personal income and disposable personal income.

(5) Know the components of gross domestic product based on the product side of the national accounts.

(6) Recognize that we need to be careful when interpreting gross domestic product as a measure of economic activity and when examining the components of gross domestic product.

1. THE INCOME AND PRODUCT ACCOUNTS

- The income side of the national accounts illustrates the relationship among GDP, GNP, national income, personal income, and personal disposable income.

- The product side of the national accounts focuses on the goods and services bought by households, firms, and governments (at all levels). The product side shows that GDP equals the sum of consumption, government purchases, investment, net exports, and changes in business inventories.

2. THE RELATIONSHIP BETWEEN GDP AND GNP

- GDP is the market value of all final goods and services produced by factors of production (i.e., labor, capital, etc.) located within the United States

- GNP is the market value of all final goods and services produced by factors of production supplied by United States residents.

- Receipts of factor income from the rest of the world represent income from United States capital or United States residents abroad.

- Payments of factor income to the rest of the world represent income received by foreign capital or foreign labor in the United States

Learning Tip

To understand the difference between GDP and GNP, recall that GDP is the value of the final goods and services produced by labor and other inputs located in the United States Some of the labor and other inputs located in the United States is supplied by foreign residents. At the same time, some of the labor and capital outside the United States is supplied by United States residents. To obtain GNP, we:

(1) first add to GDP receipts of factor income from the rest of the world and then

(2) subtract from GDP payments of factor income to the rest of the world.

This leaves us with GNP.

3. COMPONENTS OF NATIONAL INCOME

National income equals the sum of the following types of income:

- Compensation of employees: wages, salaries, and other adjustments

- Corporate profits

- Net interest: net interest paid by firms and net interest paid by the rest of the world

- Proprietors' income: income of individuals who are self-employed

- Rental income: actual rents plus imputed rents on homes and apartments that are owner-occupied

4. NATIONAL INCOME, PERSONAL INCOME, AND PERSONAL DISPOSABLE INCOME

Not all of national income goes to households. To go from national income to personal income, we must:

- subtract corporate profits
- add back that portion of corporate profits which individuals receive as personal dividend income
- subtract all net interest payments by firms
- add back the net interest payments by firms that households receive
- add transfers.

Personal income is income actually received by households. To obtain personal disposable income, we must:

- subtract from personal income personal taxes and non-tax payments.

Personal disposable income represents income that is available to households after taxes.

5. THE PRODUCT SIDE VIEW OF GDP

To understand this view of GDP, simply think about the final goods and services bought by households, government, and firms.

- Personal consumption expenditures (consumption) equals the sum of goods and services bought by persons resident in the United States and includes the purchase of:

  (1) durable goods;
  (2) nondurable goods; and
  (3) services.

- Gross private domestic fixed investment (investment) is the sum of nonresidential investment (new plants, equipment, and machinery) and residential investment (the purchase of new homes or apartments by persons).

- Government purchases equal (at the federal, state, and local levels) the purchase of goods and services by governments plus the compensation of government employees.

Learning Tip

- Why include compensation of government employees? You should view the employees as selling their labor services to the government.
- Government purchases do NOT include transfer payments or interest payments on the debt.

- Net exports (the trade balance) equals exports minus imports where:

  (1) Exports equal the foreign purchase of United States goods; and
  (2) Imports equal United States residents' purchase of foreign goods.

- Changes in business inventories equal the change in the physical volume of inventories held by businesses. It also equals production minus sales and, therefore, can be positive, negative, or zero.

6. WARNINGS

- GDP and GNP are not perfect measures of aggregate economic activity. Why? Some economic activity (e.g. household chores done in the home by the homeowner) occurs outside formal markets and, therefore, is excluded from both GDP and GNP.

- The classification of some expenditures seems inconsistent. For example,

  (1) The purchase of new machinery by firms (which will produce goods in the future) is investment while the purchase of education (which will allow the individual to produce goods and services in the future) is viewed as consumption; and

  (2) The purchase of a new home or apartment is investment while housing services are included in consumption.

REVIEW PROBLEMS

1. Define gross national product (GNP).

2. Based on the product side view of the national income accounts, what are the components of GDP?

3. Give two reasons why national income does not equal personal income.

4. Why is personal disposable income less than personal income?

5. What are the two components of gross private domestic investment?

6. What are the three components of consumption?

7. Can net exports be negative? If so, briefly explain.

8. a. In a given year, is it possible for a country's GNP to be greater than the country's GDP? If so, briefly explain.
b. In a given year, is it possible for a country's GNP to be less than the country's GDP? If so, briefly explain.

MULTIPLE CHOICE QUESTIONS

1. If GNP exceeds GDP, we know with certainty that:

a. a budget deficit exists
b. a trade deficit exists
c. receipts of factor income from the rest of the world exceed payments of factor income to the rest of the world
d. receipts of factor income from the rest of the world are less than payments of factor income to the rest of the world

2. Net national product (NNP) is equal to:

a. GDP minus consumption of fixed capital
b. GNP minus consumption of fixed capital
c. personal disposable income plus net interest payments
d. personal income plus net interest payments

3. Which of the following is NOT a component of national income?

a. wages and salaries
b. corporate profits
c. rental income
d. indirect taxes

4. Which of the following is NOT a component of consumption?

a. purchase of a new home
b. durable goods
c. housing services
d. education services

5. Which of the following activities would NOT be included in the official measure of GDP?

a. the purchase of a new home
b. a firm's purchase of a new plant
c. a firm's purchase of a new machine
d. wages and salaries received by government employees
e. government purchases at the state and local level
f. the purchase of intermediate goods

6. Changes in business inventories will be positive when:

a. production exceeds sales
b. production is less than sales
c. production is equal to sales
d. a budget deficit exists
e. a trade deficit exists

7. Which of the following is NOT a component of investment?

a. education expenses
b. a firm's purchase of a new plant
c. a firm's purchase of a new machine
d. the purchase of a new home

8. If imports exceed exports, we know with certainty that:

a. GNP exceeds GDP
b. GDP exceeds GNP
c. a budget deficit exists
d. a trade deficit exists

CHAPTER 3.
THE GOODS MARKET

OBJECTIVES, REVIEW, AND TUTORIAL

After working through the chapter and the following material, you should be able to:

(1) Understand the interaction among demand, aggregate production and income.

(2) Become familiar with the composition of GDP and with the relative size of each of its components.

(3) Know the distinction between endogenous and exogenous variables.

(4) Understand the characteristics of the consumption function.

(5) Discuss and explain what is meant by equilibrium output.

(6) Know the difference between autonomous spending and the other components of spending that depend on income.

(7) Recognize that models have three equations: (1) behavioral equations; (2) equilibrium conditions; and (3) identities.

(8) Graphically illustrate and explain the effects of changes in autonomous spending on demand and on equilibrium output.

(9) Discuss and explain the multiplier.

(10) Explain the relationship between investment and the sum of private and public saving.

(11) Explain what is meant by the paradox of saving.

1. INTERACTION AMONG AGGREGATE PRODUCTION, INCOME, AND DEMAND

To understand the interaction among aggregate production, income, and demand, think about the following scenario: suppose the economy is in equilibrium (i.e., a situation where there is no pressure for output to change). Now assume that some event occurs that causes an increase in the demand for goods at each level of output (e.g. an increase in government spending).

• Firms respond to this increase in demand by increasing production. As we observed in Chapter 2, income equals production.

• This increase in income will cause a second increase in demand as households increase their purchase of goods and services (i.e., as consumption increases).

• Firms will respond to this second increase in demand by producing even more goods and services.

• This process continues until a new equilibrium output level is achieved.

2. COMPONENTS OF GDP

Three different agents exist in the economy: households (both domestic and foreign), firms, and governments (at all levels). To understand the components of GDP, think about the expenditures of these three groups.

- Consumption (C)

Households buy goods and services. The purchase of these goods by households represents consumption (C). Consumption also happens to represent the largest component of GDP. Note: some of the goods and services bought by households represent foreign goods.

- Investment (I)

Investment represents the purchase of new plants and equipment by firms (nonresidential investment) and the purchase of new homes and apartments by households (residential investment). The sum of residential and nonresidential investment is called fixed investment (I).

> **Learning Tip**
>
> Be careful when referring to investment. From this point on, investment will refer to the sum of residential and nonresidential investment. Investment does <u>not</u> refer to the purchase of stocks or bonds or to the amount of funds a student has in his or her savings account, for example.

- Government spending (G)

Government spending (G) represents the purchase of goods and services by governments at the federal, state and local levels.

> **Learning Tip**
>
> G does <u>not</u> include transfer payments such as social security payments or unemployment compensation.

- Net Exports (X - IM)

Some of the goods and services bought by households, firms, and governments may be foreign goods. These purchases of foreign goods and services represent imports (IM). Some of the goods and services produced in the country are sold to foreign households, firms, and governments (can you think of relevant examples?). The sale of domestically produced goods and services to foreign agents represents exports (X). The difference between X and IM represents net exports; net exports are also often called the trade balance. If $X > IM$, a trade surplus exists. If $IM > X$, a trade deficit exists.

- Inventory Investment (I_S)

Inventory investment (I_S) is the difference between production and sales. I_S, therefore, can be positive, negative, or zero. For example, if production exceeds sales, I_S is positive and firms' inventories of goods must be rising. While these goods are not purchased during the current period, they have obviously been produced and, therefore, should be included in our measure of economic activity (i.e., GDP).

3. DISTINCTION BETWEEN EXOGENOUS AND ENDOGENOUS VARIABLES

An endogenous variable is a variable that is determined within (or by) the model. In Chapter 3, output (Y) is an endogenous variable. An exogenous variable is a variable we take as given (i.e., determined outside the model). Changes in exogenous variables (e.g. changes in consumer confidence) will cause changes in endogenous variables (e.g. C and Y). Changes in endogenous variables, however, will not cause changes in exogenous variables.

4a. THE CONSUMPTION FUNCTION

We assume that consumption is an increasing function of disposable income (Y_D). That is, increases in disposable income will cause increases in consumption. C is represented by the following behavioral equation:

$C = c_0 + c_1 Y_D$ where c_0 and c_1 are both parameters.

c_1 represents the effect of a given change in disposable income on consumption. For example, if $c_1 = .85$, a \$1 increase in disposable income will cause an 85-cent increase in consumption [Question: What happens to the remaining 15-cent increase in disposable income? We answer this below in part 4b]. c_1 is referred to as the marginal propensity to consume and equals $\Delta C/\Delta Y_D$ where ΔC and ΔY_D represent the change in consumption and the change in disposable income (Δ is read as "change in"). Since $Y_D = C + S$, any change in disposable income is divided between consumption and saving. Hence, c_1 will be greater than 0 and less than 1.

c_0 represents the level of consumption which occurs when $Y_D = 0$. How can there be positive consumption when $Y_D = 0$? This will occur via dissaving (individuals will either drawn down their assets or borrow). c_0 can also be referred to as autonomous consumption, that portion of consumption that is independent of income.

Graphically, we have:

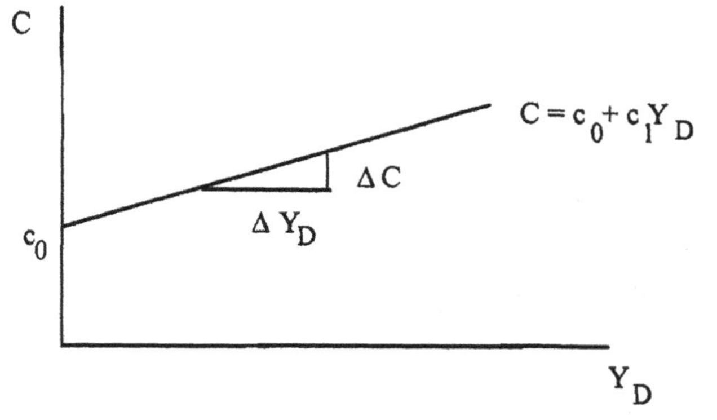

Learning Tip
• If c_0 increases (due to, for example, an increase in consumer confidence), the consumption function will shift up by the change in c_0 (note: the slope does not change when c_0 changes).

- If c_1 increases, the consumption function becomes steeper. What is the intuition behind this result? Any given increase in Y_D now would cause an even greater increase in consumption - this is represented by a steeper consumption function.
- Any change in Y_D will cause movements along the consumption function. Y_D (i.e., $Y_D = Y - T$) will increase when total income (Y) increases and/or taxes (T) fall.
- Given the definition for disposable income, the consumption function can be rewritten as $C = c_0 + c_1[Y - T]$.

4b. THE SAVING FUNCTION

The saving and consumption functions are closely related since $Y_D = C + S$. Furthermore, any increase in disposable income will cause an increase in consumption and an increase in saving. The extent to which consumption and saving will increase depends on the marginal propensity to consume. As we saw in the text, the saving function is given by the following:

$$S = -c_0 + (1 - c_1)[Y - T].$$

If we set $Y_D = 0$ (i.e., $Y - T = 0$), we see that $S = -c_0$. As we discussed above, $C = c_0$ if $Y_D = 0$.

Learning Tip

- How can consumption occur when $Y_D = 0$? Individuals must either be drawing down their assets or borrowing. Either situation represents dissaving, a situation where $S < 0$.
- What does the expression $(1 - c_1)$ represent? Let $c_1 = .85$. If Y_D increases by \$1, consumption will increase by 85 cents. What happens to the remaining 15 cents of additional disposable income? It must be used to increase saving. The expression $(1 - c_1)$, therefore, represents the marginal propensity to save. The marginal propensity to save measures the extent to which saving changes for a given change in disposable income.

Graphically, we have:

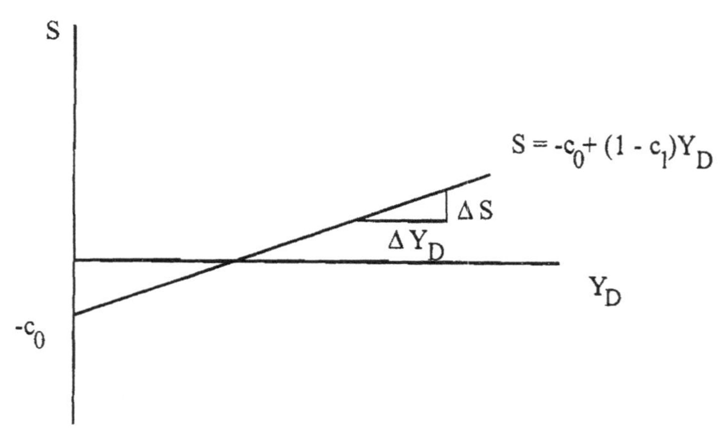

Learning Tip

- Any increase in c_0 (i.e., an increase in autonomous consumption) will cause the saving function to shift down by the amount of the change in c_0.
- Any increase in c_1 will cause the saving function to become flatter (the slope of the saving function decreases).
- Changes in Y_D will cause movements along the saving relationship.

5. MODEL ASSUMPTIONS AND DEMAND (Z)

In this chapter, it is assumed that:

a. firms do not hold inventories;
b. the economy is closed (i.e., X = IM = 0);
c. firms produce the same good, we can then look at the market for this one good; and
d. firms are willing to supply any amount of the good at a given price.

For this economy, the demand for goods (Z) is defined as Z = C + I + G. After substituting the consumption function for C, we have:

$Z = c_0 + c_1[Y - T] + I + G.$

Learning Tip

Recall that both I and G (and, for that matter, T) are exogenous. Furthermore, c_0, T, I, and G will be referred to as autonomous expenditures. Autonomous expenditures are those expenditures that are independent of income. You should note that total consumption (C) is not autonomous because it does depend on income.

Equilibrium in the goods market will occur when production (Y) equals demand (Z). This equilibrium condition (i.e., Y = Z) helps explain the interaction among aggregate production, income, and demand. Any event that causes an increase in autonomous expenditures will cause an increase in income. As Y increases, Z will increase as a result of the income-induced increase in consumption. There is, however, only one level of output (for given values of c_0, c_1, T, I, and G) that will satisfy the equilibrium condition.

6. EQUILIBRIUM OUTPUT

The equilibrium condition indicates that firms will set production so that it equals demand. As we saw in the text, the equilibrium level of output is represented by the following:

$Y = [1/(1 - c_1)][c_0 - c_1T + I + G]$.

> **Learning Tip**
>
> If you have trouble following the steps described in the text, think back to the algebra course you completed in high school. We have one equation (i.e., Y = Z) and one unknown variable (i.e., Y).

The above equation represents the equilibrium level of output given the parameters (c_0 and c_1) and the exogenous variables in the model (T, I, and G). You should understand that if any of these parameters or exogenous variables changes, the equilibrium level of output will also change.

> **Learning Tip**
>
> - The expression in brackets, $c_0 - c_1T + I + G$, has a simple interpretation. This represents the level of demand that would occur if Y were zero. It also represents the level of demand that does not depend on income; hence, it represents autonomous spending.
> - The other term, $1/(1 - c_1)$, will be some number greater than one since $c_1 < 1$. For example, if $c_1 = .8$, the term equals 5. This term "multiplies" the effect of autonomous spending and is, therefore, called the multiplier. You should also understand that as c_1 increases, the multiplier will increase. To verify this, calculate the multiplier if c_1 increases to .9.

Equilibrium output can also be illustrated graphically. To do this, we will first plot the demand function Z in Z-Y space (i.e., a graph with Z on the vertical axis and Y on the horizontal axis), this is represented by the line ZZ in the figure below:

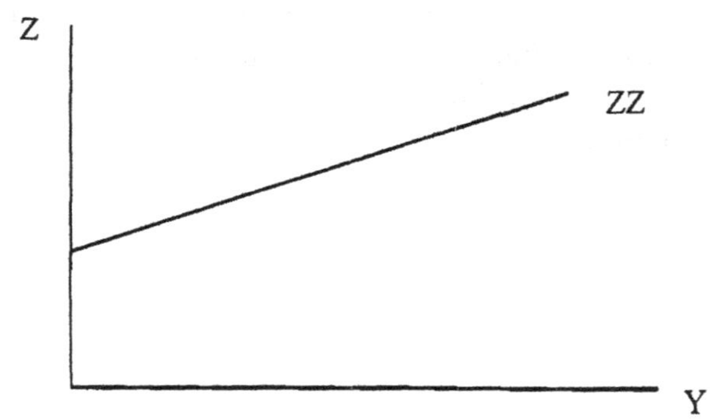

Learning Tip

- The vertical intercept is simply autonomous spending (i.e., if $Y = 0$, $Z = c_0 - c_1T + I + G$).
- This line is upward sloping because as Y increases, households increase consumption. This increase in consumption causes an increase in demand. The slope of ZZ is, therefore, equal to the marginal propensity to consume (c_1).
- Any change in autonomous spending will cause ZZ to shift. A change in c_1 will cause the slope of ZZ to change.

To determine equilibrium output, we will now include in the figure a 45-degree line that has a slope of 1. This 45-degree line illustrates the relationship between production and income. Since production and income are the same, a 1-unit increase in income will equal, by definition, a 1-unit increase in production.

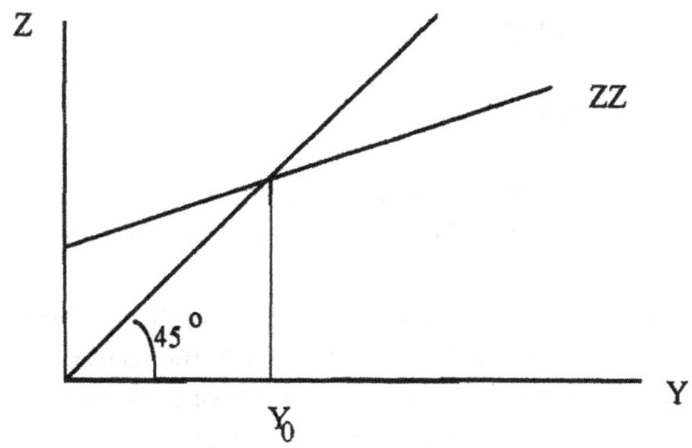

As we can see graphically, there is only one level of output that yields a level of demand (Z) that is equal to income; this occurs at Y_0. For any other level of output, Z will not equal Y. If output exceeds Y_0, then $Y > Z$. If output is less than Y_0, $Z > Y$. Review problem #9 will help reinforce this concept.

7. THE MULTIPLIER

What happens to output if autonomous spending changes? We will examine this both graphically and algebraically. Suppose government spending falls by 100. Further assume that the marginal propensity to consume is .8. Algebraically, the change in output caused by this reduction in G equals $1/(1-.8)(-100) = -500$. That is, every one-dollar change in G causes a \$5 change in equilibrium output. Graphically, we observe that the reduction in G causes a dollar-for-dollar reduction in autonomous spending. This decline in G, therefore, causes the demand relation, ZZ, to shift down by 100.

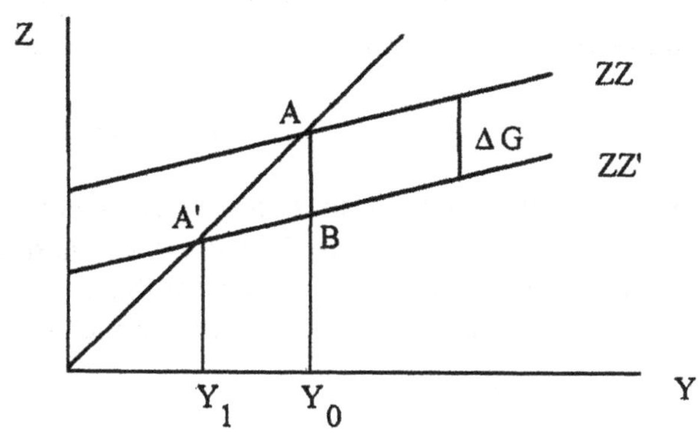

This initial decline in G causes a decrease in demand to point B. As demand falls, production changes by 100. As income falls, demand falls again as we move along the new ZZ line. Production changes again, and the process continues until the economy is at point A' where Y = Z at the lower level of output. Both graphically and intuitively, we observe that this one-time, permanent reduction in G causes the drop in Y to exceed the initial drop in autonomous spending. The multiplier indicates the extent to which Y will change for a given change in autonomous spending. In this case, the multiplier is 5.

8. SAVING, INVESTMENT AND THE PARADOX OF SAVING

Equilibrium output can be obtained using the Y = Z equilibrium condition. Equilibrium output can also be illustrated using an approach that focuses on the relationship between investment and saving. As we saw in Chapter 3, S = I + G - T when the economy is in equilibrium. Rearranging this equation yields I = S + (T - G). This equation allows us to obtain an alternative interpretation of equilibrium output:

- S represents private saving by households.
- T - G represents public saving.
- The sum of private and public saving represents national saving.
- In short, the economy is also in equilibrium when investment equals national saving.

A basic understanding of this investment-saving relationship combined with an understanding of the model presented above will shed light on the paradox of saving. In particular, what are the effects of an increase in saving? Any autonomous increase in saving will be represented by an equal reduction in autonomous consumption ($\Delta c_0 < 0$).

Learning Tip

If you understand the link between consumption and saving, the answer to the above question is obvious.

- A decline in c_0 (increase in autonomous saving) will cause an equal reduction in demand at each level of output.
- This reduction in demand will cause a decline in production equal to the change in c_0 times the multiplier.

What happens to saving? Since I, G, and T are all autonomous, they do not change as income falls. This implies, given, the alternative interpretation of equilibrium (S = I + (G - T)), that the level of saving will remain unaffected by the initial change in saving. Any attempt to increase saving will cause: (1) a reduction in output; and (2) no permanent change in the level of saving. These two results are referred to as the paradox of saving. Review problem #12 will allow you to work through a numerical problem to illustrate these two results.

Learning Tip

Appendix 3 (An Introduction to Econometrics) contains a useful introduction to statistical analysis. The example that is used to illustrate these concepts is the marginal propensity to consume. Some instructors might emphasize this material. If so, you should carefully read this appendix. To help you understand this, I have included a summary of this material in the next section.

SELF-TEST QUESTIONS

1. What is the largest component of GDP (1)?

2. Explain the difference among exogenous, endogenous and autonomous variables (2).

3. What is the difference between fixed investment and inventory investment (1)?

4. Can inventory investment take on negative (positive) values? If so, explain (1).

5. Explain what the marginal propensity to consume is (2).

6. What effect, if any, will an increase in consumer confidence have on: (1) the consumption function; and (2) the demand line (ZZ) (3)?

7. What variables determine the vertical intercept and slope of the ZZ line (3)?

8. Why is the demand line (ZZ) upward sloping (3)?

9. Explain what is meant by the multiplier (3).

REVIEW PROBLEMS

1. The table below includes information about real GDP (measured in billions of 1987 dollars) for the United States in 1993 and 1994.

	1993	1994
Consumption (C)	3459	3579
Investment (I)	805	903
Nonresidential	592	672
Residential	213	231
Government Spending (G)	930	923
Exports (X)	603	655
Imports (IM)	676	769
Inventory Investment (I_S)	15	52

a. Calculate the level of GDP for 1993 and 1994. Then calculate the rate of GDP growth between 1993 and 1994. Based on your calculations, briefly explain what happened to economic activity between 1993 and 1994.

b. Calculate the rate of growth/decline in each of the components of GDP between 1993 and 1994. Which of the components of GDP grew the fastest and slowest between these two periods? Calculate each component's share of GDP in 1993 and 1994. Did any of the components of GDP experience any changes in their size relative to total output? Briefly comment.

c. Based on the information in these two tables, what happened, if anything, to the size of the United States trade deficit between these two years? If the deficit did change, did it occur primarily because of changes in exports or imports? Explain.

2. The definition of GDP includes (or, equivalently, takes into account) the value of changes in inventories (i.e., inventory investment). Suppose we developed an alternative measure of GDP that ignored inventory investment. First, describe and explain a situation in which the exclusion of inventory investment would cause the value of this alternative (and, by the way, incorrect!) measure of GDP to be <u>greater</u> than the value of output obtained using the current definition's measure of GDP. Second, describe and explain a situation in which the exclusion of inventory investment would cause the value of this alternative measure of GDP to be <u>less</u> than the value of output obtained using the current definition's measure of GDP. Finally, given your analysis, <u>briefly</u> discuss why it is important to include inventory investment when measuring the value of current output.

3. The definition of GDP includes (or, equivalently, takes into account) the value of net exports (X - IM). Suppose we developed an alternative measure of GDP that ignored net exports. First, describe and explain a situation in which the exclusion of net exports would cause the value of this alternative (and, by the way, incorrect!) measure of GDP to be <u>greater</u> than the value of output obtained using the current definition's measure of GDP. Second, describe and explain a situation in which the exclusion of net exports would cause the value of this alternative measure of GDP to be <u>less</u> than the value of output obtained using the current definition's measure of GDP. Finally, given your analysis, <u>briefly</u> discuss why it is important to include net exports when measuring the value of current output.

4. Suppose consumption in the United States is represented by the following equation:

$C = 200 + .5Y_D$ where $Y_D = Y - T$ and $T = 200$.

a. What is the level of consumption in this economy if $Y_D = 0$? Briefly explain how individuals "pay for" this consumption when $Y_D = 0$.
b. Given the above parameters, calculate the level of consumption if Y = 1200. Suppose Y increases to 1300. What happens to the level of Y_D as Y increases to 1300 (i.e., calculate the change in Y_D)? What happens to the level of consumption when Y rises to 1300? Based on this analysis, what is the marginal propensity to consume for this economy?
c. Write out the saving function for this economy. What is the level of saving (S) when $Y_D = 0$? Explain how and why this occurs. What is the marginal propensity to save for this economy? How do you know?

5. Suppose the following information represents current economic conditions and behavior in some economy:

$C = 400 + .75Y_D$ where $Y_D = Y - T$
$T = 400$ and $Y = 2000$.

a. First, graphically depict the above consumption function in C - Y_D space (with C on the vertical axis and Y_D on the horizontal axis). What does the vertical intercept represent? Explain. What is the slope of this consumption function? Explain. With Y = 2000, what is the level of consumption for this economy?

b. Assuming that Y does not change, graphically illustrate (in the above graph), and explain the effects of a reduction in the marginal propensity to consume to .5. Calculate what happens to the level of consumption.

6. Suppose the United States economy is represented by the following equations:

$Z = C + I + G$	$C = 400 + .5Y_D$	$T = 400$	$I = 200$
$Y_D = Y - T$	$G = 600$		

a. What is the marginal propensity to consume for this economy? What is the marginal propensity to save?

b. Write out the equation that indicates how demand (Z) is a function of income (Y) and the remaining autonomous expenditures. What will be the level of demand if Y = 0? What does this level of demand represent? Furthermore, given your equation, what will happen to the level of demand (Z) as Y increases by $1? What does this number represent?

c. Based on your answer in part (b), calculate the level of demand (Z) for the following levels of income: Y = 1600, Y = 1800, Y = 2000, Y = 2200, and Y = 2400. Now compare the level of demand that you calculated at each level of income with the corresponding level of income. Is the economy in equilibrium at any of these levels of income? Explain.

d. Use your calculations in part (c) to answer this question. When Y = 1600, compare the levels of income and demand. How will firms respond to this situation? Briefly explain. When Y = 2400, compare the levels of income and demand. How will firms respond to this situation? Briefly explain.

7. Suppose the United States economy is represented by the following equations:

$Z = C + I + G$	$C = 300 + .5Y_D$	$T = 400$	$I = 200$
$Y_D = Y - T$	$G = 1000$		

a. Given the above variables, calculate the equilibrium level of output. Hint: First specify (using the above numbers) the demand equation (Z) for this economy. Second, using the equilibrium condition, equate this expression with Y. Once you have done this, solve for the equilibrium level of output. Using the ZZ-Y graph (i.e., a graph that includes the ZZ line and 45-degree line with Z on the vertical axis, and Y on the horizontal axis), illustrate the equilibrium level of output for this economy.

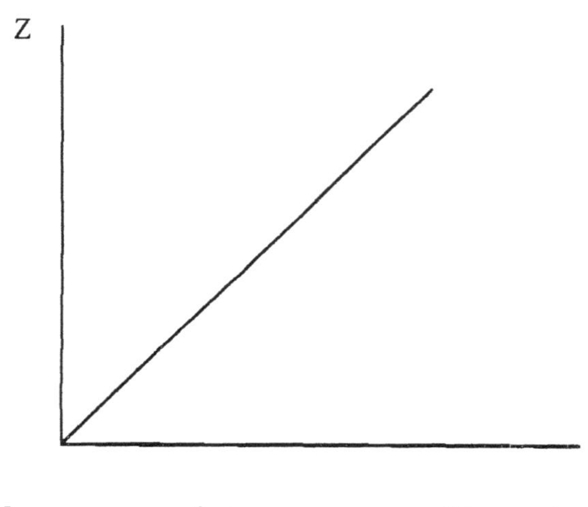

b. Now, assume that consumer confidence increases causing an increase in autonomous consumption (c_0) from 300 to 400. What is the new equilibrium level of output? How much does income change as a result of this event? What is the multiplier for this economy?

c. Graphically illustrate (in the above graph) the effects of this change in autonomous consumption on the demand line (ZZ) and Y. Clearly indicate in your graph the initial and final equilibrium levels of output.

d. Briefly explain why this increase in output is greater than the initial increase in autonomous consumption.

8. Repeat the analysis in question 7, parts (a) - (c). This time, however, assume that the marginal propensity to consume is .8.

a. See #7, part (a).
b. See #7, part (b).
c. What happened to the slope of the ZZ line as a result of the increase in the marginal propensity to consume? Explain.
d. What happened to the changes in output and, therefore, the size of the multiplier as a result of the increase in c_1? Explain.
e. Graphically illustrate using the ZZ-Y graph the effects of an increase in c_1 on equilibrium output.

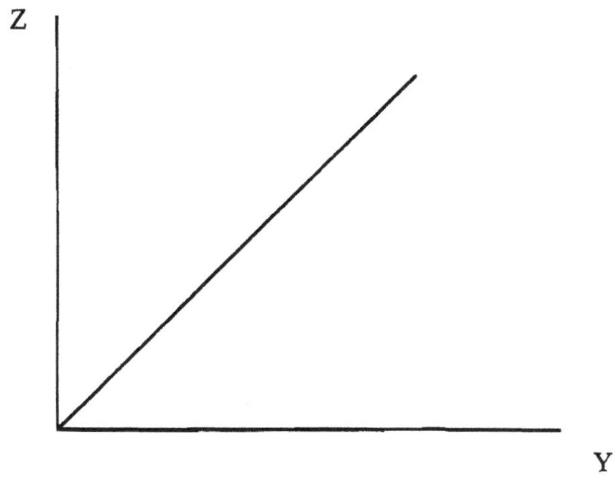

9. Use the ZZ-Y graph found below to answer the following questions:

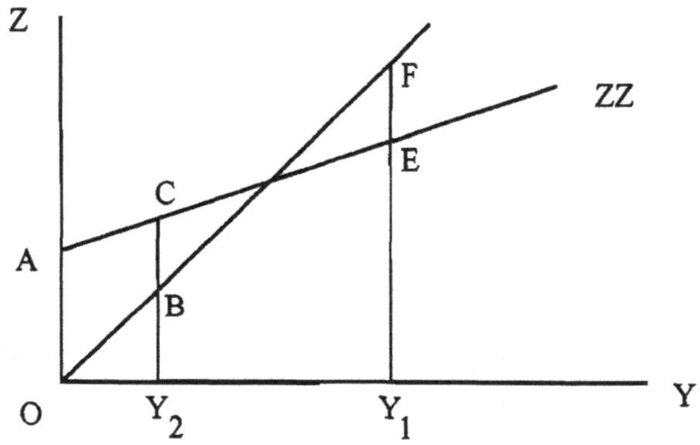

a. What does the distance OA represent? Briefly discuss and explain what events could occur in this model that would cause the distance OA to decrease.
b. Briefly explain what the following distances represent: OY_1, Y_1E, Y_1F. Is the economy in equilibrium when output equals Y_1? Explain.
c. Briefly explain what the following distances represent: OY_2, Y_2B, Y_2C. Is the economy in equilibrium when output equals Y_2? Explain.
d. Given your analysis in parts (b) and (c), what is the level of equilibrium output? What must occur for the economy to be in equilibrium? Illustrate this condition in the above graph.

10. a. Calculate the multiplier for each of the following values of the marginal propensity to consume: $c_1 = .4$, $c_1 = .5$, $c_1 = .6$, $c_1 = .8$, and $c_1 = .9$. Briefly explain what happens to the multiplier as the marginal propensity to consume increases.
b. Explain what happens, if anything, to the demand line (ZZ) as the marginal propensity to consume takes on the following values: $c_1 = .4$, $c_1 = .5$, $c_1 = .6$, $c_1 = .8$, and $c_1 = .9$. Briefly explain what happens to equilibrium output as the marginal propensity to consume increases.
c. Suppose policy makers want to increase equilibrium output by 1000. For each of the following values of the marginal propensity to consume, calculate the required change in government spending which would yield the desired change in equilibrium output: $c_1 = .4$, $c_1 = .5$, $c_1 = .6$, $c_1 = .8$, and $c_1 = .9$.

11. Suppose there are two different economies, both represented by the model presented in Chapter 3. Further assume that the equilibrium level of output is the same in both countries. For simplicity, we can illustrate the equilibrium for both economies in the same graph. The demand line for economy A (B) is represented by ZZ_A (ZZ_B). I have depicted this situation in the following graph.

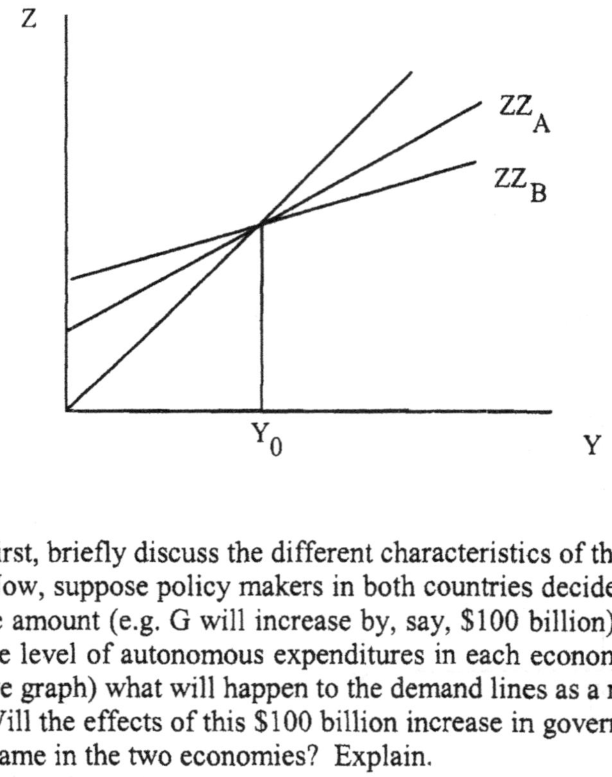

a. First, briefly discuss the different characteristics of the demand lines for these two economies.
b. Now, suppose policy makers in both countries decide to increase government spending by the same amount (e.g. G will increase by, say, $100 billion). First, briefly explain what will happen to the level of autonomous expenditures in each economy. Second, graphically illustrate (in the above graph) what will happen to the demand lines as a result of this identical increase in G.
c. Will the effects of this $100 billion increase in government spending on equilibrium output be the same in the two economies? Explain.

12. Suppose the United States economy is represented by the following equations:

$Z = C + I + G$	$C = 300 + .9Y_D$	$T = 1000$
$Y_D = Y - T$	$G = 2000$	$I = 200$

a. Calculate the equilibrium level of output.
b. After you have calculated equilibrium income, calculate the level of consumption at this level of output. Hint: Since you know the level of taxes and income, you can easily obtain the level of disposable income to calculate consumption.

c. Write out the saving function for this economy. Then, calculate the level of saving that occurs at the equilibrium level of output.
d. Now, suppose households decide to increase their autonomous saving by 100. Equivalently, households have decided to cut their autonomous consumption by 100. Calculate the new equilibrium level of output that occurs as a result of the decrease in autonomous consumption of 100. Has this increased desire to save had a positive or negative effect on economic activity? Explain.
e. Based on your analysis in part (d), calculate the level of saving that occurs at this new equilibrium level of output. Compare this level of saving with the level of saving obtained in part (c). What has happened to the level of saving in this economy as a result of the increased desire to save? Explain.

13. For each of the following events, explain what effect each event has on: (1) autonomous expenditures; (2) equilibrium output; (3) the slope of ZZ; and (4) the multiplier.

a. decrease in business confidence that results in a reduction in nonresidential investment
b. increase in consumer confidence that results in an increase in residential investment
c. Congress passes a budget that requires a reduction in government spending
d. an increase in the marginal propensity to consume
e. an increase in the marginal propensity to save

MULTIPLE CHOICE QUESTIONS

1. A reduction in government spending (G) can occur if:

a. government spending at the state level declines
b. government spending at the local level declines
c. government spending at the federal level declines
d. all of the above

2. Assume that the United States economy is an open economy. Given this information, we would expect that:

a. exports (X) exceed imports (IM)
b. X < IM
c. X = IM = 0
d. United States households (in addition to the government and business sectors) trade goods and services with individuals/firms from other countries

3. In this chapter, we studied the difference between endogenous and exogenous variables. Which of the following is (are) an endogenous variable(s) in our model of the goods market?

a. consumption and saving
b. government spending and consumption
c. investment and saving
d. taxes
e. all of the above
f. none of the above

4. Which of the following is (are) an exogenous variable(s) in our model of the goods market?

a. saving and investment
b. government spending and taxes
c. disposable income and taxes
d. demand for goods (Z)
e. all of the above
f. none of the above

5. Which of the following variables is (are) an endogenous variable(s) in our model of the goods market?

a. autonomous consumption and the marginal propensity to consume
b. government spending
c. taxes
d. consumption

Answer the following four questions (i.e., questions 6 - 9) using the information included in the following behavioral equation:

$$C = 200 + .75Y_D$$

6. For this economy, a one-time, permanent increase in disposable income (Y_D) of 200 will cause consumption to rise by:

a. 150
b. 200
c. less than 150
d. more than 200

7. If $Y_D = 0$, we know that:

a. saving equals 0
b. saving equals 200
c. saving equals -200
d. saving and consumption are both equal to 0

8. The saving function for the above economy would be:

a. $S = 200 + .25Y_D$
b. $S = .75Y_D$
c. $S = 200 + .25Y_D$
d. $S = -200 + .25Y_D$

9. The multiplier for this economy is equal to:

a. .75
b. .25
c. 4
d. 1.33
e. 1

10. When the economy is in equilibrium, we know with certainty that:

a. private saving equals investment
b. public saving equals investment
c. the federal budget is balanced (i.e., G = T)
d. income equals demand
e. consumption equals private saving

11. An increase in the marginal propensity to save will tend to cause:

a. an increase in the multiplier and a given change in government expenditures to have a smaller effect on equilibrium output
b. an increase in the multiplier and a given change in government expenditures to have a greater effect on equilibrium output
c. a reduction in the multiplier and a given change in government expenditures to have a smaller effect on equilibrium output
d. a reduction in the multiplier and a given change in government expenditures to have a greater effect on equilibrium output

12. An increase in the marginal propensity to consume will tend to cause:

a. an increase in the multiplier and a given change in government expenditures to have a smaller effect on equilibrium output
b. an increase in the multiplier and a given change in government expenditures to have a greater effect on equilibrium output
c. a reduction in the multiplier and a given change in government expenditures to have a smaller effect on equilibrium output
d. a reduction in the multiplier and a given change in government expenditures to have a greater effect on equilibrium output

Answer the following five questions (i.e., 13 - 17) using the following information. Suppose the United States economy is represented by the following behavioral equations:

$Z = C + I + G$ $\quad$ $C = 300 + .5Y_D$ $\quad$ $T = 1600$ $\quad$ $I = 200$

$Y_D = Y - T$ $\quad$ $G = 2000$

13. The endogenous variables in this economy are:

a. government expenditures (G)
b. taxes (T)
c. fixed investment (I)
d. consumption and saving (C and S)

14. Given the above variables, the equilibrium level of output for this economy is:

a. 900
b. 1800
c. 1700
d. 2500
e. 3400

15. The multiplier for the above economy is:

a. .5
b. 1
c. 2
d. 4

16. Suppose fiscal policy makers implemented a policy that causes government spending to increase by 200 (i.e., the new level of government spending would be 2200). Based on our understanding of the above economy, we would expect that equilibrium output will:

a. increase by 200
b. increase by less than 200
c. increase by 400
d. increase by 100

17. In addition to using disposable income for consumption, households also will use a portion of disposable income for saving. The saving function for the above economy which summarizes the behavior of households is given by:

a. $S = 300 + .5Y_D$
b. $S = -300 - .5Y_D$
c. $S = -300 + .5Y_D$
d. $S = 300 + .5Y$
e. $S = -300 + .5Y$

18. Assume that households experience a reduction in confidence. Further assume that this reduction in confidence causes a reduction in autonomous consumption (c_0). This reduction in c_0 will cause

a. no change in output and no change in the final level of consumption
b. a reduction in output and a reduction in the level of saving
c. no change in output if the level of saving does not change
d. no change in the level of saving

19. An increase in the marginal propensity to consume will cause:

a. an increase in output and an increase in the multiplier
b. a reduction in output and a reduction in the multiplier
c. an increase in output and a reduction in the multiplier
d. a reduction in output and an increase in the marginal propensity to save

20. An increase in fixed investment (I) will cause:

a. a reduction in output and a reduction in the multiplier
b. an increase in output and an increase in the multiplier
c. an increase in output and no change in the multiplier
d. no change in the multiplier and, therefore, no change in output

APPENDIX 3. AN INTRODUCTION TO ECONOMETRICS

OBJECTIVES, REVIEW, AND TUTORIAL

After working through the appendix and the following material, you should be able to:

(1) Understand and explain the relationship between $(\Delta C_t - \overline{\Delta C})$ and $(\Delta Y_{Dt} - \overline{\Delta Y_D})$.

(2) Explain how econometrics is used to obtain estimates of the marginal propensity to consume.

(3) Understand and explain the results obtained with the use of econometrics.

(4) Explain the difference between correlation and causality using the consumption and disposable income example.

(5) Interpret a consumption equation that includes lagged values of disposable income.

1. THE RELATIONSHIP BETWEEN $(\Delta C_t - \overline{\Delta C})$ AND $(\Delta Y_{Dt} - \overline{\Delta Y_D})$

How can we obtain an estimate of c_1? If we estimate (more on how we do this below) the effects of changes in the level of disposable income on the level of consumption, we would obtain a marginal propensity to consume close to 1 and, therefore, a very high multiplier.

Learning Tip

Verify this for yourself. What is the multiplier when $c_1 = .8$; $c_1 = .9$; and $c_1 = .95$; $c_1 = .99$?

To avoid this problem, we can measure the effects of changes in disposable income above or below normal on consumption. To do this:

- Obtain the average quarterly change in consumption (ΔC). Since C has generally risen over time, $\Delta C > 0$;
- Obtain the average quarterly change in disposable income (ΔY_D). Since Y_D has generally risen over time, $\Delta Y_D > 0$;
- Obtain the actual change in C for each quarter (ΔC_t); and
- Obtain the actual change in Y_D for each quarter (ΔY_{Dt}).

We use the above data to calculate:

(1) $(\Delta C_t - \overline{\Delta C})$. This represents the change in C as a deviation from its mean; this expression can be positive, negative, or equal to zero; and

(2) $(\Delta Y_{Dt} - \overline{\Delta Y_D})$. This represents the change in Y_D as a deviation from its mean; this expression can also be positive, negative, or equal to zero.

Analysis of the above data indicates that there is a positive relationship between $(\Delta C_t - \overline{\Delta C})$ and $(\Delta Y_{Dt} - \overline{\Delta Y_D})$. When disposable income increases above normal, consumption increases above normal as well.

2. HOW DO WE OBTAIN AN ESTIMATE OF THE MARGINAL PROPENSITY TO CONSUME?

We use econometrics to obtain a line which best fits the data. The "best" line is chosen to minimize the sum of the squared distance of the points to the line. This process is called ordinary least squares.

- The estimated equation is called the regression.
- The line is called the regression line.

Learning Tip

Suppose you are given the following equation:

$$(\Delta C_t - \overline{\Delta C}) = 0.34(\Delta Y_{Dt} - \overline{\Delta Y_D}) + \text{residual}.$$

How would you interpret it?

- The estimate, 0.34, indicates that an increase in disposable income of \$1 billion above normal would cause an increase in consumption of \$0.34 billion above normal. 0.34 also represents the slope of the regression line and, therefore, is the estimated value of the marginal propensity to consume ($c_1 = 0.34$).
- The relationship between $(\Delta C_t - \overline{\Delta C})$ and $(\Delta Y_{Dt} - \overline{\Delta Y_D})$ is not perfect (i.e., all points do not lie on the regression line). A change in consumption can be decomposed into that part caused by changes in disposable income and those changes caused by other factors. The residual represents this other component.
- If changes in consumption are caused primarily by changes in disposable income, the better is the fit of the regression line and, therefore, the smaller is the residual.

3. INTERPRETATION OF ECONOMETRIC RESULTS

Suppose you are given the following information:

$$(\Delta C_t - \overline{\Delta C}) = 0.42(\Delta Y_{Dt} - \overline{\Delta Y_D}) \qquad \overline{R}^2 = 0.20$$
$$(5.46)$$

Sample Period: 1960:1 to 1995:4
Usable observations: 144
Degrees of Freedom: 143

How do we interpret this information? Review problem #10 will help you understand this material.

- Dependent variable: The variable we are trying to explain (here it is $(\Delta C_t - \overline{\Delta C})$).
- Independent variables: Variables used to explain the dependent variable (here, it is $(\Delta Y_{Dt} - \overline{\Delta Y_D})$).
- Coefficient: This is the estimated coefficient, 0.42 (in this case, the estimated marginal propensity to consume). A \$1 billion increase in disposable income (above its mean) in period t will cause a \$0.42 billion increase in consumption (above its mean) in period t. The marginal propensity to consume is 0.42.
- t-statistic: For each estimated coefficient, a t-statistic is obtained. The t-statistic tells us how confident we can be that the true value of the estimated coefficient is different from zero. The t-statistic for the above equation is the number in parentheses below the estimated coefficient (i.e., 5.46).
    - If the t-statistic exceeds 2, we can be 95% sure that the estimated coefficient is different from zero.
    - If the t-statistic exceeds 5.2, we can be 99.99% sure that the estimated coefficient is different from zero.
- $\overline{R}^2$: A measure of how well the regression line fits the data. $\overline{R}^2$ is between 0 and 1. The higher is $\overline{R}^2$, the better the line fits the data.
- Usable observations: The number of observations of data in the sample period (all quarters from 1960:1 to 1995:4 which is 144).
- Degrees of freedom: Usable observations minus the number of estimated coefficients (143 here).

4. CORRELATION AND CAUSALITY

The estimated marginal propensity to consume indicates that consumption and disposable income move together (i.e., are positively correlated). We have interpreted these results as suggesting that changes in Y_D **cause** changes in C. There are, however, two possible explanations for such a result.

- As Y_D increases, people do increase consumption; changes in Y_D do cause changes in consumption.

• If individuals decide to increase consumption as a result of, for example, an increase in consumer confidence, demand, output, and, therefore, disposable income will increase. In this case, changes in Y_D do not cause changes in consumption. In fact, it is the change in consumption that causes the change in Y_D.

The estimated coefficient and, therefore, the estimated value of the marginal propensity to consume might "pick up" (i.e., include) some of the effects of C on Y_D. To avoid this problem, economists use instrumental variable estimation. How is this done?

• First, find exogenous variables, variables that affect output (and, therefore, Y_D) but are not affected by changes in output.

• Second, examine the changes in consumption in response to changes in Y_D that are caused by exogenous variables. Ignore the changes in Y_D that are caused by changes in consumption

• These estimates will reflect the effect of changes in Y_D on consumption and not the other way around.

Learning Tip

• The exogenous variables used in instrumental variable estimation are called instruments.
• Instrumental variable estimation will generally yield lower estimates when compared to estimates obtained using ordinary least squares estimation. Why? This approach eliminates the effect of consumption on Y_D. Hence the estimated value of the marginal propensity to consume will be lower (and so will the size of the multiplier).
• The interpretation of the results of an equation estimated using instrumental variable methods is the same as before.

SELF-TEST QUESTIONS

1. Suppose you are given data for the following variable ($\Delta C_t - \overline{\Delta C}$). What do the data measure?

2. What is a regression line, and how is it obtained?

3. What is the difference between an independent and dependent variable?

4. How can changes in consumption cause changes in disposable income?

REVIEW PROBLEMS

1. Suppose you are given the following information:

$$(\Delta C_t - \overline{\Delta C}) = 0.49\,(\Delta Y_{Dt} - \overline{\Delta Y_D}) \qquad \overline{R}^2 = 0.24$$
$$(3.34)$$

Sample Period: 1960:1 to 1997:4

a. How many usable observations exist for this study?
b. How many degrees of freedom exist for this study?
c. How do we interpret the number, 0.49?
d. How confident can we be that the true coefficient is different from zero? Why?
e. What does the size of $\overline{R}^2$ mean?
f. Does the above value of $\overline{R}^2$ suggest a good or bad fit? Briefly explain.
g. If you were to graph the above regression line with $(\Delta C_t - \overline{\Delta C})$ on the vertical axis and $(\Delta Y_{Dt} - \overline{\Delta Y_D})$ on the horizontal axis, what does the coefficient represent?

2. Suppose we estimate the consumption equation for the United States and Canada and obtain the following results:

Results for the United States: $(\Delta C_t - \overline{\Delta C}) = 0.60\,(\Delta Y_{Dt} - \overline{\Delta Y_D})$ $\qquad \overline{R}^2 = 0.20$
$$(3.34)$$

Results for Canada: $(\Delta C_t - \overline{\Delta C}) = 0.50\,(\Delta Y_{Dt} - \overline{\Delta Y_D})$ $\qquad \overline{R}^2 = 0.24$
$$(3.98)$$

a. What is the marginal propensity to consume and multiplier in the United States?
b. What is the marginal propensity to consume and multiplier in Canada?
c. What are the independent variables in these two equations?
d. What are the dependent variables in these two equations?
e. Which of these two equations represents a "better" fit? Explain.

MULTIPLE CHOICE QUESTIONS

1. An $\overline{R}^2$ with a value between 2 and 5.2:

a. cannot occur
b. suggests that the regression line represents a good fit
c. indicates that we can be at least 95% sure that the true coefficient is different from zero
d. suggests that the instrumental variable method should be used

2. The regression line obtained using the ordinary least squares process is chosen to:

a. maximize the size of the estimated coefficient
b. minimize the sum of the squared distances of the points to the regression line
c. maximize the size of the multiplier
d. minimize the size of the multiplier

3. A t-statistic close to zero indicates that:

a. the regression line fits the data well
b. the regression does not fit the data well
c. the residual is small
d. we cannot be 95% sure that the true coefficient is different from zero

4. The instrumental variable method is used when:

a. changes in the dependent variable are believed to cause changes in the independent variable
b. changes in the independent variable are believed to cause changes in the dependent variable
c. the $\overline{R}^2$ is low
d. none of the above

CHAPTER 4.
FINANCIAL MARKETS

OBJECTIVES, REVIEW, AND TUTORIAL

After working through the chapter and the following material, you should be able to:

(1) Know the distinction between money and bonds.

(2) Recognize the difference among saving, savings, wealth, income, and investment.

(3) Understand the difference between stock and flow variables.

(4) Explain the determinants of money demand.

(5) Explain the determinants of the interest rate, and be familiar with the LM relation.

(6) Discuss the balance sheet of banks and the balance sheet of the central bank.

(7) Understand the components and determinants of the money supply.

(8) Explain the dynamic effects of open market operations on the money supply.

(9) Understand the determinants of the interest rate based on the market for central bank money.

1. DISTINCTION BETWEEN MONEY AND BONDS

In this chapter, we assume that there are only two financial assets: money and bonds.

(1) Money

Money is a financial asset that can be used for transactions and pays no interest. There are several definitions of money (i.e., M1, M2, etc.). M1, which will be used here, consists of:

(1) currency (CU): coins and bills issued by the central bank; and
(2) checkable deposits: deposits (at banks) on which one can write a check.

Learning Tip
M1 also includes travelers' checks. In much of the discussion that follows, travelers' checks will be ignored since they represent less than 1% of M1.

(2) Bonds

Bonds are financial assets that pay an interest rate (i) but cannot be used for transactions. You must be careful not to confuse money and bonds with the following variables:

- saving: that part of disposable income not consumed
- wealth (\$Wealth): value of financial assets minus value of financial liabilities
- income: payments one receives for working, rental income, and interest and dividends
- investment: the purchase of new plants and machinery by firms and the purchase of new homes and apartments by homeowners

Learning Tip

It is easy to confuse the above variables because they are often used interchangeably (and incorrectly!!). For example, think about what is wrong with the following statements. How would we correct them?

(1) "I expect to earn a lot of money after graduation."
(2) "She has a lot of investment in the stock market."

(3) Stock versus flow variables

We can use the above variables to distinguish between flow and stock variables.

- A flow variable is a variable that must be expressed per unit of time. Examples: income per year; saving per quarter; and budget deficits per year.

- A stock variable can be measured at a given point in time. Wealth and money are stock variables since they can be measured at a given moment in time.

2. THE CHOICE BETWEEN HOLDING MONEY AND BONDS

Individuals decide how to allocate their wealth between money and bonds. Two extreme cases will illustrate the factors that affect this decision.

- Case 1. Suppose all of your wealth will be held in bonds. This portfolio allocation will:
(1) maximize interest income; but also
(2) maximize the costs (transaction fees) associated with converting bonds to money when you wanted to buy something.

- Case 2. Suppose all of your $Wealth were held in money. This allocation would:
(1) minimize the costs (in fact, they would be zero) associated with converting bonds into money; but also
(2) minimize the interest income received on your wealth (interest income would be zero).

Individuals will, therefore, hold both money and bonds.

3. THE DETERMINANTS OF MONEY DEMAND (M^d)

Money demand (M^d) depends on:

(1) Level of transactions: As the level of transactions increases, individuals will allocate a greater proportion of their portfolio to money. We include nominal income ($Y) in place of the level of transactions. Why? Unlike the level of transactions, $Y can be measured. As $Y increases, the level of transactions rises causing M^d to increase as well.

(2) The interest rate on bonds (i): As i increases, individuals are willing to accept the additional costs of converting bonds into money in order to benefit from the higher interest rate on bonds. As i increases, M^d falls.

M^d is, therefore, an increasing function of \$Y and a decreasing function of i.

M^d is written as: $M^d = \$YL(i)$. How do we interpret this?

(1) M^d is proportional to \$Y. If your nominal income rises by 5%, your demand for money will increase by 5%.
(2) Increases in the interest rate cause a reduction in money demand. This effect is captured by the function, L(i).

M^d is shown graphically in Figure 4-1. You must know the following about M^d:

(1) Each money demand curve is drawn for a given level of \$Y;
(2) Money demand is downward sloping because, as i increases, individuals increase their bond holdings and reduce their money holdings (the curve does NOT shift!); and
(3) Changes in \$Y will cause changes in money demand and, therefore, cause shifts in the money demand curve.

Learning Tip

Credit cards do NOT represent money. Credit cards allow you to combine the payments of goods and services on one day each month.

4. INTEREST RATE DETERMINATION: THE MONEY MARKET APPROACH

(1) Introduction

Financial markets are in equilibrium when the supply of money (M) equals money demand: $M = \$YL(i)$. This equilibrium condition is called the LM relation. What does this LM relation mean? For equilibrium to occur, the interest rate must be at a level that causes individuals to hold an amount of money (M^d) equal to the existing stock of money (i.e., $M = M^d$). Figure 4-2 illustrates this.

Learning Tip

If $M = M^d$, we also know that the supply of bonds (B) equals bond demand. Why?

- Assume the stocks of money and bonds are given.
- $M^d + B^d = \$Wealth$
- We also know that M + B = \$Wealth.
- Therefore, $M^d + B^d = M + B$.
- If $M^d = M$, B^d must equal B.

Make sure you can explain why the money supply curve is vertical. Answer: Changes in the interest rate do not cause changes in the supply of money. Changes in the money supply WILL cause shifts in the money supply curve.

(2) Changes in i

The interest rate will change when \$Y or the money supply changes.

- Changes in \$Y. An increase in \$Y causes an increase in M^d. At the initial interest rate, M^d exceeds the supply of money ($M^d > M$). i must increase to reduce the amount of money individuals want to hold. This occurs at i' in Figure 4-3. At the higher i, M once again equals money demand.

Learning Tip

Note: The increase in \$Y causes a shift in the money demand curve. The increase in the interest rate causes a movement along the now, higher money demand curve. Make sure you understand the distinction between a shift versus a movement along a curve.

- Changes in the money supply. An increase in the money supply causes a rightward shift in the money supply curve. At the initial interest rate i, the money supply now exceeds money demand. i must fall to induce individuals to hold more money. This occurs at i' in Figure 4-4. At the lower i', M once again equals money demand.

5. MONETARY POLICY, OPEN MARKET OPERATIONS, AND THE BOND MARKET

(1) The bond market

In the bond market:

- Individuals who sell bonds (in exchange for money) want to increase the proportion of money in their portfolio;
- Individuals who buy bonds want to reduce the proportion of money in their portfolios; and
- In equilibrium, the interest rate is such that $B = B^d$ (or, as we saw earlier, $M = M^d$).

(2) The central bank and the bond market

The central bank can change the stock of money by buying and selling bonds in the bond market (i.e., open market operations).

- Increase the money supply: The central bank buys bonds and pays for the bonds by creating money. This has two effects on the central bank's balance sheet:
  (1) the increased bond holdings represent an increase in the central bank's assets; and
  (2) the increased money in circulation represents an increase in the central bank's liabilities.

- Decrease the money supply: The central bank sells bonds and receives money as payment for these bonds. This has two effects on the central bank's balance sheet:
  (1) the reduced bond holdings represent a reduction in the central bank's assets; and
  (2) the reduced money in circulation represents a reduction in the central bank's liabilities.

Learning Tip

You should understand the relationship between the price of a bond ($\$P_B$) and the interest rate. On a one-year bond which promises a fixed, nominal payment of \$100 in one year, the interest rate is defined as:

$i = (\$100 - \$P_B)/\$P_B$.

This definition indicates that the higher is $\$P_B$, the lower will be the interest rate. The lower is $\$P_B$, the higher will be the interest rate. This makes sense because, for example, as $\$P_B$ falls, the numerator (your gain), $\$100 - \$P_B$, gets larger AND the denominator, $\$P_B$, gets smaller. i, therefore, rises. Alternatively, the return per dollar allocated to bonds rises as the price of the bond falls.

(3) Policy

- Expansionary open market operations. This central bank purchase of bonds will increase the demand for bonds, raise the price of bonds, reduce the interest rate, and increase the supply of money

- Contractionary open market operations. This central bank sale of bonds will increase the supply of bonds, reduce the price of bonds, raise the interest rate, and reduce the supply of money.

6. BANKS AND THE MONEY SUPPLY

(1) Introduction

Banks are financial institutions. They receive funds by offering checkable deposits (D) and use these funds to buy bonds, issue loans, and hold reserves (R). The deposits are the bank's liabilities. The bonds, loans, and reserves are the bank's assets.

In the presence of banks, the central bank continues to control central bank money. Central bank money (i.e., the monetary base) is given by:

$H = CU + R$; where

- H is the monetary base (central bank money);
- CU is currency (coins and bills);
- c is a parameter representing the proportion of money demand that individuals wish to hold as CU;
- therefore, $CU = cM^d$
- R is reserves;
- θ is the reserve ratio (the proportion of deposits banks wish to hold as reserves);
- therefore, $R = \theta D$.

Learning Tip

In previous courses, you might have discussed a parameter called the currency-deposit ratio. The parameter c in this text is NOT the currency-deposit ratio. The currency-deposit ratio represents the proportion of deposits that individuals wish to hold as currency. Here, c represents the proportion of money (the sum of currency and checkable deposits) that individuals wish to hold as currency.

(2) Case 1: CU = 0

When CU = 0, H = R and M = D. The amount of checkable deposits is given by $D = (1/\theta)R$. If $\theta = .2$ and R = \$100 million, the supply of checkable deposits will be \$500 million. Why? When $\theta = .2$, banks hold \$20 of reserves for every \$100 dollars of checkable deposits. If R = \$100 million, banks can issue \$500 million of checkable deposits.

Since M = D, we know that

$M = (1/\theta)R.$

The money supply equals the money multiplier, $(1/\theta)$, times the monetary base, R.

(3) Case 2: CU > 0

In the presence of CU, we know that:

(1) $H = CU^d + R^d$ (i.e., the supply of central bank money = the demand for central bank money);
(2) $H = cM^d + \theta(1\text{-}c)M^d = [c + \theta(1\text{-}c)]M^d$; and, therefore,
(3) $H/[c + \theta(1\text{-}c)] = M^d$;
(4) When the money market is in equilibrium, we know that: $H/[c + \theta(1\text{-}c)] = M^d = M$.

The expression, $1/[c + \theta(1\text{-}c)]$, is the money multiplier. Suppose c = .6 and $\theta = .2$. The money multiplier is 1.47. A \$1 change in H will cause a \$1.47 change in the money supply.

Learning Tip

The central bank's balance sheet is essentially the same in the presence of currency. The central bank still controls the amount of central bank money. Central bank money can now be held in the form of currency and reserves.

- The central bank can increase the amount of central bank money by buying bonds.
- The central bank can reduce the amount of central bank money by selling bonds.

(4) Summary of M

The money supply is a function of:

- the monetary base (H):
- the reserve ratio (θ); and
- the parameter c.

If any of these three parameters/variables changes, the money supply will change.

For example, if the Fed buys $200 million of bonds, H increases by $200 million. The eventual change in the money supply will be equal to the money multiplier times the $200 million change in the monetary base. Review problems #14 and #15 will focus on this issue.

7. DETERMINATION OF INTEREST RATES: MARKET FOR CENTRAL BANK MONEY

You can use the money market (i.e., the supply and demand for money) presented above to examine the determinants of the interest rate. You can also use the market for central bank money to examine the determination of the interest rate.

(1) Supply of central bank money (H)

The Fed has complete control over the supply of central bank money (H). To change H, the Fed will either buy or sell bonds.

(2) Demand for central bank money

There are two components of the demand for central bank money: the demand for currency and the demand for reserves.

- Currency demand: CU^d. This is given by: $CU^d = cM^d$.
- Demand for reserves: R^d. This is given by: $R^d = \theta D = \theta(1\text{-}c)M^d$.
- Demand for central bank money: This is the sum of the above two components, $CU^d + R^d$.

(3) The market for central bank money

The interaction between the supply and demand for central bank money can also be used to examine the determinants of the interest rate. That is, the interest rate will adjust to equate H and $[CU^d + R^d]$. This is shown graphically in Figure 4-8.

Learning Tip

There are several characteristics of the market for central bank money that you must know.

- The quantity of central bank money, H (not M), is measured along the horizontal axis.
- The Fed controls the supply of H using open market operations.
- The demand for central bank money is a decreasing function of the interest rate because as i increases, individuals will hold less money. As M^d decreases, both currency demand (by individuals) and reserve demand (by banks) will fall.
- The demand for central bank money is drawn for a given level of income. If income changes, money demand, and, therefore, currency demand and reserve demand will change.

(4) Determination of the interest rate

The interest rate will adjust to clear this market for central bank money. This model can be used to examine what would cause a change in the equilibrium interest rate.

- Open market operations. The Fed's purchase or sale of bonds will cause a change in the supply of central bank money and, therefore, a new equilibrium interest rate.

- Changes in \$Y. Any change in income will cause a change in money demand, a change in currency and reserve demand, and, therefore, a change in the demand for central bank money. For example, an increase in the demand for central bank money will cause an increase in the interest rate.

Learning Tip

- You should become familiar with both models of interest rate determination: (1) the money market; and (2) the market for central bank money. To practice this, you can examine, for both models, the effects of a change in the parameters c and θ.
- You may also want to spend some time reviewing the discussion of the market for reserves. Some instructors might emphasize this interpretation of the material. An understanding of this market for reserves will allow you to understand the determination of the federal funds rate.

SELF-TEST QUESTIONS

1. Compare the characteristics of money and bonds (1).

2. Define each of the following: wealth and saving (1).

3. Explain the difference between a stock and flow variable (1).

4. What effect will an increase in the interest rate (i) have on the demand for money? Briefly explain (1).

5. What effect will an increase in nominal income (\$Y) have on the demand for money? Briefly explain (1).

6. Why is the money demand curve downward sloping (1)?

7. If the Fed wants to increase the money supply, should it buy or sell bonds? Briefly explain (1).

8. What does the LM relation represent (2)?

9. What effect will an increase in the money supply have on the interest rate? Show this graphically (2).

10. What effect will an increase in nominal income have on the interest rate? Show this graphically (2).

11. What effect will a contractionary open market operation have on the price of bonds, the interest rate and the money supply (2)?

12. Define central bank money (i.e., the monetary base) and explain what the money multiplier is (3).

13. In the presence of currency, the money supply is determined by three variables/parameters? What are they (3)?

14. What is the market for central bank money (3)?

15. What is the Federal funds market (3)?

REVIEW PROBLEMS

1. The purpose of this question is to make sure that you understand the definitions of several variables discussed in this chapter.

a. Is it possible for someone to have zero income and a large amount of wealth? Briefly explain.

b. Is it possible for someone to have zero saving and positive wealth? Briefly explain.

c. Can wealth ever be negative for an individual? Explain.

2. The following is a list of variables you have now studied: wealth, saving, investment, business inventories, the money supply, capital, and income.

a. Which of the above variables is a flow variable?

b. Which of the above variables is a stock variable?

3. What effect will a reduction in nominal income have on money demand? Explain.

4. Briefly explain what happens to money demand and the money supply as a result of each of the following events:

a. a 10% increase in $Y

b. a reduction in i

c. expansionary open market operation

5. Note: only work on this problem is your instructor has discussed velocity in your class. This question is based on material presented in a previous edition of Blanchard and, therefore, may not be presented by some instructors.

Use the information and space provided below to answer the following questions.

Year$Y	M	i	$Wealth	Velocity
1964	648.0	160.3	4.03	1997.2
1974	1458.6	274.3	7.82	4078.9
1984	3777.2	552.1	11.89	11409.6
1994	6736.9	1147.6	6.27	19493.4

$Y is nominal GDP measured in billions; M is M1 measured in billions; $Wealth is nominal wealth (the figure for $Wealth in 1994 is the value of $Wealth in 1993); and i is the interest rate on 3-year U.S. Treasury securities. Source: *The Economic Report of the President*, 1995.

a. Calculate velocity for the above four years. Briefly comment on what has happened, if anything, to velocity during the above period.
b. Assume that the above changes in the interest rate represent the only change in financial markets. Are the changes in velocity that you calculated consistent with what you would expect given our assumption about money demand? Explain.
c. Based on the model of money demand presented in this chapter, what effect did the above changes in $Wealth have on velocity? Briefly explain.

6. Use the graph provided below to answer the following question.

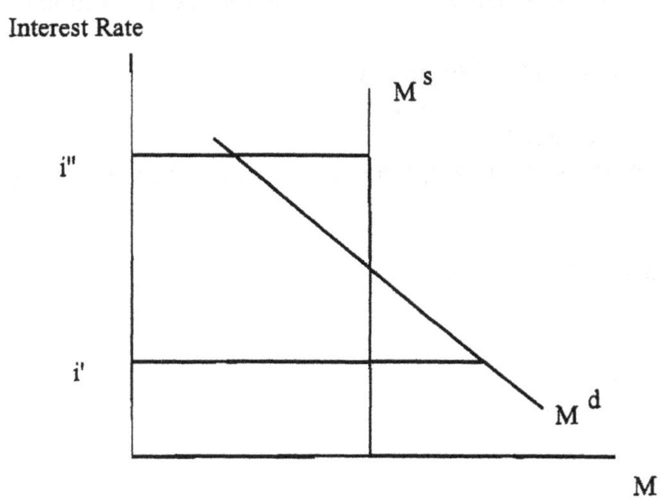

a. Given money demand and money supply, explain what type of situation exists when the interest rate equals i". At this interest rate, how much money do individuals want to hold? At this interest rate, how much money actually exists?
b. Based on your analysis in part (a), what must happen to the interest rate for financial market equilibrium to occur? What happens to money demand and money supply as i changes?

c. Given money demand and money supply, explain what type of situation exists when the interest rate equals i'. At this interest rate, how much money do individuals want to hold? At this interest rate, how much money actually exists?
d. Based on your analysis in part (c), what must happen to the interest rate for financial market equilibrium to occur? What happens to money demand and money supply as i changes?

7. Use the graph provided below to answer the following questions.

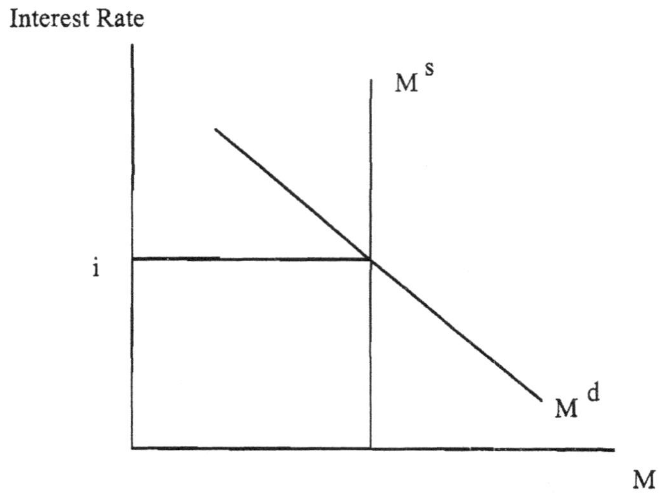

a. How much money do individuals hold at the initial interest rate (i)? Show this in the graph.
b. Suppose there is a reduction in \$Y. What effect will this have on money demand and on the interest rate? Show this graphically.
c. At the initial interest rate of i, what has happened to money demand?
d. What must happen to the interest rate to restore equilibrium?
e. As i changes, what happens to money demand?
f. How much money do individuals hold at this new interest rate? Compare your answer here with your answer to part (a).

8. Use the space provided below to answer this question.

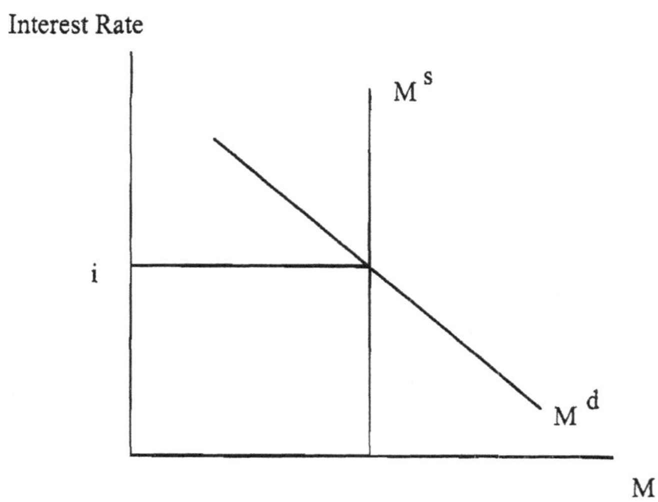

a. How much money do individuals hold at the initial interest rate (i)? Show this in the graph.
b. Suppose there is a reduction in the money supply. What effect will this have on the money supply curve and on the interest rate? Show this graphically.
c. At the initial interest rate of i, what has happened to the actual quantity of money?
d. What must happen to the interest rate to restore equilibrium?
e. As i changes, what happens to money demand?
f. How much money do individuals hold at this new interest rate? Compare your answer here with your answer to part (a).

9. Suppose a bond pays $200 in one year. Calculate the interest rate on this bond when the price of the bond ($\$P_B$) is:
a. $150
b. $160
c. $180
d. $195
e. What happens to the interest rate as the price of the bond falls?

10. Suppose a bond pays $1000 in one year. Calculate the price of the bond when the interest rate is:
a. 5% (.05)
b. 10% (.10)
c. 15% (.15)
d. What happens to the price of the bond as the interest rate increases?

11. For this question, assume that all money is held in the form of currency. Assume that central bank money is initially equal to $100 million. Now suppose that the Fed pursues an expansionary open market operation equal to $10 million. Given this information, explain what effect this has on:
a. the amount of the Fed's assets
b. the amount of the Fed's liabilities
c. the price of bonds
d. the interest rate
e. the money demand curve
f. central bank money
g. the money supply curve

12. For this question, assume that all money is held in the form of currency. Again, assume that central bank money is initially equal to $100 million. Now suppose that the Fed pursues a contractionary open market operation equal to $20 million. Given this information, explain what effect this has on:
a. the amount of the Fed's assets
b. the amount of the Fed's liabilities
c. the price of bonds
d. the interest rate
e. the money demand curve
f. central bank money
g. the money supply curve

13. For this question, assume that individuals do not hold currency and that the reserve ratio (θ) is 0.2. Also assume that the monetary base equals $500 million. Given this information, calculate:
a. the amount of reserves
b. the amount of checkable deposits
c. the money supply
d. the money multiplier

14. Based on your analysis in #13, calculate what happens to the following variables if the Fed buys $50 million of bonds:

a. the monetary base
b. the amount of reserves
c. the amount of checkable deposits
d. the money supply

15. Based on your analysis in #13 (and using the original numbers), calculate what happens to the following variables if the Fed sells $10 million of bonds:

a. the monetary base
b. the amount of reserves
c. the amount of checkable deposits
d. the money supply

16. The expression, $(1/\theta)$, represents the money multiplier when CU = 0.

a. Calculate the money multiplier for of the following values of θ: .1, .2, .3, .4, and .5.
b. What happens to the size of the money multiplier when θ increases?
c. Provide a brief, intuitive explanation of the effects of an increase in θ on the money multiplier.

17. Use the information provided below to answer the following questions:

R = 50 CU = 250 D = 500

a. Calculate the reserve ratio.
b. Calculate the value of the parameter c.
c. Calculate the size of the monetary base.
d. Calculate the size of the money supply.
e. Calculate the money multiplier.
f. In the space below, fill in the information about the banks' and central bank's balance sheets. Specifically, what is the dollar value of the bonds held by banks? What is the dollar value of the bonds held by the central bank?

Banks' Balance Sheet

Assets	Liabilities

Central Bank Balance Sheet

Assets	Liabilities

18. Use your calculations in #17 to answer these questions.

a. Suppose the Fed wishes to increase by money supply by $100 million. What type of open market operation should it pursue? What should the dollar amount of the Fed purchase or sale of bonds be in order for M to increase by $100 million?
b. What effect will this Fed action have on the price of bonds? Explain.
c. Suppose the Fed wants to reduce the money supply by $40 million. What type of open market operation should it pursue? What should the dollar amount of the Fed purchase or sale of bonds be in order for M to fall by $40 million?
d. What effect will this Fed action have on the price of bonds? Explain.

19. a. Suppose c = .2. Calculate the money multiplier for each of the following values of the reserve ratio (θ): .1, .2, and .5.
b. What happens to the money multiplier when the reserve ratio increases?
c. Provide an intuitive explanation of the effects of an increase in the reserve ratio on the money multiplier.

20. a. Suppose θ = .1. Calculate the money multiplier for each of the following values of c: .1, .2, and .5.
b. What happens to the money multiplier when the parameter c increases?
c. Provide an intuitive explanation of the effects of an increase in c on the money multiplier.

21. Use the market for central bank money to answer the following questions. Graphically illustrate and briefly explain the effects of the following events on the interest rate. Briefly note whether your conclusions here are any different from those you would obtain if you used the money market to examine these events.
a. an open market sale by the Fed
b. a reduction in income
c. an increase in the reserve ratio, θ

MULTIPLE CHOICE QUESTIONS

1. Which of the following variables is NOT a stock variable?

a. the money supply
b. $Wealth
c. investment
d. the monetary base

2. An increase in nominal income ($Y) will cause:

a. an increase in money demand
b. an increase in central bank money
c. an increase in the monetary base
d. an increase in the money supply

3. The U.S. government currently insures each bank account up to what level?

a. $25,000
b. $50,000
c. $75,000
d. $100,000

4. An increase in the interest rate (i) will cause:

a. a rightward shift in money demand
b. a leftward shift in money demand
c. an increase in the money supply
d. a reduction in money demand

5. Which of the following events will cause a reduction in the interest rate?

a. a Fed sale of bonds
b. a reduction in the money supply
c. a reduction in $Y
d. an increase in money demand

6. Which of the following variables is an asset on a bank's balance sheet?

a. reserves
b. checkable deposits
c. the monetary base
d. currency

7. Which of the following variables is a liability on a bank's balance sheet?

a. currency
b. checkable deposits
c. bonds
d. reserves

8. Which of the following variables is a liability on the Fed's balance sheet?

a. checkable deposits
b. bonds
c. currency
d. loans

9. A central bank purchase of bonds will cause which of the following to occur?

a. a reduction in the monetary base
b. an increase in the monetary base
c. a reduction in the price of bonds
d. an increase in the price of bonds

10. An expansionary open market operation will tend to cause:

a. an increase in bond prices ($\$P_B$) and an increase in the interest rate (i)
b. an increase in $\$P_B$ and a reduction in i
c. a reduction in $\$P_B$ and a reduction in i
d. a reduction in $\$P_B$ and an increase in i

11. A contractionary open market operation will cause:

a. a reduction in the money supply
b. an increase in the money supply
c. an increase in the monetary base
d. the interest rate to fall

12. Which of the following will occur when the interest rate increases?

a. the price of bonds will fall
b. the money demand curve shifts to the left
c. the money demand curve shifts to the right
d. the money supply curve shifts to the right

13. Suppose a bond pays $1000 in one year. If the price of the bond is $750, we know that the interest rate on this bond is:

a. 7.5%
b. 15%
c. 25%
d. 33%

14. Suppose money demand is greater than money supply at the current interest rate. Given this information, we know that:

a. the interest rate (i) must fall to restore equilibrium
b. i must increase to restore equilibrium
c. the bond market is in equilibrium at the current interest rate
d. none of the above

15. Suppose individuals do not hold currency and that the banks' reserve ratio is 0.25. The money multiplier is:

a. 1/(1-.25) = 1.33
b. 2.5
c. 4
d. 5

16. Suppose the ratio of currency to checkable deposits is 0.5 and the reserve ratio (θ) is 0.25. The money multiplier is:

a. 1/.75 = 1.33
b. 1.6
c. 1/(1-.75) = 4
d. 5

17. Which of the following events will cause an increase in the money multiplier?

a. an increase in the reserve ratio
b. an increase in the parameter c
c. a reduction in the reserve ratio
d. an increase in the monetary base

18. Which of the following events will cause an increase in the money supply?

a. an increase in the interest rate
b. an increase in the reserve ratio
c. a Fed purchase of bonds
d. an increase in the parameter c

19. The federal funds rate is determined in which of the following markets?

a. the market for central bank money
b. the market for reserves
c. the money market
d. the bond market

20. Suppose individuals hold both currency and checkable deposits. Given this information, which of the following expressions represents the money multiplier?

a. $1/[c + \theta(1-c)]$
b. $1/\theta$
c. $[c + \theta(1-c)]$
d. $1/[1-c]$
e. $1/[1-\theta]$

CHAPTER 5. GOODS AND FINANCIAL MARKETS: THE IS-LM MODEL.

OBJECTIVES, REVIEW, AND TUTORIAL

After working through the chapter and the following material, you should be able to:

(1) Understand the determinants of investment.

(2) Interpret and explain the IS relation.

(3) Understand how the IS curve is derived; explain its shape; and explain what factors cause it to shift.

(4) Explain the relationship between the real money supply and real money demand.

(5) Understand how the LM curve is derived; explain its shape; and explain what factors cause it to shift.

(6) Understand what is meant by equilibrium in the IS-LM model.

(7) Examine the effects of fiscal policy in the IS-LM model.

(8) Examine the effects of monetary policy in the IS-LM model.

(9) Discuss what is meant by the "policy mix."

(10) Explain how factors other than monetary and fiscal policy can affect the IS-LM model.

(11) Re-examine the implications of the IS-LM model when dynamics are introduced.

1. THE DETERMINANTS OF INVESTMENT

Investment is now assumed to be:

(1) an increasing function of sales; and
(2) a decreasing function of the interest rate.

• Sales. As sales rise, firms will increase their purchase of equipment and will build new plants. As sales decrease, firms will cut back on investment.

Learning Tip
In this chapter, we assume that output always equals sales. Therefore, investment is an increasing function of output.

• The interest rate. As i increases, the cost of borrowing rises. As the cost of borrowing increases, some firms will not purchase new equipment since the now higher cost of borrowing is greater than the additional profits from the new equipment.

2. THE IS RELATION AND THE IS CURVE

(1) Introduction

The equilibrium condition in the goods market is represented by the IS relation:

$Y = C(Y\text{-}T) + I(Y,i) + G$.

We use the IS relation to derive the IS curve.

• The IS curve represents the relationship between the interest rate and the equilibrium level of output in the goods market.

(2) Slope of the IS curve

- A reduction in the interest rate causes an increase in investment.
- The increase in I causes an increase in demand (Z).
- The increase in Z causes an increase in equilibrium output through the multiplier effect.
- A lower i, therefore, leads to an increase in equilibrium output in the goods market. The IS curve is downward sloping to reflect this.

Learning Tip

The IS curve is derived by examining the effects of changes in i on I and on Y. Changes in i and Y do NOT cause shifts in the IS curve, only movements along the IS curve.

(3) Shifts in the IS curve

Any factor, other than a change in i, that causes a change in Y in Figure 5-1 (i.e., the ZZ-45° degree line graph) will cause a shift in the IS curve.

- The IS curve shifts to the right when government purchases (G) increase, taxes (T) fall, consumer confidence increases, etc.
- The IS curve shifts to the left when G falls, T increases, consumer confidence falls, etc.

Learning Tip

To understand shifts, consider the following example. Suppose G falls by 100. Let's also keep i arbitrarily fixed. The drop in G causes Y to fall by an amount equal to the change in G times the multiplier. At the same i, equilibrium output is now lower. We now need a new IS curve to reflect this. The IS curve then shifts left with the horizontal distance equal to the change in G times the multiplier.

3. REAL MONEY SUPPLY, REAL MONEY DEMAND, AND THE LM RELATION

(1) Introduction

The financial markets equilibrium condition is now expressed in real terms. That is, equilibrium occurs when the interest rate equates the real supply of money with real money demand. This is represented by the following LM relation:

$M/P = YL(i)$.

Learning Tip

- M/P is the real supply of money.
- YL(i) is real money demand.
- A 5% increase in real income causes a 5% increase in real money demand.
- An increase in the interest rate (i) causes a reduction in real money demand.

- The LM curve represents the relationship between income (Y) and the equilibrium interest rate in the financial markets.

(2) Slope of the LM curve

- An increase in income causes an increase in real money demand.
- At the initial interest rate, money demand now is greater than the supply of money.
- i must rise to restore equilibrium in the financial markets.
- A higher Y, therefore, requires an increase in the interest rate to maintain financial markets equilibrium. The LM curve is upward sloping to reflect this.

(3) Shifts in the LM curve

The LM curve will shift whenever the financial markets equilibrium interest rate changes because of factors other than a change in Y.

- The LM curve is drawn for a given value of the real money supply (M/P).
- A change in M/P causes a change in the equilibrium interest rate at every level of output.
- The LM curve shifts down when M/P increases because a lower i is needed to maintain equilibrium in the financial markets.
- The LM curve shifts up when M/P decreases because a higher i is needed to maintain equilibrium in the financial markets.

Learning Tip

- M/P can increase when M increases or when P falls.
- Changes in M (or P) will, therefore, cause shifts in the LM curve.
- A change in Y (or a change in i) does NOT cause shifts in the LM curve, only movements along the curve.
- If you do not understand how changes in M/P cause shifts in the LM curve, return to Figure 5-5.
    - For a given level of Y, change M/P.
    - This change in M/P causes a change in i.
    - This change in i determines the extent to which the LM curve shifts up or down.

4. EQUILIBRIUM IN THE IS-LM MODEL

- The IS curve represents the relationship between the interest rate and the level of output that maintains equilibrium in the goods market.
- The LM curve represents the relationship between the interest rate and the level of output that maintains equilibrium in the financial markets.
- Refer to Figure 5-6. There is only one **i** and one level of output which simultaneously maintain equilibrium in BOTH the goods and financial markets. This equilibrium is called the overall equilibrium.
- Since the economy is operating on both the IS and LM curves, we know that the goods and financial markets are in equilibrium.

Learning Tip

Recall that:
(1) The IS curve can shift when, for example, G, T, or consumer confidence changes. Any shift in the IS curve will yield a new overall equilibrium;
(2) The LM curve can shift when the real money supply changes. Any shift in the LM curve will yield a new overall equilibrium;
(3) As the IS and LM curves shift, the interest rate, the level of output, and the composition of output may also change.

5. FISCAL POLICY

- A fiscal expansion occurs when government purchases (G) increase or when taxes are cut.
- A fiscal contraction occurs when government purchases are cut or when taxes are increased.

Consider the effects of a reduction in G in the IS-LM model; the graphical analysis is identical to that found in Figure 5-7.

- The cut in G causes the IS curve to shift left. The size of the horizontal shift equals the change in G times the multiplier.
- The leftward shift in the IS curve yields a new equilibrium at the intersection of the new IS curve and the original LM curve.
- This cut in G causes a reduction in Y and a reduction in i.

Learning Tip

You must be able to explain intuitively these shifts and the economy's response to these shifts.

- The decrease in G causes a reduction in demand (Z)
- The decrease in demand causes firms to cut production.
- As Y falls, individuals reduce their demand for money.
- As money demand falls, the interest rate must fall to restore equilibrium in the financial markets.
- At the lower i, money demand once again equals the money supply.
- Question: Why doesn't Y fall to Y_C? Answer: as i falls, some of the drop in Y is offset by the positive effects of the lower i on investment.

To summarize, a fiscal contraction will cause:

- a reduction in Y
- a lower i
- a reduction in consumption and saving via the reduction in disposable income
- ambiguous effects on investment
  - the lower i causes an increase in I
  - the lower Y causes a reduction in I

Learning Tip

- Make sure you can explain the effects of a fiscal expansion. Review problem #9 will examine this.
- The above analysis applies to any leftward shift in the IS curve (e.g. increases in taxes, reductions in consumer confidence, etc.).

6. MONETARY POLICY

- A monetary expansion occurs when the money supply increases.
- A monetary contraction occurs when the money supply falls.

A Fed purchase of bonds (i.e., a monetary expansion) will cause:

- an increase in the money supply and a rightward shift in the money supply curve
- the increase in the money supply requires a reduction in the interest rate to induce individuals to hold the larger quantity of money
- the drop in i causes the LM curve to shift down
- the shift down in the LM curve yields a new equilibrium with a lower i and higher Y

Other results/explanations of a monetary expansion:

- Why does Y increase? The lower i causes an increase in investment which has a positive, multiplier effect on Y.
- Consumption and saving both increase via the increase in disposable income.
- Investment increases for two reasons. Both the reduction in i and increase in Y cause I to increase.

Learning Tip

- Does the increase in the money supply or the reduction in the interest rate cause the IS curve to shift? NO!! We move along the IS curve.
- Make sure you can explain the opposite example (a monetary contraction).
- You must understand that changes in the reserve ratio (θ) and the parameter c (the ratio of currency to checkable deposits) will also cause changes in the money supply and, therefore, cause the LM curve to shift.
- A shift in money demand caused by factors other than changes in Y will also cause the LM curve to shift. Review problem #8 will allow you to examine this.

7. THE MONETARY AND FISCAL POLICY MIX

- The combination of monetary policy and fiscal policy is called the monetary-fiscal policy mix.
- The policy mix refers to situations where both the LM and IS curves shift.
- There are four possible cases of the policy mix:
  - Case 1: Expansionary monetary policy and expansionary fiscal policy (LM shifts down, and the IS shifts right).
  - Case 2: Expansionary monetary policy and contractionary fiscal policy (LM shifts down, and the IS shifts left).
  - Case 3: Contractionary monetary policy and contractionary fiscal policy (LM shifts up and, the IS shifts left).
  - Case 4: Contractionary monetary policy and expansionary fiscal policy (LM shifts up and, the IS shifts right).

Learning Tip

- In each case, the effects of the policy mix on one of the endogenous variables (Y or i) will always be ambiguous (unless we know the exact magnitude of the policy changes).
- The effect on the other endogenous variable will be known. For example:
  - For Case 2, i unambiguously falls with the change in Y depending on the size of the shifts in the IS and LM curves.
  - In the figure associated with the German Unification example (Case 4), i unambiguously increases, and the change in Y again depends on the size of the shifts.
- Make sure you can explain the effects of each combination of monetary and fiscal policy.
- Also make sure you can explain the effects of the policy mix on consumption, saving, and investment.

8. INTRODUCTION OF DYNAMICS TO THE IS-LM MODEL

When the IS curve shifts, Y will not immediately adjust to its new equilibrium level for three reasons:

(1) Y will respond with a lag to changes in demand
(2) C will respond with a lag to change in disposable income
(3) Investment may respond with a lag to changes in sales

Financial markets will, however, adjust rapidly to changes in supply and demand. We can assume that the economy is always on the LM curve.

Learning Tip

- The assumption about rapid adjustment in the financial markets is not unrealistic. Think about how quickly the bond market responds to any change in supply or demand conditions.
- Pay particular attention to the analysis that immediately follows. Attempt to repeat this for a change in the money supply where we assume that financial markets are always in equilibrium and output responds slowly to changes in demand.

The dynamic effects of an increase in government purchases are shown in the graph below:

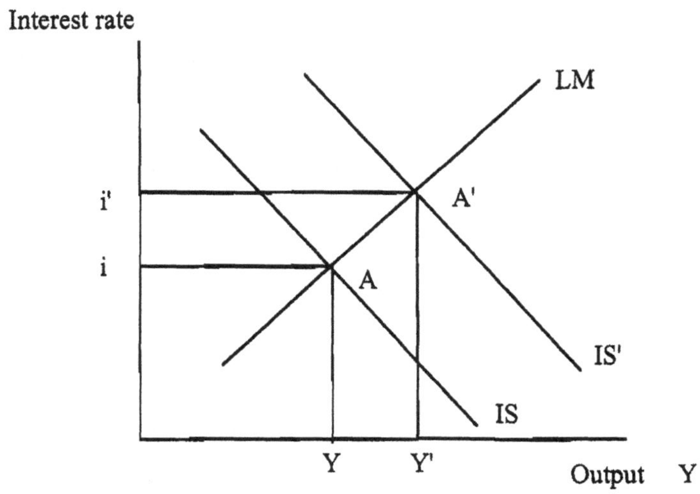

- The increase in G causes an increase in demand (Z).
- Firms respond by slowly increasing Y.
- As soon as Y begins to increase, money demand rises and i rises to maintain financial markets equilibrium.
- Therefore, as Y increases, the economy moves along the LM curve. Y continues to increase (and i rises) until the new equilibrium is reached at A'.

9. THE LM RELATION AS AN INTEREST RATE RULE

The appendix ("An Alternative Derivation of the LM Relation as an Interest Rate Rule?") contains an excellent discussion of how an interest rate rule policy can be incorporated in the IS-LM model. Specifically, the LM curve can be adjusted to reflect different interest rate rules chosen by the central bank. To do so, one must alter slightly the definition of the LM relation.

When the central bank is pursuing an interest rate policy, one must recognize the following change in the definition of the LM relation:

- The LM relation illustrates the relation between the interest rate and income when the central bank is pursuing an interest rate rule.

Also, note the following:

- This new LM relation will be flatter when the central bank pursues an interest rate rule.
- This new LM relation will be horizontal, at the targeted interest rate, when the central bank attempts to keep the interest rate equal to some targeted interest rate.
- Make sure you understand the differences among three different LM curves in Figure 1 (i.e., LM, LM'', and LM') of the appendix.
- To test your understanding of the implications of interest rate rules, examine the effects of a given increase in government spending for each of the three different LM curves in Figure 1 of the appendix.

SELF-TEST QUESTIONS

1. What are the two determinants of investment (1)?

2. What does the IS curve represent (1)?

3. Why is the IS curve downward sloping (1)?

4. Changes in what variables cause the IS curve to shift (1)?

5. What does the LM curve represent (2)?

6. Why is the LM curve upward sloping (2)?

7. Changes in what variables cause the LM curve to shift (2)?

8. What is meant by overall equilibrium in the IS-LM model (3)?

9. Why are the effects of fiscal policy on investment ambiguous (3)?

10. What effect will a fiscal expansion have on Y and i (3)?

11. What effect will a monetary expansion have on Y and i (3)?

12. What is meant by the policy mix (4)?

13. In the IS-LM model which incorporates dynamics, which market (goods or financial) will respond more quickly to a change in the money supply (4)?

14. What effect does an interest rate rule have on the LM relation (appendix)?

REVIEW PROBLEMS

1. Suppose investment is represented by the following expression:

$I = 200 - 20i + .1Y$.

a. Let Y = 5000. Calculate the level of investment for the following values of i: 5%, 10%, and 15%. Let i = 5 when the interest rate is 5%, and so on. What happens to investment as i increases?
b. Let i = 5. Calculate the level of investment for the following values of Y: 5500, 6000 and 6500. What happens to I as Y increases?

2. Suppose the goods market is represented by the following equations:

$C = 180 + .7Y_D$ $\qquad Y_D = Y - T$ $\qquad T = 400$
$I = 100 - 18i + .1Y$ $\qquad G = 400$
$Y = C + I + G$

a. Solve for the equilibrium level of output. That is, obtain an equation with Y on the left hand side and all other variables on the right hand side.
b. Calculate the level of output that occurs when the interest rate is: 5%, 10%, 15%, and 20% (i.e., i = 5, and so on). On a separate piece of paper, plot these 4 combinations of i and Y. What does this curve represent?
c. As the goods market adjusts to these increases in i, what happens to consumption, saving, and investment? Briefly explain why each variable changes.
d. Calculate the equilibrium level of output when i = 8% (let i = 8). Where is this point on your graph? Assume that i continues to be 8%. Calculate the equilibrium level of output when G increases by 100 (to 500). What is the size of the multiplier?
e. What does your analysis in part (d) suggests happens to the IS curve depicted in your graph? Briefly explain.

3. Assume the goods market is represented by the equations provided in question #2. Note: no calculations are needed here, just provide brief explanations. Briefly explain what would happen to the IS curve as a result of each of the following events:
a. reduction in the interest rate
b. increase in the interest rate
c. a reduction in c_0 from 180 to 100
d. an increase in taxes

4. Assume that money is represented only by coins and bills held by individuals (i.e., there are no checkable deposits). Suppose an individual, given her current income, always wants to hold enough currency to buy three bottles of her favorite beverage each day.
a. Suppose a can of this beverage costs $1. How much currency will this individual hold? This is her nominal money demand.
b. Now suppose that the price of the beverage increases to $1.20. What happens to her nominal money demand? How much currency (in nominal terms) will she now hold? Explain.
c. For simplicity, assume that the GDP deflator increases from 1 to 1.2 during this same period. What happened to the individual's real money demand? Briefly explain.
d. Now suppose that her real income increases. Briefly explain what will happen to her consumption (including her consumption of this beverage). What do you think will happen to her real demand for money? Briefly explain.

5. Use the graphs provided below to answer the following questions.

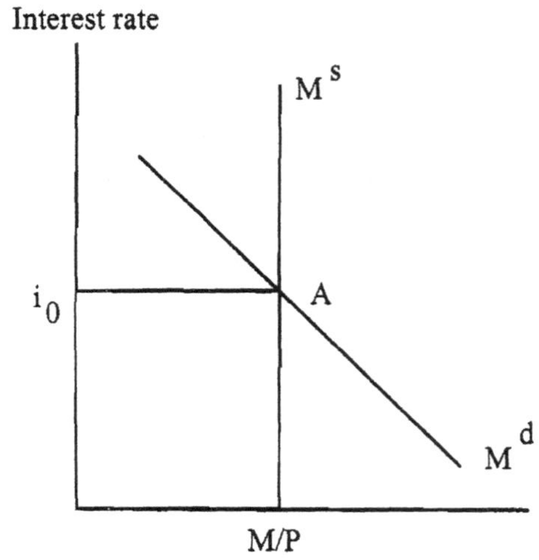

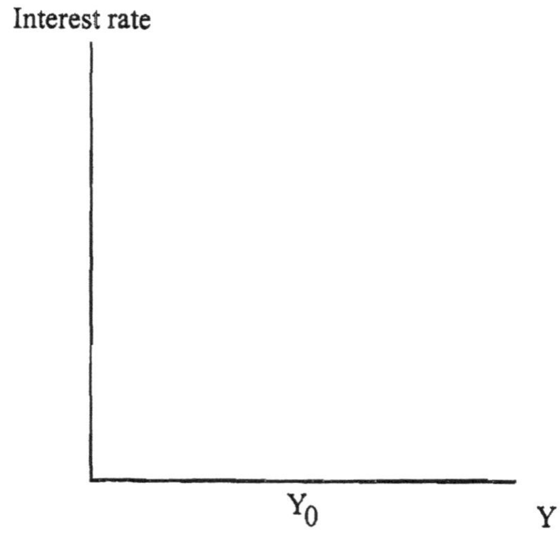

a. Initially let $i = i_0$ and $Y = Y_0$. Suppose Y falls to Y_1. Illustrate what happens to money demand as a result of this drop in Y. At the initial interest rate, what type of situation exists? Briefly explain.
b. What must happen to i as a result of this drop in Y? Briefly explain. Label this new equilibrium A'. In the graph to the right, plot the points A and A'.
c. Repeat the analysis in (a) and (b) assuming that Y falls even further to Y_2. Label this point A" and plot it in the graph to the right.
d. What does this plot of points in the above graph represent? Explain.

6. Use the graphs provided below to answer the following questions.

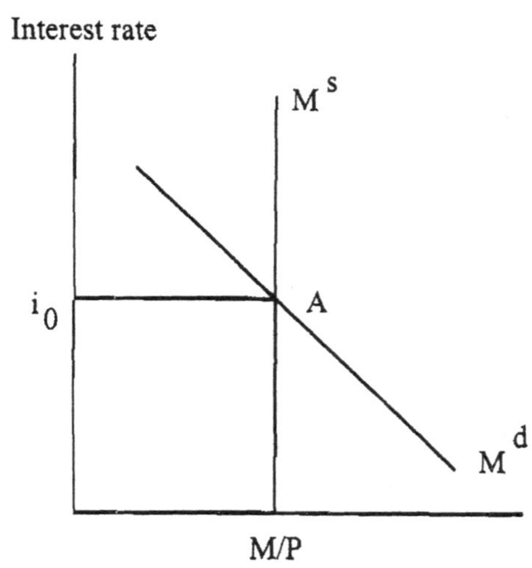

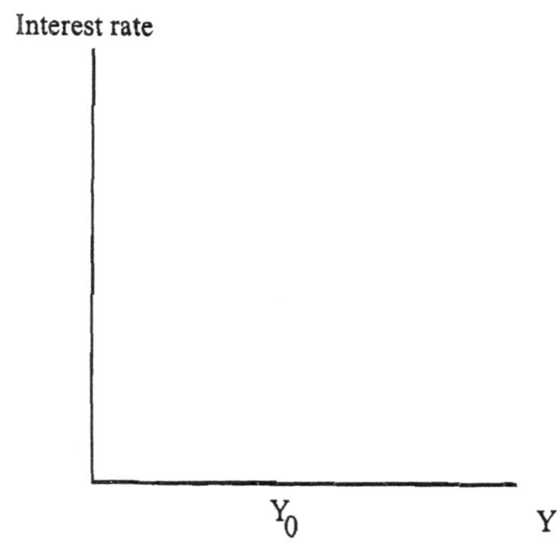

a. Initially let $i = i_0$ and $Y = Y_0$. Suppose the real money supply <u>falls</u> to M'/P. Illustrate what happens to the real money supply curve as a result of this drop in M/P. At the initial interest rate, what type of situation exists? Briefly explain.
b. What must happen to i as a result of this drop in the real money supply? Briefly explain. Label this new equilibrium A'.
c. What effect does this drop in the real money supply have on the position of the LM curve? Illustrate this in the above graph.

7. Suppose real money supply and real money demand are represented by the following equations:

$M^d = 6Y - 120i$ $\quad\quad$ $M^s = 5400$

a. Equate the above expressions for real money demand and real money supply, and solve for i. That is, i should appear on the left hand side with all other variables on the right hand side.
b. Calculate i when Y equals: 1000, 1100, and 1200. On a separate piece of paper, plot these combinations of i and Y. What does this curve represent?
c. Calculate i when Y = 1400. Where is this point on the curve? Assume that Y remains at 1400. Suppose the real money supply falls to 5000. Calculate the new equilibrium i when M falls by 400. How much does i change?
d. What does your analysis in part (c) suggest happens to the LM curve? Briefly explain.

8. Use the graph provided below to answer this question. Suppose the financial markets are in equilibrium and that Y does not change.

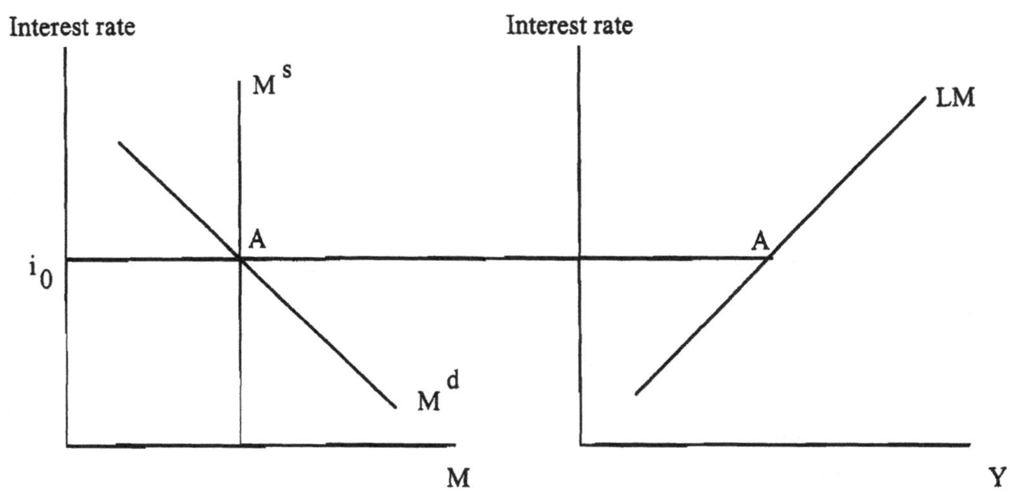

a. What effect has the increased use and availability of credit cards had on money demand? Briefly explain.
b. Illustrate the effects of this on money demand in the above graph. Briefly explain what must happen to i to restore equilibrium.
c. What does your analysis suggest happens to the position of the LM curve <u>given</u> that income (Y) has not changed?
d. During holiday periods, individuals will often increase their holdings of money even though the interest rate and their incomes have not changed. What effect would this behavior have on the LM curve? Briefly explain.

9. Use the IS-LM model to answer this question.
a. Suppose government purchases increase. What effect will this have on the IS curve and on the LM curve?
b. What effect will this increase in G have on i and Y?
c. What effect will this increase in G have on consumption and saving? Briefly explain.
d. What effect will this increase in G have on investment?
Note: Make sure you can illustrate graphically the effects of this change in G.

10. Use the IS-LM model to answer this question.

a. Suppose the money supply decreases. What effect will this have on the IS curve and on the LM curve?

b. What effect will this decrease in M have on i and Y?

c. What effect will this decrease in M have on consumption and saving? Briefly explain.

d. What effect will this decrease in M have on investment?

Note: Make sure you can illustrate graphically the effects of this change in M.

11. The effects of a fiscal expansion on investment are ambiguous.

a. Why is this so?

b. Is it possible for investment to increase when government purchases increase? Explain.

c. Is it possible for investment to increase when G falls? Explain.

12. Suppose the economy is represented by the following equations (these are identical to those included in questions #2 and #7).

$M^d = 6Y - 120i$ $\quad\quad$ $M^s = 5400$

$C = 180 + .7Y_D$ $\quad\quad$ $Y_D = Y - T$ $\quad\quad$ $T = 400$

$I = 100 - 18i + .1Y$ $\quad\quad$ $G = 400$

$Y = C + I + G$

a. Write out the equation for equilibrium in the goods market. Specifically, solve for the equilibrium level of output. That is, obtain an equation with Y on the left-hand side and all other variables on the right-hand side. You did this in part (a) of #2.

b. Write out the equation for equilibrium i in the financial market. Specifically, equate the above expressions for real money demand and real money supply and solve for i. That is, i should appear on the left-hand side with all other variables on the right-hand side. You did this in part (a) of #7.

c. Substitute the expression for i (in part (b)) into your equation for Y in part (a). Calculate the overall equilibrium level of output.

d. Calculate the equilibrium i by substituting the value of Y from (c) into your equation in (b).

e. At this equilibrium, what is the level of consumption and investment?

f. Calculate the new equilibrium value of Y, i, C, and I when G increases by 10 (from 400 to 410). What happened to investment as a result of this fiscal expansion? Briefly comment.

g. Using the original values of the variables, calculate the new equilibrium values of Y, i, C, and I when M increases by 200 (from 5400 to 5600). What happened to investment as a result of this monetary expansion?

13. Use the graph provided below to answer the following questions. Suppose the economy is initially at point A in the graph. Assume that government spending increases.

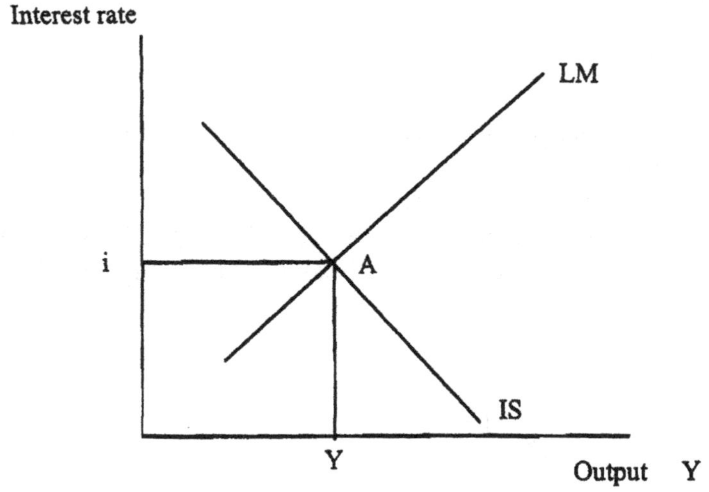

a. What effect will this increase in G have on the IS curve?
b. Suppose the Fed wants to maintain i at the initial level. What type of policy must the Fed pursue (i.e., contractionary or expansionary) to maintain the interest rate at its initial level? What effect will this Fed policy have on the LM curve? Illustrate the effects of the higher G and Fed response on the IS and LM curves. In your graph, clearly label the new equilibrium.
c. What happens to consumption, saving, and investment as a result of this policy mix? Briefly explain.

14. Use the graph provided below to answer the following questions. Suppose the economy is initially at point A in the graph. Assume that taxes are reduced.

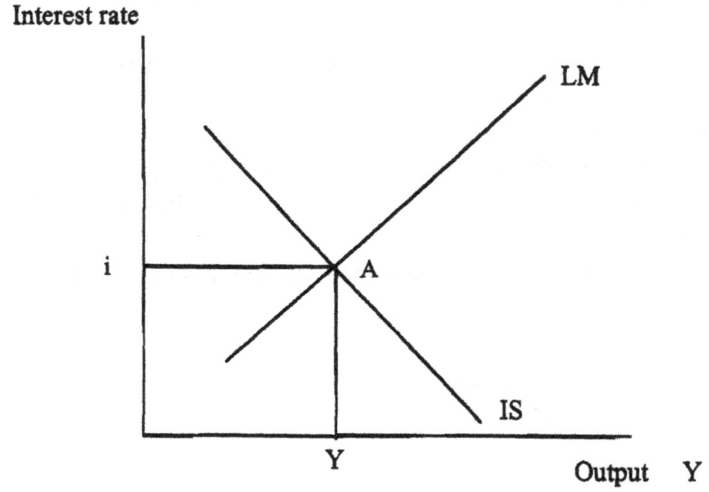

a. What effect will this cut in T have on the IS curve?
b. Suppose the Fed wants to maintain Y at the initial level. What type of policy must the Fed pursue (i.e., contractionary or expansionary) to maintain output at its initial level? What effect will this policy have on the LM curve? Illustrate the effects of the lower T and Fed response on the IS and LM curves. In your graph, clearly label the new equilibrium.
c. What happens to consumption, saving, and investment as a result of this policy mix? Briefly explain.

15. Briefly discuss what effect each of the following events will have on the IS curve, the LM curve, output, the interest rate, consumption, and investment.
a. an increase in consumer confidence
b. a reduction in consumer confidence
c. an increase in the use of credit cards

16. Assume that Y responds slowly to changes in demand (i.e., take into account dynamics). Assume that there is an increase in taxes.
a. What effect will this have on the IS curve? Briefly explain.
b. Use the graph provided below to answer this question. In your IS-LM graph, trace out the path the economy takes in response to this increase in taxes. What will be the final equilibrium? Show this in your graph.

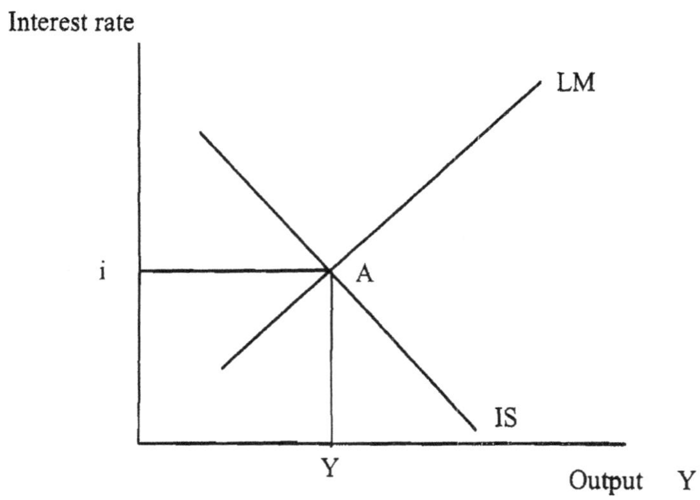

c. What happens to consumption, the interest rate, and investment during this adjustment?

17. Assume that Y responds slowly to changes in demand (i.e., take into account dynamics). Assume that there is an increase in the money supply.
a. What effect will this have on the LM curve? Briefly explain.
b. Use the graph provided below to answer this question. In your IS-LM graph, trace out the path the economy takes in response to this increase in the money supply. What will be the final equilibrium? Show this in your graph.
c. What happens to consumption, the interest rate, and investment during this adjustment?

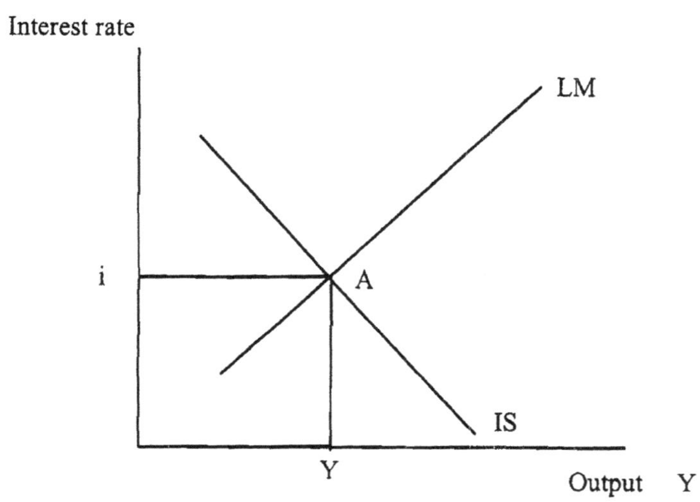

18. Suppose investment is independent of the interest rate. That is, changes in i have no effect on I.

a. What would the IS curve look like for such an economy? Briefly explain.

b. In such an economy, to what extent would changes in the money supply affect output? Explain.

c. In such an economy, to what extent would changes in G (or taxes) affect output? Explain.

MULTIPLE CHOICE QUESTIONS

1. In the IS-LM model, an increase in income (Y), all else fixed, will cause:

a. an increase in consumption
b. an increase in money demand
c. an increase in investment
d. all of the above

2. In the IS-LM model, an increase in the interest rate, all else fixed, will cause:

a. an increase in the money supply
b. a reduction in investment
c. a reduction in the money supply
d. none of the above

3. A tax cut will cause:

a. the IS curve to shift to the right
b. the IS curve to shift to the left
c. the LM curve to shift down
d. the LM curve to shift up

4. A reduction in government purchases will cause:

a. the IS curve to shift to the right
b. the IS curve to shift to the left
c. the LM curve to shift down
d. the LM curve to shift up

5. An increase in consumer confidence will cause:

a. the IS curve to shift to the right
b. the IS curve to shift to the left
c. the LM curve to shift down
d. the LM curve to shift up

6. A reduction in the money supply will cause:

a. the IS curve to shift to the right
b. the IS curve to shift to the left
c. the LM curve to shift down
d. the LM curve to shift up

7. An increase in money demand caused by factors other than a change in income (or the interest rate) will cause:

a. the IS curve to shift to the right
b. the IS curve to shift to the left
c. the LM curve to shift down
d. the LM curve to shift up

8. The IS curve is downward sloping because:

a. an increase in government purchases causes an increase in income
b. an increase in the money supply causes an increase in income
c. a reduction in the interest rate causes an increase in investment and income
d. an increase in the interest rate causes a reduction in money demand

9. The LM curve is upward sloping because:

a. an increase in Y causes an increase in money demand and an increase in the interest rate
b. an increase in the money supply causes a reduction in the interest rate
c. a reduction in the money supply causes an increase in the interest rate
d. all of the above

10. A Fed purchase of bonds will cause:

a. the LM curve to shift up
b. the LM curve to shift down
c. a lower interest rate, an increase in investment, and a rightward shift in the IS curve
d. a higher interest rate, a reduction in investment, and a leftward shift in the IS curve

11. In the IS-LM model presented in this chapter, we know with certainty that a fiscal expansion will cause:

a. an increase in the interest rate and an upward shift in the LM curve
b. an increase in the interest rate and an increase in output
c. an increase in the interest rate and a reduction in investment
d. an increase in output and an increase in investment

12. A monetary contraction will cause:

a. an increase in the interest rate and a reduction in investment
b. an increase i, a reduction in I, and a leftward shift in the IS curve
c. the LM curve to shift down
d. a reduction in Y, a reduction in money demand, and a reduction in the interest rate

13. A monetary expansion combined with a fiscal expansion will cause:

a. an increase in Y with ambiguous effects on i
b. a reduction in Y with ambiguous effects on i
c. an increase in i with ambiguous effects on Y
d. a reduction in i with ambiguous effects on Y

14. A monetary expansion combined with a fiscal contraction will cause:

a. an increase in Y with ambiguous effects on i
b. a reduction in Y with ambiguous effects on i
c. an increase in i with ambiguous effects on Y
d. a reduction in i with ambiguous effects on Y

15. A monetary contraction combined with a fiscal expansion will cause:

a. an increase in Y with ambiguous effects on i
b. a reduction in Y with ambiguous effects on i
c. an increase in i with ambiguous effects on Y
d. a reduction in i with ambiguous effects on Y

16. A monetary contraction combined with a fiscal contraction will cause:

a. an increase in Y with ambiguous effects on i
b. a reduction in Y with ambiguous effects on i
c. an increase in i with ambiguous effects on Y
d. a reduction in i with ambiguous effects on Y

17. In the IS-LM model which incorporates the dynamic adjustment of the goods market, we know that a change in the money supply will cause:

a. an immediate change in the interest rate with no change in output
b. an immediate change in both the interest rate and output
c. shifts in both the IS and LM curves
d. none of the above

18. In the IS-LM model which incorporates the dynamic adjustment of the goods market, we know that a reduction in the money supply will cause:

a. the interest rate to adjust immediately to the final, overall equilibrium level
b. the interest rate to initially rise above its final, overall equilibrium level
c. output to adjust immediately
d. none of the above

19. In the IS-LM model which incorporates the dynamic adjustment of the goods market, we know that a fiscal expansion will cause:

a. the interest rate to adjust immediately to the final, overall equilibrium level
b. the interest rate to initially rise above its final, overall equilibrium level
c. output and, therefore, the interest rate to adjust slowly over time
d. an increase in the interest rate and a leftward shift in the IS curve

CHAPTER 6.
THE LABOR MARKET

OBJECTIVES, REVIEW, AND TUTORIAL

After working through the chapter and the following material, you should be able to:

(1) Understand the difference among the participation rate, unemployment rate and the non-employment rate.

(2) Be familiar with the three characteristics of the large flow of workers.

(3) Explain the effects of movements in the unemployment rate on individual behavior.

(4) Explain how bargaining power, labor market conditions, and efficiency wage considerations affect wages.

(5) Explain the relationship among output, employment, wages, and prices.

(6) Understand both the WS and PS relations.

(7) Explain what is meant by the equilibrium real wage and the natural rate of unemployment.

(8) Explain what the natural level of employment and the natural level of output represent.

1. A REVIEW OF LABOR MARKET STATISTICS

You should be familiar with the following definitions:

- labor force = unemployed + employed
- participation rate = (labor force)/(noninstitutional civilian population)
- unemployment rate = unemployed/labor force
- non-employment rate = (population - employment)/population

2. THREE CHARACTERISTICS OF THE LARGE FLOWS OF WORKERS

(1) Employment

- Flows into employment come from: (1) unemployment; and (2) out of the labor force.
- Flows out of employment go: (1) to unemployment; and (2) out of the labor force.

(2) Unemployment

- Flows out of unemployment: (1) go to employment; and (2) leave the labor force.
- Flows into unemployment come from: (1) layoffs; (2) out of the labor force.

(3) Labor force

• These flows include retirees, those who finish school, and those who enter the labor force for the first time.
• These flows also include those who switch between participation and nonparticipation.

3. EFFECTS OF MOVEMENTS IN THE UNEMPLOYMENT RATE

Firms can reduce employment by:

(1) hiring fewer workers; and
(2) laying off existing workers.

(1) Decreased hires

A reduction in hires causes:

• a reduction in the chances that an unemployed worker gets a job
• fewer job openings
• a higher unemployment rate and more applicants; and
• an increase in the duration of unemployment.

(2) Decreased hires <u>and</u> more layoffs

This will cause an increase in unemployment. This increase in unemployment implies:

• a reduction in the chances that an unemployed worker gets a job; and
• a higher chance that employed workers will lose their jobs.

Learning Tip

• The proportion of unemployed finding a job each month tends to decrease when the unemployment rate rises.
• The separation rate tends to increase when the unemployment rate rises
• You should be aware that these changes occur differently for different groups.

4. WAGE DETERMINATION

Learning Tip

You should understand that:
(1) Workers are typically paid a wage that exceeds their reservation wage; and
(2) Wages depend on labor market conditions.

(1) Bargaining power

Many employed workers have bargaining power. When unemployment is low, their bargaining power increases.

(2) Efficiency wages

Firms may want to pay workers above their reservation wages:

- to increase the chances that productive workers will stay with the firm; and
- to increase the cost of workers losing their jobs if they are found shirking.

Learning Tip

Labor market conditions will also affect the firms' decisions to change wages. When unemployment decreases, firms may increase wages:
(1) to reduce the probability that workers will quit; and
(2) to deter shirking (with low unemployment, the cost of losing a job is lower).

You must also be able to interpret the following wage equation: $W = P^eF(u, z)$; where W is the nominal wage, P^e is the expected price level, u is the unemployment rate, and z is a catch-all variable.

(3) Expected price level

Both workers and firms care about the real wage (W/P). Since P is not known when W is set, the nominal wage depends on P^e. An increase in P^e will cause a proportionate increase in W.

(4) Unemployment

When u increases, bargaining power falls, and workers will accept lower wages.

(5) Other factors

Unemployment insurance, structural change, and changes in minimum wage legislation will also affect W.

5. RELATION AMONG OUTPUT, EMPLOYMENT, W, AND P

The production function, $Y = N$, implies that:
(1) an increase in employment will cause an equal increase in output; and
(2) the cost of producing one more unit of output equals the cost of employing one more worker.

Firms set their price according to:

$P = (1 + \mu)W$ where W is the cost of labor and μ is the markup of price over cost.

Learning Tip

- With perfect competition, firms set price equal to cost, so $\mu = 0$.
- When $\mu = 0$, P must equal W.
- Since many goods markets are not perfectly competitive, some firms can set P above W.
- Note: As markets become more competitive, μ decreases and P is closer to W.

6. THE WAGE-SETTING AND PRICE-SETTING RELATIONS

(1) The WS relation

Assume that nominal wages depend on the actual price level (P). The WS relation is represented by the following:

$W/P = F(u, z)$.

This equation indicates that there is a negative relation between the real wage and unemployment. As u increases, workers have less bargaining power and W/P is lower. This is represented by the WS relation in Figure 6-6.

(2) The PS relation

The PS relation is given by:

$W/P = 1/(1 + \mu)$.

Price-setting decisions determine the real wage paid by firms. An increase in the markup, μ, causes firms to increase P, given W. The real wage, therefore, falls when μ increases. The PS relation in Figure 6-6 is a horizontal line. Why? Changes in u have no effect on μ and, therefore, no effect on the real wage implied by price-setting behavior.

Learning Tip

- Make sure you can explain the shape of the WS and PS relations.
- The WS relation will shift up if the catch-all variable increases (e.g. if unemployment compensation increases, or the minimum wage increases).
- The PS relation will shift up if μ falls.

7. EQUILIBRIUM REAL WAGE, EMPLOYMENT, AND UNEMPLOYMENT

Equilibrium in the labor market requires that the real wage implied by the WS relation be equal to the real wage implied by the PS relation:

$F(u, z) = 1/(1 + \mu)$.

This is represented by the point in the following graph where the two relations intersect:

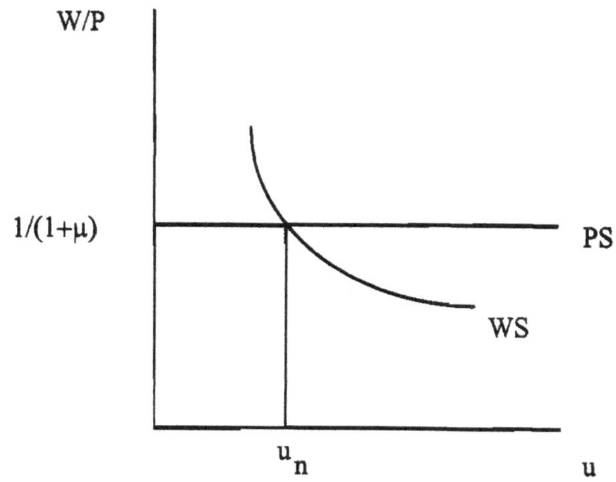

The unemployment rate consistent with equilibrium is the natural rate of unemployment (u_n).

Learning Tip

- Shifts in the WS and PS relations will cause:
  - changes in u_n
  - and, in the case of shifts in PS, changes in the real wage
- For example, changes in μ, unemployment compensation, minimum wages, etc. will yield new equilibria.
- Make sure you can explain intuitively the slope of the WS and PS relations.
- Make sure you can explain intuitively what factors cause shifts in the WS and PS relations.

Since $u = (L - N)/L$, $u = 1 - (N/L)$. Given u_n, there are corresponding natural levels of employment (N_n) and output (Y_n). Specifically, $Y_n = N_n = L(1 - u_n)$.

8. THE WS, PS, LABOR DEMAND, AND LABOR SUPPLY RELATIONS

In previous economics courses, you might have examined the labor market using supply and demand curves for labor. In this labor demand/labor supply framework, the market for labor determines both the equilibrium real wage and equilibrium level of employment. The model presented in this chapter can be modified so that it resembles what you might have seen previously.

(1) The WS curve when N is on the horizontal axis

- An increase in employment will cause a reduction in the unemployment rate.
- A reduction in u will cause an increase in bargaining power.
- The increase in bargaining power will cause an increase in the nominal wage.
- Given the aggregate price level, the rise in W will cause an increase in W/P.
- The WS curve, with N on the horizontal axis, is upward sloping.
- The WS curve appears similar to the labor supply curve.

(2) The PS curve when N is on the horizontal axis.

- An increase in N will cause a reduction in u.
- A reduction in u has no effect on the markup.
- Because P does not change, the real wage does not change either when N changes.
- Hence, the PS curve (with N on the horizontal axis) is horizontal.

(3) Determination of equilibrium u, N, and W/P

- The interaction of the WS and PS relations will determine the equilibrium levels of N and W/P.
- There is only one level of N that equates the real wage from wage-setting and price-setting behavior.
- These levels of N and W/P are the equilibrium levels of employment and real wage.
- Changes in z and the markup will have similar effects on the curves, u, and W/P.

Learning Tip

- The horizontal PS curve is similar to a labor demand curve when the marginal product of labor is constant.
- With Y = N (the production function), the marginal product of labor is constant.
- If labor exhibited diminishing marginal returns (i.e., the marginal product of labor falls as N increases), the PS curve in Figure 6-6 would be upward sloping. The PS curve in the figure associated with the Focus material would then be downward sloping.
- While these curves appear similar to labor supply and labor demand curves, there are several importance differences. You should review that section of the Focus that discusses these issues.

SELF-TEST QUESTIONS

1. What are the two components of the labor force (1)?

2. What is the difference between the participation rate and the unemployment rate (1)?

3. What are "separations," and what are the two reasons they occur (1)?

4. What is the non-employment rate (1)?

5. Monthly separation rates tend to be high for which groups (1)?

6. What is the relation between the proportion of unemployed workers finding a job each month and the unemployment rate (2)?

7. What does the reservation wage represent (3)?

8. How does bargaining power affect wage determination (3)?

9. What is meant by "efficiency wages" (3)?

10. Why do firms and workers care about real wages (3)?

11. Why do nominal wages depend on the expected price level (3)?

12. An increase in the unemployment rate will have what effect on wages (3)?

13. When the production function is given by Y = N, what is the marginal cost of production (4)?

14. Why is P > W (4)?

15. Why is the wage-setting relation downward sloping (5)?

16. Why is the price-setting relation a horizontal line (5)?

17. What is the natural rate of unemployment (5)?

18. What effect will an increase in unemployment benefits have on the real wage and on the natural rate of unemployment (5)?

REVIEW PROBLEMS

1. Use the information provided below to answer the following questions.

Civilian noninstitutional population	250
Employed	150
Unemployed	12

a. What is the size of the labor force?
b. How many individuals are "out of the labor force"?
c. Calculate the participation rate.
d. Calculate the unemployment rate.
e. Calculate the nonemployment rate.

2. Based on your understanding of the efficiency wage theory, explain what effect an increase in the wage would have on the following: (a) quits; (b) productivity.

3. Explain what must occur for the average duration of unemployment to increase.

4. Explain what must occur for the separation rate to increase.

5. What are the basic differences between the primary and secondary labor markets?

6. Using the wage equation (equation (15.1)), briefly explain how each of the following events will affect the nominal wage.
a. reduction in P^e
b. reduction in the unemployment rate
c. a reduction in unemployment insurance

7. Briefly explain how each of the following events will affect the price set by firms.
a. increased merger activity causes markets to become less competitive
b. increased anti-trust legislation leads to increased competition
c. a reduction in the nominal wage

8. This question focuses on the wage-setting (WS) relation.
a. Briefly explain what effect a reduction in the unemployment rate will have on the real wage.
b. Why is the WS relation downward sloping?
c. What effect will a reduction in unemployment benefits have on the WS curve?
d. What effect will an increase in the rate of structural change have on the WS curve?
e. What effect will an increase in the price level have on the WS relation?

9. For the following values of μ, calculate the real wage.
a. $\mu = .1, .2, .3$, and $.4$.
b. What happens to the real wage as μ increases?
c. Explain why the real wage changes as μ increases.

10. Suppose all markets are perfectly competitive.
a. What is the value of μ when perfect competition exists?
b. What will be the real wage paid by firms when all markets are perfectly competitive?

11. Use the WS and PS relations to examine the effects of the following events on the natural rate of unemployment and on the real wage. Be sure to explain the effects of the event on the WS and PS relations.
a. reduction in unemployment insurance
b. increase in the rate of structural change in the labor market
c. less stringent antitrust legislation
d. increase in the minimum wage

12. Based on your analysis in #11, explain what effect each event will have on the level of employment and output.

MULTIPLE CHOICE QUESTIONS

Use the information provided below to answer questions 1 - 4.

Civilian noninstitutional population	200 million
Employed	100 million
Unemployed	6 million

1. The labor force for this economy is:

a. 100 million
b. 106 million
c. 194 million
d. 200 million

2. The unemployment rate for this economy is:

a. 6/100 = 6%
b. 6/106 = 5.7%
c. 6/194 = 3.1%
d. 6/200 = 3%

3. The labor force participation rate is:

a. 100/200 = 50%
b. 94/200 = 47%
c. 94/100 = 94%
d. 106/200 = 53%

4. The nonemployment rate for this economy is:

a. 100/200 = 50%
b. 106/200 = 53%
c. 100/106 = 94.3%
d. 194/200 = 97%

5. Suppose the average monthly flows out of unemployment is 3 million. Further assume that the average number of individuals who are unemployed in any month is 6 million. The average duration of unemployment will be:

a. 2 months
b. 3 months
c. 6 months
d. one half of a month

6. Which of the following variables would be included in separations?

a. quits
b. layoffs
c. new hires
d. all of the above
e. both a and b

7. Which of the following represented the largest share of the total population in the United States in 2006?

a. individuals officially out of the labor force
b. the unemployed
c. the employed
d. the civilian labor force

8. Suppose firms decide to hire fewer workers. This will tend to:

a. increase the chances of losing a job if currently employed
b. decrease the chances of an unemployed worker finding a job
c. all of the above
d. none of the above

9. An increase in the unemployment rate will tend to be associated with:

a. an increase in the proportion of unemployed workers finding a job
b. a reduction in the proportion of unemployed workers finding a job
c. an increase in wages
d. an increase in bargaining power

10. A reduction in the unemployment rate will tend to be associated with:

a. a reduction in the separation rate
b. an increase in the separation rate
c. a reduction in wages
d. a reduction in bargaining power

11. If an individual is offered a wage <u>below</u> her/his reservation wage, we would expect:

a. the individual will prefer to work at that wage
b. the individual will prefer not to work at that wage
c. is indifferent to working or being employed (at the offered wage)
d. none of the above

12. Suppose workers and firms expect P to increase by 5%. Given this information, we would expect that:

a. the nominal wage will increase by more than 5%
b. the nominal wage will increase by less than 5%
c. the nominal wage will increase by exactly 5%
d. the real wage will increase by 5%

13. In a graph with the real wage on the vertical axis and the unemployment rate on the horizontal axis, which of the following statements is true?

a. the PS relation is downward sloping
b. the PS relation is upward sloping
c. the WS relation is horizontal
d. none of the above

14. A reduction in unemployment insurance will cause:

a. the PS relation to shift up
b. the PS relation to shift down
c. the WS relation to shift up
d. the WS relation to shift down

15. As markets become more competitive, we know that:

a. the PS relation will shift up
b. the PS relation will shift down
c. the WS relation will shift up
d. the WS relation will shift down

16. An increase in the markup of price over cost will cause:

a. the PS relation to shift up
b. the PS relation to shift down
c. the WS relation to shift up
d. the WS relation to shift down

17. If the markup over cost is zero ($\mu = 0$), we know that:

a. the real wage is 1
b. the real wage is greater than 1
c. the real wage is less than one
d. the PS relation is upward sloping

18. Less stringent antitrust legislation will tend to cause:

a. an increase in u_n and an increase in W/P
b. an increase in u_n and a reduction in W/P
c. a reduction in u_n and a reduction in W/P
d. a reduction in u_n and an increase in W/P

19. An increase in u_n will be associated with:

a. an increase in N
b. an increase in Y
c. a reduction in N
d. none of the above

CHAPTER 7. PUTTING ALL MARKETS TOGETHER: THE AS-AD MODEL

OBJECTIVES, REVIEW, AND TUTORIAL

After working through the chapter and the following material, you should be able to:

(1) Understand the derivation and interpretation of the AS relation.

(2) Understand the derivation and interpretation of the AD relation.

(3) Be able to explain why output returns to the natural level of output in the medium run.

(4) Explain the short-run and medium-run effects of a change in monetary policy.

(5) Explain the short-run and medium-run effects of a change in fiscal policy.

(6) Explain the short-run and medium-run effects of a change in oil prices.

1. A REVIEW OF THE AS RELATION AND THE AS CURVE

The AS relation is represented by the following:

$P = P^e(1 + \mu)F(1 - (Y/L), z)$.

You need to understand two key characteristics of the AS relation.

(1) An increase in the expected price level causes a proportionate increase in the actual price level.

Learning Tip

- If P^e increases by 5%, the nominal wage will increase by 5% and firms will raise prices by 5%.
- If P^e falls, the opposite occurs.
- A key issue is how individuals form expectations of the price level. When the actual price level does not equal the expected price level, wage setters will revise their expected. In general, when $P > P^e$, we would expect that individuals would revise upwards their expected price level. When $P < P^e$, we would expect that individuals would revise downwards their expected price level. One example of how individuals form expectations of the aggregate price level is given by the following, $P^e_t = P_{t-1}$. In this case, the expected price for period t is equal to the price level that occurred in the previous period.

(2) An increase in Y causes an increase in P.

Learning Tip

- The positive relation between Y and P is represented by the upward sloping AS curve.
- Why is the AS curve upward sloping?
    - As output increases, employment (N) increases.
    - As N increases, u falls.
    - Reductions in u cause increases in bargaining power and an increase in nominal wages.
    - As nominal wages increase, firms raise prices.
    - Therefore, an increase in Y is associated with higher prices.

You also need to understand the relation among P, P^e, Y_n, and the AS curve. These characteristics are:

(1) Each AS curve is drawn for a given P^e.

(2) If $P = P^e$, Y must equal Y_n.

(3) When $Y > Y_n$, P exceeds P^e (Tighter labor markets cause W to increase. The increase in W causes P to increase above P^e).

(4) When $Y < Y_n$, P is less than P^e (for the opposite reasons).

Learning Tip

- If you draw a vertical line at Y_n, each AS curve intersects this vertical line at the point where $P = P^e$.
- If P^e changes, the AS curve shifts by the amount of the change in P^e.
- As the AS curve shifts, it shifts along the vertical line where $Y = Y_n$.

2. A REVIEW OF THE AD RELATION AND THE AD CURVE

The AD curve captures the effects of P on Y, given equilibrium in the goods and financial markets. You must understand two characteristics of the AD curve: (1) why it is downward sloping; and (2) what causes it to shift.

(1) Slope

- A drop in P will cause the LM curve to shift down.
- This shift in the LM curve causes i to fall.
- As i falls, Y increases to maintain equilibrium in the two markets.
- A drop in P, therefore, causes Y to increase and the AD curve is downward sloping.

Learning Tip

You can also explain the slope of the AD curve in the following way:

- A lower P causes a decline in nominal money demand.
- As money demand drops, i must fall to maintain equilibrium in the financial markets.
- The lower i causes an increase in the demand for goods and an increase in Y.

(2) Shifts

Any event, other than a change in P, which shifts the IS or LM curves will cause a shift in the AD curve.

- Increases in G, M, consumer confidence, and reductions in T will cause Y to increase and, therefore, cause the AD curve to shift right.
- The opposite of these changes will cause the AD curve to shift to the left.

Learning Tip

- Make sure you understand that a change in P causes only a movement along the AD curve.
- Other shifts in the IS or LM curves cause the AD curve to shift.

3. ADJUSTMENT TO Y_n

To understand the adjustment of Y, you must understand that:

(1) The AS curve this year depends on the expected price level for this year (P^e_t);

(2) $P^e_t = P_{t-1}$; and, therefore,

(3) The position of this year's AS curve depends on last year's price level.

The adjustment when Y is above Y_n:

- For Y to exceed Y_n, $P > P^e$.
- At the end of this year, the expected price level will increase causing the AS curve to shift up.
- This shift in the AS curve causes P to increase and Y to fall.
- As long as $Y > Y_n$ [and, therefore, $P > P^e$], prices continue to increase as the AS curve shifts up.
- P will no longer increase when $Y = Y_n$.

Learning Tip

- Make sure you can explain what happens when $Y < Y_n$.
- Recall that next year's AS curve depends on this year's price level.
- As P changes, we move along the AD curve; the AD curve does NOT shift.
- In the short run, Y can deviate from Y_n.
- In the long run, $Y = Y_n$.

4. THE EFFECTS OF MONETARY EXPANSIONS AND CONTRACTIONS

Assume Y initially equals Y_n.

- An increase in the nominal money supply causes an increase in aggregate demand and an increase in Y.
- The increase in Y causes an increase in P (above P^e).
- As expectations of P adjust, nominal wages and the price level increase as the AS curve shifts up.
- As long as $Y > Y_n$, expectations adjust and the AS curve shifts up.
- The shifts in AS will cause P to increase and Y to fall.
- The adjustment stops when $Y = Y_n$.

Learning Tip

- The change in M has no effect on Y and the real interest rate in the medium run.
- M is said to be "neutral" in the medium run.
- For example, a 10% increase in M will eventually lead to a 10% increase in P.
- The LM curve also returns to its original position leaving the interest rate unchanged.
- In the short run, the interest rate does fall. In the medium run, however, as P increases, the real money stock returns to its original level.
- The short-run effects of a change in M on Y will depend on the slope of the AS curve.
- Make sure you can explain the short-run and medium-run effects of a reduction in M.
- More generally, make sure you understand the difference between the short run and the medium run.

5. THE EFFECTS OF A FISCAL EXPANSION AND CONTRACTION

Changes in G or T will cause changes in aggregate demand. These changes in aggregate demand will affect the level of Y and P in the same way that changes in M did:

(1) An increase in G will cause Y to increase in the short run.
(2) Eventually, Y returns to Y_n at a higher price.

Learning Tip

- The short-run effects of a reduction in G on Y and P are similar to the short-run effects of a drop in M: Y decreases and P decreases.
- The medium-run effects of a reduction in G on Y and P are similar to the medium-run effects of a drop in M: Y returns to Y_n, and P is permanently lower.

While M is neutral in the medium run, changes in G, T, or consumer confidence are not.

- A decrease in G causes a leftward shift in the IS curve and drop in i.
- As P continues to fall, the real money stock increases and the LM curve shifts down, further depressing i.
- We know that P decreases until Y returns to Y_n.
- This implies that all of the drop in G will be offset by an equal increase in I in the medium run (via the drop in i).

Learning Tip

- Changes in G, T, and consumer confidence will have no medium-run effects on the level of output.
- Changes in these variables will, however, affect i and the composition of output.

6. THE EFFECTS OF CHANGES IN THE PRICE OF OIL

(1) Medium-run effects

Firms produce goods with labor and other inputs (e.g. oil). When the price of oil increases, we know that:

- the firm's nonlabor costs increase
- given wages, firms respond by increasing prices
- this increase in P represents an increase in the markup (μ).

An increase in μ causes:

- a lower real wage implied by price-setting behavior (the PS relation shifts down)
- a reduction in the equilibrium real wage
- an increase in u_n
- As u_n falls, Y_n falls. This increase in the price of oil, therefore, causes a reduction in Y_n.
- An increase in μ causes an increase in P at each level of output. The AS curve, therefore, shifts up.

Learning Tip

You must understand the shift in the AS curve.

- The new AS curve goes through the point where output equals the new Y_n at a price level of P_{t-1}.
- The horizontal distance between the first two AS curves represents the change in Y_n.

(2) Short-run effects

An increase in the price of oil causes:

- the AS curve to shift up, Y to fall, and P to increase
- Y initially remains above the now lower Y_n
- as expectations adjust, the AS curve will continue to shift until $Y = Y_n'$
- an increase in the price of oil, therefore, causes an increase in P and a permanent reduction in Y
- the increase in the price of oil also causes an increase in u_n and a reduction in W/P

Learning Tip

- It is assumed that changes in the price of oil do not cause changes in the AD curve.
- Make sure you can explain the effects of a reduction in the price of oil.

SELF-TEST QUESTIONS

1. What does the AS relation represent and how is it derived (1)?

2. Why does an increase in output cause an increase in the price level (1)?

3. Based on the AS relation, what effect does a 4% increase in the expected price level have on the actual price level (1)?

4. What does the AD relation represent, and how is it derived (2)?

5. Suppose $Y > Y_n$. Compare u with u_n and P with P^e (3).

6. If $P = P^e$, compare Y and Y_n (1).

7. Money is believed to be neutral in the medium run. What does that mean (4)?

8. In the medium run, what effect will a decrease in G have on Y, I, and i (5)?

9. What effect does an increase in the price of oil have on μ (5)?

10. What effect does an increase in the price of oil have on W/P, u_n, Y_n, and the AS curve (6)?

11. What are the medium-run effects of an increase in the price of oil on P and Y (6)?

12. What is meant by stagflation (6)?

13. What is meant by propagation mechanisms (7)?

14. Suppose $P_t > P_{t-1}$. What will happen to the AS curve next year (3)?

15. Approximately how long does it take for the output effects of a change in the money supply to disappear (4)?

REVIEW PROBLEMS

1. Using the AS relation, explain how each of the following events will affect the price level.

a. 5% increase in P^e
b. 2% reduction in P^e
c. increase in μ
d. decrease in μ
e. increase in Y
f. decrease in Y

2. Concisely explain why the AS relation is upward sloping.

3. In the following graph, illustrate the effects of a reduction in the price level on output. Explain what effect the drop in P has on M, M/P, nominal money demand, i, and I.

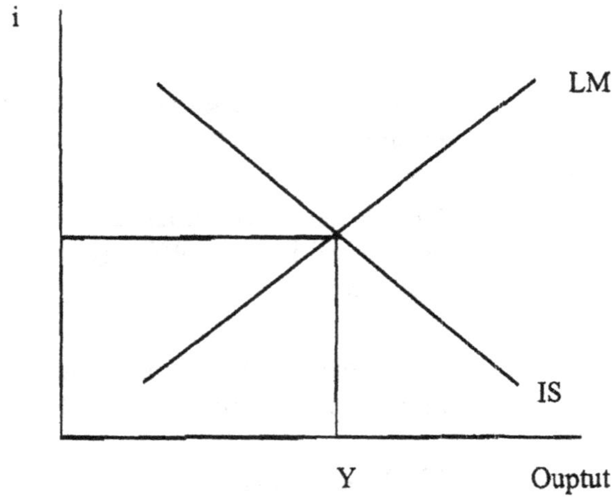

4. Concisely explain why the AD relation is downward sloping.

5. Explain what effect each of the following events has on the IS curve, the LM curve, and the AD curve.

a. increase in G
b. decrease in G
c. increase in M
d. decrease in M
e. rise in consumer confidence
f. drop in consumer confidence
g. increase in T
h. decrease in T
i. increase in P
j. decrease in P

6. Suppose $Y > Y_n$.

a. In this case, compare u with u_n, N with N_n, and P with P^e.
b. What will happen to the expected price level for next year?
c. What will happen to the nominal wage for next year?
d. What happens to the AS curve for next year?

7. Suppose $Y < Y_n$.

a. In this case, compare u with u_n, N with N_n, and P with P^e.
b. What will happen to the expected price level for next year?
c. What will happen to the nominal wage for next year?
d. What happens to the AS curve for next year?

8. a. In #6, as the AS shifts, what happens to M, M/P, i, I, and Y?
b. In #7, as the AS shifts, what happens to M, M/P, i, I, and Y?

9. Suppose the economy is initially operating at Y_n. Now suppose the Fed conducts a monetary contraction where the nominal money supply falls.

a. Use the following graph to illustrate the initial equilibrium, dynamic adjustment, and medium-run equilibrium. In your graph, illustrate the equilibrium for the next two periods (in addition to the medium-run equilibrium).

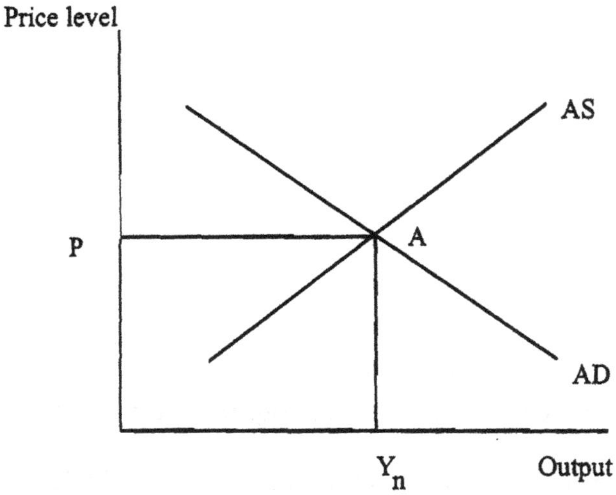

b. What are the initial effects of the drop in M on P, M/P, i, I, and Y?

c. What happens to u and Y relative to their natural levels during: the short run, the dynamic adjustment, and the medium run?

d. When Y is less than Y_n, what happens to the AS curve for the next year? Explain.

e. As the AS curve shifts, what happens to P, M/P, i, I, and Y?

f. What are the medium-run effects of the drop in M on P, M/P, i, I, and Y?

g. Does Y return to Y_n? If so, what does this suggest about P and P^e in the medium run?

10. The following questions are based on your analysis in #9. Suppose M fell by 6% in #9.

a. How much did P and P^e fall in the medium run?

b. Did the drop in M have any medium-run effects on real variables (i, Y, I, etc.)?

c. What are the medium-run effects on the nominal and real wages?

11. Suppose the economy is initially operating at Y_n. Now suppose G increases.

a. Use the graph below to illustrate the initial equilibrium, dynamic adjustment, and medium-run equilibrium. In your graph, illustrate the equilibrium for the next two periods (in addition to the medium-run equilibrium).

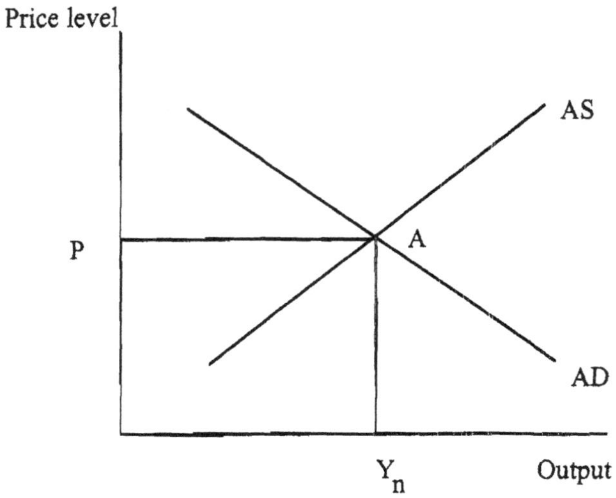

b. What are the initial effects of the increase in G on P, M/P, i, I, and Y?
c. What happens to u and Y relative to their natural levels during: the short run, the dynamic adjustment, and the medium run?
d. When Y is greater than Y_n, what happens to the AS curve for the next year? Explain.
e. As the AS curve shifts, what happens to P, M/P, i, I, and Y?
f. What are the medium-run effects of the increase in G on P, M/P, i, I, and Y?
g. Does Y return to Y_n? If so, what does this suggest about P and P^e in the medium run?

12. Did the increase in G in #11 have any effects on real variables in the medium run? Explain.

13. An increase in the price of oil was found to raise the price level and reduce the level of output.
a. Use the IS-LM graph, on a separate piece of paper, to illustrate the effects of the increase in the price of oil on the interest rate.
b. Based on your analysis, what happens to C and I as a result of the increase in the price of oil?

14. During the mid-1980s, the price of oil in the United States fell. Using the following graph, explain what effect a reduction in the price of oil will have on μ, the real wage and u_n.

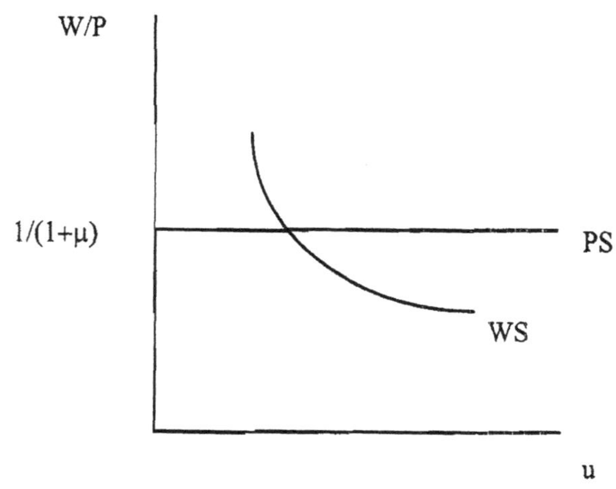

15. Using the AS and AD graph and the IS-LM graph, illustrate and explain the short-run and medium-run effects of a reduction in the price of oil. Explain what happens to P, Y, i, W/P, I, and u.

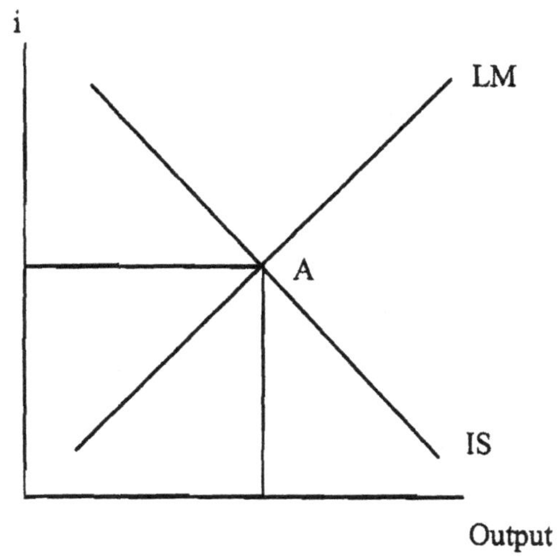

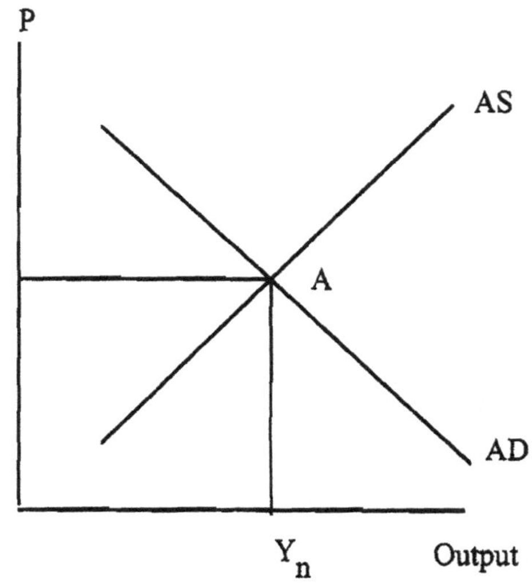

16. Using the AS and AD, WS and PS, and IS-LM graphs, illustrate and explain the short-run and medium-run effects of a reduction in unemployment benefits. Explain what happens to P, Y, i, W/P, I, and u. Use a separate piece of paper to show your graphs.

MULTIPLE CHOICE QUESTIONS

1. Based on the AS relation, an increase in which of the following variables will cause an increase in the price level (P)?

a. P^e
b. μ
c. output
d. all of the above

2. Based on the AS relation, a 4% increase in P^e will cause:

a. P will increase by more than 4%
b. P will increase by less than 4%
c. P will increase by exactly 4%
d. no change in P

3. We have assumed that wage setters expect the price level for period t to be equal to:

a. the actual P in period t
b. the actual P in period t-1
c. the expected P in period t-1

4. When $Y = Y_n$, we know that:

a. $P > P^e$
b. $P < P^e$
c. $P = P^e$
d. none of the above

5. When $Y < Y_n$, we know that:

a. $P > P^e$
b. $P < P^e$
c. $P = P^e$
d. none of the above

6. The AD curve is downward sloping because of the effects of:

a. G on the IS curve
b. the nominal money supply on the LM curve
c. P on M/P
d. G on i

7. Which of the following events will cause a rightward shift in the AD curve?

a. increase in P
b. decrease in P
c. increase in T
d. increase in M

8. An increase in the money supply will cause which of the following to occur in the short run?

a. i will increase
b. $P > P^e$
c. $u > u_n$
d. a decrease in i and a rightward shift in the IS curve

9. An increase in M will cause which of the following to occur in the medium run?

a. no change in the real wage
b. no change in the composition of output
c. a higher nominal wage
d. all of the above

10. A reduction in M will cause:

a. a proportionate drop in P in the medium run
b. a reduction in i in the short run
c. an increase in I in the medium run
d. a reduction in W/P in the medium run

11. Money is said to be "neutral" because it has no effect on:

a. nominal variables in the medium run
b. real variables in the medium run
c. nominal variables in the short run
d. real variables in the short run

12. A reduction in G will have which of the following effects in the short run?

a. increase in P
b. increase in i
c. $P > P^e$
d. $P < P^e$

13. A reduction in G will have which of the following effects in the medium run?

a. no change in i
b. an increase in I
c. a reduction in P
d. all of the above
e. both b and c

14. A tax cut will have which of the following effects in the short run?

a. a lower i
b. a higher i
c. a leftward shift in the AD curve
d. $P < P^e$

15. A $100 (real) billion increase in G will have which of the following effects in the medium run?

a. no change in I or Y
b. drop in I equal to $100 billion
c. drop in I greater than $100 billion
d. drop in I less than $100 billion

16. An increase in the price of oil will tend to cause which of the following in the short run?

a. decrease in Y and decrease in P
b. increase in P and a leftward shift in the AD curve
c. decrease in Y and an increase in P
d. increase in the real wage

17. An increase in the price of oil will tend to cause which of the following in the medium run?

a. increase in i
b. decrease in W/P
c. decrease in Y and an increase in P
d. all of the above

18. A reduction in the price of oil will tend to cause which of the following in the medium run?

a. increase in Y and an increase in P
b. increase in Y and a drop in P
c. lower i
d. both a and b
e. both b and c

19. When $P > P^e$, we know that:

a. $Y > Y_n$
b. $u > u_n$
c. $N < N_n$
d. all of the above

CHAPTER 8. THE NATURAL RATE OF UNEMPLOYMENT AND THE PHILLIPS CURVE

OBJECTIVES, REVIEW, AND TUTORIAL

After working through the chapter and the following material, you should be able to:

(1) Explain what the original Phillips curve illustrates.

(2) Based on the aggregate supply relation, explain what factors determine inflation.

(3) Be familiar with the Phillips curve when expected inflation is zero.

(4) Understand what two factors caused the original Phillips curve to vanish.

(5) Understand the Phillips curve when expected inflation depends on last period's inflation rate.

(6) Define the natural rate of unemployment (u_n) and explain the determinants of u_n.

(7) Know what effect wage indexation has on the Phillips curve.

(8) Recognize that u_n varies across countries and over time.

1. INFLATION, EXPECTED INFLATION, AND UNEMPLOYMENT

The aggregate supply relation indicates that π_t can be represented as:

$\pi_t = \pi^e_t + (\mu + z) - \alpha u_t$.

There are three factors that affect inflation.

• Expected inflation (π^e_t). Higher expected inflation causes an increase in nominal wages that causes an increase in the rate at which P increases.

• $(\mu + z)$. An increase in the markup (μ) or an increase in factors which determine wages (z) will increase inflation.

• Unemployment (u). As u increases, wages decrease and inflation will decrease.

2. THE ORIGINAL PHILLIPS CURVE

The relation between unemployment and inflation first discovered by Phillips, Solow, and Samuelson is represented by:

$\pi_t = (\mu + z) - \alpha u_t$.

- This equation indicates a negative relation between the <u>level</u> of inflation and the <u>level</u> of the unemployment rate.
- The equation is based on the assumption that expected inflation is zero.
- A high unemployment rate leads to lower wages and lower inflation.
- A lower unemployment rate leads to higher wages and higher inflation.

Learning Tip

- The parameter α indicates how responsive inflation is to a given (in this case) level of unemployment.
- You must understand that the original Phillips curve is a relation between the unemployment rate and the rate of inflation.
    - A low u will cause a high (but constant) rate of inflation.
    - A high u will cause a low (but constant) rate of inflation.
- This original Phillips curve vanished because of: (1) high oil prices in the 1970s; and (2) firms and workers changed the way they formed expectations.

3. THE (MODIFIED) PHILLIPS CURVE

As inflation became persistent, rather than expect this year's price level to be equal to last year's price level ($P^e_t = P_{t-1}$), workers and firms formed expectations about inflation using the following: $\pi_t = \theta\pi_{t-1}$.

Learning Tip

- When $\pi > 0$, individuals would always <u>underpredict</u> this period's price level if they used the following relation to form expectations: $P^e_t = P_{t-1}$.
- As inflation became more persistent, θ became larger and approached 1.

When $\theta > 0$, π_t will depend on π_{t-1}. Why? Because the nominal wage will change based on expected inflation. If prices increased 5% last year, workers will expect prices to increase by some fraction of 5% this year. Nominal wages increase by some percentage causing prices to increase this period as well.

Learning Tip

- When $\theta = 0$, we obtain the original Phillips curve.
- We will assume that $\theta = 1$.

When $\theta = 1$, the AS relation becomes:

$\pi_t = \pi_{t-1} + (\mu + z) - \alpha u_t$; or

$\pi_t - \pi_{t-1} = (\mu + z) - \alpha u_t$.

Learning Tip

- This relation implies that π_t is a function of π^e_t, $(\mu + z)$ and u_t.
- In particular, when π_{t-1} increases (i.e., when expected inflation increases), inflation this period will increase by the same amount.
- Why does this occur? As expected inflation increases, nominal wages rise. As nominal wages rise, firms raise prices causing an increase in the actual inflation rate.

The natural rate of unemployment, u_n, is the unemployment rate such that actual inflation (π_t) equals expected inflation (π^e_t). As explained in the text, $u_n = (\mu + z)/\alpha$.

The AS relation becomes:

$\pi_t - \pi_{t-1} = -\alpha(u_t - u_n)$.

There are several features of the AS relation you must understand:

(1) When $u_t < u_n$, the rate of inflation will increase;
(2) When $u_t > u_n$, the rate of inflation will decrease; and
(3) When $u_t = u_n$, the rate of inflation is constant (i.e., $\pi_t = \pi_{t-1}$).

Learning Tip

- If u were kept below the natural rate, inflation would increase each year (above the previous year's rate).
- Inflation will be constant only when $u_t = u_n$. It is for this reason that u_n is also called the nonaccelerating inflation unemployment rate.
- To reduce inflation, u, therefore, must exceed the natural rate.

4. OTHER ISSUES

You should also understand: (1) the effects of wage indexation on inflation; and (2) the determinants of u_n.

(1) Wage indexation

As the proportion (λ) of labor contracts which are indexed increases, changes in unemployment will have a greater effect on inflation. Why?

- When u falls, wages increase.
- As wages increase, prices increase.
- With wage indexation, some wages will increase within the same period as prices rise.
- This indexation-induced increase in wages causes a second increase in prices within the same period.
- Therefore, the same drop in u causes a greater increase in π.

(2) Differences in u_n across countries

The natural rate of unemployment is given by the following expression:

$u_n = (\mu + z)/\alpha$.

Therefore, differences in μ, z, and/or α will cause u_n to vary across countries.

(3) European Unemployment

Critics argue that "labor market rigidities" cause high unemployment in Europe. Several possible explanations for these labor market rigidities exist:

- Generous unemployment insurance
- A high degree of employment protection
- Relatively high minimum wages
- Bargaining rules that increase bargaining power.

Learning Tip

- While each of the above factors would cause an increase in unemployment, a number of European countries have low unemployment.
- The explanation for the varying unemployment rates across Europe requires a deeper understanding of a possible relationship between institutions and shocks and how these different "rigidities" affect labor markets in each country.

(4) Differences in u_n over time

The natural rate of unemployment in the United States increased during the 1950-1989 period. During the 1990s, this trend appears to have changed. There are several possible causes of the simultaneous drop in unemployment and drop in inflation in the United States during this period:

- a reduction in benefits paid to workers;
- the drop in the price of imports caused by an appreciation of the dollar; and
- the drop in the price of raw materials (e.g. oil).

SELF-TEST QUESTIONS

1. What are the determinants of inflation (1)?

2. Given the original Phillips curve, why is there a negative relation between inflation and the unemployment rate (1)?

3. What is meant by the "wage-price spiral" (2)?

4. Give the two reasons why the original Phillips curve vanished (2).

5. How does the original Phillips curve differ from the modified Phillips curve (2)?

6. What happens to inflation when the unemployment rate is low (2)?

7. Define the natural rate of unemployment (2).

8. List the determinants of u_n (2).

9. What happens to inflation when $u > u_n$? What happens to inflation when $u < u_n$ (2)?

10. What is the level of u_n today in the United States (2)?

11. What does wage indexation represent (3)?

12. What effect does an increase in wage indexation have on the relation between the unemployment rate and changes in inflation (3)?

13. Explain the labor market rigidities that affect European labor markets (3).

14. What has happened to u_n in the United States since the 1960s (3)?

REVIEW PROBLEMS

1. For each of the following variables explain how a reduction in the variable affects the inflation rate: (a) π^e_t; (b) μ; and (c) z.

2. Use the original Phillips curve to answer the following questions.
a. Suppose policy makers wish to reduce the unemployment rate. What must happen to π? Explain.
b. Suppose policy makers wish to reduce π. What must happen to u? Explain.

3. Let $\pi^e_t = \theta\pi_{t-1}$. Suppose $\pi_{t-1} = 10\%$.
a. For each of the following values of θ, calculate π^e_t: $\theta = 0.4, 0.6, 0.8$ and 1.0.
b. What happens to π^e_t as θ increases? Explain.

4. Suppose the Phillips curve is represented by the following:

$\pi_t = \pi^e_t + 0.10 - 2u_t$ where $\pi^e_t = \theta\pi_{t-1}$.

a. Assume $\theta = .25$. Calculate u_n.
b. Now assume $\theta = 1$. Calculate u_n.
c. What happens to u_n as θ changes? Briefly explain.

5. Suppose the Phillips curve is represented by the following:

$\pi_t = \pi^e_t + 0.20 - 2u_t$ where $\pi^e_t = \theta\pi_{t-1}$.

a. Assume $\theta = .5$, $\pi_{t-1} = .06$ (6%) and $u_t = .08$ (8%). Calculate π_t.
b. Suppose u_t increases to 10%. Calculate what happens to π_t. How much does π_t change? Briefly explain why inflation in t changes as u_t changes.
c. What happens to π^e_t as u_t increases? Briefly explain.

6. Assume $\pi^e_t = \pi_{t-1}$ and that the Phillips curve for the United States is given by the following: $\pi_t - \pi_{t-1} = -1.5(u_t - u_n)$. Suppose $u_t = .06$, $u_n = .05$ and $\pi_{t-1} = .04$.
a. Calculate π_t. Is π_t greater than, less than or equal to π_{t-1}?
b. Calculate π_t for each of the following values of u_t: .07, .08, and .09.
c. What happens to the change in inflation in t for each 1% increase in u_t?
d. As u_t increases, is inflation in period t increasing or decreasing?

7. Assume $\pi^e_t = \pi_{t-1}$ and that the Phillips curve for the United States is given by the following: $\pi_t - \pi_{t-1} = -1.5(u_t - u_n)$. Suppose $u_t = .07$, $u_n = .08$ and $\pi_{t-1} = .04$.
a. Calculate π_t. Is π_t greater than, less than or equal to π_{t-1}?
b. Calculate π_t for each of the following values of u_t: .06, .05, and .04.
c. What happens to the change in inflation in t for each 1% reduction in u_t?
d. As u_t falls, is inflation in period t increasing or decreasing?

8. Assume $\pi^e_t = \pi_{t-1}$ and that the Phillips curve for the United States is given by the following: $\pi_t - \pi_{t-1} = -1.5(u_t - u_n)$. Suppose $u_t = .06$, $u_n = .06$ and $\pi_{t-1} = .04$.

a. Calculate π_t. Is π_t greater than, less than or equal to π_{t-1}?

b. Calculate π_t for each of the following values of π_{t-1}: .03 and .06.

c. Given your analysis in b, compare π_t with π_{t-1} when $u_t = u_n$.

9. Use your analysis in questions 6, 7, and 8 to answer the following questions.

a. Suppose inflation is increasing in a country. Given this information, is u_t greater than, less than or equal to u_n? Explain.

b. Suppose inflation is decreasing in a country. Given this information, is u_t greater than, less than or equal to u_n? Explain.

c. Suppose inflation is constant in a country. Given this information, is u_t greater than, less than or equal to u_n? Explain.

10. Suppose there are two economies: A and B where $u^A_t = 6\%$ and $u^B_t = 5\%$.

a. Given this information, what can you say, if anything, about the change in inflation in these two economies? Specifically, what happened to π_t (relative to π_{t-1}) in these two economies? Briefly explain.

b. Suppose $\pi^A_t < \pi^A_{t-1}$. Given this information, where is u^A_t relative to the natural rate of unemployment?

c. Suppose $\pi^B_t > \pi^B_{t-1}$. Given this information, where is u^B_t relative to the natural rate of unemployment?

11. a. Suppose policy makers keep u less than u_n. What will happen to inflation over time?

b. Suppose policy makers keep u above than u_n. What will happen to inflation over time?

12. Suppose the proportion of contracts that are indexed in the United States declines. Will a given reduction in unemployment now have a greater or smaller effect on inflation? Explain.

13. Suppose the benefits paid to workers (e.g. health care) by firms decreases. What effect will this have on the equilibrium real wage and u_n? Explain.

14. Explain how an increase in the price of oil might have no effect on the natural rate of unemployment. Based on your analysis, will this change in the price of oil have any effect on the natural level of output and the equilibrium real wage?

MULTIPLE CHOICE QUESTIONS

1. An increase in which of the following variables will cause an increase in π_t?

a. μ
b. z
c. π^e_t
d. all of the above

2. An increase in which of the following variables will cause a reduction in π_t?

a. Phillips curve
b. z
c. u_t
d. none of the above

3. The original Phillips curve represented a relation between:

a. changes in inflation and changes in unemployment
b. inflation and unemployment
c. changes in inflation and unemployment
d. inflation and changes in unemployment

4. Which of the following equations represents the (modified) Phillips curve?

a. $\pi_t = \pi^e_t + (\mu + z) - \alpha u_t$
b. $\pi_t - \pi_{t-1} = \mu + z - \alpha u_t$
c. all of the above
d. none of the above

5. Suppose the Phillips curve is represented by the following equation:

$\pi_t - \pi_{t-1} = 12 - 2u_t$.

The natural rate of unemployment in this economy is:

a. 12%
b. 6%
c. the unemployment which occurs when inflation is rising
d. 5.5%

6. The natural rate of unemployment is represented by the following expression:

a. $\alpha/(\mu + z)$
b. $\mu/(z + \alpha)$
c. $z/(\mu + \alpha)$
d. $(\mu + z)/\alpha$

7. An increase in which of the following variables will cause a reduction in u_n?

a. μ
b. z
c. α
d. π^e

8. Which of the following equations represents the Phillips curve?

a. $\pi_t = \pi^e_t - \alpha(u_n - u_t)$
b. $\pi^e_t = \pi_t - \alpha(u_t - u_n)$
c. $\pi_t = \pi^e_t - \alpha(u_t - u_n)$
d. none of the above

9. The natural rate of unemployment in the United States is believed to be:

a. around 10%
b. around 8%
c. around 6%
d. around 4%

10. Suppose $u_n = 7\%$ and that $\pi_{t-1} = 4\%$. If $u_t = 8\%$, we know that:

a. inflation in t will be less than 4%
b. inflation in t will equal 4%
c. inflation in t will be greater than 4%
d. more information is needed to answer this question

11. Suppose $u_n = 7\%$ and that $\pi_{t-1} = 4\%$. If $u_t = 6\%$, we know that:

a. inflation in t will be less than 4%
b. inflation in t will equal 4%
c. inflation in t will be greater than 4%
d. more information is needed to answer this question

12. Suppose $u_n = 7\%$ and that $\pi_{t-1} = 4\%$. If $u_t = 7\%$, we know that:

a. inflation in t will be less than 4%
b. inflation in t will equal 4%
c. inflation in t will be greater than 4%
d. more information is needed to answer this question

13. Which of the following helps explain why the original Phillips curve vanished?

a. wage indexation
b. higher oil prices
c. low-wage jobs
d. all of the above
e. none of the above

14. As the proportion of indexed contracts decreases, we would expect that a reduction in the unemployment rate will cause:

a. a larger increase in inflation
b. a smaller increase in inflation
c. a larger reduction in inflation
d. a smaller reduction in inflation

15. As the proportion of indexed contracts gets closer to 1, we would expect:

a. small changes in unemployment will cause large changes in inflation
b. expected inflation will have no effect on actual inflation
c. small changes in unemployment will cause small changes in inflation
d. none of the above

16. Which of the following is NOT a possible explanation for the labor market rigidities that exist in Europe?

a. relatively low unemployment insurance
b. relatively high minimum wages
c. relatively high degree of employment protection
d. bargaining rules that increase bargaining power

17. Which of the following is NOT believed to explain the relative low price inflation and increase in wage inflation in the United States during the 1990s?

a. Fed policy during the period
b. a reduction in benefits paid to workers by firms
c. the cheaper price of imports
d. the drop in the price of raw materials

18. Suppose the unemployment rate in Canada is 8.9%. If the rate of inflation in Canada is decreasing, we know that the natural unemployment rate in Canada:

a. is greater than 8.9%
b. equals 8.9%
c. is less than 8.9%
d. could be greater than, less than, or equal to the actual unemployment rate

CHAPTER 9. INFLATION, ACTIVITY, AND NOMINAL MONEY GROWTH

OBJECTIVES, REVIEW, AND TUTORIAL

After working through the chapter and the following material, you should be able to:

(1) Understand and interpret the Okun's Law relation.

(2) Understand and interpret the aggregate demand relation.

(3) Understand the relation among inflation, unemployment, output growth, and nominal money growth in the medium run.

(4) Explain what is meant by disinflation policy, point-years of excess unemployment, and the sacrifice ratio.

(5) Explain how the economy adjusts to a reduction in nominal money growth (i.e., a disinflation).

(6) Discuss how expectations and credibility (i.e., the Lucas critique) can alter how the economy adjusts to a reduction in nominal money growth.

(7) Discuss how nominal rigidities and contracts can alter the effects of a disinflation policy.

(8) Discuss and explain the 1979-1985 U.S. disinflation.

1. OKUN'S LAW

Okun's law summarizes the relation between output growth and the change in unemployment:

$u_t - u_{t-1} = -0.4(g_{yt} - 3\%)$.

There are three features of Okun's law that you should know.

(1) Inverse relation. Increases in output growth will cause reductions in u. Why? To increase output, firms must increase employment. As employment increases, u will fall.

(2) Okun's coefficient. A 1% increase in the growth rate will cause u to fall by less than 1%. Why? First, labor hoarding occurs. Second, labor force participation changes as employment changes.

(3) Normal growth rate ($\overline{g}_y$). Actual output growth must exceed $\overline{g}_y$ (3%) for u to fall. Alternatively, g_{yt} must equal $\overline{g}_y$ for u to remain constant. Why? First, employment must grow at the same rate as the labor force. Second, labor productivity is growing each year.

2. THE AGGREGATE DEMAND RELATION

Aggregate demand is an increasing function of the real money stock. The growth rate of output is given by the following:

$g_{yt} = g_{mt} - \pi_t$.

Learning Tip

- When $g_{mt} > \pi_t$, we know that $g_{yt} > 0$.
- When $g_{mt} < \pi_t$, we know that $g_{yt} < 0$.
- When $g_{mt} = \pi_t$, we know that $g_{yt} = 0$.

3. INFLATION, UNEMPLOYMENT, AND THE GROWTH RATE IN THE MEDIUM RUN

Suppose $\bar{g}_m = 6\%$. What are the values of π, y, and g_{yt} in the medium run?

- Since u will return to some constant level, from Okun's law, we know that $g_{yt} = \bar{g}_y = 3\%$.
- If $g_{yt} = \bar{g}_y$, from the AD relation, we know that $\pi = \bar{g}_m - \bar{g}_y = 6\% - 3\% = 3\%$. Recall that adjusted money growth is $\bar{g}_m - \bar{g}_y$.
- Since π does not change, from the Phillips curve, we know that $u = u_n = 6\%$.
- In the medium run, $u = u_n$, $g_y = \bar{g}_y$, and $\pi = \bar{g}_m - \bar{g}_y$.

What are the medium run effects of a change in money growth? Changes in g_m will affect inflation only in the medium run. In fact, there is a one-for-one relation between changes in g_m and π.

Learning Tip

- For example, a 3% decrease in g_m will cause inflation to fall by 3%. u and g_y will not be affected in the medium run.
- Once again, we see that money (in this case, a change in nominal money growth) is neutral in the medium run.

4. INTRODUCTION TO DISINFLATION POLICY

You must understand three concepts.

(1) Disinflation refers to a decrease in inflation. This can occur only when $(u_t - u_n) > 0$. That is, u must rise above u_n for inflation to decrease.

(2) A point-year of excess of unemployment is a difference between u and u_n of one percentage point for one year. The number of point-years of excess unemployment is given by (the number of years that u is above u_n) times $(u-u_n)$.

Learning Tip

- Assume $\alpha = 1$ and that the central bank wants to reduce inflation by 8%.
- From the Phillips curve we have $\Delta\pi = -1(u - u_n)$.
- Since $\Delta\pi = -8$, $u - u_n = 8$.
- The number of point-years of excess unemployment is 8.
- Any combination of years and $u - u_n$ which yields 8 will achieve the 8% drop in inflation.
- The central bank CAN choose the distribution of excess unemployment over time.
- The central bank CANNOT change the total amount of point-years of excess unemployment.

(3) The sacrifice ratio is the number of point-years of excess unemployment needed to reduce inflation by 1%.

- The change in inflation equals -1.
- Given the Phillips curve relation, we have : $-1 = -\alpha(u - u_n)$.
- The sacrifice ratio is, therefore, $1/\alpha$ (which equals $u - u_n$).

5. DISINFLATION: THE TRADITIONAL APPROACH

Learning Tip

- The best way to learn this is to work through the material in the chapter step-by-step.
- It is crucial that you understand the material corresponding to Table 9-1.
- Review problem #15 will allow you to practice this.

There are three periods associated with a disinflation: (1) the pre-period; (2) the disinflation; and (3) the post-period.

To complete a table similar to 9-1, simply follow these steps:

(1) Determine the target path of inflation.
(2) Given (1), use the Phillips curve relation to calculate the required path of u (for each year).
(3) Given the required path of u, use the Okun's law relation to calculate the required growth rate of output.
(4) Now that you have the target path of inflation and the growth rate of output for each year, use the AD relation to calculate the required nominal money growth for each year.

Learning Tip

There are several features of the traditional approach you need to understand.
- u must first rise above u_n to begin a period in which π falls.
- Once π is at its desired level, u can return to u_n.
- g_{yt} must first decrease to cause the increase in u. g_{yt} returns to normal as long as u does not have to change. g_{yt} then increases above normal to cause u to fall to u_n.
- g_{mt} must first drop to cause the drop in g_{yt}. g_{mt} will then change to keep g_{yt} at 3%. Consequently, as π falls, g_{mt} falls as well. At the end, g_{mt} must increase to push u back to u_n.

6. THE LUCAS CRITIQUE, NOMINAL RIGIDITIES, AND CONTRACTS

(1) The Lucas Critique

Lucas argued that wage setters' expectations would incorporate the effects of policy changes. A Fed policy to reduce inflation (IF credible) could reduce inflation without any increase in unemployment. Wage setters would adjust expectations causing wages and, therefore, prices to change. Note that credibility is the key ingredient to a disinflation without a recession.

(2) Nominal Rigidities and Contracts

The fact that wages and prices are set in nominal terms suggests that a decrease in money growth (even if credible) would cause an increase in unemployment.

The staggering of wage decisions would also cause a rapid decrease in money growth to result in an increase in u.

(3) Conclusion

- Announce in advance the disinflation policy.
- Reduce money growth slowly at first to allow those few contracts that are negotiated to take this policy into account.
- Over time, money growth can be reduced more quickly.

7. THE U.S. DISINFLATION OF 1979-1985

Learning Tip

- You should become familiar with this example.
- To do so, you should re-read this section in the chapter.
- Two issues stand out:
    - The Fed lost credibility because of its actions in 1980.
    - The sacrifice ratio by 1984 and 1985 was higher than that observed in the traditional approach (i.e., this disinflation caused a substantial increase in unemployment).

SELF-TEST QUESTIONS

1. What relation does Okun's Law represent (1)?

2. What relation does aggregate demand represent (1)?

3. To keep the unemployment rate constant, annual output growth has to be at least 3%. What are the two factors which explain this (1)?

4. What is meant by the "normal growth rate" of output (1)?

5. Output growth of 1% in excess of the normal growth rate causes unemployment to decline by less than 1%. Why is this so (1)?

6. The AD relation indicates that the growth rate of output is equal to what (1)?

7. Output must grow at what rate in the medium run (2)?

8. What determines inflation in the medium run (2)?

9. Define "adjusted nominal money growth" (2).

10. What will unemployment be in the medium run (2)?

11. What effect does a reduction in nominal money growth have on u, output growth and inflation in the medium run (2)?

12. What must happen to the unemployment rate in the short run for the inflation rate to fall (2)?

13. Explain what is meant by a "point-year of excess unemployment" (3).

14. What is meant by the sacrifice ratio (3)?

15. Briefly discuss the Lucas critique (3).

16. What is meant by the "credibility of monetary policy" (3)?

17. What are nominal rigidities (3)?

18. What does the staggering of wage decisions represent (3)?

19. How did the Fed's behavior in 1980 affect the credibility of the Fed (3)?

20. Research by Laurence Ball indicates that faster disinflations have what effect on the sacrifice ratio (3)?

REVIEW PROBLEMS

1. a. Suppose labor productivity is growing 2% a year. Given this, calculate, for each of the following rates of growth in the labor force, what output growth must be to keep u constant: 0, 1%, 2% and 3%.
b. Briefly explain what happens to the normal growth rate as the rate of growth in the labor force increases.
c. Suppose the labor force is growing at 1% per year. Given this, calculate, for each of the following rates of growth in labor productivity, what output growth must be to keep u constant: 0, 1%, 2% and 3%.
d. Briefly explain what happens to the normal growth rate as labor productivity increases.

2. Use the following Okun's law relation to answer these questions:

$u_t - u_{t-1} = -0.4(g_{yt} - 3\%)$. Assume $u_{t-1} = 6\%$.

a. Calculate the change in u ($u_t - u_{t-1}$) for each of the following values of g_{yt}: 4%, 5% and 6%. What happens to the change in unemployment for each 1% increase in output growth?
b. Calculate the change in u ($u_t - u_{t-1}$) for each of the following values of g_{yt}: 2%, 1% and 0. What happens to the change in unemployment for each 1% decrease in output growth?
c. Calculate the change in u ($u_t - u_{t-1}$) when output growth is 3%. What must the growth rate of output be to keep u_t from changing?

3. Suppose the normal growth rate is 2% and that output growth is currently 1%. Explain why this output growth of 1% below normal leads to an increase in u of less than 1%.

4. The Okun's law coefficient has increased for a number of countries. Does this increase cause u to be more or less sensitive to deviations of output growth from normal? Briefly explain.

5. Use the AD relation to answer this question.
a. Assume $\pi_t = 3\%$. Calculate output growth for each of the following values of nominal money growth: 7%, 5%, 3% and 1%. What happens to g_{yt} as money growth falls?
b. Assume nominal money growth is 6%. Calculate output growth for each of the following values of inflation: 6%, 4%, and 2%. What happens to g_{yt} as the inflation rate falls?

6. This question focuses on the medium run. Suppose $\bar{g}_m = 7\%$, $u_n = 6\%$ and $\bar{g}_y = 2\%$.
a. What will g_{yt} and u_t be in the medium run? Briefly explain.
b. Calculate what the rate of inflation and adjusted nominal money growth will be in the medium run.

7. Suppose the central bank decides to reduce $\bar{g}_m$ from 7% to 3%. Using the original numbers in question 6, answer the following questions.
a. What happens to g_{yt} and u_t in the medium run as a result of the decrease in money growth?
b. What happens to the rate of inflation and to adjusted nominal money growth in the medium run as a result of the reduction in money growth?

8. Suppose a central bank decides to increase $\bar{g}_m$ by 3%. What will be the medium run effects of this on g_{yt}, u_t and π_t?

9. Suppose $u_n = 6\%$ and that $u_t = 8\%$. Calculate the point-years of excess unemployment for each of the following number of years assuming that u_t remains at 8%: 1, 2, 3, 4 and 5. What happens to the point-years of excess unemployment as the number of years for which u = 8% increases?

10. Suppose the central bank wishes to reduce inflation by 8%.
a. Calculate the point-years of excess unemployment needed to reduce inflation by 8% for each of the following values of α: 1.5, 1.4, 1.15 and 1.
b. What happens to the point-years of excess unemployment as α decreases in size. Briefly explain.

11. Suppose the central bank would like to reduce inflation by 9%.
a. If $\alpha = 1.15$, what is the number of point-years of excess unemployment?
b. Given the goal of reducing inflation by 9%, can the central bank affect the number of point-years of excess unemployment calculated in a? Briefly explain.
c. Can the central bank choose the distribution of excess unemployment over time? If so, give three examples.

12. Let $\beta = 0.5$, $\bar{g}_y = 2\%$ and $u_{t-1} = 6\%$.
a. To reduce u_t by 2%, what must g_{yt} be?
b. To increase u_t by 3%, what must g_{yt} be?

13. a. Define the sacrifice ratio.
b. Calculate the sacrifice ratio for each of the following values of α: 1.5, 1.3, 1.15, 1, and .9.
c. What happens to the size of the sacrifice ratio as α declines? Explain.

14. Assume $\beta = 0.5$, $\alpha = 1$, $\bar{g}_y = 3\%$, $u_n = 6\%$ and $u_{t-1} = 6\%$. Suppose the central bank wants to reduce inflation by 8% and wants this to occur in one year.
a. Calculate what u_t must be to achieve the 8% decline in inflation.
b. Given Okun's law and your answer to part a, calculate output growth in t needed to reduce inflation by 8%.

15. Suppose $\pi = 18\%$, $u_n = 6\%$, $\alpha = 1$, $\bar{g}_y = 3\%$, $\beta = 0.5$. Assume in year 0 that u = 6% and that the central bank decides that it wants to begin a disinflation in year 1 to reduce inflation to 3%. Assume that the desired path of inflation is: inflation starts at 18% in year 0 (before the change in monetary policy) and decreases 3% a year until it reaches 3%.
a. Given this information, construct a table similar to Table 9-1 in the chapter. Include in your table for years 0 - 8 the values of inflation, unemployment, output growth and money growth.
b. Briefly explain the path of each variable in your table. Specifically, why do they change as they do?

16. Given the Lucas critique, do you think the central bank should announce in advance a policy to reduce inflation? Explain.

17. Are the sacrifice ratios for 1983, 1984 and 1985 (included in table 1 of the discussion, "The U.S. Disinflation, 1979-1985") consistent with the sacrifice ratios of: (1) the traditional approach; and (2) the Lucas critique? Explain.

MULTIPLE CHOICE QUESTIONS

1. Which of the following equations represents the Phillips curve relation?

a. $g_{yt} = g_{mt} - \pi_t$
b. $u_t - u_{t-1} = -\beta(g_{yt} - 3\%)$
c. $\pi_t - \pi_{t-1} = -\alpha(u_t - u_n)$
d. none of the above

2. Which of the following equations represents the Okun's law relation?

a. $u_t - u_{t-1} = -\beta(g_{yt} - 3\%)$
b. $u_t - u_{t-1} = -\beta(3\% - g_{yt})$
c. $\pi_t - \pi_{t-1} = -\alpha(u_t - u_n)$
d. $g_{yt} = g_{mt} - \pi_t$

3. Which of the following represents the AD relation?

a. $\pi_t - \pi_{t-1} = -\alpha(u_t - u_n)$
b. $g_{yt} = g_{mt} - \pi_t$
c. $u_t - u_{t-1} = -\beta(g_{yt} - 3\%)$
d. $u_t - u_{t-1} = -g_{yt}$

4. Which of the following expressions represents adjusted nominal money growth?

a. M/P
b. $g_{mt} - \pi_t$
c. g_{mt}
d. $\bar{g}_m$
e. $\bar{g}_m - \bar{g}_y$

5. Which of the following does NOT explain why output growth of 1% in excess of normal growth leads to a 0.4% reduction in unemployment?

a. labor hoarding
b. changes in labor force participation
c. the parameter α does not equal 1
d. none of the above

6. The normal rate of growth of the economy in the United States is approximately:

a. 4%
b. 1.15%
c. 3%
d. 6%
e. 0.4%

7. Let nominal money growth be 10% and the inflation rate be 3%. Given this information, we know that the growth rate of output is:

a. 4%
b. 3%
c. 6%
d. 7%
e. 9%

8. Given a certain rate of nominal money growth, an increase in inflation will cause output growth to:

a. increase
b. decrease
c. remain constant
d. more information is needed to answer this question

9. Which of the following events will cause an increase in the size of the sacrifice ratio?

a. an increase in β
b. a reduction in β
c. an increase in α
d. a reduction in α

10. Which of the following events will cause an increase in adjusted nominal money growth?

a. a reduction in π
b. an increase in $\bar{g}_y$
c. a reduction in $\bar{g}_y$
d. a reduction in $\bar{g}_m$

11. Which of the following variables will be affected in the medium run by a change in $\bar{g}_m$?

a. u
b. u_n
c. g_y
d. π

12. In the medium run, which of the following expressions determines the rate of inflation?

a. $\bar{g}_m - \bar{g}_y$
b. $\bar{g}_y - \bar{g}_m$
c. $u - u_n$
d. $g_y - \bar{g}_y$

13. Suppose the central bank wants to reduce inflation by 12%, $u_n = 6\%$, and $\alpha = 1.2$. How many point-years of excess unemployment will be needed to reduce inflation by 12%?

a. 10
b. 12
c. 6
d. 10.8

14. If $\alpha = 1.5$, the sacrifice ratio is approximately:

a. .5
b. .67
c. 2
d. 3

15. Suppose unemployment must increase by 5% to reduce inflation by 5%. Assume $u_n = 6\%$, $\beta = 0.4$, $\overline{g}_y = 3\%$ and $u_{t-1} = 6\%$. Output growth must be equal to what rate for one year to increase in u by 5% (in year t)?

a. -9.5%
b. -15.5%
c. -2%
d. -11%

16. The Lucas critique suggests that an announced disinflation policy will:

a. have no effect on u
b. have no effect on g_{yt}
c. yield a sacrifice ratio of 0
d. all of the above
e. none of the above

17. The traditional approach to disinflation requires which of the following conditions to reduce inflation?

a. $u_t > u_n$
b. $\alpha > 1$
c. $u_t < u_n$
d. none of the above

18. Research by John Taylor on the staggering of wage decisions indicates which of the following actions by the central bank should be taken to reduce inflation?

a. a rapid, unannounced reduction in g_m
b. a slow, unannounced reduction in g_m
c. a rapid, announced reduction in g_m
d. a slow (but gradually faster), announced reduction in g_m

19. Nominal rigidities refer to which of the following?

a. disinflation policy
b. the fact that many wages and prices are set in nominal terms
c. the fact that changes in nominal money growth cause changes in inflation
d. contracts which index wages to inflation

CHAPTER 10.
THE FACTS OF GROWTH

OBJECTIVES, REVIEW, AND TUTORIAL

After working through the chapter and the following material, you should be able to:

(1) Make the distinction between fluctuations and growth.

(2) Understand what is meant by the standard of living and how it is measured.

(3) Understand the two main conclusions about growth in rich countries.

(4) Understand the three main conclusions about growth across time and about growth across a larger number of countries.

(5) Explain the characteristics of the aggregate production function.

(6) Discuss the two sources of growth.

1. MEASURING THE STANDARD OF LIVING

Economists care about growth because they care about the standard of living. The standard of living is generally measured as output per person (or output per capita).

(1) Calculation of output per person

To compare output across countries, one could use exchange rates convert the values of output to a common measure. However, there are two problems with this approach:

- Exchange rates vary a lot.
- Price levels can differ across countries.

To avoid these issues, economists obtain purchasing power parity numbers.

(2) Purchasing Power Parity (PPP) Numbers

To correct for the variations in exchange rates and systematic differences in price levels, economists use a common set of prices for all countries when calculating output per person across countries. These calculations yield measures of purchasing power across time and across countries.

Learning Tip

- You should understand how the use of exchange rates to obtain measures of GDP can exaggerate differences in the standard of living across countries.
- To eliminate these problems, economists use purchasing power parity numbers in order to obtain measures of GDP across countries.
- You should review the discussion of purchasing power parity in the text. Review problem #6 will allow you to work on this.
- You should also review the material in the box, "Growth and Happiness."

2. SUMMARY OF CONCLUSIONS

(1) Rich countries since 1950

There are two conclusions you should understand about the level of output per capita and about growth in output per capita for these countries.

- Growth has been strong (i.e., there have been significant increases in the standard of living).

- The levels of output per capita have converged over time.

(2) A broader look at growth

This section of the chapter examines growth over longer periods of time and for a larger number of countries. There are three main conclusions you should understand.

- The observed convergence of OECD countries to the United States may be a prelude to "leapfrogging."

- Convergence has occurred for most Asian countries.

- Convergence is not the rule for all African countries.

Learning Tip

- Convergence indicates that there will be a negative relation between initial levels of output per capita and the rate of growth in output per capita.
- Growth did not occur in Europe prior to 1500.
- More recently, growth has been negative for some countries in Africa.

3. THE AGGREGATE PRODUCTION FUNCTION

There are several characteristics of the aggregate production function ($Y = F(K,N)$) that you must understand.

(1) Constant returns to scale

This implies that if the quantities of all inputs (N and K), for example, double in size, output will also double. Alternatively, if N and K both fall by 5%, Y will drop by exactly 5%.

(2) Decreasing returns to capital and decreasing returns to labor

An increase in K will cause Y to increase. An increase in N will cause Y to increase. Decreasing returns to capital and labor imply that:

- equal increases in K, given N, will lead to smaller and smaller increases in Y
- equal increases in N, given K, will lead to smaller and smaller increases in Y.

Learning Tip

- For example, a 5% increase in K, given N, will cause Y to increase but by less than 5%.
- The state of technology indicates how much output is produced, given N and K.
- Improvements in the state of technology are call technological progress.

(3) Output per worker (Y/N) and capital per worker (K/N)

- Constant returns to scale allow us to obtain the following relation between Y/N and K/N: Y/N = F(K/N,1).
- Increases in K/N cause Y/N to increase.
- Because of decreasing returns to capital, equal increases in K/N will cause smaller and smaller increases in Y/N.

4. SOURCES OF GROWTH

(1) Capital accumulation

Capital accumulation cannot sustain increases in growth forever. Why?

- Steady increases in Y/N would require larger and larger increases in K/N.
- To increase capital, the saving rate (the proportion of income that is saved) must rise.
- The saving rate cannot rise forever.
- Therefore, capital accumulation cannot be the source of growth forever.

Learning Tip

- Increases in the saving rate will have no long-run effect on the growth of output per capita.
- Increases in the saving rate WILL cause increases in the level of output per capita.

(2) Technological progress

Technological progress will cause sustained increases in growth. This is shown in Figure 10-6. Specifically, increases in technological progress will cause shifts in the aggregate production function. These same increases in technological progress will cause increases in output per capita.

SELF-TEST QUESTIONS

1. What is meant by "growth" (Introduction)?

2. Define output per capita (1).

3. What are the two main reasons for focusing on output per capita rather than the level of output (1)?

4. What is meant by purchasing power parity numbers and how are they obtained (1)?

5. What are the two main conclusions about growth for the five rich countries discussed in this chapter (2)?

6. What is convergence (2)?

7. What is the relation between the initial level of output per capita and the rate of growth for OECD countries (2)?

8. Prior to the year 1500, what was the rate of growth of output per capita in Europe (3)?

9. For which group of countries does convergence tend not to occur (3)?

10. Write down the aggregate production function. What are the two determinants of aggregate output (4)?

11. What is meant by the state of technology (4)?

12. Explain what is meant by constant returns to scale (4).

13. Explain what is meant by decreasing returns to capital and decreasing returns to labor (4).

14. Output per worker is determined by changes in what variable (4)?

15. What are the two sources of growth (4)?

16. Define technological progress (4).

17. Define what is meant by an economy's saving rate (4).

18. Will capital accumulation and/or technological progress sustain output growth forever (4)?

REVIEW PROBLEMS

1. Suppose you receive $1000 at the age of 20.
a. Calculate what this $1000 will yield in 40 years if invested at the following interest rates: 2.2% (0.022), 1.7% (0.017), 1.2% (0.012), and 0.7% (0.007).
b. What happens in (a) as the interest rate falls?

2. Between 1950 and 1973, output per capita grew 2.2% per year in the United States. Between 1973 and 1992, it grew by 1.2% per year. In 1992, real per capita output was $17,945.
a. Assuming this lower rate of growth remains constant over the next 40 years, calculate what real output per capita will be in 40 years.
b. Now assume that real output per capita grows by the higher rate of 2.2% per year over the next 40 years. Calculate what real output per capita will be in 40 years.
c. Compare your answers in a and b. What does your analysis suggest happens to the standard of living as the growth rate in per capita output declines?

3. Look at Table 10-1. List the two main conclusions about the growth of per capita output for these countries.

4. Suppose convergence occurs. Based on the 2004 levels of per capita output included in Table 10-1, which of these countries should experience the highest rate of growth in per capita output in the future? Which of these countries should experience the lowest rate of growth in per capita output in the future? Explain.

5. Suppose the U.S. growth rate of per capita output 1950 and 2004 had grown at the same rate as in Japan during the same period (i.e., at 4.6% rather than 2.6%).
a. Calculate what U.S. output per capita would have been in 2004 if this had occurred.
b. How much larger is the measure of output calculated in (a) than the actual level that occurred in 2004?

6. Assume the typical consumer in the United States and in Mexico buys only two types of goods: (1) food; and (2) durable goods. Use the information provided below to answer the following questions.

	Price of food	Quantity of food consumed	Price of durables	Quantity of durables consumed
United States	$2	4000	$4	8000
Mexico	2 pesos	2000	20 pesos	1000

a. Calculate U.S. consumption per capita in dollars ($).
b. Calculate Mexican consumption per capita in pesos.
c. Assume the exchange rate is .10 (i.e., $0.10 per peso). Using the exchange rate method, calculate Mexican consumption per capita in dollars. What is the relative consumption per capita in Mexico compared to that in the United States?
d. Use the purchasing power parity method to calculate Mexican per capita consumption in dollars. Using this method, what is the relative consumption per capita in Mexico compared to that in the United States?
e. To what extent does the relative standard of living (or, in this case, consumption) between these two countries depend on the method used to obtain measures of Mexican consumption?

7. Suppose the aggregate production function is given by the following: $Y = (K^{1/2})(N^{1/2})$ where $K^{1/2}$ and $N^{1/2}$ are the square roots of K and N.

a. Calculate Y when K = 200 and N = 100.
b. Calculate Y when K = 400 and N = 200. What is the percentage increase in N, K and Y?
c. Calculate Y when K = 220 and N = 110. What is the percentage increase (compared to the calculations in a) in N, K and Y?
d. Does the above aggregate production function represent constant returns to scale? Explain.
e. Given the above aggregate production function, if N and K both increase by 2.7%, what will be the percentage increase in Y? Briefly explain.

8. Suppose the aggregate production function is given by the following: $Y = (K^{1/2})(N^{1/2})$ where $K^{1/2}$ and $N^{1/2}$ are the square roots of K and N.

a. Divide both Y and the right-hand side of the equation by N. [Hint: Let X be some positive number. $(X^{1/2})/X = (X^{1/2})(X^{-1}) = X^{-1/2} = 1/X^{1/2}$.] What does your answer suggest determines the level of output per capita?

b. Let K = 200 and N = 100. Calculate output per worker and capital per worker.

c. Calculate output per worker for each of the following levels of capital per worker: 2, 3 and 4. What happens to output per worker as capital per worker increases? Does it increase at an increasing, decreasing or constant rate?

d. What does the relation between Y/N and K/N look like? Draw it in the following graph.

Output per worker, Y/N

Capital per worker, K/N

9. Use the graph provided below to answer this question.

Output per capita
(log scale)

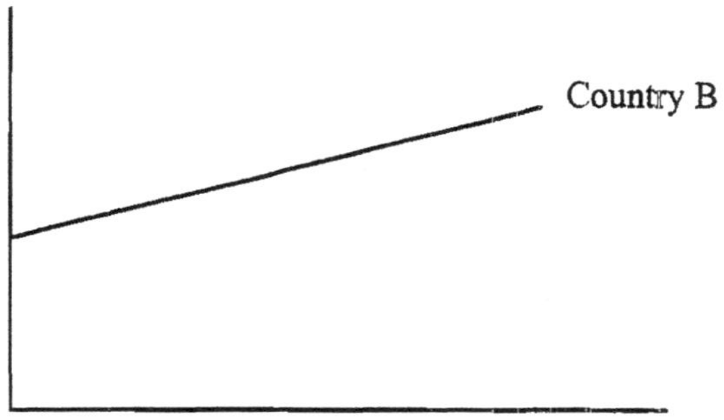

Time

a. The curve for country B is upward sloping. What does this suggest is occurring over time in country B?

b. What would cause this curve to shift up? Briefly explain.

c. What would cause this curve to shift down? Briefly explain.

d. What does the slope of the line represent?

e. What would cause the slope of this line to increase?

g. What would the above curve look like for Europe prior to the year 1500?

10. Use the graph provided below to answer the following questions.

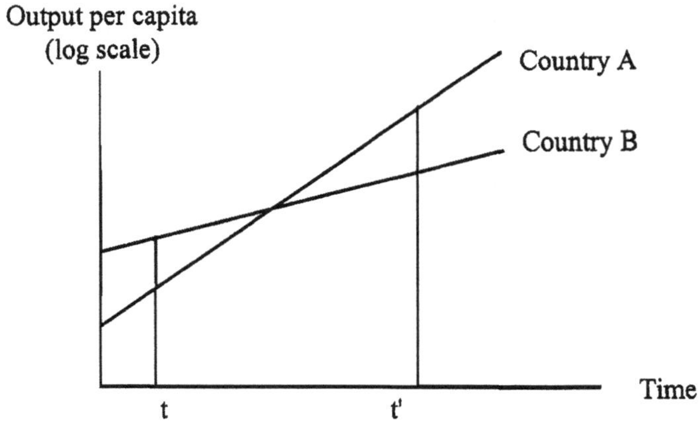

a. At time t, which country has the highest level of output per capita?
b. At time t, which country has highest rate of growth in output per capita?
c. At time t', which country has the highest level of output per capita?
d. At time t', which country has highest rate of growth in output per capita?

MULTIPLE CHOICE QUESTIONS

1. Which of the following variables provides the best measure of the standard of living?

a. level of real output
b. nominal output per capita
c. capital per worker
d. real output per capita

2. A comparison of output per capita for the five rich countries included in the chapter reveals that:

a. Japan had the highest level of output per person in 2004
b. the levels of output per capita have converged
c. growth has generally not occurred for all five countries
d. all of the above

3. When calculating and comparing GDP across countries, economists generally use:

a. per capita measures of real output
b. exchange rates to measure output
c. purchasing power parity numbers to measure output
d. all of the above
e. both a and c

4. <u>After</u> adjusting U.S. and Indian GDP figures using the purchasing power parity numbers, we see that:

a. the difference in the two countries GDP per capita is greater
b. the difference in the two countries GDP per capita is smaller
c. the difference in the two countries GDP per capita is about the same
d. the difference in the two countries GDP per capita disappears

5. When comparing the initial level of output per capita in 1950 with the rate of growth since 1950 for OECD countries, we observe:

a. a negative relation
b. a positive relation
c. no relation
d. no evidence of convergence

6. Purchasing power parity numbers:

a. use exchange rates to calculate GDP
b. use a common set of prices to calculate GDP across countries
c. provide relatively less accurate information about GDP
d. overstate, for example, U.S. output per capita

7. An analysis of GDP growth over long periods of time and across many countries indicates which of the following (circle all that apply)?

a. growth in output per capita has not always occurred
b. convergence does occur for all countries
c. some countries tend to "leapfrog" one another in terms of growth
d. growth was greatest prior to 1500

8. For which of the following groups of countries has convergence NOT occurred?

a. the five richest countries
b. OECD countries
c. African countries
d. Asian countries
e. none of the above

9. Which of the following events will cause an increase in aggregate output?

a. an increase in N
b. an increase in K
c. technological progress
d. all of the above

10. Constant returns to scale suggests that if K and N both increase by 5%, we know that:

a. Y will increase by more than 5%
b. Y will increase by exactly 5%
c. K/N increases by exactly 5%
d. K/N will decrease

11. Decreasing returns to capital indicates that a 10% increase in K will cause:

a. a reduction in K/N
b. a reduction in Y/N
c. Y to increase by exactly 10%
d. Y to increase by less than 10%

12. Which of the following events will cause an increase output per worker (Y/N)?

a. a reduction in K
b. an increase in K
c. a reduction in K/N
d. all of the above

13. Based on the aggregate production function presented in the chapter, equal increases in capital per worker (K/N) over time will cause:

a. no change in Y/N
b. equal increases in Y/N
c. smaller and smaller increases in Y/N
d. reductions in Y/N over time

14. Which of the following events most likely explains sustained output growth forever?

a. capital accumulation
b. an increase in the saving rate
c. technological progress
d. all of the above

15. An increase in the saving rate will tend to cause:

a. an increase in the level of output per capita
b. no change in the level of output per capita
c. a permanently higher growth rate of output per capita
d. a permanently lower growth rate of output per capita

Use the following graph to answer questions 16 and 17.

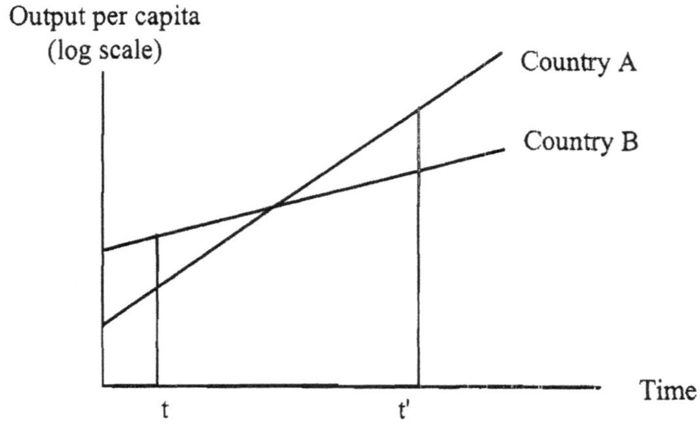

16. At time t,

a. country B has a relatively faster rate of growth in output per capita
b. country B has a relatively lower level of output per capita
c. country A has a relatively faster rate of growth in output per capita
d. country A has a relatively higher level of output per capita

17. By time t', which of the following events, given the current situation shown in the above graph, would cause the level of output per capita in country A to be <u>less</u> than output per capita in B?

a. a reduction in the saving rate in B
b. an increase in technological progress in A
c. a reduction in technological progress in B
d. a reduction in the saving rate in A

CHAPTER 11.
SAVING, CAPITAL ACCUMULATION, AND OUTPUT

OBJECTIVES, REVIEW, AND TUTORIAL

After working through the chapter and the following material, you should be able to:

(1) Understand the relation among capital, output, saving, investment, and changes in the capital stock.

(2) Understand the graphical representation of output per worker, saving per worker and depreciation per worker.

(3) Discuss the dynamics of capital and output.

(4) Explain what is meant by the "steady state of the economy" and the steady-state values of output and capital.

(5) Explain the effects of changes in the saving rate on the level of output, the growth of output in the short run, and the growth of output in the long run.

(6) Discuss what is meant by the golden rule level of capital.

(7) Discuss the possible effects of changes in the saving rate on consumption per worker in the steady state.

(8) Explain what effect changes in human capital have on output per worker.

1. OVERVIEW OF THE MODEL

The model can be summarized by the following equations:

- Output (per worker): $Y_t/N = f(K_t/N)$
- Saving/Investment (per worker): $I_t/N = s(Y_t/N)$
- Capital Accumulation (per worker): $(K_{t+1}/N) - (K_t/N) = s(Y_t/N) - \delta(K_t/N)$

Learning Tip

- S = I when the budget deficit is zero AND the economy is closed.
- More generally, I = S + (T-G).
- If G = T, we know that investment must equal saving (I = S).
- If G does not equal T, the interpretation of saving must be more general. In fact, we would then discuss national saving.
- National saving consists of two components: (1) private saving; and (2) public saving.
    - Private saving is that portion of household disposable income not consumed.
    - Public saving is simply T-G (can be positive, negative, or zero).

Learning Tip

- Capital stock per worker increases when I > depreciation.
- Capital stock per worker decreases when I < depreciation.
- Capital stock per worker is constant when I = depreciation.

2. THE DYNAMICS OF CAPITAL AND OUTPUT

(1) The graph

Make sure you completely understand all aspects of the graph found below:

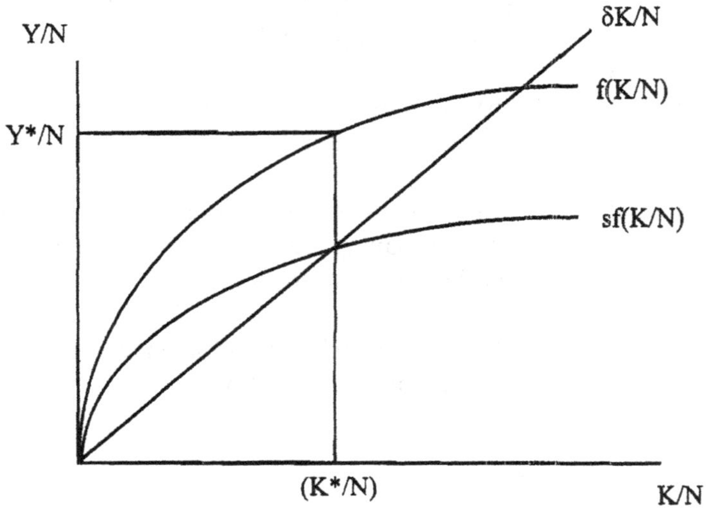

- <u>The production function</u> [f(K/N)]. Output per worker increases at a decreasing rate as K/N increases. Why? Answer: We assume decreasing returns to capital.
- <u>Investment per worker</u> [sf(K/N)]. Since saving is a proportion of income and since S = I, the investment per worker line has the same shape as the production function.
- <u>Depreciation per worker</u> [δ(K/N)]. Since depreciation increases in proportion to capital per worker, the line is upward sloping with a slope equal to δ.

(2) The adjustment to the steady state when $K_t/N < K^*/N$

- As you can see in the above graph, investment exceeds depreciation at all levels of capital per worker when $K_t/N < K^*/N$.
- When investment exceeds depreciation, K/N will increase.
- As K/N increases, Y/N also increases.
- K/N and Y/N will continue to increase until $K/N = K^*/N$ and $Y/N = Y^*/N$.
- At K^*/N, investment equals depreciation and K/N (and Y/N) is constant.

(3) The adjustment to the steady state when $K_t/N > K^*/N$

- As you can see in the above graph, investment is less than depreciation at all levels of capital per worker when $K_t/N > K^*/N$.
- When investment is less than depreciation, K/N will decrease.
- As K/N decreases, Y/N also decreases.
- K/N and Y/N will continue to decrease until $K/N = K^*/N$and $Y/N = Y^*/N$.
- At K^*/N, investment equals depreciation and K/N (and Y/N) is constant.

3. THE STEADY STATE

- The steady state occurs when K/N is constant.
- The steady state, therefore, occurs at K^*/N where investment equals depreciation.
- Since K/N is constant in the steady state, Y/N will also be constant in the steady state.
- If investment does not equal depreciation, the capital stock per worker will change until steady state is reached.

4. THE SAVING RATE AND GROWTH

Assume the economy is in steady state for a given saving rate. An increase in the saving rate will cause:

- investment to exceed depreciation at the initial level of K/N.
- K/N will increase until a new steady state is reached.
- During the adjustment, the increase in s will cause higher growth in output.
- In the long run, the higher saving rate causes an increase in Y/N and K/N.
- In the long run, the increase in the saving has **NO** effect on the rate of growth in output.

Learning Tip

- In this model, once a steady state is reached, the rate of growth in output (Y) is zero.
- Make sure you understand the effects of changes in the saving rate.
- You should also be able to examine the effects of a reduction in the saving rate.
- You should understand that there are two parameters in the model: s and δ (the saving rate and rate of depreciation).

Learning Tip

- Changes in δ and s will cause a new steady state to occur.
- Make sure you can explain the effects of changes in the rate of depreciation as well.
- Some instructors might emphasize this issue; therefore, you need to understand it.
- Changes in δ will cause the slope of the depreciation line to change.
- At the initial K/N, investment and depreciation will not be equal.
- K/N will then change until a new steady state is reached.
- To understand this concept, you should examine graphically and explain the effects of a reduction in δ.

5. THE GOLDEN RULE

The golden rule level of capital is the level of capital at which consumption is maximized in the long run. There exists a corresponding saving rate consistent with the golden rule level of capital. There are two cases to consider.

(1) K/N below the golden rule level of K/N

Here, s must increase. As s increases, consumption will increase at the new steady state (i.e., consumption will increase in the long run). In the short run, however, since K and Y do not immediately change in response to the increase in s, an increase in the saving rate will cause a reduction in consumption.

(2) K/N above the golden rule level of K/N

Here, the saving rate must fall. As s falls, consumption will increase at the new steady state. In the short run, consumption will also increase since s is now lower.

(3) Graphical analysis of the golden rule

Figure 11-6 illustrates (for a given value of δ and for a given aggregate production function) all possible levels of steady state per capita consumption. There are several features of this figure that you must understand.

- If s = 0, steady state consumption is zero. Why? If s = 0, there will be no investment, no capital, no output, and, therefore, no consumption.
- If s = 1, steady state consumption is zero. Why? If s = 1, all income is saved. If all income is saved, consumption is zero.
- There is a unique value of s that maximizes consumption in the steady state. This is represented by s_G.
- The figure indicates that an increase in the saving rate will cause an increase in C/N if s is initially less than s_G.
- Increases in the saving rate above s_G, however, will cause reductions in C/N.
- It is, therefore, possible to save "too much."

Learning Tip

- The United States (like most economies) is most likely below the golden rule level of capital.
- To increase consumption, these countries must increase the saving rate. This policy, however, will reduce consumption in the short run.
- Because individuals care about consumption (rather than output), such a policy which reduces consumption (in the short run) may not be preferred.
- You should review the numerical example in the chapter.

6. HUMAN CAPITAL AND GROWTH

- Human capital is the set of skills possessed by workers.
- Aggregate output can be represented by Y = F(K, N, H) where H is human capital.
- Constant returns to scale allow us to obtain the following: Y/N = F(K/N, H/N).
- Increases in H/N (like increases in K/N caused by an increase in the saving rate) will cause an increase in output per worker.
- Increases in H/N occur via education and on-the-job training.

Learning Tip

- You should review the short discussion of models of endogenous growth.
- In these endogenous growth models, growth DOES depend on the saving rate and on spending on education in the long run.

SELF-TEST QUESTIONS

1. What effect does an increase in K/N have on Y/N (1)?

2. Equal increases in K/N have what effect on Y/N (1)?

3. The saving rate (s) can take on what values (1)?

4. When the budget deficit is zero and the economy is closed, what does saving equal (1)?

5. The amount capital in period t + 1 is determined by what variables and represented by what equation (1)?

6. What determines the change in the capital stock per worker (1)?

7. Why is the depreciation per worker line upward sloping in Figure 13-2 (2)?

8. Discuss what happens to K/N when depreciation is less than investment (2).

9. Discuss what happens to K/N when depreciation is greater than investment (2).

10. What is the "steady state" of the economy (2)?

11. What happens to K/N and Y/N when the economy is in the steady state (2)?

12. What effect does an increase in s have on the growth rate of Y/N in the long run (2)?

13. What effect does an increase in s have on the level of Y/N in the long run (2)?

14. What effect does an increase in s have on the growth rate of Y/N in the short run (2)?

15. What can the government do to increase the saving rate (2)?

16. When s = 0, what is the level of K/N, Y/N and consumption per worker (2)?

17. When s = 1, what is the level of K/N, Y/N and consumption per worker (2)?

18. What is meant by the "golden rule" level of capital (2)?

19. On which side of the golden rule is the United States (3)?

20. What is human capital (4)?

21. What determines human capital accumulation (4)?

22. What is meant by "endogenous growth" (4)?

REVIEW PROBLEMS

1. In period t, suppose Y/N = 2 and K/N = 4.
a. Calculate K/N in period t+1 when s = .4 and δ = .1.
b. Now assume that s = .6 and δ = .1. Calculate K/N in period t+1. What happens to capital accumulation as s increases? Briefly explain.
c. Now assume that s = .4 and δ = .2. Calculate K/N in period t+1. What happens to capital accumulation as δ increases? Briefly explain.

2. "When $I_t > 0$, we know that the capital stock will increase between period t and t+1 ($K_{t+1} > K_t$)." Is this statement true, false or uncertain? Explain.

3. Saving per worker and depreciation (per worker) determine capital accumulation.
a. Compare saving per worker and depreciation when the change in the capital stock is positive.
b. Compare saving per worker and depreciation when the change in the capital stock is negative.
c. Compare saving per worker and depreciation when there is no change in the capital stock.

4. Assume δ = .1.
a. Calculate depreciation (per worker) for the following values of K/N: 2, 3, 4, and 5.
b. What happens to depreciation (per worker) as K/N increases? Does it change at an increasing, decreasing or constant rate?

5. Use the graph provided below to answer the following question.

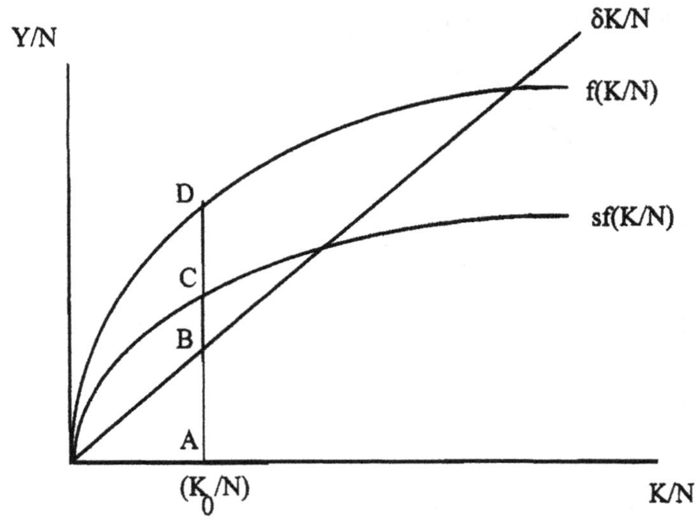

a. What do the distances AB, AC, AD, CB and CD represent?
b. What will happen to K/N and Y/N over time? Explain.
c. Is the economy in steady state at K_0/N?
d. What will be the final levels of K/N and Y/N?

6. Use the graph provided below to answer the following question.

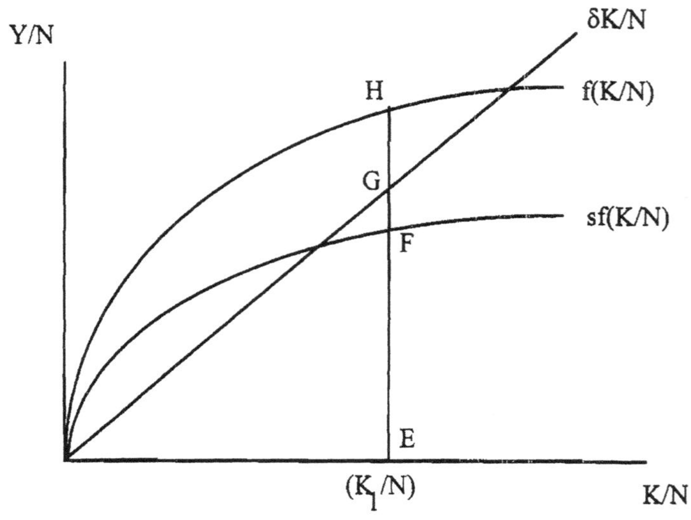

a. What do the distances EF, EG, EH, FG and FH represent?
b. What will happen to K/N and Y/N over time? Explain.
c. Is the economy in steady state at K_1/N?
d. What will be the final levels of K/N and Y/N?

7. Use the graph provided below to answer the following questions.

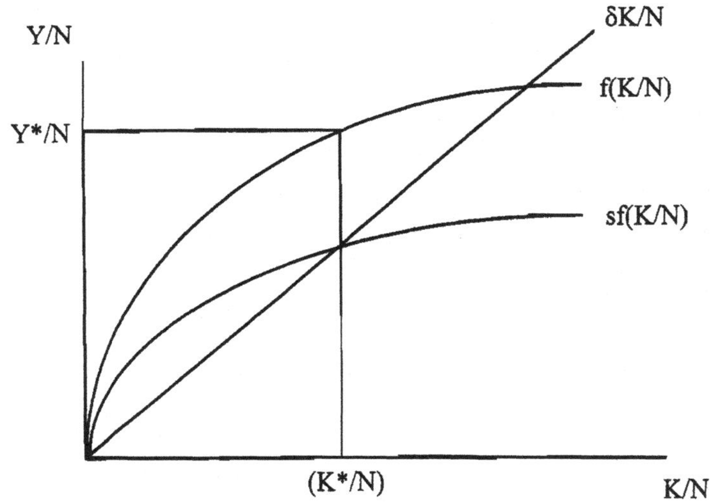

a. Graphically illustrate the effects of a reduction in the saving rate in period t.
b. In period t, what happens to K/N, Y/N, S/N and C/N as a result of the reduction in the saving rate?
c. Explain what happens to K/N and Y/N over time.
d. What are the short-run effects of this reduction in s on the growth rate of Y/N?
e. What are the long-run effects of this reduction in s on the growth rate of Y/N?
f. What are the long-run effects of this reduction in s on the level of Y/N?

8. a. Explain what effect a reduction in the rate of depreciation (δ) will have on the depreciation per worker line.
b. Based on (a), what effect will a reduction in δ have on K/N and Y/N over time? Briefly explain.

9. a. To achieve the highest level of output per worker, what must the saving rate be?
b. Do you see any disadvantages of a policy that seeks to maximize output per worker?

10. a. An increase in s in period t will have what effect on K/N, Y/N and C/N in period t?
b. What effect will this increase in the saving rate have on Y/N, K/N and C/N in the long run?

11. a. A reduction in s in period t will have what effect on K/N, Y/N and C/N in period t?
b. What effect will this reduction in the saving rate have on Y/N, K/N and C/N in the long run?

12. Assume that $Y/N = (K/N)^{1/2}$; Y/N equals the square root of K/N.
a. Calculate Y/N for the following values of K/N: 1, 2, 3, 4, and 5.
b. Does Y/N increase at an increasing, decreasing or constant rate for each additional (and equal) increase in K/N?
c. Does this production function exhibit constant returns to scale?

13. Assume that $Y/N = (K/N)^{1/2}$ and let $\delta = .05$.
a. For each of the following saving rates, calculate the steady-state levels of K/N and Y/N: s = .1, .3, .5, .7, and .9.
b. Given (a), calculate the steady-state levels of C/N for each value of s.
c. What happens to the steady-state level of C/N as s increases from .1 to .5?
d. What happens to the steady-state level of C/N as s increases from .5 to .9?
e. What are the golden rule levels of K/N, C/N and s?

14. Suppose the current saving rate is .2 and that the golden rule saving rate is .5.
a. What can the government do to achieve the golden rule level of K/N?
b. What effect will this policy have on C/N in the short run?
c. What effect will this policy have on C/N in the long run?

15. Let $Y/N = (K/N)^{1/2}(H/N)^{1/2}$ where H/N is human capital per worker.
a. Calculate Y/N when K = 400, N = 100 and H = 400.
b. Does this production function exhibit constant returns to scale?
c. Does this production function exhibit decreasing returns to physical capital?
d. Does this production function exhibit decreasing returns to human capital?

16. Let $Y/N = (K/N)^{1/2}(H/N)^{1/2}$.
a. Given N, what are the two determinants of Y/N? Briefly explain.
b. What must occur for the steady state level of K/N to increase?
c. What must occur for H/N to increase?

17. Provide an intuitive explanation of the shape of the curve in Figure 11-6.

MULTIPLE CHOICE QUESTIONS

1. Suppose K/N increases from 2 to 3. We know that this increase in K/N will cause:

a. Y/N to fall
b. Y/N to remain constant
c. Y/N to increase

2. When the budget deficit is zero and the economy is closed, we know that:

a. $S = I$
b. $S > I$
c. $S < I$
d. the economy is not in the steady state

3. An <u>increase</u> in which of the following will cause K_{t+1} to <u>fall</u>?

a. δ
b. I_t
c. K_t
d. all of the above

4. If the capital stock per worker does not change, we know that:

a. $Y/N = I/N$
b. the economy is NOT in steady state
c. $S/N = \delta(K/N)$
d. none of the above

5. If $K_{t+1} > K_t$, we know that:

a. saving per worker equals depreciation per worker
b. saving per worker is less than depreciation per worker
c. saving per worker is greater than depreciation per worker
d. the saving rate fell in period t

6. The change in the capital stock equals:

a. consumption - depreciation
b. output - depreciation
c. investment - saving
d. investment - depreciation

7. When the economy is in steady state, we always know that:

a. saving per worker equals depreciation (per worker)
b. $s = \delta$
c. consumption per worker is at its highest level
d. the capital stock per worker is increasing

Use the graph provided below to answer questions 8 - 11.

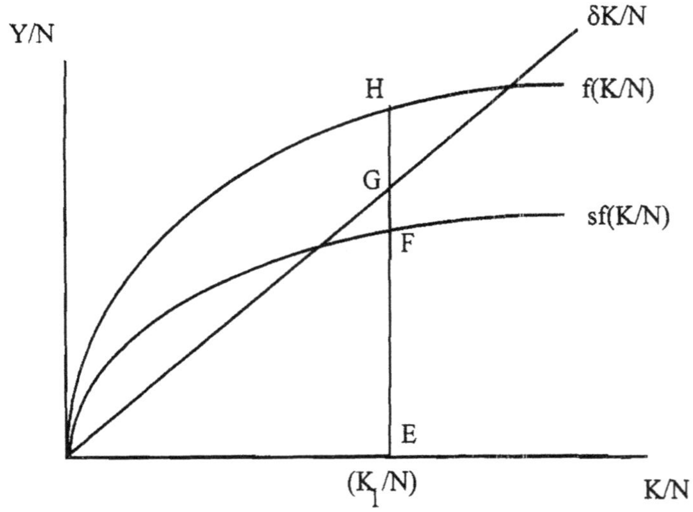

8. This distance EF is:

a. C/N
b. S/N
c. Y/N
d. the change in the capital stock

9. The distance FG is:

a. S/N
b. C/N
c. I/N
d. the change in the capital stock

10. The distance FH is:

a. S/N
b. C/N
c. I/N
d. the change in the capital stock

11. Given the situation at K_1/N, which of the following will tend to occur over time?

a. S/N will decrease
b. K/N will decrease
c. Y/N will decrease
d. all of the above

12. Assume the economy is initially in the steady state. We know with certainty that a reduction in the saving rate will cause:

a. an increase in C/N in the long run
b. a reduction in C/N in the long run
c. no change in C/N in the long run
d. more information is needed to answer this question

13. Assume the economy is initially in the steady state. We know with certainty that a reduction in the saving rate will:

a. cause a reduction in the rate of growth in Y/N in the long run
b. have a negative effect on the rate of growth in Y/N in the short run
c. have no effect on the level of Y/N in the long run
d. cause an increase in the level of Y/N in the long run

14. Assume the economy is initially in the steady state. We know with certainty that an increase in the saving rate will cause:

a. an increase in C/N in the long run
b. a reduction in C/N in the long run
c. no change in C/N in the long run
d. ambiguous effects on C/N in the long run

15. Which of the following represents the effects in period t of an increase in the saving rate in period t?

a. a reduction in consumption
b. no change in Y/N
c. no change in K/N
d. all of the above

16. Which of the following represents the effects in period t of a reduction in the saving rate in period t?

a. output will fall
b. investment will be less than depreciation
c. consumption will fall
d. all of the above

17. The golden rule level of capital is the level of capital which:

a. maximizes output per worker
b. maximizes saving per worker
c. maximizes consumption per worker
d. yields a constant level of capital per worker

18. Assume that the economy is in the steady state and that the current level of capital per worker does not equal the golden rule level of capital. Which of the following actions should be taken to achieve the golden rule level of capital?

a. increase the saving rate
b. reduce the saving rate
c. the economy will achieve the golden rule level of capital by itself
d. more information is needed to answer this question

19. Assume that the economy is in the steady state and that the current level of capital per worker is greater than the golden rule level of capital. Which of the following actions should be taken to achieve the golden rule level of capital?

a. increase the saving rate
b. reduce the saving rate
c. the economy will achieve the golden rule level of capital by itself
d. more information is needed to answer this question

20. Which of the following will cause an increase in Y/N?

a. increase in education
b. increase in on-the-job training
c. increase in the saving rate
d. all of the above

21. Human capital represents:

a. the set of skills of skilled workers
b. the set of skills of unskilled workers
c. all of the above
d. none of the above

22. Models of endogenous growth suggest that growth depends in the long run on:

a. the saving rate
b. the rate of spending on education
c. all of the above
d. none of the above

CHAPTER 12.
TECHNOLOGICAL PROGRESS AND GROWTH

OBJECTIVES, REVIEW, AND TUTORIAL

After working through the chapter and the following material, you should be able to:

(1) Understand what determines the level of research and development and the rate of technological progress.

(2) Explain how technological progress (the state of technology) is included in the production function.

(3) Understand the relation between output per effective worker and capital per effective worker.

(4) Explain the dynamics of capital and output (per effective worker).

(5) Discuss what happens to Y/NA, K/NA, the growth rate of output, output per worker, and the capital stock when the economy is in steady state (balanced growth).

(6) Examine the effects of changes in the saving rate on Y/NA, K/NA, the growth rate of output, output per worker, and the capital stock.

(7) Explain whether changes in growth are caused by capital accumulation or technological progress.

(8) Discuss and understand the facts of growth.

1. SUMMARY OF RESEARCH AND DEVELOPMENT (R&D) AND TECHNOLOGICAL PROGRESS

- Technological progress is the result of R&D spending.
- Increases in R&D spending increase the probability a firm will develop a new product or method to produce a product.
- Patent laws give a firm the right to exclude other firms from producing a newly developed product.
- The fertility of research tells us how R&D spending translates into new ideas and products.
- The appropriability of research results captures the extent to which a firm benefits from the results of R&D.

Learning Tip

- If research is very fertile, R&D spending will increase; the opposite is also true.
- If appropriability is high, firms will increase R&D spending; the opposite is also true.

2. OVERVIEW OF THE MODEL

(1) A review of the variables

- The state of technology: A
- The amount of effective labor: NA
- Aggregate output: Y = F(K,N,A)
- Capital per effective worker: K/NA
- Output per effective worker: Y/NA = f(K/NA)
- Saving/Investment per effective worker: I/NA = sf(K/NA)
- Required investment per effective worker: $(\delta + g_N + g_A)$K/NA
- Output per worker: Y/N
- Capital per worker: K/N

Learning Tip

- The amount of effective labor increases for two reasons:
  (1) The number of workers (N) grows at rate g_N.
  (2) Technological progress grows at rate g_A.

- To maintain a constant level of capital per effective worker, investment per effective worker must take into account:

  (1) the depreciation of capital (δ);
  (2) the fact that N grows at rate g_N; and
  (3) the fact that technological progress grows at rate g_A.

- Effective labor grows at rate $(g_N + g_A)$.
- To keep K/NA constant, K must increase at the same rate as NA $(g_N + g_A)$.
- An increase in δ, g_N, or g_A will increase the amount of required investment.
- The slope of the required investment line is $(\delta + g_N + g_A)$.

(2) The graph

Make sure you completely understand all aspects of the following graph.

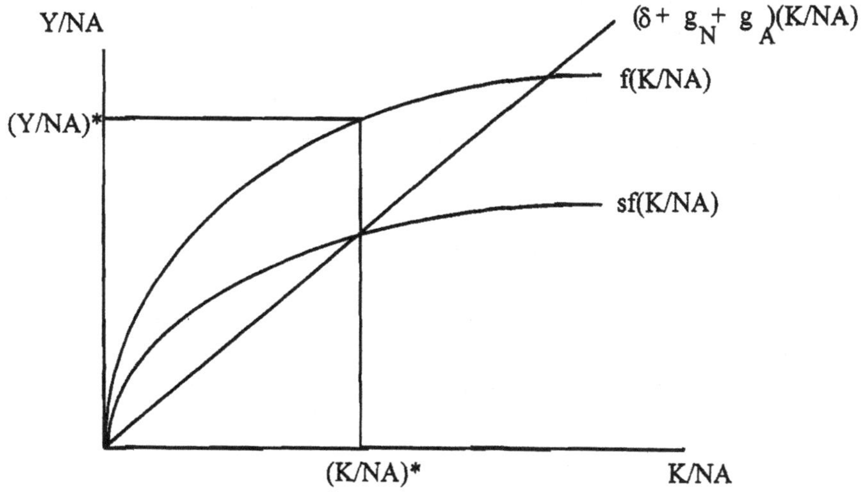

Note:
- The production function continues to exhibit constant returns to scale.
- The production function also continues to exhibit decreasing returns to K, N and A.

(3) The adjustment to the steady state when K/NA < (K/NA)*

- In this case, investment exceeds required investment and K/NA will increase.
- As K/NA increases, Y/NA will also increase.
- K/NA and Y/NA will rise until K/NA = (K/NA)* and Y/NA = (Y/NA)*.
- At (K/NA)*, Y/NA and K/NA are constant.

(4) The adjustment to the steady state when K/NA > (K/NA)*

- In this case, investment is less than required investment and K/NA will fall.
- As K/NA decreases, Y/NA will also decrease.
- K/NA and Y/NA will fall until K/NA = (K/NA)* and Y/NA = (Y/NA)*.
- At (K/NA)*, Y/NA and K/NA are constant.

3. SUMMARY OF THE STEADY STATE: BALANCED GROWTH

Learning Tip

You must understand the following two characteristics of the steady state to understand the characteristics of the balanced growth path:

(1) once the steady state is reached, we know that Y/NA and K/NA are constant; and
(2) N grows at rate g_N and technological progress grows at rate g_A; NA, therefore, grows at rate $(g_N + g_A)$.

Suppose $g_A = 2\%$ and $g_N = 4\%$. On the balanced growth path:

(1) The rate of growth of output per effective worker is zero since Y/NA is constant.
(2) The rate of growth of capital per effective worker is zero since K/NA is constant.
(3) When Y/NA is constant, the level of output (Y) grows at the same rate as NA which equals 6% $(g_N + g_A)$.
(4) When K/NA is constant, the capital stock (K) grows at the same rate as NA which equals 6% $(g_N + g_A)$.
(5) Since Y grows at 6% and N grows at 4%, output per worker (Y/N) grows at 2% (g_A).
(6) Since K grows at 6% and N grows at 4%, capital per worker (K/N) grows at 2% (g_A).

Learning Tip

- What is constant in the steady state is Y/NA and K/NA.
- Since Y/NA and K/NA are constant in the steady state (i.e., on the balanced growth path), we know that Y, K and NA all grow at the same rate which is $(g_N + g_A)$.

4. THE EFFECTS OF CHANGES IN THE SAVING RATE

Assume the economy is initially in steady state. An increase in the saving rate will have the following effects:

(1) Investment will exceed required investment so K/NA will increase.
(2) K/NA and Y/NA will increase until the new steady state is reached.
(3) As K/NA and Y/NA increase, Y and K grow faster than $(g_N + g_A)$.
(4) As K/NA and Y/NA increase, Y per worker and K per worker grow faster than g_A.
(5) Once the steady state is reached, Y and K grow at $(g_N + g_A)$ and Y per worker and K per worker grow at g_A.
(6) Changes in the saving rate have no long-run effect on growth rates (of any of the variables).
(7) An increase in s WILL cause a permanent change in the levels of Y/NA and K/NA.

Learning Tip

Make sure you can explain the effects of a reduction in the saving rate.

5. OTHER ISSUES

(1) Causes of high growth

• When growth is caused by technological progress, we expect output per worker (Y/N) to grow at g_A (i.e., balanced growth).
• When growth is caused by increases in capital accumulation (caused by, for example, an increase in s), we would expect output per worker to grow at a rate that exceeds g_A.

Learning Tip
• So, if growth in Y/N > g_A, growth is from capital accumulation.
• If growth in Y/N = g_A, growth is from technological progress.

(2) Facts of growth

The period of high growth (1950-73), the growth slowdown (between 1973 and 2000), and the convergence of Y/N all appear to be caused by technological progress NOT from changes in capital accumulation.

(3) The Solow residual

The Solow residual is given by the following:

$$\text{residual} = g_Y - [\alpha g_N + (1 - \alpha)g_K]$$

The Solow residual can be used to obtain estimates of the rate of technological progress:

$$g_A = \text{residual}/\alpha.$$

6. FINAL ADVICE

Depending on your instructor, you might be asked to examine the effects of changes in δ, g_N, and g_A in the model.

• Increases in δ, g_N, and g_A cause the required investment line to become steeper and cause Y/NA and K/NA to fall.
• In the cases of changes in g_N and g_A, changes in the rate of growth at the new steady state will also occur.

Learning Tip

- Make sure you understand the graph, the dynamic adjustment to steady state and the characteristics of the steady state (balanced growth).
- As suggested above, you might want to examine and discuss the effects of an increase (or decrease) in each of the following variables: δ, g_N, and g_A.
- Changes in these three parameters will cause changes in the slope of the required investment line and, therefore, changes in the steady state levels of K/NA and Y/NA.
- Changes in the depreciation rate and rate of growth of the population will not cause permanent changes in the rate of growth in Y/N.
- As discussed above, changes in the rate of technological progress will cause permanent changes in the rate of growth of Y/N.
- To test your understanding of this material, you might want to examine graphically and then explain changes in each of these parameters.

SELF-TEST QUESTIONS

1. Technological progress is primarily the result of what activity (2)?

2. What is the difference between the purchase of a machine and spending on R&D (2)?

3. What are patents (2)?

4. What is meant by the fertility of research (2)?

5. What is meant by the appropriability of research results (2)?

6. What are the different dimensions of technological progress (1)?

7. Given the production function, what are the three determinants of output (1)?

8. What determines "effective labor" (1)?

9. What determines the level of output per effective worker (1)?

10. What determines the level of investment per effective worker (1)?

11. What is the expression which indicates how much investment is needed to maintain a given level of capital per effective worker (1)?

12. What happens to output per effective worker and capital per effective worker in the steady state (1)?

13. What happens to Y and K in the steady state? If they are changing, at what rate do they change in the steady state (1)?

14. What happens to output per worker in the steady state (1)?

15. What is meant by "balanced growth" (1)?

16. In steady state, what determines the rate of growth in output (1)?

17. What effect does an increase in the saving rate have on Y/NA and K/NA in the long run (1)?

18. What are the short-run and long-run effects of an increase in the saving rate on the growth rate of output and capital (1)?

19. Compare the rate of growth of output per worker with the rate of technological progress if growth reflects high balanced growth (3).

20. Compare the rate of growth of output per worker with the rate of technological progress if growth reflects capital accumulation (3).

21. The rate of growth in output per person for rich countries since 1950 was primarily caused by what (3)?

22. The rate of growth in output per person for China since 1980 was primarily caused by what (3)?

23. Convergence of output per capita has come from what (3)?

24. List the three hypotheses that attempt to explain the reduction in the rate of technological progress (3).

REVIEW PROBLEMS

1. To what extent do patents affect: (1) the fertility of research; and (2) the appropriability of research results? Explain.

2. Briefly explain why relatively poor patent protection might affect spending on R&D and technological progress.

3. Suppose N = 100.
a. Calculate the amount of effective labor (NA) for the following values of A (the state of technology): 1, 1.1, 1.2, 1.3, 1.5.
b. What happens to the amount of effective labor as A increases? Why?

4. Suppose $Y = (K)^{1/2}(NA)^{1/2}$.
a. Calculate Y when K = 100 and NA = 100.
b. Calculate Y when K = 200 and NA = 200. When K and NA both increase by a factor of 2, what happens to Y? Does this production function exhibit constant returns to scale?
c. Assume NA = 100 and does not change. Calculate Y for each of the following values of K: 100, 150 and 200. Does this production function exhibit decreasing returns to K?
d. Assume K = 100 and does not change. Calculate Y for each of the following values of NA: 100, 140 and 180. Does this production function exhibit decreasing returns to NA?

5. Using equation (24.1), discuss what factors determine the level of output.

6. Assume $\delta = .10$, $g_N = .03$ and $g_A = .02$.
a. Calculate the level of investment needed to maintain the level of capital at each of the following values of K: 100, 110, 120 and 130.
b. What happens to this level of investment for each 10-unit increase in K? Does it increase at an increasing, decreasing or constant rate?

7. Assume $\delta = .10$, $g_N = .05$ and $g_A = .05$.
a. Calculate the amount of "required investment" (per effective worker) for each of the following levels of K/NA: 10, 20, 30 and 40.
b. What happens to required investment for each 10-unit increase in K/NA? Does it increase at an increasing, decreasing or constant rate?

8. Briefly explain how an increase in each of the following variables will affect required investment:

a. g_N

b. g_A

c. δ

9. Assume $\delta = .10$, $g_N = .03$, $g_A = .02$ and K/NA = 10.

a. Given this information, calculate "required investment."

b. Suppose the current I/NA = 2. Given your answer in (a) what will happen, if anything, to K/NA? Briefly explain.

c. Suppose the current I/NA = 1. Given your answer in (a), what will happen, if anything, to K/NA? Briefly explain.

d. What must I/NA be to maintain K/NA at 10?

10. Use the graph provided below to answer the following questions.

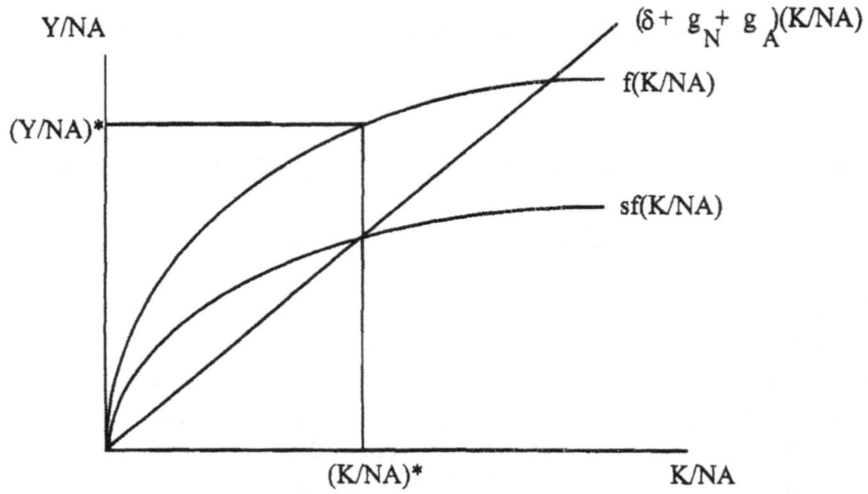

a. If K/NA < (K/NA)*, explain what happens to K/NA and Y/NA over time.

b. If K/NA > (K/NA)*, explain what happens to K/NA and Y/NA over time.

c. Is (K/NA)* the steady state level of K/NA? Briefly explain.

11. Assume $\delta = .10$, $g_N = .03$, $g_A = .02$ and K/NA = 10. Assume the economy is in steady state.

a. What is the rate of growth in Y/NA and K/NA in steady state?

b. What is the rate of growth in Y and K in steady state?

c. What is the rate of growth in N in steady state?

d. What is the rate of growth in capital per worker in steady state?

e. What is the rate of growth in output per worker in steady state?

12. a. What can cause the rate of growth in output (Y) to increase in the steady state?
b. What can cause the rate of growth in the output per worker to increase in the steady state?

13. Use the graph provided below to answer the following questions.

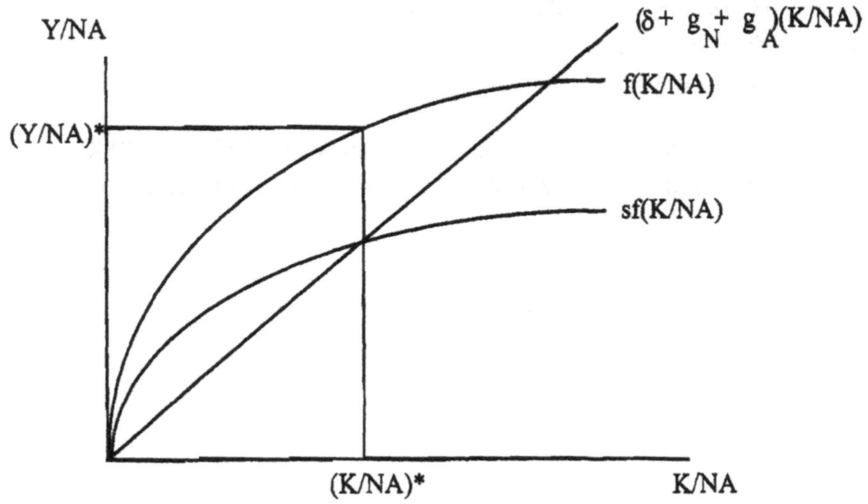

a. Graphically illustrate the effects of a reduction in the saving rate.
b. Explain what happens to K/NA and Y/NA over time.
c. What are the long-run effects on the level of Y/NA and K/NA?
d. Prior to the drop in s, what was the rate of growth in output per worker?
e. What are the short-run effects of this reduction in s on the growth rate of output per worker?
f. Once the new steady state is reached, what is the rate of growth in output per worker?

14. "A reduction in the saving rate will cause a permanent reduction in the rate of growth of output per worker." Is this statement true, false, or uncertain? Explain.

15. In the steady state, what determines the rate of growth of Y, K, output per worker and capital per worker?

16. Discuss the long-run effects of an increase in the rate of technological progress on the rate of growth of output per worker.

17. Discuss the short-run and long-run effects of an increase in the saving rate on K/NA and on the rate of growth in output per worker.

18. Suppose output per worker is growing at 6% and $g_A = 2\%$.
a. Is the economy in steady state? Why or why not?
b. What is causing this relatively high rate of growth in output per worker?

19. Suppose output per worker is growing at 2% and $g_A = 4\%$.

a. Is the economy in steady state? Why or why not?

b. What is causing this relatively low rate of growth in output per worker?

20. Suppose output per worker is growing at 2% and $g_A = 2\%$.

a. Is the economy in steady state? Why or why not?

b. What is causing this rate of growth in output per worker?

21. Was the slowdown in the rate of growth in output per worker between 1973 and 2000 caused by a slowdown in capital accumulation or a slowdown in the rate of technological progress? Explain.

MULTIPLE CHOICE QUESTIONS

1. Industrial R&D expenditures account for what percentage of GDP in each of the 5 major rich countries?

a. 2-3%
b. 10%
c. 15%
d. 25-26%

2. Patent laws will:

a. increase the fertility of research
b. increase the appropriability of research results
c. all of the above
d. none of the above

3. The fertility of research tells us:

a. how R&D spending translates into new ideas
b. how R&D spending translates into new products
c. the extent to which firms benefit from the results of their R&D
d. both a and b
e. none of the above

4. The appropriability of research results tells us:

a. how R&D spending translates into new ideas
b. how R&D spending translates into new products
c. the extent to which firms benefit from the results of their R&D
d. both a and b
e. none of the above

5. Which of the following represents the dimensions of technological progress?

a. larger quantities of output given N and K
b. better products
c. new products
d. all of the above

6. An increase in which of the following variables will cause an increase in output (Y)?

a. N
b. K
c. A
d. all of the above

7. Which of the following expressions represents the amount of effective labor?

a. N
b. NA
c. N/A
d. A/N

8. Output per effective worker is equal to:

a. Y/N
b. Y/A
c. Y/NA
d. none of the above

9. Suppose A increases by 50% and N decreases by 50%. Given this information, we would expect that:

a. Y will increase
b. Y will decrease
c. Y will not change
d. the amount of effective labor will increase

10. If K and NA both increase by 10%, we know that:

a. Y will increase by exactly 10%
b. Y will increase by less than 10%
c. Y will increase by more than 10%
d. there will be no change in Y

11. Which of the following expressions represents required investment per effective worker?

a. $(\delta + g_N + g_A)K/NA$
b. $(\delta + g_N + g_A)Y/NA$
c. $(g_N + g_A)K/NA$
d. $(\delta + g_N)K/NA$

Use the information provided below to answer questions 12-19:

$\delta = .10$ (10% per year) $g_N = .03$ (3% per year) $g_A = .02$ (2% per year).

12. Effective labor grows at what rate?

a. 2%
b. 3%
c. 5%
d. 10%
e. 15%

13. The number of workers is growing at what rate?

a. 1%
b. 2%
c. 3%
d. 5%

14. The level of investment per effective worker needed to maintain a constant level of capital per effective worker (K/NA) is:

a. .02(K/NA)
b. .03(K/NA)
c. .05(K/NA)
d. .10(K/NA)
e. .15(K/NA)

15. The steady state rate of growth of Y/NA is:

a. 0
b. 2%
c. 3%
d. 5%
e. 10%
f. 15%

16. The steady state rate of growth of output per worker is:

a. 0
b. 2%
c. 3%
d. 5%
e. 10%

17. The steady state rate of growth of output (Y) is:

a. 0
b. 2%
c. 3%
d. 5%
e. 10%

18. The steady state rate of growth of capital per effective worker (K/NA) is:

a. 0
b. 2%
c. 3%
d. 5%
e. 10%

19. The steady state rate of growth of capital (K) is:

a. 0
b. 2%
c. 3%
d. 5%
e. 10%

20. An increase in the saving rate will cause:

a. a permanent increase in Y/NA
b. a permanent increase in K/NA
c. a temporary increase in the rate of growth in output per worker
d. all of the above

21. A reduction in the saving rate will cause:

a. a permanent reduction in the rate of growth of output per worker
b. no change in K/NA
c. a permanent reduction in the rate of growth of output (Y)
d. all of the above
e. none of the above

22. Which of the following will cause a permanent increase in the rate of growth of output per worker?

a. increase in g_A
b. increase in s
c. reduction in s
d. none of the above

23. Which of the following will cause a permanent reduction in the rate of growth of output per worker?

a. increase in s
b. reduction in s
c. reduction in g_A
d. none of the above

24. In the model presented in this chapter, balanced growth occurs when:

a. Y and K are constant
b. output per worker is constant
c. output per effective worker is increasing
d. the number of workers, output and capital grow at the same rate

25. If the growth rate of output per worker is greater than the rate of technological progress, we know that:

a. the high growth is caused by high balanced growth
b. the high growth is caused by capital accumulation
c. the economy is in steady state
d. none of the above

26. If the growth rate of output per worker is equal to the rate of technological progress, we know that:

a. the high growth is caused by high balanced growth
b. the high growth is caused by capital accumulation
c. the economy is NOT in steady state
d. none of the above

CHAPTER 13. TECHNOLOGICAL PROGRESS: THE SHORT, THE MEDIUM, AND THE LONG RUN

OBJECTIVES, REVIEW, AND TUTORIAL

After working through the chapter and the following material, you should be able to:

(1) Understand the short run effects of changes in productivity on output, employment, and unemployment.

(2) Understand the effects of changes in productivity on the natural rate of unemployment (and on the real wage).

(3) Explain how a reduction in the rate of growth in technological progress can cause an increase in the natural rate of unemployment.

(4) Discuss how changes in technological progress can affect wage inequality.

(5) Understand the role that institutions can play in determining economic growth.

1. SHORT-RUN EFFECTS OF PRODUCTIVITY ON OUTPUT, EMPLOYMENT, AND UNEMPLOYMENT

(1) Review of the production function

The production function is represented as: Y = NA.

- Each worker produces A units of output.
- The variable A represents the state of technology.
- The variable A also represents labor productivity since A = Y/N.

Learning Tip

- An increase in A, given N, causes an increase in Y.
- An increase in A allows firms to produce the same level of output with less N.

(2) Increases in A and employment

Since Y = NA, employment can be written as: N = Y/A. Will an increase in A cause N to increase? There are three possible cases:

- N increases if the percentage change in Y > percentage change in A.
- N decreases if the percentage change in Y < percentage change in A.
- N remains constant if the percentage change in Y = percentage change in A.

(3) Technological progress and aggregate supply

- An increase in A reduces the amount of labor needed to produce some fixed level of output.
- This increase in A, therefore, reduces costs.
- Firms respond by reducing their prices at any level of output.
- The aggregate supply curve, therefore, shifts down when A increases.

(4) Technological progress and aggregate demand (2 cases)

<u>Case 1</u>

- Productivity coming from the widespread use of new technologies may cause consumers to raise their expectations of future income and firms to raise their expectations of future profits.
- Consumption, investment and, therefore, aggregate demand will increase.

<u>Case 2</u>

- Productivity coming from a more efficient use of existing technology may cause firms to cut costs and eliminate jobs.
- Such reorganization may increase uncertainty about job security and cause consumption to fall.
- The drop in consumption will cause aggregate demand to fall.

(5) Productivity and output

Suppose productivity increases. This increase in A will shift the AS curve down. The increase in A may cause aggregate demand to increase or decrease.

<u>Case 1: AD increases</u>

- Here, the increase in A causes the AS curve to shift down and the AD curve to shift to the right.
- Output unambiguously increases (Note: P could increase, decrease or remain the same).
- Will employment increase (and unemployment fall)? Since the change in A could be greater than, less than, or equal to the change in Y, the effects on N are ambiguous.

<u>Case 2: AD falls</u>

- The drop in AD acts to offset the effects of the increase in A on the AS curve.
- The extent to which Y increases depends on how significant the drop in aggregate demand is.

Learning Tip

- Could Y fall? In theory, yes. The leftward shift in the AD curve would have to be large enough to more than offset the shift down in the AS curve. We will ignore this unlikely case.
- The empirical evidence indicates that increases in productivity have ambiguous effects on employment and the unemployment rate in the short run.

2. THE EFFECTS OF PRODUCTIVITY ON U_n

To examine the long-run effects of changes in productivity on unemployment, we use the WS and PS relations presented earlier.

(1) Effects of productivity on the PS relation

- Each worker produces A units of output.
- One unit of output requires 1/A workers.
- The cost of producing one unit of output is the wage times 1/A which equals W/A.
- Firms set prices as a markup over cost, therefore:

$P = (1 + \mu)W/A$.
The real wage as determined by the above price-setting equation is:

$W/P = A/(1 + \mu)$.

- An increase in A reduces costs and, therefore, reduces P, given W.
- As P falls, given W, the real wage increases.
- An increase in A, therefore, causes an increase in W/P and the PS relation to shift up by the change in A.

(2) Effects of productivity on the WS relation

- Wages (W) are set to reflect increases in productivity.
- The wage-setting equation is $W = A^eP^eF(u,z)$.
- For example, a 5% increase in the expected level of productivity will cause a 5% increase in W and, given P, a 5% increase in the real wage.
- Increases in productivity, therefore, cause the WS relation to shift up by the change in A.

(3) Productivity and u_n

Assume expectations of A and P are correct ($P^e = P$ and $A^e = A$). An increase in A will cause:
- The WS relation to shift up by the change in A.
- The PS relation to shift up by the change in A.
- No change in u_n since the WS and PS relations both shift by the same amount.
- An increase in W/P equal to the change in A.

3. EFFECTS OF PRODUCTIVITY ON U_n WHEN EXPECTATIONS ARE SLOW TO ADJUST

(1) Introduction

- The PS relation is the same.
- The WS relation now includes A^e since expectations of A are slow to adjust: $W/P = A^eF(u,z)$.

(2) <u>Case 1</u>: The percentage change in A = the percentage change in A^e
- Suppose A and A^e are both increasing at the same rate.
- Since A and A^e are both increasing at the same rate, the WS and PS relations are both shifting up by the same amount each period.
- In this case, u_n does not change and the real wage increases each period as A rises.

(3) Case 2: The percentage change in A < the percentage change in A^e

- Suppose A and A^e have been both increasing at, say, 4% each year.
- Suppose productivity growth suddenly declines in period t; A increases by only 2%.
- The PS relation now shifts up by only 2%.
- The WS relation, based on expectations of A, continues to shift up by 4%.
- As seen in Figure 13-6, u_n increases here.
- The real wage increases by 2%.

Learning Tip

- This analysis can explain why there appears to be a negative relation between productivity growth and unemployment.
- Over time, expectations of A will adjust and the WS relation's position will be based on the actual level of A returning unemployment to the original u_n.

4. TECHNOLOGICAL PROGRESS AND WAGE INEQUALITY

- Technological progress is a process of structural change.
- Technological progress has caused an increase in wage inequality (i.e., the gap between the wages of skilled workers and unskilled workers has increased).
- The primary cause of the increased wage inequality has been the increase in the relative demand for skilled workers.
- This increase in the relative demand for skilled workers has been caused by:
    (1) international trade; and
    (2) skill-biased technological progress.

5. THE ROLE OF INSTITUTIONS

In addition to factors such as geography, climate, and culture, institutions may also affect economic growth. The following are considered to be some of the institutions that may have the greatest effect on growth: property rights, the quality of a country's political and judicial system, and the effectiveness of a country's anti-trust laws.

Learning Tip

- You should become familiar with the discussion of the sources of growth in China.
- Make sure you can explain how each of the following has affected China's growth:
    a. the Confucian tradition;
    b. the role of markets in the Chinese economy; and
    c. the guarantee of property rights to foreign investors.
- Future growth in China, however, may be hindered by an inefficient banking system and property rights that are not well established.

SELF-TEST QUESTIONS

1. What is meant by technological unemployment (Introduction)?

2. What are the two highlighted dimensions of technological progress in this chapter (Introduction)?

3. What does the process of "creative destruction" represent (Introduction)?

4. What are the two interpretations of A in this chapter (Introduction)?

5. Y = NA. What is the expression for labor productivity (1)?

6. An increase in productivity (A) has what effect on the aggregate supply curve (1)?

7. In the short run, for N to increase when A increases, what must happen to Y (1)?

8. What type of increase in A would cause an increase in aggregate demand (1)?

9. What type of increase in A would cause a decrease in aggregate demand (1)?

10. Why do increases in output growth in the short run cause increases in productivity (1)?

11. What effect does an increase in A have on firms' costs (2)?

12. An increase in productivity will have what effect on the wage (W) as determined by wage setters (2)?

13. Given the price-setting equation, an increase in A will have what effect on the real wage and on the PS relation (2)?

14. Given the wage-setting equation, an increase in A will have what effect on the real wage and on the WS relation (2)?

15. When expectations of P and A are correct, a 10% increase in A will have what effect on the WS relation, the PS relation, the real wage, and on the natural rate of unemployment (2)?

16. Over long periods of time in the United States, what type of relation appears to exist between productivity growth and unemployment (2)?

17. When workers' expectations of productivity growth adjust slowly, a slowdown in productivity growth will have what effect on the WS relation, the PS relation, the real wage, and on the natural rate of unemployment (2)?

18. What is meant by technological unemployment (2).

19. What is meant by the "churning process" (3)?

20. What do most economists believe is the cause of the increase in wage inequality (3)?

21. Explain what hysteresis means(3).

22. Explain what eurosclerosis means (3)?

23. What are several of the factors behind the relative decline in demand for unskilled workers (3)?

24. What is skill-biased technological progress (3)?

25. What are the effects of institutions on economic growth (4)?

26. Provide some examples of institutions that can affect economic growth (4)?

27. What are some of the sources of growth in China (4)?

REVIEW PROBLEMS

Note: Unless specified otherwise, assume Y = NA for all of the review problems and for all of the multiple choice questions.

1. a. Suppose N = 100. Calculate the level of output for each of the following values of A: 1, 1.2, 1.4 and 1.6.
b. What happens to labor productivity as A increases? Briefly explain.

2. a. Suppose output remains constant at 2000. Calculate how many workers will be needed to produce this level of output for each of the following values of A: 1, 1.25, 1.5 and 2.
b. What happens to N as A increases? Briefly explain.

3. a. To produce one more unit of output, how many additional workers will be needed for each of the following values of A: .5, .75, 1, and 1.5.
b. Explain why N changes as A changes.
c. For a fixed nominal wage, what happens to the cost of producing this one unit of output as A increases? Briefly explain.

4. Assume productivity (A) increases by 5%.
a. Discuss what happens to N in the short run for each of the following percentage changes in output: 2%, 4%, 5%, 6% and 7%.
b. Based on a, under what conditions will an increase in A result in a reduction in N?
c. Based on a, under what conditions will an increase in A result in an increase in N?
d. Based on a, under what conditions will an increase in A result in no change in N?

5. Briefly explain how an increase in A affects the aggregate supply curve.

6. Briefly explain how an increase in A can cause an increase in aggregate demand. Specifically, explain what happens to the components of aggregate demand.

7. Briefly explain how an increase in A can cause a reduction in aggregate demand. Specifically, explain what happens to the components of aggregate demand.

8. "The model of aggregate supply and demand indicates that increases in productivity will always result in higher output in the short run." Is this statement true, false or uncertain? Explain.

9. "The model of aggregate supply and demand indicates that increases in productivity will always cause the aggregate price level (P) to fall in the short run." Is this statement true, false or uncertain? Explain.

10. Assume P = 1 and $\mu = .10$.
a. Using the PS equation, calculate the real wage for each of the following values of A: .5, .75, 1, 1.5.
b. What happens to the real wage as A increases? Briefly explain.
c. What happens to the PS relation as A increases?
d. Based on your analysis, a 7% increase in A will have what effect on the real wage (as determined by the PS relation)?

11. Assume P = 1, u = .05 and W = AP(1 - u).

a. Using the above WS equation, calculate the real wage for each of the following values of A: .5, .75, 1, 1.5.

b. What happens to the real wage as A increases? Briefly explain.

c. What happens to the WS relation as A increases?

d. Based on your analysis, a 7% increase in A will have what effect on the real wage (as determined by the WS relation)?

12. Assume that expectations of prices and productivity are correct. Using the graph found below, illustrate and discuss what effect a 3% increase in A will have on the PS relation, WS relation, real wage and natural rate of unemployment.

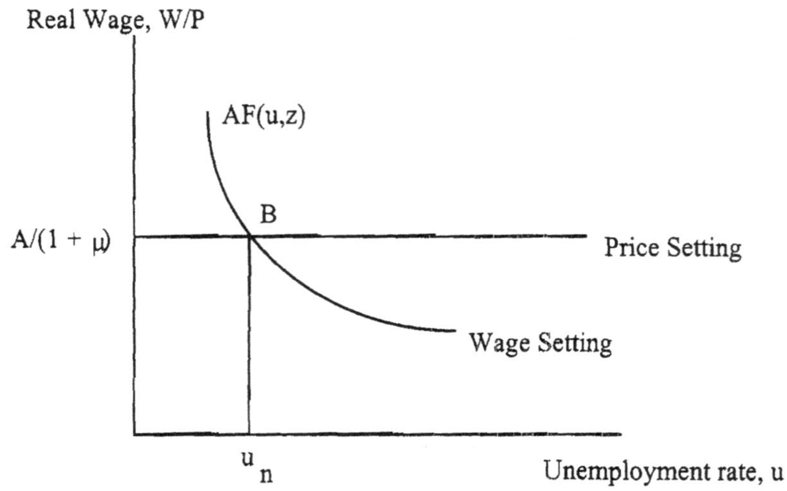

13. Assuming that expectations of A and P are correct, what effect will a reduction in A have on u_n and on the real wage? Briefly explain.

14. Assume that expectations of productivity adjust slowly. Further assume that productivity growth has been 7% per year over the past 10 years. In period t, assume that productivity growth suddenly declines to 3%.

a. Using the following graph, illustrate and discuss what effect this productivity growth slowdown
will have on the PS relation, WS relation, real wage and natural rate of unemployment in period t.

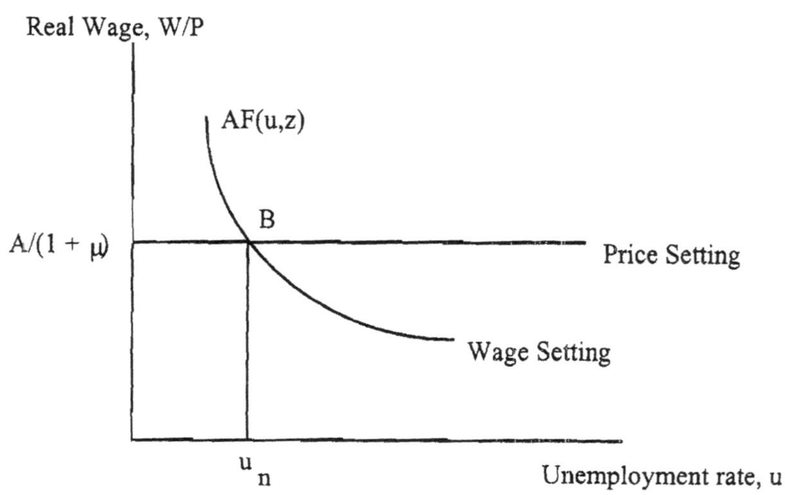

b. Assume that productivity growth will remain at 3% per year. What effect will this productivity growth slowdown have over time on the PS relation, WS relation, real wage and natural rate of unemployment?

15. Assume expectations of productivity adjust slowly. Figure 13-6 in the chapter illustrates what happens when productivity growth declines.

a. What will happen to the WS and PS relations over time as expectations of this slowdown adjust?

b. What will happen over time to the real wage and the natural rate of unemployment as expectations of the productivity growth slowdown adjust?

16. Briefly explain why the CPI has increased faster than the GDP deflator.

17. The relative demand for skilled workers increased during the 1960s and 1970s. However, the relative wage of skilled workers did not change significantly. Why?

MULTIPLE CHOICE QUESTIONS

1. We know that technological progress:

a. allows for greater quantities of output given the currently existing quantities of labor (and capital)
b. leads to the production of new goods
c. leads to the disappearance of old goods
d. all of the above

2. Who is responsible for first emphasizing the process of "creative destruction"?

a. Solow
b. Schumpeter
c. Phillips
d. Friedman

3. Which of the following represents the production function used in this chapter?

a. Y = N
b. Y = NA
c. Y = K/NA
d. Y = K/N

4. Increases in A can be interpreted as:

a. technological progress
b. labor productivity growth
c. all of the above
d. none of the above

5. Given Y, an increase in the level of productivity will cause:

a. an increase in N
b. a reduction in N
c. no change in N

6. Labor productivity is represented as:

a. Y
b. Y/A
c. A
d. NA
e. N/A

7. Employment is represented as:

a. Y
b. Y/A
c. A/Y
d. A

8. An increase in productivity will <u>always</u> cause:

a. the aggregate supply curve to shift down
b. the aggregate supply curve to shift up
c. the aggregate demand curve to shift to the right
d. the aggregate demand curve to shift to the left

9. An increase in productivity causes the aggregate supply curve to shift because it:

a. increases the amount of labor needed to produce a unit of output
b. causes consumers to feel more optimistic about future income
c. increases uncertainty and, therefore, reduces consumption
d. none of the above

10. Suppose an increase in productivity causes Y to increase in the short run. Given this information, we know with certainty that:

a. N increases
b. N falls
c. N remains the same
d. the effects on N are ambiguous

11. Suppose productivity increases by 4%. We know that employment (N) increases if:

a. Y does not change
b. Y rises by exactly 4%
c. Y rises by more than 4%
d. Y rises by less than 4%

12. Suppose A = 0.5. How many workers will be needed to produce one unit of output?

a. 0.5
b. 1
c. 2
d. none of the above

13. If the nominal wage is W, the cost of producing one unit of output is:

a. W
b. W/A
c. WA
d. A/W

14. The price-setting equation is given by:

a. $P = (1 + \mu)A/W$
b. $P = (1 + \mu)W/A$
c. $P = (1/(1 + \mu))W/A$
d. $P = (1/(1 + \mu))A/W$

15. The wage-setting equation is given by:

a. $W = A^eP^eF(u,z)$
b. $W = P^eF(u,z)/A^e$
c. $W = A^eF(u,z)/P^e$
d. $W = A^eP^e/F(u,z)$

16. Assume expectations of P and A are correct. A 4% increase in A will cause:

a. the PS relation to shift up by 4%
b. the WS relation to shift up by less than 4%
c. the PS relation to shift down by 4%
d. the WS relation to shift down by 4%

17. Assume expectations of P and A are correct. A 2% increase in A will cause:

a. a 2% increase in the real wage and an increase in the natural rate of unemployment
b. a 2% increase in the real wage and no change in the natural rate of unemployment
c. no change in the real wage and an increase in the natural rate of unemployment
d. no change in the real wage and a reduction in the natural rate of unemployment

18. Assume expectations of P and A are correct. A reduction in productivity (A falls) will cause:

a. the PS relation to shift down
b. the PS relation to shift up
c. the WS relation to shift up
d. an increase in the real wage

19. Suppose expectations of productivity are slow to adjust. Further assume that A had been increasing by 6% a year. Now suppose A increases by only 3% in period t. This slowdown in productivity growth will cause:

a. the PS relation to shift more than the WS relation
b. the WS relation to shift more than the PS relation
c. the natural rate of unemployment will fall
d. the real wage will fall

20. Suppose expectations of productivity are slow to adjust. A slowdown in productivity growth will cause:

a. an increase in the real wage and an increase in u_n
b. an increase in the real wage and a reduction in u_n
c. a reduction in the real wage and an increase in u_n
d. a reduction in the real wage and a reduction in u_n

21. Since 1890 in the United States, increases in labor productivity tend to be associated with:

a. increases in unemployment
b. reductions in unemployment
c. no change in unemployment
d. reductions in output

22. Which of the following does NOT help explain the increase in the relative demand for skilled workers?

a. international trade
b. skill-biased technological progress
c. decrease in the demand for skilled workers
d. all of the above

CHAPTER 14. EXPECTATIONS: THE BASIC TOOLS

OBJECTIVES, REVIEW, AND TUTORIAL

After working through the chapter and the following material, you should be able to:

(1) Understand the difference between nominal and real interest rates.

(2) Explain how the real interest rate is calculated.

(3) Recognize that the real interest rate affects investment and, therefore, that the real interest rate belongs in the IS relation.

(4) Explain why the nominal interest rate, not the real interest rate, influences the individual's decision to hold money and bonds.

(5) Understand that the LM relation depends on the nominal interest rate.

(6) Explain the short-run and medium-run effects of changes in money growth on output, inflation, the real interest rate, and the nominal interest rate.

(7) Explain what is meant by the Fisher effect.

(8) Explain the effects of changes in expected inflation in the IS-LM model.

(9) Understand the concept of expected present discounted value (i.e., present value).

(10) Explain what factors influence the present value of a sequence of payments.

(11) Become familiar with the equations used to calculate present value.

Learning Tip

- To best understand the material in this chapter, you should carefully read the appendix to the chapter and the first few pages of Appendix 2 ("A Math Refresher").
- When reading this material, take notes and work through the equations. It is important that you become comfortable with the equations.

1. DISTINCTION BETWEEN NOMINAL AND REAL INTEREST RATES

- The nominal interest rate (i_t) indicates how many dollars ($1 + i_t$) one repays in the future in exchange for one dollar today. Alternatively, one dollar today is worth $1 + i_t$ dollars in the future.

- The real interest rate (r_t) indicates how many goods ($1 + r_t$) one repays next year in exchange for one good today.

2. CALCULATION OF THE REAL INTEREST RATE

You must understand why $1 + r_t$ is expressed as follows:

$1 + r_t = (1 + i_t)/(1 + \pi^e_t)$.

Learning Tip

Let P_t be the price of a basket of goods (similar to the Consumer Price Index).

- To buy a basket of goods today, you borrow P_t.
- Next year, you must repay $(1 + i_t)P_t$ dollars (i.e., P_t, the amount borrowed, plus i_tP_t the nominal interest payment).
- To convert $(1 + i_t)P_t$ dollars to baskets of goods, simply divide by the price of the basket you expect to occur next year (P^e_{t+1}).
- This yields: $(1 + i_t)P_t/P^e_{t+1}$.
- This expression represents the amount of goods you must pay next year in exchange for one basket today.

How do you go from $(1 + i_t)P_t/P^e_{t+1}$ to $(1 + i_t)/(1 + \pi^e_{t+1})$?

- $\pi^e_{t+1} = (P^e_{t+1} - P_t)/P_t$.
- Add 1 to both sides:
  $1 + \pi^e_{t+1} = ((P^e_{t+1} - P_t)/P_t) + P_t/P_t \; (P_t/P_t = 1)$
- The right hand side simplifies to P^e_{t+1}/P_t
- Therefore, $1 + \pi^e_{t+1} = P^e_{t+1}/P_t$ and $P_t/P^e_{t+1} = 1/(1 + \pi^e_{t+1})$.
- Replace this expression for P_t/P^e_{t+1} above and you have $(1 + i_t)/(1 + \pi^e_{t+1})$.
- So, $1 + r_t = (1 + i_t)/(1 + \pi^e_{t+1})$

The exact definition of the real interest rate (r_t) is given by:

$r_t = (1 + i_t)/(1 + \pi^e_{t+1}) - 1$.

A close approximation of the real interest rate is given by:

$r_t = i - \pi^e_t$.

Learning Tip

- $i = r$ only when $\pi^e = 0$.
- Since π^e is generally greater than zero, i is generally greater than r.
- If $i = \pi^e$, $r = 0$. For example, if $i = 20\%$ and $\pi^e = 20\%$, a dollar today yields 1.20 dollars in one year. One dollar in a year, however, is worth 20% less in terms of goods. The real cost of borrowing and the real return from lending are zero.

3. NOMINAL INTEREST RATES, THE REAL INTEREST RATE AND THE IS-LM MODEL

You must understand that: (1) investment, the IS relation, and the IS curve depend on the real interest rate; and (2) individuals' portfolio decisions (money versus bonds) depend on the nominal interest rate.

(1) Investment, the real interest rate, and the IS curve

When firms borrow to finance an investment project, they care about how much they will repay in terms of goods. The real interest rate (NOT the nominal interest rate) determines investment.

Learning Tip

There are several key issues that you must understand.

(1) Changes in r cause changes in investment.

(2) When the real interest rate (r) is on the vertical axis:

- A change in r causes a movement along the IS curve.
- A change in the nominal interest rate (i) will have no effect on investment and the IS curve.

(3) When the nominal interest rate (i) is on the vertical axis:

- A change in i, given expected inflation, will cause a movement along the IS curve.
- A change in expected inflation, given i, will cause a change in r and a shift of the IS curve.
- In particular, the IS curve is drawn for a given expected rate of inflation.

(2) Money, bonds, the nominal interest rate, and expected inflation

Recall that: (1) bonds pay a nominal interest rate (i); and (2) money pays a zero nominal interest rate. Changes in i, therefore, affect money demand and bond demand.

- When i increases, the opportunity cost of holding money increases and money demand falls (and bond demand increases).
- When i falls, the opportunity cost of holding money falls and money demand increases (bond demand falls).
- In general, it is the difference between the rate of return on bonds and the rate of return on money which determines money demand. This difference in returns equals i ($i - 0 = i$).

Learning Tip

Changes in expected inflation (π^e) have no effect on money demand. Why? Changes in π^e do not affect the opportunity cost (measured in nominal or real terms) of holding money. Let i = 10% and $\pi^e = 0$.

- The opportunity cost of holding money in nominal terms is 10%.
- The real rate of return on bonds is 10% and the real rate of return on money is 0.
- The opportunity cost of holding money is still 10%.

Suppose π^e increases to 5% and i remains fixed at 10%.

- The opportunity cost of holding money (in nominal terms) is still 10%.
- The real rate of return on bonds is now 5% and the real rate of return on money is now -5% (0 - 5% = -5%).
- The opportunity cost of holding money in real terms, despite the increase in π^e, is still 10% (5% - (-5%) = 10%).

You should now realize that:

- Changes in expected inflation have no effect on money demand.
- Money demand is a function of i (NOT the real interest rate).
- The LM relation, therefore, is also a function of i (NOT r).
- i (NOT r) will adjust to maintain financial market equilibrium: M/P = YL(i).

4. MONEY GROWTH, INFLATION, OUTPUT, AND INTEREST RATES

(1) Short-run effects

In the short run, an increase in money growth will cause:

- a reduction in the nominal interest rate (see Figure 14-4);
- a reduction in the real interest rate for a given expected rate of inflation; and
- an increase in output.

(2) Medium-run effects

In the medium run, an increase in money growth will cause:

- no change in output (Y returns to the natural level of output)
- no change in the real interest rate (r returns to the natural real interest rate)
- an equal increase in inflation
- an equal increase in the nominal interest rate (i.e., the Fisher effect)
- the Fisher effect summarizes the medium-run effects of a change in inflation on the nominal interest rate.

Learning Tip

There are several issues that you <u>must</u> understand in this section.

(1) Determinants of inflation.

- $\pi = g_m - g_Y$. If $g_Y = 0$, we have $\pi = g_m$.

(2) The natural real interest rate: r_n.

- r_n is the real interest rate that occurs, for given G and T, when $Y = Y_n$.

- To determine r_n, simply determine the position of the IS curve. Then, determine Y_n. r_n is the real rate that occurs at this level of output.
- Note: r_n will change as G and T (and Y_n) change.

(3) The nominal interest rate
- In general, $i = r + \pi^e$.
- In the medium run, $r = r_n$ and $\pi = \pi^e = g_m$ (assuming $g_Y = 0$).
- Therefore, in the medium run, $i = r_n + g_m$.

(3) From the short run to the medium: the adjustment process

An increase in money growth will cause:
- a reduction in both i and r in the short run; and
- no change in r and an increase in i in the medium run.

During the adjustment process, the increase in money growth causes:
- Y to rise initially above Y_n
- expected inflation to rise with $Y > Y_n$
- with $Y > Y_n$, eventually inflation will exceed money growth
- with real money growth negative, i must increase
- for given π^e, r must also rise as i rises (see Figure 14-5)
- eventually, r returns to r_n and i is permanently higher (i.e., medium-run effects).

Learning Tip

How do we know that inflation will eventually exceed money growth during the adjustment process? There are two ways to explain this.

- If we use the IS-LM model with r on the vertical axis, the analysis is easy. The initial increase in money growth causes a reduction in r. Given previous analysis, we know that money is neutral in the medium run. In other words, the LM curve will shift up as the price level (and inflation increases). For the LM curve to shift up, inflation must exceed money growth so that the real supply of money falls.
- Recall that $\pi = g_m - g_Y$. In the short run, output growth is positive. As expectations adjust, however, Y will return to the natural level causing g_Y to be negative. If $g_Y < 0$, the above equation implies that $\pi > g_m$.

5. EXPECTED INFLATION AND THE IS-LM MODEL

(1) Review

When $\pi^e = 0$, the nominal and real interest rates are the same (i.e., a change in i represents an equal change in r) and the IS-LM model is unchanged.

- Reductions in i (or r) cause increases in investment and movements along the IS curve.
- Increases in income cause increases in money demand, increases in the interest rate and movements along the LM curve.

When $\pi^e > 0$, we need to do two things. First, we need to determine which interest rate (i or r) belongs on the vertical axis in the IS-LM model. And second, we need to examine the effects of changes in expected inflation on the IS-LM model.

Learning Tip

The IS-LM model can be presented with either the nominal interest rate (i) or the real interest rate (r) on the vertical axis. The following discussion includes i on the vertical axis. You might want to think carefully about how this analysis differs if the real interest rate is on the vertical axis.

(2) Which interest rate?

We will measure the nominal interest rate (i) on the vertical axis. Changes in i cause only movements along the LM curve and, for a given rate of expected inflation (π^e), movements along the IS curve.

(3) Changes in π^e and the IS curve.

The IS curve shifts when expected inflation changes. For a given i, an increase in expected inflation causes an (measured in absolute terms) reduction in the real interest rate. As the real interest rate falls, I increases and the equilibrium level of output in the goods market at a given i is higher. This is represented as a rightward shift in the IS curve.

(4) Changes in π^e and the LM curve.

Suppose i = 10%. An increase in π^e from 0 to 5% will not affect money demand. The nominal interest rate, therefore, does not change initially since financial markets remain in equilibrium. The LM curve does not shift as a result of a change in expected inflation.

(5) The macroeconomic effects of an increase in expected inflation.

An increase in π^e will cause:

- an initial reduction in r equal to the change in π^e
- a rightward shift in the IS curve
- an increase in investment as r falls
- the increase in investment causes an increase in output and an increase in money demand
- as money demand increases, i will rise (a movement along the LM curve)
- output continues to increase until equilibrium is reached

Here is a summary of the final effects of the change in expected inflation:

- expected inflation is higher
- the real interest rate falls
- the nominal interest rate rises (but by less than the change in π^e)
- investment and output increase

Learning Tip

- Make sure you can graphically illustrate and explain the effects of a reduction in expected inflation on the IS-LM model.
- Note the difference between the effects of changes in the price level (P) and changes in expected inflation (π^e).
  - An increase in P causes a reduction in the real supply of money, an increase in the nominal interest rate and an upward shift in the LM curve.
  - An increase in expected inflation causes, as described above, a rightward shift in the IS curve. Changes in expected inflation do not reflect changes in the current price level; consequently, changes in expected inflation do not cause changes in the real supply of money.

6. INTRODUCTION TO EXPECTED PRESENT DISCOUNTED VALUE (PV): ONE AND TWO PERIOD CASES

The expected present discounted value is the value today of a sequence of payments. You can examine two examples.

(1) The one period example

If you lend one dollar today, you receive $1 + i_t$ dollars in one year (i.e., the one dollar (1) plus interest on the dollar (i_t)). If you borrow one dollar today, you will repay $1 + i_t$ dollars in one year. One dollar today is, therefore, worth $1 + i_t$ dollars next year. And, $1 + i_t$ dollars next year are worth one dollar today.

- One dollar next year is worth $1/(1 + i_t)$ dollars today.
  - If you lend $1/(1 + i_t)$ dollars today, you receive one dollar in a year [to prove this, simply multiply this expression by $(1 + i_t)$].
  - $1/(1 + i_t)$ is called the discount factor.

Learning Tip

- If $i_t = 20\%$, 1 dollar today is worth 1.20 dollars in a year.
- One dollar next year is worth 83 cents today.
  - When $i_t > 0$, having a dollar next year is worth less than having a dollar today.
  - As i_t increases, a dollar next year is worth less today. That is, an increase in the interest rate reduces the present value of a future dollar.

(2) The two period example

If you lend one dollar for two years, you receive $(1 + i_t)(1 + i_{t+1})$ dollars in two years. Why?

- In one year, the one dollar is worth $(1 + i_t)$ dollars.
- If you lend the $1 + i_t$ dollars for one more year, you receive the $1 + i_t$ plus interest (at a rate of i_{t+1}) on the $1 + i_t$ dollars (i.e., $i_{t+1}(1 + i_t)$) in two years.
- Therefore, you receive $1 + i_t + i_{t+1}(1 + i_t)$ in two years.
- Factor out $(1 + i_t)$ and you have $(1 + i_t)(1 + i_{t+1})$.

Learning Tip

- Let $i_t = i_{t+1} = 5\%$.
- The PV of a dollar received one year from now is 95 cents.
- The PV of a dollar received two years from now is 91 cents.
- As i_t and/or i_{t+1} increases, the PV of a future payment decreases.
- Having a dollar two years from now is worth less than having a dollar one year from now which is worth less than having one dollar today.
- The PV of one dollar received in one year is: $1/(1 + i_t)$.
- $1/(1 + i_t)$ is the relevant discount factor for a payment received in one year.
- The PV of one dollar received in two years is: $1/(1 + i_t)(1 + i_{t+1})$.
- $1/(1 + i_t)(1 + i_{t+1})$ is the relevant discount factor for a payment received in two years.

7. EXPECTED PRESENT DISCOUNTED VALUE: OTHER CASES

Individuals will not always know with certainty: (1) future interest rates; and/or (2) future payments. Individuals, therefore, must form expectations of the future interest rate (i^e_{t+2}) and of future payments ($\$z^e_{t+2}$). The general formula for expected present discounted value of a sequence of payments is given by:

$$\$V_t = \$z_t + (1/(1 + i_t))\$z^e_{t+1} + (1/(1 + i_t)(1 + i^e_{t+1}))\$z^e_{t+2} + \ldots$$

Each expected payment (the z^e variables) is adjusted by the appropriate discount factor. There are several implications of this equation that you must know.

$V will decline:

- the higher the interest rate(s)
- the more distant the payment, that is, $1000 ten years from now is worth less than $1000 five years from now
- the lower the expected payment $\$z^e$

Learning Tip

- If you understand this equation and understand the material presented in the appendices, you will understand all of the applications of PV analysis.
- If we know the future payments with certainty, replace $\$z^e$ with $\$z$.
- If we know the future interest rates with certainty, replace i^e with i
- If i and $\$z^e$ are constant, the above expression simplifies to the expression found in the text.
- To calculate real PV, simply replace i with r and $z with z. This yields V_t.

There are two final cases to consider.

- Case 1: Consol bond. A consol bond is a bond that promises to make some payment ($z) each year forever. Such a bond never matures.
    - The PV of an infinite series of fixed payments to begin next period is given by $\$V_t = \$z/i$.
    - The PV of a consol increases when:
        (1) i falls; and/or
        (2) $z increases.

- Case 2: Zero interest rates. When the interest rate is zero, all of the discount factors equal 1. That is, the PV of a sequence of payments simply equals the sum of the payments.

Advice/Warning

Some instructors will want you to understand the concept of present value. Others might require you to use many of the formulas found in this chapter. In the latter case, students must work through these calculations. You should, therefore, carefully work through each step in the derivation of the equations. The only way to become comfortable with these expressions is to work through them yourself.

SELF-TEST QUESTIONS

1. Define the nominal interest rate (1).

2. Define the real interest rate (1).

3. Can the real interest rate equal the nominal interest rate? Explain (1).

4. If the real interest rate is 3% and the expected inflation rate is 7%, what is the nominal interest rate (1)?

5. Which interest rate (nominal or real) affects investment (2)?

6. Which interest rate (nominal or real) affects money demand (2)?

7. What initial effect will an increase in expected inflation have on money demand (3)?

8. What effect will a reduction in expected inflation have on the IS curve and on the LM curve (3)?

9. What determines inflation in the medium run (3)?

10. What effect does an increase in money growth have on the real interest rate and nominal interest rate in the short run (3)?

11. What effect does an increase in money growth have on the real interest rate and nominal interest rate in the medium run (3)?

12. What is meant by the Fisher effect (3)?

13. What is meant by the natural real interest rate (3)?

14. What does "expected present discounted value" measure? Explain (4).

15. What effect does an increase in the interest rate (i) have on the present value of a dollar you receive next year (4)?

16. Suppose you are offered $1000 at the end of two years. How would you calculate the present value of the $1000 (4)?

17. The present value of a sequence of payments is a weighted sum of current and expected future payments. What happens to the size of the weights through time (4)?

18. What type of bond is a consol (4)?

19. How does one calculate the real present value of future payments (4)?

REVIEW PROBLEMS

1. Use the information provided below to answer the following questions. Assume the nominal interest rate is 10% ($i_t = .10$) and that the average price of goods (as measured by the Consumer Price Index) equals 1.0 ($P_t = 1.0$). Using the definition of expected inflation (π^e) and the exact definition of the real interest rate (r), calculate expected inflation and r for each of the following price levels which are expected to prevail in the next period (P^e_{t+1}).

a. 1.0
b. 1.03
c. 1.05
d. 1.07
e. 1.10
f. In which of these cases is i = r? Explain.
g. In which of these cases is i > r? Explain.
h. In which of these cases is r = 0? Explain.

2. Repeat the analysis in #1 for parts (a) - (e); ignore parts (f), (g) and (h). This time, however, use the approximate definition of the real interest rate (see equation (14.4) in the chapter). Are any of your calculations of r different from those obtained in #1? Briefly explain.

3. a. For each of the following pairs of expected inflation and the nominal interest rate, calculate the real interest rate using: (1) the exact definition (call this r^I); and (2) the "approximate" definition of the real interest rate (call this r^{II} , see equation (14.4)). Use the space below to write down your answers.

i	π^e	r^I	r^{II}
2%	0		
5%	3%		
10%	8%		
15%	13%		
20%	18%		
50%	48%		
100%	98%		

b. What happens to the ability of the approximate definition (r^{II}) to measure accurately the actual real interest rate (r^{I}) as i and π^e increase? Briefly explain.

4. Based on the definition of the real interest rate, the real interest rate can increase for two reasons. What are they? Briefly explain.

5. Is it possible for the nominal interest rate to fall and the real interest rate to increase during the same period? Explain.

6. Suppose you will receive $100,000 each year for the next two years, beginning in one year. Calculate the present value of this sequence of payments when the interest rate is:
a. 0
b. 4%
c. 8%
d. What happens to the present value of this sequence of payments as the interest rate increases? Explain.

7. Suppose individual A will receive $50,000 each year for the next three years beginning one year from now. Suppose individual B also receives three annual payments of $50,000. She, however, receives the first $50,000 today, the second $50,000 payment a year from now and the final $50,000 payment two years from now.
a. Suppose the nominal interest rate is expected to be constant for the next three years. Which of these two individuals will receive the larger present value given these two sequences of payments? Explain.
b. Under what condition, if any, would the present value of these two sequences of payments be equal? Explain.

8. Suppose a friend of yours wins the lottery and must choose among three different payment options:

option 1: receive $100,000 in one year
option 2: receive $100,000 in two years
option 3: receive $100,000 in three years

Your friend asks you to determine which option is best. Suppose the nominal interest rate is expected to remain constant at 10% for each of the next three years.
a. Calculate the present value of option 1
b. Calculate the present value of option 2
c. Calculate the present value of option 3
d. Discuss what happens to the present value as the same payment occurs further into the future.

9. Suppose a college introduces a payment plan in which incoming first-year students can: (1) make a one-time payment on the first day of classes in their first year; or (2) pay $20,000 on the first day of classes in their first year, pay $22,000 at the beginning of their second year, pay $25,000 at the beginning of their third year and pay $28,000 at the beginning of their fourth year. Assume that the interest rate is assumed to remain constant at 10% over the next four years.
a. Suppose it is the first day of classes of the first year. Calculate (separately) the present value of each of the four yearly payments.
b. Based on your analysis in part a, what is the maximum one-time payment you would recommend that this student make if he chooses the one-time payment plan? Explain.

10. Suppose you have $100,000 and want to calculate what it will be worth at the end of three years given the following three different interest rate scenarios:

	i_t	i_{t+1}	i_{t+2}
Case 1:	0	0	0
Case 2:	10%	12%	14%
Case 3:	10%	8%	6%

a. Calculate what the $100,000 will be worth at the end of three years in each of the above three cases.
b. Which of these three cases would be preferred if you wish to maximize what the $100,000 will be worth in three years? Explain.

11. Suppose bonds pay a nominal interest rate of 9% and that expected inflation is initially 0. Recall that money pays a zero nominal interest rate.
a. What is the opportunity cost of holding money?
b. When $\pi^e = 0$, what is the real interest rate on bonds? What is the real interest rate on money?
c. For each of the following values of expected inflation, calculate the real rates of return on bonds and on money: 1%, 3%, 7% and 9%.
d. As expected inflation increases, what happens to the opportunity cost (measured in nominal terms) of holding money? Briefly explain.
e. Given the nominal interest rate of 9%, what happens to the opportunity cost of holding money (measured in nominal terms) when expected inflation increases? Briefly explain.
f. Given your analysis in c, d and e, what does your analysis suggest happens to money demand when expected inflation or the real interest rate change? Explain.

12. Use the graph provided below to answer the following questions. Initially assume that the nominal interest rate which maintains financial market equilibrium is 10% and that expected inflation is 0. Since $\pi^e = 0$, the nominal interest rate is initially equal to the real interest rate.

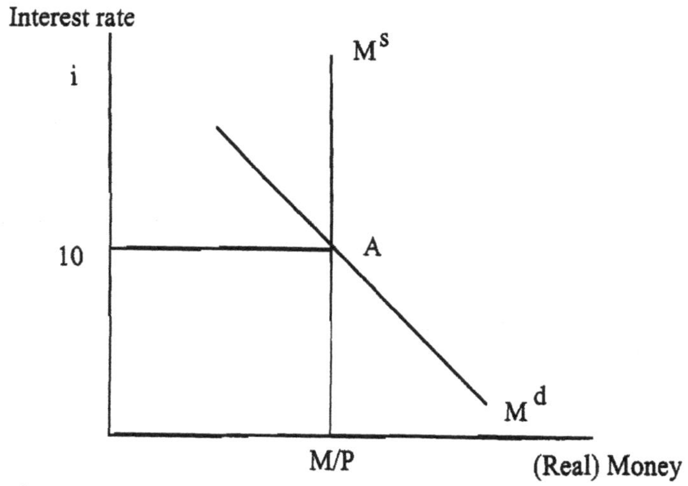

a. If expected inflation is 0, what must the real interest rate be to maintain financial market equilibrium?
b. Suppose expected inflation increases from 0 to 2%. Given your analysis in #11, what effect does this have on money demand and on the nominal interest rate? What is the real interest rate consistent with financial market equilibrium when $\pi^e = 2\%$?
c. Repeat the analysis in part b with expected inflation now equal to 5%.

13. Explain the short-run and medium-run effects of a reduction in money growth on output, inflation, the nominal interest rate and the real interest rate.

14. Discuss what effect each of the following events will have on the natural real interest rate (r_n):
a. a reduction in government spending
b. a reduction in taxes
c. a reduction in the price of oil

15. Suppose the goods and financial markets are in equilibrium and that the initial equilibrium nominal interest rate in the financial markets is 8% and that expected inflation is 6%. Also assume that financial markets are always in equilibrium (i.e., the economy is always on the LM curve).
a. Given the above information, what is the initial equilibrium real interest rate? That is, what is the real interest rate which maintains equilibrium in the goods market and is consistent with equilibrium in the financial markets?
b. Use the following graph to answer the following questions.

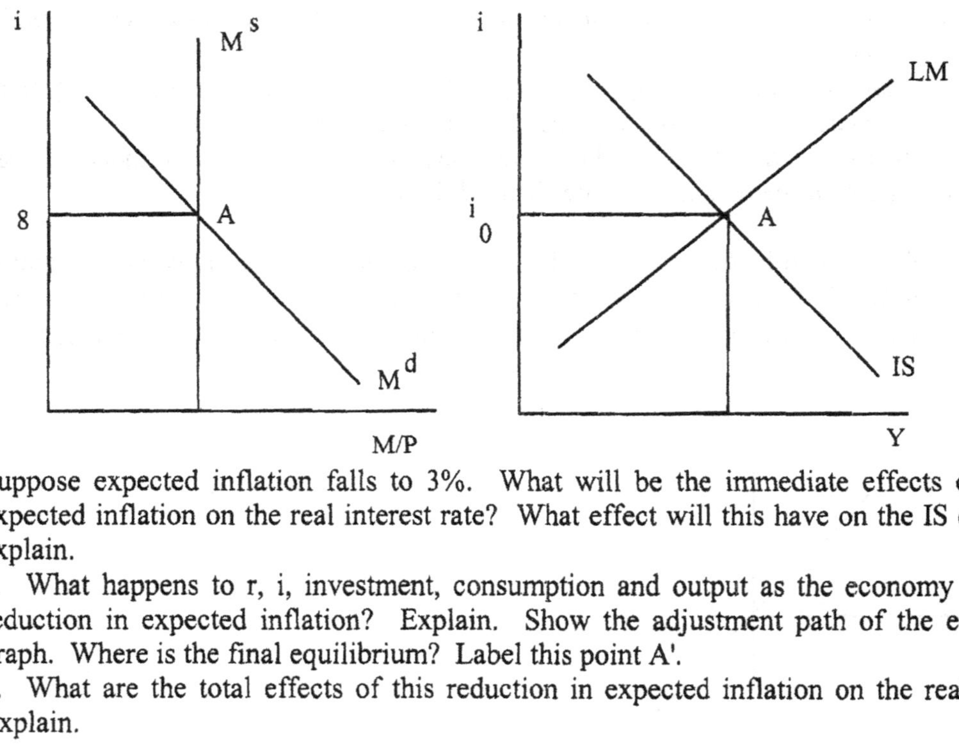

Suppose expected inflation falls to 3%. What will be the immediate effects of this drop in expected inflation on the real interest rate? What effect will this have on the IS curve? Briefly explain.
c. What happens to r, i, investment, consumption and output as the economy adjusts to this reduction in expected inflation? Explain. Show the adjustment path of the economy in the graph. Where is the final equilibrium? Label this point A'.
d. What are the total effects of this reduction in expected inflation on the real interest rate? Explain.

MULTIPLE CHOICE QUESTIONS

1. The nominal interest rate:

a. measures the cost of borrowing in terms of goods
b. is approximately equal to the real interest rate minus the expected rate of inflation
c. measures the cost of borrowing 1 dollar today in terms of how many dollars one repays in one year
d. measures the rate of return on money

2. Which of the following expressions represents the exact definition of the real interest rate?

a. $i - \pi^e$
b. $i - \pi^e$
c. $(1 + i)/(1 + \pi^e)$
d. $[(1 + i)/(1 + \pi^e)] - 1$

3. Suppose the nominal interest rate is fixed. An increase in expected inflation will cause:

a. an increase in the real interest rate
b. a reduction in the real interest rate
c. no change in the real interest rate since the nominal interest rate is fixed
d. none of the above

4. If $\pi^e = 0$, we know that:

a. $r > i$
b. $r < i$
c. $r = i$
d. $i > 0$ and $r = 0$

5. Suppose $\pi^e = 5\%$ and does not change. We know with certainty that:

a. $r > i$
b. $r < i$
c. $r = i$
d. $r < 5\%$
e. $i > 5\%$

6. Suppose the real interest rate does not change while the nominal interest rate falls during a given period. This would suggest that:

a. π^e increased
b. the change in $\pi^e >$ the change in i
c. the change in $\pi^e =$ the change in i
d. the change in $\pi^e <$ the change in i

7. Suppose you will receive $100 one year from now and that i = 10%. The present value (PV) of this $100 is:

a. $110
b. $100
c. $90.91
d. $90

8. Suppose you borrow $1000 today and will repay the $1000 in one year. If the nominal interest rate is 15%, what will you repay in one year?

a. $1150
b. $1015
c. $869.56
d. $850

9. Assume the nominal interest rate equals 5% and does not change. The PV of $1000 to be received at the end of two years is:

a. $1102.50
b. $952.38
c. $907.03
d. $900

10. Suppose you are to receive a sequence of future payments. The PV of this sequence of payments will increase as:

a. the nominal interest rate increases
b. the nominal interest rate falls
c. the higher the value of the future payments
d. both b and c

11. Suppose you are to receive a sequence of future payments. The PV of this sequence of payments will be lower:

a. the higher the nominal interest rate
b. the lower the nominal interest rate
c. the later you receive the payment
d. both a and c

12. Suppose you are to receive a one-time payment of $1000 at the end of ten years. Also assume that the nominal and real interest are zero and expected to remain at this level for the next 10 years. We know that:

a. the PV of this payment is greater than $1000
b. the PV of this payment is less than $1000
c. the PV of this payment is equal to $1000
d. none of the above

13. Suppose you hold a consol which promises to pay you $100 each year, forever, starting next year. If the nominal interest rate is 10% and not expected to change, the PV of this consol is:

a. $110
b. $900
c. $1000
d. will increase as the nominal interest rate increases

14. Suppose expected inflation is greater than zero. Which of the following statements is correct about the IS-LM model?

a. the nominal interest rate belongs in the IS relation
b. the nominal interest rate belongs in the LM relation
c. the real interest rate belongs in the LM relation
d. none of the above

15. Suppose the nominal interest rate is fixed. An increase in expected inflation will cause:

a. the IS curve to shift to the right
b. the IS curve to shift to the left
c. an increase in investment and an increase in output
d. a decrease in investment and a reduction in output
e. a reduction in the real interest rate and a rightward shift in the IS curve

16. In the financial market (that is, in the money supply and money demand graph), an increase in expected inflation will cause:

a. an immediate drop in i
b. an immediate increase in i
c. a reduction in the real interest rate associated with financial market equilibrium
d. an increase in the real interest rate associated with financial market equilibrium

17. A reduction in expected inflation will cause:

a. the LM curve to shift down
b. the LM curve to shift up
c. the IS curve to shift to the right
d. the IS curve to shift to the left

18. Which of the following statements is correct concerning the decision individuals make about how much money and bonds to hold?

a. an increase in expected inflation will cause an individual to hold more bonds and less money
b. an increase in the nominal interest rate will cause an increase in the opportunity cost of holding money
c. a reduction in expected inflation will cause an individual to hold more money and fewer bonds
d. both a and c

19. An increase in expected inflation will cause:

a. the LM curve to shift down, a reduction in r and an increase in investment
b. the LM curve to shift up, an increase in r and a reduction in investment
c. the IS curve to shift to the right, a reduction in r and an increase in output
d. the IS curve to shift left, a reduction in r and a reduction in output

Use the IS-LM model to answer the next three questions.

20. An increase in expected inflation will result:

a. a lower r and higher i
b. a lower r and lower i
c. a higher r and higher i
d. a higher r and lower i

21. A reduction in expected inflation will cause:

a. the LM curve to shift down, a reduction in r and an increase in investment
b. the LM curve to shift up, an increase in r and a reduction in investment
c. the IS curve to shift to the right, an increase in r and an increase in output
d. the IS curve to shift left, a reduction in r and a reduction in output

22. A reduction in expected inflation will cause:

a. a lower r and higher i
b. a lower r and lower i
c. a higher r and higher i
d. a higher r and lower i

23. An increase in government spending will cause:

a. the natural real interest rate to increase
b. the natural real interest rate to decrease
c. no change in the natural real interest rate
d. ambiguous effects on the natural real interest rate

24. An increase in taxes will cause:

a. the natural real interest rate to increase
b. the natural real interest rate to decrease
c. no change in the natural real interest rate
d. ambiguous effects on the natural real interest rate

25. In the short run, an increase in money growth will cause:

a. an increase in i and an increase in r
b. an increase in i and a reduction in r
c. a reduction in i and a reduction in r
d. a reduction in i and an increase in r

26. In the medium run, an increase in money growth will cause:

a. an increase in i and an increase in r
b. an increase in i and a reduction in r
c. a reduction in i and a reduction in r
d. a reduction in i and an increase in r
e. none of the above

CHAPTER 15. FINANCIAL MARKETS AND EXPECTATIONS

OBJECTIVES, REVIEW, AND TUTORIAL

After working through the chapter and the following material, you should be able to:

(1) Understand that the price of a bond is equal to the present value of the payments on the bond.

(2) Explain how arbitrage is used to examine the relationship between the expected returns on two assets.

(3) Explain the relationship between current long-term interest rates, current short-term interest rates, and future expected short-term interest rates.

(4) Explain what is meant by yield to maturity and the yield curve.

(5) Explain what upward sloping and downward sloping yield curves suggest about expected future short-term interest rates.

(6) Use the IS-LM model to make predictions about future short-term interest rates and, therefore, make predictions about the shape of the yield curve.

(7) Explain the determinants of current stock prices.

(8) Explain how anticipated and unanticipated changes in both economic activity and fiscal and monetary policy affect stock prices.

(9) Explain what is meant by the fundamental value of a stock price.

(10) Understand the difference between rational speculative bubbles and fads.

1. BOND MARKET VOCABULARY

- Risk premium. Bonds with a higher probability of default generally have a higher interest rate. The difference between the interest rate on a relatively risky bond and the interest rate on a bond with a relatively low probability of default is the risk premium.

- Junk bonds. These are bonds with a relatively high probability of default and, therefore, a relatively high risk premium.

- Coupon bond. These are bonds which promise multiple payments prior to maturity and one payment (the face value) at maturity. These payments are called coupon payments.

- Coupon rate. The coupon rate is the ratio of the coupon payments to the face value.

- Current yield. The current yield is the ratio of the coupon payment to the current price of the bond.

- Indexed bonds. These are bonds that promise payments adjusted for inflation.

Learning Tip

There are several other terms you might want to review in this chapter. Depending on the preferences of your instructor, you might be expected to know, for example, the differences among short-term, medium-term, and long-term bonds. It would be worthwhile to quickly review these and other terms and definitions.

2. BOND PRICES AND PRESENT VALUE

Assume that all bonds promise to pay $100 upon maturity.

- One-year bond. The price of a one-year bond ($\$P_{1t}$) is given by:

  $\$P_{1t} = \$100/(1 + i_{1t})$ where i_{1t} is the nominal one-year interest rate.

- Two-year bond. The price of a two-year bond ($\$P_{2t}$) is given by:

  $\$P_{2t} = \$100/[(1 + i_{1t})(1 + i^e_{1t})]$.

3. ARBITRAGE AND EXPECTED RETURNS

(1) Returns from one-year bond held for one year.

- For every dollar you put in a one-year bond, you receive $1 + i_t$ dollars in one year.

(2) Returns from two-year bond held for one year.

- For every dollar you put in a two-year bond, you receive $1/\$P_{2t}$ two-year bonds today.
- When you sell your two-year bond in one year, the bond will become a one-year bond since it has just one more year until maturity.
- Your proceeds from selling $1/\$P_{2t}$ two-year bonds in one year at an expected price for one-year bonds are $\$P^e_{1t}/\$P_{2t}$.

(3) Arbitrage relation.

The market for one- and two-year bonds will only be in equilibrium when the above returns are equal:

$$1 + i_{1t} = \$P^e_{1t}/\$P_{2t}.$$

Learning Tip

- If the returns from holding the one-year bond are greater than the returns from holding the two-year bond, no one would hold two-year bonds.
- If the returns from holding the two-year bond are greater than the returns from holding the one-year bond, no one would hold one-year bonds.
- Therefore, the two bonds must offer the same expected returns.

As shown in the text, the above arbitrage relation can be rearranged to yield:

$$\$P_{2t} = \$100/[(1 + i_{1t})(1 + i^e_{1t})]$$

Arbitrage between these two bonds implies that the price of the two-year bond is the present value of the \$100 payment using i_{1t} and i^e_{1t+1}.

4. YIELD TO MATURITY AND THE YIELD CURVE

- The yield to maturity on an n-period bond (i.e., the n-year interest rate) is the interest rate which makes the price of the bond equal to the present value of the future payments of the bond (using the n-year interest rate). For example, i_{2t} and i_{3t} are the yields to maturity (as defined below) on two-year and three-year bonds:

$$\$P_{2t} = \$100/(1 + i_{2t})^2$$

$$\$P_{3t} = \$100/(1 + i_{3t})^3$$

- The yield curve (or term structure of interest rates) plots the relation between yields and maturity.

Learning Tip

- Don't be confused by the definition of the yield curve. The yield curve is simply a graph with time (maturity) on the horizontal axis and the yield to maturity on the vertical axis.
- The yield curve shows what rates are on the one-year, three-year, ... bonds.
- The yield curve is generally (though not always) upward sloping.

Does the yield curve provide any information about future interest rates? Yes!! The arbitrage relation between one-year and two-year bonds indicates that the price of a two-year bond is:

$$\$P_{2t} = \$100/[(1 + i_{1t})(1 + i^e_{1t+1})].$$

The definition of the yield to maturity on a two-year bond indicates that:

$$\$P_{2t} = \$100/(1 + i_{2t})^2.$$

Equating these two expressions for $\$P_{2t}$ and rearranging yields:

$$(1 + i_{2t})^2 = (1 + i_{1t})(1 + i^e_{1t+1}).$$

An approximation of this relation is:

$$i_{2t} = (i_{1t} + i^e_{1t+1})/2.$$

Learning Tip

How do we get the approximate relation? If you expand both sides of the above equation, you obtain:

$$1 + 2i_{2t} + (i_{2t})^2 = 1 + i_{1t} + i^e_{1t+1} + (i_{1t})(i^e_{1t+1}).$$

- Subtract one from both sides.
- As shown in the "Math Refresher" appendix, the terms $(i_{2t})^2$ and $(i_{1t})(i^e_{1t+1})$ will be small so we can ignore them.
- That leaves us with $2i_{2t} = i_{1t} + i^e_{1t+1}$.
- Divide by 2 and we have the above approximation.

The above equation has a very simple interpretation:

- i_{2t} is (approximately) an average of the current one-year rate and one-year rate expected to occur next year.
- More generally, the n-year rate is the average of the current one-year rate and expected future one-year rates over the next n-1 periods.

The above equation can also be used:

(1) to explain the slope of the yield curve; and
(2) to provide information about what financial markets expect the future one-year rate to be.

- Upward sloping yield curve.
  - The yield curve is upward sloping when $i_{2t} > i_{1t}$.
  - If $i_{2t} > i_{1t}$, financial markets expect the one-year rate to increase in the future (above its current level).

- Downward sloping yield curve.
  - The yield curve is downward sloping when $i_{1t} > i_{2t}$.
  - If $i_{1t} > i_{2t}$, financial markets expect the one-year rate to decrease in the future (above its current level).

Learning Tip

What will i^e_{t+1} be?

- After rearranging the above equation, we obtain: $i^e_{t+1} = 2i_{2t} - i_{1t}$.
- Given i_{1t} and i_{2t}, we can infer what financial markets expect the future one-year rate to be.

5. EXPECTATIONS, THE YIELD CURVE, AND THE IS-LM MODEL

Assume: (1) expected inflation is 0; and (2) the one-year rate is on the vertical axis of the IS-LM graph. Given these assumptions, what determines i^e_{t+1} and, therefore, the slope of the yield curve? The answer is relatively easy.

The positions of the IS and LM curves that financial markets expect to occur in one year determine the equilibrium interest rate in one year (this happens to be i^e_{t+1}). There are at least four types of events that can occur which will cause i^e_{t+1} and the slope of the yield curve to change.

Case 1: An expected monetary contraction. This expected future reduction in the money supply will cause the LM curve to shift up, the future one-year rate to increase and the yield curve to become steeper.

Case 2: An expected monetary expansion. This expected future increase in the money supply will cause the LM curve to shift down, the future one-year rate to decrease and the yield curve to become flatter.

Case 3: An expectation that consumer confidence and, therefore, consumption will increase (or, equivalently, an expected increase in G or expected reduction in T). This expected future increase in spending will cause the IS curve to shift to the right, the future one-year rate to increase and the yield curve to become steeper.

Case 4: An expectation that consumer confidence and, therefore, consumption will decrease (or, equivalently, an expected reduction in G or expected increase in T). This expected future reduction in spending will cause the IS curve to shift to the left, the future one-year rate to decrease and the yield curve to become flatter.

In general, any expectation of a future shift in the IS or LM curves will cause a change in i^e_{t+1}.

Learning Tip

How does the current long-term rate respond to a given change in the current short-term rate?

- An increase in i_{1t} will cause an increase in i_{2t} since i_{2t} is an average of i_{1t} and i^e_{t+1}.
- The change in i_{2t} is generally smaller than the change in i_{1t} because some of the change in i_{1t} is not expected to last (i.e., $\Delta i_{1t} > \Delta i^e_{t+1}$).

6. DETERMINANTS OF STOCK PRICES

Stocks pay dividends. Dividends: (1) are paid from profits; and (2) generally increase when profits increase.

Learning Tip

Firms' profits increase when sales increase. Increases in income cause increases in sales.

- Therefore, increases in Y generally will cause increases in dividends.
- Increases in expected future income will cause increases in expected future profits and, therefore, increases in expected future dividends.

The current price of stock ($\$Q_t$) is given by the present value of the expected future dividends using the current one-year rate and expected future one-year rates. This is also called the fundamental value of the stock price.

The nominal stock price ($\$Q_t$) will increase when:

(1) Expected future nominal dividends increase; and/or
(2) The current and expected future nominal one-year rates decrease.

The real stock price (Q_t) will increase when:

(1) Expected future real dividends increase; and/or
(2) The current and expected future real one-year rates decrease.

Learning Tip

Make sure you understand the material presented in the appendix to this chapter. In particular, you should understand how the arbitrage relation between stocks and bonds is used to show that the price of stock is the present value of future dividends.

7. ECONOMIC ACTIVITY, MACROECONOMIC POLICY, AND STOCK PRICES

You must recognize that: (1) major movements in stock prices cannot be predicted; and (2) fully anticipated changes in interest rates and economic activity will have no effect on stock prices.

(1) Why anticipated events do not matter

Suppose the Fed decreases the money supply causing the one-year rate to increase and income to fall. If this policy were fully anticipated, the current stock price would already reflect:

- the expectation of the increase in the interest rate; and
- the expectation of the reduction in output and the reduction in expected dividends.

Hence, the stock price does not change in response to this anticipated reduction in the money supply.

Learning Tip

- Conclusion #1. For the current stock price to change in response to a change in the current one-year interest rate or to a change in current output, at least some of the change must be unanticipated.
- Conclusion #2. Changes in expected future interest rates and in expected future output (and, therefore, expected future dividends) will cause changes in stock prices.

You must also understand that:

- unanticipated changes in monetary policy cause unambiguous changes in stock prices; and
- unanticipated shifts in the IS curve have ambiguous effects on stock prices.

(2) Unexpected changes in monetary policy

An increase in the money supply that is at least partially unexpected causes financial markets to expect:

• a reduction in the expected future one-year interest rate. The lower expected future one-year rate causes, via the definition of the stock price, an increase in $\$Q_t$; and
• an increase in income, an increase in sales, an increase in profits and, therefore, an increase in $\$Q_t$.

Both of these effects will cause $\$Q_t$ to increase.

(3) Unexpected shifts in the IS curve

An unexpected increase in consumption (or an unexpected increase in G or cut in T) will cause the IS curve to shift to the right. The effects on stock prices are ambiguous for two reasons.

• Reason 1: The higher Y causes an increase in profits and dividends; therefore, stock prices will tend to increase. The higher Y, however, causes the one-year interest rate to rise as money demand increases. The higher interest rates will cause stock prices to fall. If the interest rate effects are large enough, stock prices could actually fall.

• Reason 2: The Fed's response to this unexpected shift in the IS curve can also influence how stock prices respond. Three cases can occur.

Case 1: The Fed does nothing. In this case, the analysis is the same as that described in Reason 1. The effects on $\$Q_t$ are still ambiguous.

Case 2: If the Fed wishes to accommodate the shift in the IS curve to keep the one-year interest rate from rising (i.e., the LM shifts down), stock prices will rise as dividends increase. Since i does not change, there is no offsetting effect of higher interest rates here.

Case 3: If the Fed contracts to keep output constant (i.e., the LM curve shifts up), stock prices fall as the one-year rate increases.

Learning Tip

The Fed does not have to respond to this shift in the IS curve for the above effects to occur. The expectation of a Fed response will affect expectations of future interest rates or future output (and, therefore, dividends). Changes in expected interest rates and expected output will affect current stock prices.

(4) The slope of the LM curve

The slope of the LM curve can influence what effect unexpected shocks to the IS curve have on stock prices. Suppose there is an unexpected increase in demand that causes the IS curve to shift to the right. There are two cases to consider.

• Case 1: Relatively flat LM curve
  • We will observe a relatively small increase in the interest rate.
  • We will also observe a relatively large increase in output.
  • Stock prices are more likely to rise in this case (the output effects are more likely to dominate the interest rate effects.

• Case 2: Relatively steep LM curve
  • We will observe a relatively large increase in the interest rate.
  • We will also observe a relatively small increase in output.
  • Stock prices are more likely to fall in this case (the interest rate effects are more likely to dominate the output effects).

8. BUBBLES AND FADS

- The fundamental value of a stock price is the present value of expected future dividends.
- Stocks can be overpriced or underpriced for two reasons: bubbles and fads.

• Rational speculative bubbles. This occurs when investors buy stock today expecting the price to be higher in the future. The expectation of increased stock prices causes stock prices to increase today. Such an episode is called a "bubble."

Result: The stock price can differ (above or below) its fundamental value.

• Fads. Sometimes stock prices increase for no other reason than stock prices have increased in the past. In this case, the change in the stock price is called a fad.

Result: The stock price can differ (above or below) its fundamental value.

SELF-TEST QUESTIONS

1. What is an indexed bond (1)?

2. What is the expression for the present value of a one-year bond which pays $100 in one year (1)?

3. What is the expression for the present value of a two-year bond which pays $100 in two years (1)?

4. What does the arbitrage relation suggest about the expected return on two assets (1)?

5. Define what is meant by the yield to maturity on an n-period bond (1)?

6. What does the yield curve represent (1)?

7. A reduction in the expected one-year interest rate, all else fixed, will have what effect on the current two-year rate (1)?

8. What does an upward sloping yield curve suggest about the financial market's expectation of future short-term interest rates (1)?

9. If individuals expect consumer confidence and consumption to decline over the next year, what will happen to the shape of the yield curve (1)?

10. A drop in current short-term interest rates of 1% will generally cause a drop in long-term rates of less than 1%. Why (1)?

11. What is the difference between debt finance and equity finance (2)?

12. List the determinants of the price of stock (2).

13. Why does fully anticipated monetary (or fiscal) policy have no effect on current stock prices (2)?

14. Why are the effects on stock prices of an unanticipated change in consumer spending ambiguous (2)?

15. What is the fundamental value of a stock price (3)?

16. Why might stock prices deviate from their fundamental values (3)?

REVIEW PROBLEMS

1. Suppose a coupon bond promises \$100 coupon payments and has a face value of \$1000. Assume that the current price of the bond is \$900.
a. What is the coupon rate for this bond?
b. What is the current yield for this bond?

2. Moody's Investors Service rates bonds. As the rating of a bond increases, its interest rate generally falls. Explain why this is so.

3. In late 1995 and early 1996, the failure of budget negotiations, some believe, raised the probability that the U.S. government would default on its bonds. What effect, if any, would this have on the interest rates on bonds issued by the U.S. government? Explain.

4. Use the information provided below to answer the following questions about one-year and two-year bonds that make a \$1000 payment upon maturity: i_{1t} = 10%; i^e_{1t+1} = 8%; let i_{1t} = .10 when i_{1t} = 10% and let i^e_{1t+1} = .08 when = 8%.
a. What is the price of the one-year bond today?
b. What is the price of the two-year bond today?
c. What is the price of the two-year bond in one year?

5. Repeat the analysis in #4. This time, however, assume that i_{1t} = 8% and i^e_{1t+1} = 6%. After you have completed parts a-c, what effect do the lower interest rates have on each of the prices you calculated (when compared to your answers in #4)?

6. Suppose the current one-year interest rate is 6%. For each of the following values of the one-year interest rate that financial markets expect to occur next year, calculate the current two-year rate and briefly explain the shape of the yield curve.
a. i^e_{t+1} = 8%
b. i^e_{t+1} = 5%
c. i^e_{t+1} = 6%

7. Repeat parts a and b in #6. This time, however, assume that:
a. i^e_{t+1} = 9%. What happens to the two-year rate as i^e_{t+1} increases (from 8% to 9%)? What happens to the shape of the yield curve? Explain.
b. i^e_{t+1} = 4%. What happens to the two-year rate as i^e_{t+1} decreases (from 5% to 4%)? What happens to the shape of the yield curve? Explain.

8. Suppose the one-year rate is 5% and that i^e_{t+1} = 7%.
a. Calculate the current two-year interest rate. What is the shape of the yield curve?
b. Now, suppose the i_{1t} increases to 6% (assume that i^e_{t+1} does not change). Calculate what happens to the two-year rate. Did i_{2t} change by more or less than the change in the one-year rate? Explain.
c. Use the original values to answer this question. Suppose i_{1t} increases to 6% and i^e_{t+1} increases to 7.5%. Calculate what happens to the two-year rate. Did i_{2t} change by more or less than the change in the one-year rate? Explain.

d. Use the original values to answer this question. Suppose i_{1t} increases to 6% and i^e_{t+1} increases to 8%. Calculate what happens to the two-year rate. Did i_{2t} change by more or less than the change in the one-year rate? Explain.
e. In parts b, c and d, you examined the effects of changes in the one-year interest rate on the two-year interest rate. In which case, if any, did the two-year rate increase by the same amount as the change in the one-year rate? Based on your analysis, what must occur for this to happen?

9. Suppose the yield curve is initially upward sloping. Briefly explain what must occur to cause each of the following events:
a. the yield curve becomes steeper
b. the yield curve becomes flat (i.e., horizontal)
c. the yield curve becomes downward sloping

10. Suppose the yield curve is initially upward sloping. Use your knowledge of the IS-LM model and the yield curve to explain what effect each of the following events will have on the shape of the yield curve.
a. financial markets expect a future reduction in consumer confidence which results in a reduction in consumer spending
b. financial markets expect a future Fed monetary expansion
c. financial markets expect a future reduction in government spending which is accompanied by a Fed monetary expansion
d. financial markets expect a future tax cut

11. Briefly explain how each of the following events will affect current stock prices.
a. financial markets expect a future monetary expansion will reduce future interest rates
b. financial markets expect a prolonged reduction in economic activity

12. a. Suppose an economic report indicates that output will increase by 5% for each of the next ten years. If financial markets already expect that this increase in Y will occur, what effect will this report have on current stock prices? Explain in detail.
b. Suppose the Fed announces that it will pursue a monetary contraction for the next two years. If financial markets already expect that this monetary contraction will occur, what effect will this announcement have on current stock prices? Explain in detail.

13. Explain how and why each of the following unanticipated events will affect current stock prices.
a. a monetary contraction
b. an increase in taxes
c. an increase in consumer confidence and spending that is accompanied by a monetary expansion (which leaves the interest rate unchanged)

14. a. Explain why unanticipated changes in monetary policy have unambiguous effects on stock prices.
b. Explain why unanticipated changes in fiscal policy have ambiguous effects on stock prices.

15. Use the graph provided below to answer the following questions. Assume that the economy is initially operating at point A. Now suppose there is an unexpected reduction in spending which causes the leftward shift in the IS curve.

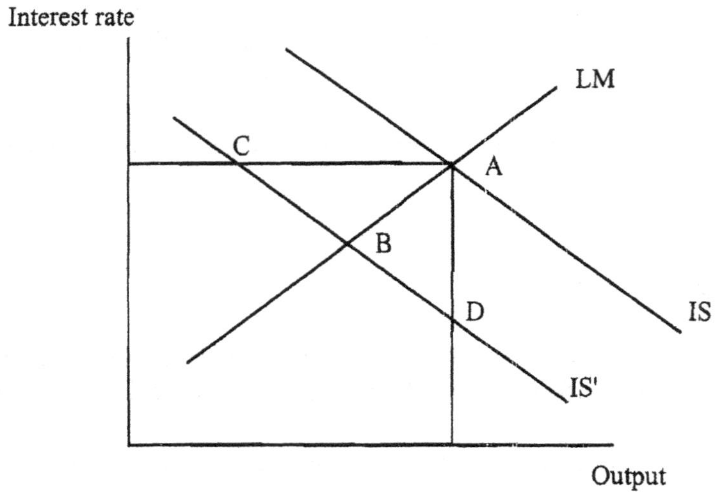

a. Explain what effect this unexpected reduction in spending will have on stock prices if the economy moves to point B.

b. Explain what type of Fed policy response financial markets expect if the economy is to move to point C.

c. Explain what type of Fed policy response financial markets expect if the economy is to move to point D.

d. Suppose the economy does move to point C (from point A). What effect will this event have on stock prices? Explain.

e. Suppose the economy does move to point D (from point A). What effect will this event have on stock prices? Explain.

MULTIPLE CHOICE QUESTIONS

1. An increase in the price of a one-year bond (which promises to pay $100 in one year) in period t will cause:

a. i_{1t} to increase
b. i_{1t} to decrease
c. a reduction in the present value of the one-year bond in period t
d. no change in the present value of the one-year bond in period t

2. Which of the following events will cause the price of a two-year bond in period t to increase?

a. an increase in i_{1t}
b. an increase in i^e_{1t}
c. a reduction in i_{1t}
d. both a and b

3. The arbitrage relation between one-year and two-year bonds indicates that:

a. $\$P_{1t} = \$P_{2t}$
b. $i_{1t} = i_{2t}$
c. the expected return from holding a one-year bond is equal to the expected return from holding a two-year bond
d. the yield to maturity on a one-year bond is equal to the yield to maturity on a two-year bond

4. An increase in the yield to maturity on a two-year bond will cause:

a. a reduction in $\$P_{2t}$
b. an increase in $\$P_{2t}$
c. the maturity on the two-year bond to increase
d. none of the above

5. The yield curve represents:

a. the yield to maturity on a particular bond over time
b. the relation between yield to maturity and maturity
c. the risk premium on a particular bond over time
d. the relation between the price of a bond and the interest rate on that bond

6. An upward sloping yield curve suggests that:

a. financial markets expect long-term rates to increase
b. financial markets expect long-term rates to fall
c. $i_{1t} > i^e_{1t}$
d. $i_{1t} < i^e_{1t}$

7. A downward sloping yield curve suggests that:

a. financial markets expect long-term rates to increase
b. financial markets expect long-term rates to fall
c. $i_{1t} > i^e_{1t}$
d. $i_{1t} < i^e_{1t}$

8. Suppose i_{1t} = 4% and i_{2t} = 5%. This suggests that the one-year rate expected to occur one year from now is:

a. 1%
b. 4.5%
c. 5%
d. 6%

9. Suppose i_{1t} is 6% and financial markets expect the one-year rate in one year to be 4%. Given this information, the interest rate on the two-year bond is:

a. 2%
b. 4%
c. 5%
d. 10%

10. Suppose the yield curve is initially upward sloping. Suppose the current one-year interest rate increases by 2% while the expected future one-year interest rate does not change. This event will tend to cause:

a. i_{2t} will increase by less than 2%
b. i_{2t} will increase by 2%
c. i_{2t} will fall by less than 2%
d. i_{2t} will fall by 2%

11. Assume that the one-year interest rate is on the vertical axis in the IS-LM model and that the yield curve is initially upward sloping. If financial markets now expect a monetary contraction in one year, we would expect that:

a. the yield curve will become steeper
b. the yield curve will become flatter
c. the yield curve to become horizontal (i.e., flat)
d. the yield curve to become downward sloping

12. Assume that the one-year interest rate is on the vertical axis in the IS-LM model and that the yield curve is initially upward sloping. If financial markets now expect an increase in taxes in one year, we would expect that:

a. the yield curve to become steeper
b. i_{2t} will decrease
c. i_{2t} will increase
d. none of the above

13. Which of the following events will cause an increase in stock prices in period t.

a. an increase in expected future dividends
b. a reduction in the current one-year interest rate
c. a reduction in the expected future one-year interest rate
d. all of the above

14. Suppose IBM announces that its profits for the next three years will drop. If this drop in profits were already expected by financial markets, we would expect that:

a. the price of IBM stock will increase as a result of this announcement
b. the price of IBM stock will decrease as a result of this announcement
c. the price of IBM stock will not change as a result of this announcement
d. the present value of expected future dividends will increase

15. A fully anticipated increase in consumer spending will cause the IS curve to shift right and:

a. current stock prices to increase
b. current stock prices to decrease
c. no change in current stock prices
d. have ambiguous effects on current stock prices

16. A fully anticipated reduction in the money supply will cause:

a. current stock prices to increase
b. current stock prices to decrease
c. no change in current stock prices
d. have ambiguous effects on current stock prices

17. A partially unexpected increase in the money supply will cause:

a. current stock prices to increase
b. current stock prices to decrease
c. no change in current stock prices
d. have ambiguous effects on current stock prices

18. Suppose the Fed is not expected to respond to the following event. A partially unexpected reduction in spending will cause:

a. current stock prices to increase
b. current stock prices to decrease
c. no change in current stock prices
d. have ambiguous effects on current stock prices

19. Suppose the Fed is expected to respond to the following event by keeping the interest rate constant (i.e., equal to its initial level). An unexpected increase in spending will cause:

a. current stock prices to increase
b. current stock prices to decrease
c. no change in current stock prices
d. have ambiguous effects on current stock prices

20. As the LM curve becomes steeper, an unexpected increase in consumer confidence:

a. will cause a relatively large increase in output and relatively large increase in the interest rate
b. will cause a relatively small increase in output and relatively small increase in the interest rate
c. is more likely to cause stock prices to rise
d. is more likely to cause stock prices to fall

CHAPTER 16. EXPECTATIONS, CONSUMPTION, AND INVESTMENT

OBJECTIVES, REVIEW, AND TUTORIAL

After working through the chapter and the following material, you should be able to:

(1) Know the components of total wealth.

(2) Explain what factors influence consumption.

(3) Explain the effects of permanent and transitory changes in income on consumption.

(4) Understand how a firm decides to buy, for example, a new machine (i.e., invest).

(5) Explain what effect changes in expected profits have on investment.

(6) Explain what is meant by the "user cost of capital."

(7) Understand why both expected profits and current profits affect investment.

(8) Explain the determinants of profits.

(9) Understand why investment is more volatile than consumption.

1. COMPONENTS AND CALCULATION OF TOTAL WEALTH

There are two types of wealth: (1) nonhuman wealth; and (2) human wealth.

(1) Nonhuman wealth

Nonhuman wealth is the sum of financial wealth and housing wealth.

- Financial wealth is the total value of an individual's stock and bond holdings, savings accounts, checking accounts, etc. MINUS any liabilities (e.g. personal loans and any outstanding balances on credit cards).
- Housing wealth is the value of one's house (minus the mortgage still due) plus the value of other goods one owns (e.g. cars, art, etc.).

(2) Human wealth

Human wealth is the expected present value of the individual's after-tax labor income: $V(Y^e_{Lt} - T^e_t)$ where Y^e_{Lt} is expected labor income and T^e_t is expected taxes.

- Total wealth = Nonhuman wealth + Human wealth.

2. THE DETERMINANTS OF CONSUMPTION

There are two cases to consider:

(1) Case 1: The very foresighted consumer

To determine her consumption, this individual would: (1) determine her total wealth; and then (2) consume a proportion of total wealth so that consumption per year is approximately the same for the rest of her life. What are the implications of this?

- Consumption is an increasing function of total wealth.
- If this constant level of consumption exceeds current (disposable) income, she borrows the difference.
- If this constant level of consumption is less than current (disposable) income, she saves the difference.

(2) Case 2: The more realistic scenario

There are four reasons why the individual might not act like the above very foresighted individual:

- Individuals might prefer to defer consumption to later periods;
- Individuals might act in a simpler, less forward-looking fashion;
- There is uncertainty about future wealth; and
- Banks are not likely to lend the amount the individual wishes to borrow to achieve this constant level of consumption.

These four reasons suggest that consumption is an increasing function of total wealth AND current disposable income.

Learning Tip

Think about all of the variables that determine total wealth and current disposable income. Specifically, think about how changes in these variables may affect consumption. For example, what effect would a reduction in housing prices (i.e., housing wealth) have on consumption?

There are two implications of this consumption relation:

(1) An increase in current income will likely cause a less than one-for-one increase in consumption. Why?

- A permanent change in income may cause a one-for-one change in consumption.
- A perceived temporary (transitory) change in income will cause a less than one-for-one change in consumption.

(2) Consumption may change even if current income does not change. These changes in consumption would be caused by changes in total wealth.

Learning Tip

In an economic expansion, income rises and consumption will rise. However, some of the change in income may be viewed as temporary. Therefore, C changes less than one-for-one.

- Permanent changes in current income cause relatively larger changes in consumption.
- Transitory changes in current income cause relatively smaller changes in consumption.

You should now understand that consumption is a function of:

- current disposable income
- financial wealth
- housing wealth
- human wealth

3. THE FIRM'S DECISION TO INVEST

When a firm decides whether to purchase a new machine (or build a new factory) it must:

(1) Determine how long the machine will last;
(2) Compute the present value of expected profits; and
(3) compare the PV of the expected profits with the price of the machine.

- Life of the machine: Machines (capital) lose their usefulness (i.e., depreciate) at a rate of δ per year. δ is the depreciation rate.

- Present value of expected profits: Π represents profit per machine in real terms. The PV of expected profits is represented by the expression $V(\Pi^e_t)$ found in the text.

Learning Tip

- Machines bought in year t become operational in year t + 1.
- $V(\Pi^e_t)$ increases when:
  (1) expected future profits increase;
  (2) the depreciation rate falls; and
  (3) the current and/or expected future real interest rate falls.

- Decision to buy the machine: Profit-maximizing firms will purchase a machine if $V(\Pi^e_t)$ is greater than the price of the machine. Firms will NOT buy the machine if $V(\Pi^e_t)$ is less than the price of the machine. The analysis suggests that investment is an increasing function of the PV of expected future profits.

Learning Tip

The ratio of the PV of expected profits to the price of the machine is referred to as Tobin's Q where Q is the ratio.

4. THE USER COST OF CAPITAL

Assume that the real interest rate is constant and that future expected profits are also constant. In this case,

$V(\Pi^e_t) = \Pi_t/(r_t + \delta)$ and, therefore, $I_t = I(\Pi_t/(r_t + \delta))$.

- User cost of capital. The expression $r + \delta$ represents the user cost of capital. An increase in r or an increase in δ will cause the user cost (or rental cost) of capital to increase.

Learning Tip

Consider the example discussed in the chapter. If a firm rents its machines (rather than purchases them), the rental agency would have to charge at least the real interest rate (r) plus the rate of depreciation. Why? Rather than rent the machine, the rental agency could hold bonds and receive r. Furthermore, given that the rental agency rents the machines, it will charge for the loss of usefulness (δ) which occurs each period.

Investment depends on the ratio of profit to the user cost of capital. Investment will increase when:
(1) profit increases;
(2) the real interest rate falls; and
(3) the rate of depreciation falls.

5. PROFIT, EXPECTATIONS, AND INVESTMENT

In addition to the PV of expected profit, investment strongly responds to changes in current profit. Current profit may affect investment for two reasons.

(1) Even if expectations of future expected profits are high, firms may be reluctant to borrow. The only way firms will invest is by using some of their retained earnings (profits) to finance this investment.

(2) Firms may be unable to borrow from banks. Firms would be able to use only current profits to finance investment.

Investment is, therefore, an increasing function of: (1) the PV of expected future profit; and (2) current profit.

Learning Tip

- Current profits are called cash flow.
- The PV of expected future profits is called profitability.
- An increase in cash flow or profitability will cause an increase in investment.

6. DETERMINANTS OF PROFIT

Profit per unit of capital is determined by:

(1) The level of sales: as sales increase, profit increases; and

(2) The existing capital stock: if the capital stock is already high, profit per unit of capital is likely to be low.

If we assume that output equals sales, profit per unit of capital can be expressed as:

$\Pi_t = \Pi(Y_t/K_t)$.

There are several implications of this:

- In a recession, output and sales decrease, causing a reduction in profit. As profit falls, investment falls.
- In an expansion, output and sales increase, causing an increase in profit. As profit increases, investment rises.
- The link between Y_t and Π_t indicates that there is a link between expected output (expected sales) and expected profit. The expectation of a long expansion causes an increase in expected profit and an increase in current investment.

7. VOLATILITY OF CONSUMPTION AND INVESTMENT

(1) Response of consumption to changes in income

- A permanent increase in income will cause consumption to increase, at most, by the increase in Y.
- A transitory increase in Y will cause a smaller increase in consumption.
- Consumption, therefore, generally responds less than one-for-one to changes in income.

Learning Tip

If consumption increases by more than the change in income, consumption would have to be cut at some point in the future. Individuals are unlikely to act this way.

(2) Response of investment to changes in income

There is no reason why firms cannot increase investment by an amount greater than the change in income (sales). Suppose a firm has a ratio of capital to annual sales of 3 (K/Sales = 3). A permanent increase in sales of \$5 million will require that the firm spend \$15 million on additional capital. If the firm responds immediately, the change in investment equals \$15 million and, therefore, exceeds the change in Y.

We can conclude that investment responds more than consumption to the same change in income.

Learning Tip

An alternative view: The Y/K-Π-I link.

An increase in income will cause:

- an increase in Y/K
- As Y/K increases, profit per unit of capital increases.
- As profit per unit of capital increases, investment will increase.
- As investment increases, the capital stock will eventually increase.
- The higher K will cause Y/K to return to normal.
- As Y/K returns to normal, so do profit per unit of capital and investment.

SELF-TEST QUESTIONS

1. What are panel data sets (1)?

2. What are the two components of nonhuman wealth (1)?

3. What are of the components of total wealth (1)?

4. What are the determinants of consumption (1)?

5. Give four reasons why individuals might not act like the "very foresighted" individual described in the chapter (1).

6. Compare the effects of permanent and temporary changes in income on consumption (1).

7. What does the depreciation rate measure (2)?

8. For a firm to buy a new machine, what must be the relationship between the present value of expected profits and the price of the machine (2)?

9. What two factors determine the user cost of capital (2)?

10. Why does current profit affect investment (2)?

11. What is meant by "profitability" and "cash flow" (2)?

12. What are the two determinants of profits (2)?

13. What effect will an increase in the existing capital stock have on profit per unit of capital (2)?

14. What effect will an increase in expected future output have on investment (2)?

15. This chapter examines both consumption and investment. Which of these two variables represents the larger share of output (3)? Which of these two variables is more volatile (3)?

REVIEW PROBLEMS

1. Use the information provided below to answer the following questions.

Financial wealth = $50,000
Housing wealth = 0
Present value of Human wealth = $1,550,000

a. Calculate the individual's total wealth.
b. Suppose the individual will live for 40 more years. If he wants to maintain the same level of consumption for each of the next 40 years, how much will the individual consume in each year?
c. Suppose the individual's current (disposable) income equals $25,000. In order to achieve the level of consumption in the current period (a level of consumption you calculated in part (b)), what will the individual have to do? Briefly explain.
d. Suppose the individual receives a one-time bonus of $10,000 in the current period. What effect will this bonus have on the individual's total wealth? What effect will this bonus have on the individual's consumption in the current period and in the future? Explain.
e. Now suppose the individual receives a permanent pay raise of $10,000; assume that she will receive this for the next 40 years. What effect will this have on the individual's total wealth? What effect will this permanent increase in income have on current and future consumption? Compare your analysis here with your analysis in part (d).

2. Explain how each of the following events will affect the components of total wealth and/or current (disposable) income.

a. a reduction in the demand for houses causes a reduction in the average price of homes
b. the 1987 stock market crash in which stock prices, on average, fell by 20%
c. a federal budget is passed which calls for a permanent increase in taxes
d. an increase in expected future nominal interest rates

3. Use the information provided below to answer the following questions.

$\delta = 10\%$ $\Pi^e_{t+1} = \$10{,}000$ $\Pi^e_{t+2} = \$12{,}000$ $r_t = 5\%$ $r^e_{t+1} = 7\%$

Let r = .05 when r = 5% and $\delta = .10$ when $\delta = 10\%$.

a. Suppose a machine is purchased in period t and is expected to yield the above levels of profits (measured in real terms). Calculate the present value, in year t, of the expected profits of this machine in year t+1.
b. Calculate the present value, in year t, of the expected profits of this machine in year t+2.
c. If this machine is used only in periods t+1 and t+2, what is the present value of the expected profits of this machine?
d. Suppose r_t and r_{t+1} both increase by 1% (to 6% and 8%). Calculate what happens (compared to your analysis in part (c)) to the present value of expected profits.
e. Use the original values to answer this question. Suppose the firm's expectations of profits in t+1 and t+2 increase by \$1000 (to \$11,000 and \$13,000). Calculate what happens (compared to your analysis in part (c)) to the present value of expected profits.
f. Again, use the original values to answer this question. Suppose the depreciation rate falls to 8%. Calculate what happens (compared to your analysis in part (c)) to the present value of expected profits.
g. What is the maximum price the firm will be willing to pay for this machine in parts (c), (d), (e) and (f)? Briefly explain.
h. What does your analysis suggest happens to the present value of expected profits of a machine as:

(1) r increases;
(2) firms revise upwards their expectations of future profits; and
(3) the depreciation rate falls.

4. Suppose firms expect both future profits (per unit of capital) and future interest rates to remain constant at the same level as today's levels where $r_t = 5\%$ and $\Pi_t = \$10{,}000$. Assume that $\delta = 10\%$. Note: when calculating PV, let r = .05 when r = 5% and $\delta = .10$ when $\delta = 10\%$.

a. Given this information, calculate the PV of expected profits. What is the highest price the firm would be willing to pay for this machine? What is the user cost of capital?
b. Repeat the analysis in part (a). This time, however, assume that $r_t = 4\%$. What happens to the user cost of capital as the real interest rate falls?
c. Repeat the analysis in part (a). This time, however, assume that $\delta = 12\%$. What happens to the user cost of capital as a result of this change in the depreciation rate?
d. Repeat the analysis in part (a). This time, however, assume that $\Pi_t = \$9{,}000$. What happens to the user cost of capital?
e. Based on your analysis, what would tend to happen to investment in parts (b), (c) and (d) as a result of these changes.

5. Intuitively explain how an increase in the user cost of capital affects the level of investment.

6. Suppose there are two firms. Firm A produces only steel. The second firm, B, has two parts (i.e., operations). The first is in steel production, and the second is in oil exploration. Suppose there is a sharp increase in the price of oil resulting in increased profits in oil exploration.
a. Suppose that only cash flows determine investment. Explain what effect this increase in the price of oil will have on investment for firm A, on investment in firm B's steel production operation, and on investment in firm B's oil exploration operation.
b. Suppose that only profitability determines investment. Explain what effect this increase in the price of oil will have on investment for firm A, on investment in firm B's steel production operation, and on investment in firm B's oil exploration operation.

7. Briefly explain how each of the following events will affect profit per unit of capital and, therefore, investment.
a. a permanent decrease in sales
b. an increase in output
c. a decline in the capital stock

8. For this question, assume that firms seek to maintain their current ratio of capital to annual sales of 4. Any deviation of the actual ratio from 4 will cause an immediate change in investment to achieve the desired ratio.
a. Suppose there is a permanent increase in sales (and, therefore, output) of $20 million in period t. Discuss what effect this increase in sales (and output) will have on investment and consumption. Which of these two variables, if either, will be most affected by this change in sales? Briefly explain.
b. In part (a), what effect will this increase in sales eventually have on the capital stock? Explain.
c. As the capital stock changes, what happens to profit per unit of capital? Briefly explain.

9. In 1990, the U.S. economy entered a recession. Based on your understanding of the material presented in this chapter, what effect do you think this recession had on: (1) sales; (2) profit per unit of capital; (3) investment; and (4) the capital stock. Briefly explain.

MULTIPLE CHOICE QUESTIONS

1. Which of the following is included in nonhuman wealth?

a. financial wealth
b. housing wealth
c. expected future taxes
d. both a and b

2. Which of the following events would cause an increase in human wealth?

a. an increase in the amount in one's savings account
b. a reduction in expected taxes
c. an increase in the value of one's house
d. an increase in the expected future real interest rate

3. Which of the following statements is true about the very foresighted consumer?

a. she will consume a proportion of total wealth so that consumption per year is approximately the same for the rest of her life
b. consumption is an increasing function of total wealth
c. if the constant level of consumption (described in (a)) is less than current (disposable) income, she saves the difference
d. all of the above

4. Which of the following explains why individuals' consumption is (in addition to total wealth) an increasing function of current income?

a. individuals might prefer to defer consumption to later periods
b. individuals might act in a simpler, less forward-looking fashion
c. banks are not likely to lend the amount the individual wishes to borrow to achieve a constant level of consumption
d. all of the above

5. For this question, assume that current income does not change. With fixed current income, current consumption will <u>fall</u> if:

a. future expected taxes decrease
b. total wealth falls
c. expected future income increases
d. none of the above

6. Which of the following events would tend to cause the greatest reduction in current consumption?

a. a one-time tax increase of $1000
b. a temporary decline in current income of $1000
c. a permanent decrease in your annual salary of $1000
d. both a and b

7. An increase in which of the following variables will cause an increase in current consumption?

a. an increase in current disposable income
b. an increase in financial wealth
c. an increase in housing wealth
d. an increase in human wealth
e. all of the above

8. When a firm makes the decision to buy a new machine, it will buy the machine if the present value of expected profit from the machine:

a. is greater than zero
b. is greater than the rate of depreciation
c. is greater than the real interest rate
d. is greater than the price of the machine

9. An increase in the rate of depreciation will cause the present value of expected profits to:

a. increase
b. decrease
c. remain unchanged if the real interest rate increases by the same amount of the increase in the rate of depreciation
d. none of the above

10. A reduction in the current and expected future real interest rates will cause:

a. the present value of expected profit to increase
b. the present value of expected profit to decrease
c. a reduction in investment
d. a reduction in the rate of depreciation

11. The rental cost of capital will decrease if:

a. the rate of depreciation increases
b. the real interest rate falls
c. the firm's expectation of future profits decrease
d. none of the above

12. Suppose firms' expect future profits and future real interest rates to remain constant at their current levels. Given this information, we know that investment will decrease if:

a. the real interest rate falls
b. the rate of depreciation falls
c. current profit falls
d. the user cost of capital decreases

13. An increase in "profitability" suggests that:

a. firms have increased their expectations of future profits
b. the real interest rate has increased
c. the rate of depreciation has increased
d. current profits have increased

14. A reduction in "cash flow" suggests that:

a. the real interest rate has increased
b. the rate of depreciation has decreased
c. the user cost of capital has increased
d. current profits have decreased

15. Which of the following statements is true?

a. sales and profits are positively related
b. income and profit are negatively related
c. expected income and expected profits are negatively related
d. the user cost of capital and investment are positively related

16. Which of the following events would cause an increase in profit per unit of capital?

a. an increase in income
b. an increase in sales
c. a reduction in the capital stock
d. all of the above

17. In a recession, we would expect that:

a. profit increases
b. investment increases
c. income and sales would decrease
d. both a and b

18. A temporary $100 million increase in output will tend to cause:

a. an equal change in consumption and investment
b. the change in consumption to be greater than the change in investment
c. the change in investment to be greater than the change in consumption
d. a reduction in profit and a reduction in investment

CHAPTER 17. EXPECTATIONS, OUTPUT, AND POLICY

OBJECTIVES, REVIEW, AND TUTORIAL

After working through the chapter and the following material, you should be able to:

(1) Explain what is meant by aggregate private spending.

(2) Explain what effect changes in current and expected future income, real interest rates and taxes have on the components of private aggregate spending and on the IS curve.

(3) Explain why the IS curve is relatively steeper when we take into account the effects of expectations.

(4) Recognize that the LM relation is NOT affected by changes in expected future income and real interest rates.

(5) Discuss how changes in monetary policy in the current period can affect expected future real interest rates.

(6) Re-examine the effects of monetary policy and explain why the IS curve can shift as a result of a monetary expansion or contraction.

(7) Explain what is meant by rational expectations, and discuss how it differs from animal spirits and adaptive expectations.

(8) Re-examine the effects of fiscal policy, and explain why the effects of, for example, deficit reduction on current output are ambiguous.

1. THE IS RELATION AND EXPECTATIONS

(1) Review of the IS relation

The IS relation is now represented by the following equation:

$$Y = A(Y, T, r, Y'^e, T'^e, r'^e) + G$$

where $A(Y, T, r, Y'^e, T'^e, r'^e)$ is aggregate private spending (i.e., consumption plus investment).

Learning Tip

- Recall that we are assuming that there are only two periods: (1) the current period; and (2) the future period.
- The future period represents all future years lumped together.

(2) Slope of the IS curve

A reduction in the current real interest rate causes an increase in spending and has a multiplier effect on output. Recall that changes in current output and the current real interest rate do not cause shifts in the IS curve (they represent movements along the curve).

(3) Shifts in the IS curve

- Current taxes (T): An increase in T causes a reduction in current consumption and a leftward shift in the IS curve.
- Expected future output (Y'^e): An increase in Y'^e will cause: (1) an increase in current consumption as the present value of human wealth increases; and (2) an increase in investment as firms expect future profits to rise. The IS curve, therefore, will shift to the right.
- Expected future r (r'^e): An increase in r'^e will cause: (1) a reduction in consumption as the present value of human wealth decreases; and (2) a reduction in investment as the present value of future profits falls. The IS curve, therefore, shifts to the left.
- Expected future taxes (T'^e): An increase in T'^e will cause a reduction in the present value of human wealth and a reduction in consumption. The IS curve, therefore, shifts to the left.
- Government spending (G): An increase in G will cause an increase in spending and a rightward shift in the IS curve.

Learning Tip

- In general, if firms and households become less confident of the future, investment and consumption will fall as expectations of future profits and income fall.
- Make sure you can explain how an increase or decrease in each of the variables in the IS relation affects the IS curve in the current period.

2. THE STEEPER SLOPE OF THE IS CURVE

When compared to the slope of the IS curve in the basic model, the slope of the IS curve is now most likely steeper for two reasons:

(1) A reduction in the current real interest rate, with future expected real interest rates unchanged, will not have much of an effect on the present value of future profits and future income; and

(2) The multiplier is likely to be smaller. The multiplier depends on how much current spending changes as a result of a given change in current income. A temporary increase in income will have a smaller effect on consumption and investment.

3. THE LM RELATION AND EXPECTATIONS

Money demand is an increasing function of current income and a decreasing function of the current nominal interest rate.

- Current money demand depends on your current level of transactions. Therefore, expected future income will have no effect on money demand and, therefore, no effect on the LM relation.

• Current money demand depends on the current opportunity cost of holding money (i.e., the nominal interest rate). What you expect the interest rate to be in one year does not affect the current opportunity cost of holding money. Therefore, future expected interest rates have no effect on current money demand and no effect on the current LM curve.

4. MONETARY POLICY, EXPECTATIONS, AND THE IS-LM MODEL

To understand the effects of monetary policy on output, you must recognize the distinction between:

(1) nominal and real interest rates; and
(2) current and expected future real interest rates.

When the Fed increases the money supply, the current nominal interest rates falls and the LM curve shifts down. The effects of the change in the current nominal interest rate on current and future expected real interest rates depend on:

(1) whether the lower nominal interest rate causes financial markets to revise their expectations of future nominal interest rates; and
(2) whether the lower nominal interest rate causes financial markets to revise their expectations of current and future inflation.

Learning Tip
• Assume that current and expected future inflation are equal to zero. • We can, therefore, ignore the second effect described above. • Since expected inflation is zero, we know that $i = r$.

There are two cases to consider.

Case 1: Financial markets do NOT adjust expectations of future interest rates.

The increase in the money supply causes the LM curve to shift down and the interest rate (both nominal and real since they are the same) to fall. As the current real interest rate falls, there is some increase in spending and output. The steeper IS curve, however, implies that the change in Y is small.

Case 2: Financial markets revise expectations of future interest rates.

• An increase in the money supply again causes the LM curve to shift down and the current interest rate to fall.
• Financial markets expect lower future interest rates.
• The lower future interest rates are expected to cause an increase in future output.
• A reduction in future expected interest rates will cause an increase in spending (both consumption and investment).
• The increase in future expected income will cause an increase in spending (both consumption and investment).
• The increased spending caused by the change in expected future interest rates and future income will cause the IS curve to shift to the right.

Learning Tip

- Monetary policy's initial effects on the economy are on the current nominal interest rate and LM curve.
- Changes in monetary policy can have significant effects on expectations of future interest rates and future income.
- These changes in expected future interest rates and future income will cause shifts in the IS curve and changes in current economic activity.

5. RATIONAL EXPECTATIONS, ANIMAL SPIRITS, AND ADAPTIVE EXPECTATIONS

How do individuals form expectations? Three approaches are presented in this chapter.

- Animal spirits. In this case, changes in expectations are taken as unexplained (or random).

- Adaptive expectations. This approach assumes that individuals base their expectations on past movements in variables. This backward-looking approach might assume, for example, that expected inflation this year will be equal to the average of actual inflation during the past two years.

- Rational expectations. This approach assumes that individuals form expectations by assessing the impact of future expected policy and then determining the implications of that policy on, for example, interest rates and income. This forward-looking approach assumes that individuals look to the future and do the best job they can in predicting it.

Learning Tip

- We assume in this chapter that firms, households, and investors have rational expectations.
- You must recognize that rational expectations does not imply that individuals know the future. It does, however, assume that individuals use information as best they can to predict future variables.

6. FISCAL POLICY, EXPECTATIONS, AND THE IS-LM MODEL

The effects of a fiscal contraction also depend on expectations. Let's examine a deficit reduction example in which T and T'^e increase. There are several cases to consider.

Case 1: No response expected from the Fed, and assume that individuals consider only the short-run effects of changes in expected future macroeconomic variables.

- The higher T and higher T'^e cause a reduction in current consumption and a leftward shift in the IS curve.
- The higher T'^e will cause the IS curve (in the future) to shift left. Individuals, therefore, expect future income and the future real interest rate to fall.
- The lower Y'^e will cause a further reduction in consumption (the present value of human wealth falls). The IS curve shifts to the left.
- The lower Y'^e also causes a reduction in investment as firms revise down their expectations of future profits. The IS curve shifts to the left.

• The lower r'^e will, however, cause an increase in both consumption and investment. This effect causes the IS curve to shift to the right.

Without knowing the magnitude of the above shifts in the IS curves, the effects of the increase in T and T'^e on current output are ambiguous. In short:

- The lower r'^e causes Y to increase (the IS curve shifts right).
- The lower Y'^e causes Y to fall (the IS curve shifts left).

Learning Tip

How do you determine the effects of future events and future policy on r'^e and Y'^e? Actually, this is easy to do. One must first determine what model individuals use to examine the effects of future events on future macroeconomic variables.

(1) Short-run analysis: Simply use the IS-LM model to evaluate the effects of the expected event on the IS and LM curves.

• If the IS curve is expected to shift to the right, Y'^e and r'^e will increase.
• If the IS curve is expected to shift to the left, Y'^e and r'^e will fall.
• If the LM curve is expected to shift down, Y'^e will increase and r'^e will fall.
• If the LM curve is expected to shift up, Y'^e will fall and r'^e will increase.
• Often, several events might be expected to occur simultaneously in the future. It might be the case that the effects on future output will be ambiguous while the effects on r'^e will be unambiguous. Or, vice versa.

(2) Medium-run analysis: Simply use the IS-LM and AS-AD model presented in Chapter 7.
• If, for example, future G is expected to fall, we know that future output will be unchanged and that the future real interest rate will be lower.

(3) Long-run analysis: Simply use the AS-AD model and your understanding of the long run model presented in Chapter 11.
• If, for example, future G is expected to fall, we know that future interest rate will be lower, investment higher, the capital stock higher, and output higher.

Case 2: Fed expected to accommodate both the current and future increase in taxes and assume that individuals consider only the short-run effects of changes in expected future macroeconomic variables.

The analysis is similar to that of Case 1 with several exceptions.

• As the IS curve shifts left as a result of the increase in T, the Fed increases the money supply to keep current output from falling.
• Individuals expect a similar response in the future. So, the future increase in T does not cause a reduction in Y'^e, only a reduction in r'^e.
• The lower T and T'^e cause current spending to decrease and the current IS curve to shift left.
• The lower r'^e, however, causes consumption and investment to increase and the IS curve to shift right.

NOTE: It is possible that current output could increase as a result of a deficit reduction package. For this to occur, the future interest rate effects must offset all other effects.

Case 3: Individuals use their understanding of the medium-run effects of a change in future taxes when forming expectations of future output and future interest rates.

• The higher T and T'^e again cause the IS curve to shift left as current consumption falls.

• The higher T'^e will cause the future real interest rate to be lower. This reduction in r'^e will cause current consumption and investment to increase, causing the IS curve to shift right in the current period.

• The higher T'^e has no effect on future expected output, however.

• The final position of the current IS curve is ambiguous. The direct effects of the higher T and T'^e on current consumption cause it to shift left. The lower r'^e will cause the IS curve to shift to the right.

Case 4: Individuals use their understanding of the long-run effects of a change in future taxes when forming expectations of future output and future interest rates.

• The higher T and T'^e again cause the IS curve to shift left as current consumption falls.

• The higher T'^e will cause the future real interest rate to be lower. This reduction in r'^e will cause current consumption and investment to increase, causing the IS curve to shift right in the current period.

• The higher T'^e will also cause future investment and the future capital stock to be higher. Expected future output will, therefore, also be higher. This increase in future expected output will cause current consumption and current investment to rise. The IS curve will shift right in the current period as a result of this.

• The final position of the current IS curve is ambiguous. The direct effects of the higher T and T'^e on current consumption cause it to shift left. The lower r'^e will cause the IS curve to shift to the right. The higher Y'^e will also cause the IS curve to shift to the right.

Learning Tip

• The less the Fed is expected to accommodate the increase in taxes, the greater will be the negative effect on current spending of the expected drop in future income.

• The deficit reduction program could be backloaded. That is, most of the tax increase (or cut in G) could occur in the future.

• If individuals do not respond much to changes in expected future taxes, the increase in T and T'^e will have little effect on current spending.

• Make sure you can explain the effects of a fiscal expansion.

• To summarize, depending on expectations, fiscal policy can have ambiguous effects on current output.

SELF-TEST QUESTIONS

1. What are the components of aggregate private spending (1)?

2. Explain what effect increases in current (and expected future) income, taxes and real interest rates have on aggregate private spending (1).

3. There are two reasons why the IS curve is now likely steeper than the IS curve in the basic model. What are they (1)?

4. What effect will an increase in expected future output have on the IS curve in the current period (1)?

5. What effect will an increase in the expected future real interest rate have on the IS curve in the current period (1)?

6. What effect will an increase in expected future taxes have on the IS curve in the current period (1)?

7. What effect does an increase in expected future income have on the LM curve in the current period (1)?

8. What effect does a reduction in the expected future real interest rate have on the LM curve in the current period (1)?

9. The extent to which the Fed (by changing the nominal interest rate) can affect current and expected future real interest rates depends on two factors. What are they (2)?

10. Why might a monetary expansion cause a rightward shift in the IS curve (2)?

11. What is meant by rational expectations (2)?

12. What are the medium-run and long-run effects of an expected future cut in government spending on future output and future real interest rates (2)?

13. What are the effects of an expected future monetary expansion on future output and future real interest rates (2)?

14. The deficit reduction package (described in the chapter) resulted in three factors shifting the IS curve. What are they (3)?

15. What is meant by a "backloaded" deficit reduction program (3)?

REVIEW PROBLEMS

1. Briefly note how each of the following events affects: (1) each of the components of current spending; (2) the position of the IS curve in the current period; and (3) the position of the LM curve in the current period.

a. reduction in expected future real dividends
b. increase in expected future real after-tax profits
c. reduction in expected future taxes
d. reduction in current cash flow
e. increase in the real money supply in the current period
f. reduction in expected future real interest rates
g. reduction in expected future income
h. increase in government spending in the current period

2. Discuss briefly how each of the following expected future events affects: (1) the position of the future IS and LM curves; and, therefore, (2) expected future income and the expected future real interest rate.

a. an expected future reduction in the money supply
b. an expected future increase in government spending
c. an expected future increase in consumer confidence that results in an increase in spending

3. a. What determines the size of the multiplier?
b. Why is the multiplier likely to be smaller in this chapter?

4. a. Why does an increase in the current real interest rate cause a reduction in spending?
b. Why is the effect of an increase in the current real interest rate, all else constant, more likely to be smaller in this chapter?

5. Briefly explain what your analysis in questions #3 and #4 suggests about the slopes of the: (a) IS curve; and (b) LM curve.

6. For each of the following events, graphically illustrate and explain the effects on: (1) the components of current spending; (2) the current IS and LM curves; and (3) the current real interest rate and income.

a. a reduction in r'^e
b. an increase in r'^e
c. an increase in Y'^e
d. a reduction in Y'^e

7. Assume that individuals consider only the short-run effects of changes in expected future macroeconomic variables. For each of the following events, graphically illustrate and explain the effects on: (1) the components of current spending; (2) the current IS and LM curves; and (3) the current real interest rate and income. NOTE: If the effects of the event on any of the current variables are ambiguous, briefly explain why this occurs.
a. an increase in the expected future money supply
b. an increase in expected future government spending
c. an increase in expected future taxes

8. Assume that individuals consider only the short-run effects of changes in expected future macroeconomic variables. Suppose that government spending is expected to increase in the future and that the Fed is expected to change the money supply to leave the future real interest rate unchanged.

a. Briefly discuss what effect this increase in future government spending and Fed response will have on r'^e and Y'^e.

b. Based on your analysis in part (a), what effect will this increase in future government spending and Fed response have on: (1) the components of current spending; (2) the position of the IS and LM curves in the current period; and (3) the current real interest rate and current output?

9. Assume that individuals consider only the short-run effects of changes in expected future macroeconomic variables. Suppose that government spending is expected to increase in the future and that the Fed is expected to change the money supply to leave future output unchanged.

a. Briefly discuss what effect this increase in future government spending and Fed response will have on r'^e and Y'^e.

b. Based on your analysis in part (a), what effect will this increase in future government spending and Fed response have on: (1) the components of current spending; (2) the position of the IS and LM curves in the current period; and (3) the current real interest rate and current output?

10. Assume that individuals consider only the short-run effects of changes in expected future macroeconomic variables. Suppose that government spending is expected to increase in the future and that the Fed is not expected to respond to this change in government spending.

a. Briefly discuss what effect this increase in future government spending and Fed response will have on r'^e and Y'^e.

b. Based on your analysis in part (a), what effect will this increase in future government spending (with no Fed response) have on: (1) the components of current spending; (2) the position of the IS and LM curves in the current period; and (3) the current real interest rate and current output?

11. You evaluated the effects of changes in expected future government spending on current output in questions 8-10.

a. In which of these three cases did current output change the most? Explain.

b. Briefly discuss how the expected Fed response (or nonresponse) to a change in expected future G can affect the current output effects of this expected fiscal policy action.

12. Assume that individuals consider only the short-run effects of changes in expected future macroeconomic variables. Suppose a budget is passed that calls for an increase in future taxes. Further assume that the Fed is not expected to alter the money supply in response to this future tax increase.

a. What effect will this expected future tax increase have on the yield curve in the current period? Explain.

b. What effect will this expected future tax increase have on future output? Explain.

c. Under what conditions will this increase in future taxes have NO effect on current output? Explain.

d. Under what conditions will this increase in future taxes cause current output to increase? Explain.

e. Under what conditions will this increase in future taxes cause current output to decrease? Explain.

13. Assume that individuals consider only the short-run effects of changes in expected future macroeconomic variables. Suppose a budget is passed that calls for an increase in current and future taxes and assume that the Fed is not expected to alter the money supply in response to this future tax increase.
a. What effect will this budget have on current output?
b. Discuss how your analysis in part (a) would differ IF financial markets and other individuals (i.e., firms and households) do not believe that taxes will increase in the future. Specifically, does current output change more or less as a result of this lack of credibility in the future tax increase? Explain.

14. Assume that individuals consider only the long-run effects of changes in expected future macroeconomic variables. Suppose there is an increase in current government spending. Also assume that individuals expect future government spending will increase.
a. What do individuals expect will happen to future output and the future interest rate? Explain.
b. Based on your analysis in part (a), what effect will this increase in current government spending and increase in expected future government spending have on current output? Explain.
c. Based on your analysis in part (b), is it possible that a budget deficit increase can lead to a recession? Explain.

15. Briefly explain how the analysis in #14 is different if we assume that individuals consider only the medium-run effects of changes in expected future macroeconomic variables.

MULTIPLE CHOICE QUESTIONS

1. Aggregate private spending (A) is equal to:

a. consumption plus government spending
b. investment plus government spending
c. consumption plus investment
d. consumption plus investment and government spending

2. An increase in expected future output will cause in the current period:

a. an increase in aggregate private spending (A) and a rightward shift in the IS curve
b. a reduction in aggregate private spending (A) and a leftward shift in the IS curve
c. a shift up in the LM curve
d. a shift down in the LM curve

3. A reduction in the expected future real interest rate will cause in the current period:

a. an increase in aggregate private spending (A) and a rightward shift in the IS curve
b. a reduction in aggregate private spending (A) and a leftward shift in the IS curve
c. a shift up in the LM curve
d. a shift down in the LM curve

4. An increase in expected future taxes (all else constant) will cause in the current period:

a. an increase in aggregate private spending (A) and a rightward shift in the IS curve
b. a reduction in aggregate private spending (A) and a leftward shift in the IS curve
c. a shift up in the LM curve
d. a shift down in the LM curve

5. A reduction in the current real interest rate is now likely to have a relatively smaller effect on current output because:

a. a change in current income, given unchanged expectations of future income, is unlikely to have much of an effect on spending
b. the LM relation depends on the nominal interest rate
c. a reduction in the current real interest rate, given unchanged expectations of future real interest rates, does not have much of an effect on spending
d. both a and c

6. An increase in future expected income will cause:

a. the LM curve to shift up in the current period
b. the LM curve to shift down in the current period
c. the LM curve in the current period to become flatter
d. have no effect on the LM curve in the current period

7. A reduction in the expected future real interest rate will cause:

a. the LM curve to shift up in the current period
b. the LM curve to shift down in the current period
c. the LM curve in the current period to become flatter
d. no effect on the LM curve in the current period

8. An increase in current income will cause:

a. an increase in the nominal interest rate and a movement along the LM curve in the current period
b. the LM curve to shift up in the current period
c. the LM curve to shift down in the current period
d. the LM curve in the current period to become flatter

9. The effects of a monetary expansion in the current period on economic activity in the current period depend on:

a. whether financial markets alter their expectations of future nominal interest rates
b. whether financial markets alter their expectations of current and future expected inflation
c. both a and b
d. none of the above

10. A reduction in expected future income will tend to cause:

a. a reduction in consumption and a leftward shift in the IS curve in the current period
b. a reduction in investment and a leftward shift in the IS curve in the current period
c. both a and b
d. a shift down in the LM curve in the current period

11. An increase in the expected future real interest rate will tend to cause:

a. a reduction in consumption and a leftward shift in the IS curve in the current period
b. a reduction in investment and a leftward shift in the IS curve in the current period
c. both a and b
d. a shift down in the LM curve in the current period

12. Suppose the Fed reduces the money supply in the current period. Further assume that individuals now expect the future real interest rate to be higher and future income to be lower. Given this information, we would expect:

a. the LM curve to shift up and the IS curve to shift left in the current period
b. the LM curve to shift down and the IS curve to shift left in the current period
c. the LM curve to shift up and the IS curve to shift right in the current period
d. the LM curve to shift down and the IS curve to shift right in the current period

13. Suppose the Fed increases the money supply in the current period. Further assume that individuals now expect the future real interest rate to be lower and future income to be higher. Given this information, we know with certainty that:

a. current income will increase
b. current real interest rate will decrease
c. current real interest rate will increase
d. current income will remain unchanged

14. Which of the following statements represents rational expectations?

a. individuals use the information they have to make predictions about the future
b. individuals know with certainty the future value of income, the interest rate, etc.
c. expectations are forward-looking
d. both a and b
e. both a and c

15. If expectations are based on animal spirits, we know that:

a. changes in expectations are random events
b. expectations are determined by backward-looking behavior
c. individuals know with certainty the future value of income, the interest rate, etc.
d. both a and b

16. If expectations are "adaptive," we know that:

a. changes in expectations are random events
b. expectations are determined by backward-looking behavior
c. individuals know with certainty the future value of income, the interest rate, etc.
d. both a and b

17. Assume that individuals consider only the short run effects of changes in expected future macroeconomic variables. Suppose individuals expect that future government spending will increase and expect that the Fed will not respond to this. Individuals will, therefore, expect:

a. future income to increase
b. future interest rates to increase
c. the IS curve to shift to the right in the future
d. all of the above

18. Assume that individuals consider only the short-run effects of changes in expected future macroeconomic variables. Suppose individuals expect a reduction in future taxes. Further assume that the Fed is not expected to respond to this reduction in future taxes. The expected reduction in future taxes will:

a. cause an increase in current income and an increase in the current real interest rate
b. cause an increase in current income and a reduction in the current real interest rate
c. cause the LM curve to shift up in the current period
d. have an ambiguous effect on the current IS curve

19. Assume that individuals consider only the short-run effects of changes in expected future macroeconomic variables. Suppose a budget is passed which calls for an increase in current and future government spending. Further assume that the Fed is not expected to respond to these changes in G. This increase in current and future G will:

a. cause an increase in current income
b. cause an increase in the current real interest rate
c. have an ambiguous effect on current income
d. both a and b

20. Assume that individuals consider only the short-run effects of changes in expected future macroeconomic variables. Suppose a budget is passed which calls for an increase in current and future government spending. Further assume that the Fed is expected to offset any effects of the changes in current and future G on current and future real interest rates. This increase in current and future G will tend to cause:

a. an increase in current income
b. an ambiguous effect on current income
c. an increase in the current real interest rate
d. a reduction in current income

21. Assume that individuals consider only the medium-run effects of changes in expected future macroeconomic variables. Suppose individuals expect that future government spending will increase and expect that the Fed will not respond to this. Individuals will, therefore, expect:

a. future income to increase
b. future interest rates to increase
c. future investment to increase
d. all of the above

22. Assume that individuals consider only the medium-run effects of changes in expected future macroeconomic variables. Suppose individuals expect that future government spending will increase and expect that the Fed will not respond to this. Given this information, we know with certainty that:

a, the IS curve in the current period will shift to the right
b. the IS curve in the current period will shift to the left
c. the IS curve in the current period will not shift
d. the effects on the position of the IS curve in the current period are ambiguous

23. Assume that individuals consider only the long-run effects of changes in expected future macroeconomic variables. Suppose individuals expect that future government spending will increase and expect that the Fed will not respond to this. Individuals will, therefore, expect:

a. future income to decrease
b. future income will not change
c. future investment to increase
d. all of the above

CHAPTER 18.
OPENNESS IN GOODS AND FINANCIAL MARKETS

OBJECTIVES, REVIEW, AND TUTORIAL

After working through the chapter and the following material, you should be able to:

(1) List and explain the three distinct notions of openness.

(2) Define the nominal exchange rate and explain what is meant by a depreciation and appreciation of the domestic currency.

(3) Define the real exchange rate and explain the determinants of the real exchange rate.

(4) Explain what the balance of payments, current account, and capital account measure.

(5) Know the distinction between GDP and GNP.

(6) Explain what factors influence an individual's decision to hold domestic versus foreign bonds.

(7) Explain what is meant by the uncovered interest parity condition.

1. THE THREE DISTINCT NOTIONS OF OPENNESS

(1) Openness in goods markets

Consumers and firms can choose between domestic and foreign goods. To restrict these choices, countries can impose <u>tariffs</u> (a tax on imported goods) or <u>quotas</u> (a restriction on the quantity of imported goods).

(2) Openness in financial markets

Financial investors can choose between domestic and foreign assets. Individuals will, therefore, compare the expected returns on U.S. and U.K. bonds. Countries can impose capital controls that restrict the flow of financial assets between countries.

(3) Openness in factor markets

This represents the opportunity of firms to choose their location and of workers to choose where they work and immigrate.

Learning Tip
You should recognize that recent developments (e.g. free trade agreements) have made economies increasingly more open in all three markets.

2. THE NOMINAL EXCHANGE RATE (E)

• The nominal exchange rate (E) equals the number of units of foreign currency you obtain with one unit of the domestic currency.
• The nominal exchange rate also represents the price of domestic currency in terms of the foreign currency.

> **Learning Tip**
>
> • The nominal exchange rate is the relative price of currencies.
> • Let E be the number of pounds one can obtain with one dollar (E = pound/\$). Suppose E = 1.8. How do we interpret this?
> - One dollar can "buy" 1.8 pounds.
> - Equivalently, it takes 1.8 pounds to buy one dollar.
> - The exchange rate, E, equals the pound price of the dollar.

An increase in E represents a nominal appreciation of the domestic currency (i.e., the dollar in this case). Suppose E increases from 1.8 to 1.9.

- This increase in E indicates that one dollar now obtains more (1.9 to be exact) pounds.
- As E increases, the dollar is now "worth" more.
- The increase in E also indicates that it takes more pounds to buy one dollar.
- The value of the pound (in terms of dollars) drops as E increases.

A reduction in E represents a nominal depreciation and has the exact opposite effects as those just described (i.e., the dollar is worth less, etc.).

> **Learning Tip**
>
> You must understand that an increase in E is a dollar appreciation while a reduction in E is a dollar deprecation. To understand this, recall the definition of E, E = pound/\$.
> - When E increases, more pounds are needed to obtain one unit of domestic currency. The value of the dollar increases and the dollar appreciates.
> - When E decreases, fewer pounds are needed to obtain one unit of domestic currency. The value of the dollar decreases and the dollar depreciates.
> - **MAJOR WARNING/ADVICE**. Previous editions of Blanchard defined the exchange rate as the dollar price of the pound (i.e., the reciprocal of E as defined above). If you look at previous exams, assignments, ... etc. based on previous editions of the text, be aware of this!

3. THE REAL EXCHANGE RATE (ε)

(1) Introduction

The real exchange rate (ε) is the price of domestic goods in terms of foreign goods. The real exchange rate is, therefore, equal to the ratio of the pound price of U.S. goods to the pound price of U.K. goods: $\varepsilon = EP/P^*$ where

- P^* is the pound price of U.K. goods.
- If we multiply P by E, we obtain the pound price of U.S. goods.
- P is the dollar price of U.S. goods.
- The ratio of EP to P^* represents the price of U.S. goods in terms of foreign goods.

(2) Real depreciation

• A reduction in ε indicates that the pound price of U.S. goods relative to the pound price of U.K. goods has decreases.
• This indicates that foreign goods have become more expensive than domestic goods.
• A reduction in ε is called a real depreciation.

(3) Real appreciation

• An increase in ε indicates that the pound price of U.S. goods relative to the pound price of U.K. goods has increased.
• This indicates that domestic goods have become more expensive than foreign goods.
• An increase in ε is called a real appreciation.

Learning Tip

• You must understand what effect changes in P, P* and E have on ε.
  • An increase in E (nominal appreciation) causes an increase in ε and a real appreciation.
  • An increase in P* causes a reduction in ε and a real depreciation.
  • An increase in P causes an increase in ε and a real appreciation.

• You must also understand that changes in ε (not E) reflect changes in the relative price of foreign and domestic goods. Why? The effects of a nominal depreciation on ε could be completely offset by a change in P and/or P* leaving ε unchanged.
• IF P and P* tend to move together, changes in E will cause similar changes in ε.

(4) Other measures of the real exchange rate

You should also understand the differences between bilateral and multilateral real exchange rates.
  • The bilateral real exchange rate measures the real exchange rate between two countries.
  • The real multilateral U.S. exchange rate (or effective real exchange rate) measures the average price of U.S. goods relative to those of its trading partners. The effective real exchange rate is a weighted average of bilateral real exchange rates. The weights used are based on import or export shares for each trading partner.

4. THE BALANCE OF PAYMENTS, THE CURRENT ACCOUNT, AND THE CAPITAL ACCOUNT

(1) Balance of payments

The balance of payments measures a country's transactions with the rest of the world.

(2) Current account

Transactions "above the line" in the balance of payments are called current account transactions. These transactions include:
• the trade balance (exports minus imports)
• net investment income
• net transfers received

The sum of these components represents the current account.

- A current account deficit implies that the United States needs to borrow from the rest of the world.
- A current account surplus implies the opposite.

(3) Capital account

Transactions "below the line" are called capital account transactions. These transactions include:

- Net increase in foreign holdings of U.S. assets (net capital flows to the United States)
- The net increase in foreign holdings of U.S. assets equals [increase in foreign holdings of U.S. assets] minus [increase in U.S. holdings of foreign assets]
- Statistical discrepancy

Learning Tip

- When the increase in foreign holdings of U.S. assets exceeds the increase in U.S. holdings of foreign assets, a capital account surplus exists.
- This capital account surplus reflects:
  - a net increase in U.S. foreign indebtedness
  - net capital flows to the United States
  - the borrowing required to finance the capital account deficit

5. DISTINCTION BETWEEN GDP AND GNP

GDP is the value added domestically (within a country).
GNP is the value added by domestically owned factors of production.
GNP = GDP plus net factor payments from the rest of the world.

Learning Tip

- For most countries, the difference between GNP and GDP is small.
- For some countries such as Kuwait, however, the difference can be significant.

6. THE DECISION TO HOLD DOMESTIC VERSUS FOREIGN FINANCIAL ASSETS

Openness in financial markets indicates that individuals have a choice of holding domestic or foreign bonds.

(1) Returns from holding one-year U.S. bonds

For every dollar you put in a one-year U.S. bond, you receive $(1 + i_t)$ dollars in one year.

(2) Expected returns from holding one-year U.K. bonds

For every one dollar you put in a one-year U.K. bond, you expect to receive $(E_t)(1 + i^*_t)/E^e_{t+1}$ dollars in one year. There are several steps required to illustrate this.

- To buy a U.K. bond, you must first obtain pounds.
- Every dollar buys E_t pounds.
- For example, if $E_t = 1.5$, one dollar obtains (or buys) 1.5 pounds.
- You take the E_t pounds and buy U.K. bonds.

- In one year, you will have $(E_t)(1 + i^*_t)$ pounds.
- Let E^e_{t+1} be the nominal exchange rate you expect to occur in one year. To convert the $(E_t)(1 + i^*_t)$ pounds back into dollars, simply divide $(E_t)(1 + i^*_t)$ by E^e_{t+1}.

(3) The interest parity condition

When we assume that financial investors want to hold only the asset with the highest rate of return, the following arbitrage relation must hold:

$$(1 + i_t) = (E_t)(1 + i^*_t)/E^e_{t+1}.$$

This relation is called the uncovered interest parity or interest parity condition.

Learning Tip

- Two factors suggest that the assumption that individuals hold only the asset with the highest return is too strong:
  (1) the existence of transaction costs of buying and selling pounds and buying U.K. bonds are ignored; and
  (2) the uncertainty (risk) about the future nominal exchange rate is ignored.

- We can ignore the decision to hold domestic versus foreign money. Why? Individuals hold money to engage in transactions. For individuals in the United States, their transactions are mostly in dollars. There is little reason to hold foreign currency since it cannot be used to buy domestic goods. Furthermore, foreign bonds would be more desirable (compared to foreign currency) since they pay interest.

7. A CLOSER LOOK AT THE INTEREST PARITY RELATION

An approximation of the arbitrage relation is:

$$i_t = i^*_t - (E^e_{t+1} - E_t)/E_t.$$

This indicates that the decision to hold domestic versus foreign bonds depends not only on a comparison of the interest rates, but also on an assessment of what will happen to the exchange rate over the next year.

- When you buy a U.K. bond, you receive interest income (i^*) and, if the dollar is expected to appreciate, you will receive pounds in one year that will be less in terms of dollars.
- The term $(E^e_{t+1} - E_t)/E_t$ represents this exchange gain or loss from an expected depreciation or appreciation of the dollar.
- The expected returns from holding U.K. bonds is, therefore, equal to the foreign interest rate ***minus*** the expected appreciation of the dollar (i.e., $i^* - (E^e_{t+1} - E_t)/E_t$).
- If the term $(E^e_{t+1} - E_t)/E_t$ is positive, individuals expect the dollar to appreciate and the pound to depreciate. There will be exchange losses from holding pound-denominated bonds.
- If the term $(E^e_{t+1} - E_t)/E_t$ is negative, individuals expect the dollar to depreciate and the pound to appreciate. There will be exchange gains from holding pound-denominated bonds.

Learning Tip

- Will you always buy U.S. bonds when $i > i^*$? Not necessarily. If the expected rate of depreciation of the dollar exceeds the interest rate differential, the return from holding U.K. bonds will be greater.
- Will you always buy U.K. bonds when $i^* > i$? Not necessarily. If the expected rate of appreciation of the dollar is greater than the interest rate differential, the expected rate of return on the U.S. bonds will be greater.

SELF-TEST QUESTIONS

1. What are the three notions of openness (Introduction)?

2. Briefly discuss what tariffs, quotas and capital controls are (1).

3. Explain how exports can exceed GDP (1).

4. Define the nominal exchange rate, E (1).

5. What effect does an increase in E have on the value of the dollar (1)?

6. When the dollar depreciates, what happens to E (1)?

7. Define the real exchange rate (1).

8. What happens to the price of U.S. goods in terms of U.K. goods when the real exchange rate increases (1)?

9. Does an increase in ε correspond to a real appreciation or real depreciation of the domestic currency (1)?

10. What does the balance of payments measure (2)?

11. How is the real multilateral U.S. exchange rate constructed (2)?

12. What are the different types of transactions included in the current account (2)?

13. What are the different types of transactions included in the capital account (2)?

14. Suppose the current nominal exchange rate between the dollar and the pound is E_t. How many pounds can you obtain with one dollar (2)?

15. What does the expression E^e_{t+1} represent (2)?

16. Suppose you have one dollar to invest in U.K. bonds. What is the expression that represents the expected return on U.K. bonds measured in dollars (2)?

17. What does the expression $(E^e - E)/E$ represent (2)?

18. Suppose the one-year nominal interest rate in the United States is 6% and 4% in Germany. Further assume that the arbitrage relation holds. Given this information, is the dollar expected to appreciate or depreciate over the coming year? How much (2)?

REVIEW PROBLEMS

1. Suppose the pound/dollar exchange rate on Monday is 1.5 and on the following Friday is 1.6.
a. Briefly discuss what has happened to the price of the domestic currency in terms of the foreign currency?
b. How many pounds can 1 dollar buy on Monday? How many pounds can 1 dollar buy on Friday?
c. Has the value of the dollar increased or decreased during the week? Briefly explain.
d. Has the dollar appreciated or depreciated during the week?
e. What happened to E during the week?

2. Suppose the nominal exchange rate, E (as defined in the chapter), decreases.
a. What does the drop in E suggest about the price of the foreign currency in terms of dollars?
b. Has the value of the dollar increased or decreased?
c. Has the dollar appreciated or depreciated?

3. Suppose the dollar/pound nominal exchange rate one week ago was 1.5.
a. If the dollar has depreciated by 10% during the past week, what is the current dollar/pound exchange rate?
b. If the dollar has depreciated by 20% during the past week, what is the current dollar/pound exchange rate?
c. If the dollar has appreciated by 10% during the past week, what is the current dollar/pound exchange rate?
d. If the dollar has appreciated by 20% during the past week, what is the current dollar/pound exchange rate?

4. Suppose a bottle of domestic (U.S.) wine is $10 and suppose a U.K. bottle of wine costs 30 pounds.
a. For each of the following dollar/pound exchange rates, calculate the ratio of the pound price of a bottle of U.S. wine to the pound price of a bottle of U.K. wine: 1.2, 1.4, and 1.6.
b. Based on your analysis, what happens to the price of a U.S. good (bottle of wine) in terms of a U.K. good (bottle of wine) as E increases?
c. Based on your analysis, what happens to the price of a U.S. good (bottle of wine) in terms of a U.K. good (bottle of wine) as E decreases?

5. Let P be the GDP deflator in the United States and P* be the GDP deflator in the U.K. Suppose $P = 1.1$ and $P^* = 1.6$.
a. Calculate the real exchange rate for each of the following dollar/pound nominal exchange rates: 1.2, 1.4, and 1.6.
b. What happens to the real exchange rate as E increases?
c. What happens to the price of U.S. goods in terms of U.K. goods as E increases? Briefly explain.
d. Does an increase in E cause a real appreciation or depreciation of the dollar?

6. Use the following information to answer this question.

	E	P	P*
1996	1.5	1.5	1.2
1997	1.6	1.65	1.25

Note: E is the pound/dollar nominal exchange rate.

a. Calculate the real exchange rate in 1996 and 1997.
b. What was the percentage change in the real exchange rate between 1996 and 1997? Does this change in the real exchange rate represent a real appreciation or depreciation?
c. Calculate the percentage change in the nominal exchange rate between the two years. Does this change represent a nominal appreciation or depreciation of the dollar?
d. Calculate the percentage change in P and P*.
e. Was the nominal appreciation (or depreciation) greater than, less than or equal to the real appreciation (or depreciation)? Explain.

7. Suppose P and P* are both increasing. Now suppose that the dollar experiences a 5% nominal depreciation.
a. Which country is experiencing the higher rate of inflation if the domestic currency experiences a real appreciation? Briefly explain.
b. Which country is experiencing the higher rate of inflation if the domestic currency experiences a real depreciation?
c. Compare the changes in P and P* if the real exchange rate does not change.

8. Use the following information and equation (18.4) in the chapter to answer this question: $i^* = .10$; $E_t = 1.5$; and $E^e_{t+1} = 1.4$
a. Based on the above information, what must the domestic interest rate be for the arbitrage relation to hold?
b. Is $i = i^*$? If i does not equal i*, which bond has the highest expected return (measured in dollars)? Explain.

9. Use the following information and equation (18.4) to answer this question: $i^* = .06$; and $E_t = 1.5$
a. Suppose $E^e_{t+1} = 1.53$. Do individuals expect the dollar to appreciate or depreciate? Calculate the expected rate of appreciation or depreciation. Based on your analysis, what must the domestic interest rate be to satisfy the arbitrage relation?
b. Now, suppose $E^e_{t+1} = 1.55$. Do individuals expect the dollar to appreciate or depreciate? Calculate the expected rate of appreciation or depreciation. Based on your analysis, what must the domestic interest rate be to satisfy the arbitrage relation?
c. Now, suppose $E^e_{t+1} = 1.45$. Do individuals expect the dollar to appreciate or depreciate? Calculate the expected rate of appreciation or depreciation. Based on your analysis, what must the domestic interest rate be to satisfy the arbitrage relation?

10. Suppose the dollar is expected to depreciate during the next year. Does the arbitrage relation indicate that the U.S. interest rate is greater than, less than or equal to the foreign interest rate? Briefly explain.

11. Suppose the dollar is expected to appreciate during the next year. Does the arbitrage relation indicate that the U.S. interest rate is greater than, less than or equal to the foreign interest rate? Briefly explain.

12. For each of the following cases, determine whether an individual should buy U.S. bonds or foreign bonds.

a. $i = 4\%$, $i^* = 6\%$, expected depreciation of the dollar of 3%
b. $i = 4\%$, $i^* = 6\%$, expected depreciation of the dollar of 1%
c. $i = 4\%$, $i^* = 6\%$, expected depreciation of the dollar of 2%
d. $i = 6\%$, $i^* = 5\%$, expected depreciation of the dollar of 3%
e. $i = 6\%$, $i^* = 5\%$, expected depreciation of the dollar of 1%
f. $i = 6\%$, $i^* = 5\%$, expected depreciation of the dollar of 2%
g. $i = 5\%$, $i^* = 5\%$, expected depreciation of the dollar of 3%
h. $i = 5\%$, $i^* = 5\%$, expected appreciation of the dollar of 1%
i. $i = 5\%$, $i^* = 5\%$, expected appreciation of the dollar of 2%
j. $i = 5\%$, $i^* = 5\%$, expected depreciation of the dollar of 0%

MULTIPLE CHOICE QUESTIONS

1. The nominal exchange rate is:

a. the number of units of foreign currency you can obtain with one unit of domestic currency
b. the price of domestic currency in terms of foreign currency
c. the number of units of domestic currency you can get from one unit of foreign currency
d. both a and b
e. both b and c

2. The real exchange rate is:

a. EP/P*
b. the price of foreign goods in terms of domestic goods
c. the price of domestic goods in terms of foreign goods
d. both a and c

3. An increase in E represents a:

a. real appreciation
b. real depreciation
c. nominal appreciation
d. nominal depreciation

4. When the value of the dollar (in terms of pounds) increases, we know that:

a. E increases
b. E decreases
c. the dollar has depreciated
d. none of the above

5. A depreciation of the dollar indicates that:

a. E has decreased
b. it takes more domestic currency to purchase one unit of foreign currency
c. E has increased
d. both a and b

6. When the dollar appreciates, we know that:

a. the dollar price of foreign currency has decreased
b. the dollar price of foreign currency has increased
c. E has decreased
d. none of the above

7. Which of the following expressions represents the real exchange rate?

a. EP*/P
b. EP/P*
c. P*/EP
d. P/EP*

8. A reduction in the real exchange rate indicates that:

a. foreign goods are now relatively more expensive compared to domestic goods
b. domestic goods are now relatively more expensive compared to foreign goods
c. a real depreciation of the domestic currency has occurred
d. both a and c

9. An increase in the real exchange rate indicates:

a. foreign goods are now relatively more expensive compared to domestic goods
b. domestic goods are now relatively more expensive compared to foreign goods
c. a real depreciation of the domestic currency has occurred
d. a real appreciation of the domestic currency has occurred
e. both b and d

10. Which of the following events would cause a real depreciation of the domestic currency?

a. reduction in E
b. increase in E
c. reduction in P*
d. increase in P

11. Which of the following events would cause a real appreciation of the domestic currency?

a. reduction in E
b. reduction in P*
c. reduction in P
d. all of the above
e. none of the above

12. Which of the following transactions is included in the current accounts?

a. statistical discrepancy
b. net investment income
c. increase in foreign holdings of U.S. assets
d. increase in U.S. holdings of foreign assets

13. Which of the following transactions is included in the capital account?

a. trade balance
b. net investment income
c. increase in foreign holdings of U.S. assets
d. all of the above
e. both b and c

14. Suppose a country has a current account deficit. Given this information, we know that:

a. this country's exports exceed its imports
b. this country lends to the rest of the world
c. a capital account deficit exists
d. a capital account surplus exists

15. Based on the definition of GDP and GNP, we know that:

a. GNP = GDP + net factor payments from the rest of the world
b. GDP = GNP + net factor payments from the rest of the world
c. GNP = GDP + the balance of payments
d. GNP = GDP + net investment income
e. GNP = GDP + net capital flows from the rest of the world

16. Which of the following expressions represents the expected return (in dollars) from holding a U.K. bond:

a. i^*
b. $(1 + i)E^e_{t+1}$
c. $(1/E^e_{t+1})(1 + i^*)E_t$
d. $(1/E_t)(1 + i^*)E^e_{t+1}$

17. Assume the interest parity condition holds. If $i = 5\%$ and $i^* = 7\%$, we know that:

a. individuals will hold only domestic bonds
b. individuals will hold only foreign bonds
c. the dollar is expected to appreciate by 2%
d. the dollar is expected to depreciate by 2%

18. Assume the interest parity condition holds. If $i = 10\%$ and $i^* = 8\%$, we know that:

a. the expected return on U.S. bonds is greater than the expected return on U.K. bonds
b. the expected return on U.S. bonds is less than the expected return on U.K. bonds
c. the dollar is expected to appreciate by 2%
d. the dollar is expected to depreciate by 2%

19. Assume the interest parity condition holds and that individuals expect the dollar to appreciate by 4% during the next year. Given this information, we know that:

a. $i > i^*$
b. $i < i^*$
c. $i = i^*$
d. individuals will hold only U.S. bonds

20. Assume the interest parity condition holds. Suppose i* = 10% and that the dollar is expected to depreciate by 2% during the next year. For every dollar an individual invests in a foreign bond, she can expect to receive how many dollars in one year?

a. 1.02
b. 1.08
c. 1.10
d. 1.12

21. Assume the interest parity condition holds. Suppose i* = 10% and that the dollar is expected to appreciate by 3% during the next year. For every dollar an individual invests in a foreign bond, she can expect to receive how many dollars in one year?

a. 1.03
b. 1.07
c. 1.10
d. 1.13

22. Suppose i = 10%, i* = 8% and the dollar is expected to depreciate by 3% during the next year. Given this information, we know that:

a. individuals will prefer to hold U.S. bonds
b. individuals will prefer to hold U.K. bonds
c. the expected return from holding a U.K. bond (measured in dollars) will equal 5%
d. the expected return from holding a U.K. bond (measured in dollars) will equal 11%
e. both a and c
f. both b and d

23. Suppose i = 10%, i* = 8% and the dollar is expected to appreciate by 3% during the next year. Given this information, we know that:

a. individuals will prefer to hold U.S. bonds
b. individuals will prefer to hold U.K. bonds
c. the expected return from holding a U.K. bond (measured in dollars) will equal 5%
d. the expected return from holding a U.K. bond (measured in dollars) will equal 11%
e. both a and c
f. both b and d

CHAPTER 19. THE GOODS MARKET IN AN OPEN ECONOMY

OBJECTIVES, REVIEW, AND TUTORIAL

After working through the chapter and the following material, you should be able to:

(1) Know the distinction between domestic demand for goods and the demand for domestic goods.

(2) Understand the determinants of imports and exports.

(3) Explain the determinants of equilibrium output and the trade balance.

(4) Examine the effects of changes in domestic demand on output and net exports.

(5) Examine and graphically illustrate the effects of foreign demand on output and net exports.

(6) Understand that the multiplier is smaller in an open economy.

(7) Explain the effects of a real depreciation on output, imports, and net exports.

(8) Examine the combined effects of changes in the exchange rate and fiscal policy on output and the trade balance.

(9) Discuss what is meant by the Marshall-Lerner condition and the J-curve.

(10) Understand the relationship among saving, investment, and the trade deficit.

1. DOMESTIC DEMAND AND THE DEMAND FOR DOMESTIC GOODS

(1) Domestic demand for goods

This represents the demand for goods by individuals, governments, and firms residing in the country. It, therefore, equals: $C + I + G$.

(2) Demand for domestic goods

Two adjustments must be made to obtain the demand for domestic goods: (1) add exports; and (2) subtract imports. It, therefore, equals: $C + I + G + X - IM/\varepsilon$.

Learning Tip

- Why add exports? X represents the demand for domestic goods that comes from abroad.
- Why subtract imports? Some of the goods bought by domestic residents, firms, and governments may include foreign goods.
- Why do we divide IM by the real exchange rate, ε? IM is the quantity of imports. To express this quantity of imports in terms of domestic goods, divide IM by the relative price of domestic goods in terms of foreign goods.

2. DETERMINANTS OF EXPORTS AND IMPORTS

(1) Imports (IM)

• As domestic income (Y) rises, C and I both increase. Some of this increase in C and I will include foreign goods. Hence, IM increases as Y increases.
• An increase in ε, the real exchange rate, represents a real appreciation of the domestic currency.
• An increase in ε also indicates that domestic goods are now relatively more expensive. An increase in the relative price of domestic goods will cause an increase in IM.

(2) Exports (X)

• As foreign income (Y*) rises, foreign C and foreign I both increase. Some of this increase in foreign C and foreign I will include U.S. goods. Hence, X increases as Y* increases.
• A real depreciation (a reduction in ε) corresponds to a decrease in the relative price of U.S. goods. The U.S. goods become more attractive (i.e., relatively cheaper), and X increases.

3. EQUILIBRIUM, THE TRADE BALANCE, AND THE MULTIPLIER

(1) Equilibrium output

Equilibrium output occurs when output equals the demand for domestic goods (Y = Z):

$Y = C + I + G + X - IM/\varepsilon$.

(2) The trade balance

The trade balance (net exports, NX) is the difference between exports and imports: $NX = X(Y^*, \varepsilon) - IM(Y, \varepsilon)/\varepsilon$. NX is shown graphically in Figure 19-1. The NX line is downward sloping because an increase in Y will cause an increase in IM. The higher IM, given X, causes NX to decline (a trade surplus will shrink, or a trade deficit will grow).

Learning Tip

There are several features of the NX line that you must understand.
• For a given value of ε and Y*, the equilibrium level of Y will determine the trade balance. Equilibrium output occurs when Y = Z.
• Equilibrium Y does NOT occur when NX = 0!
• An increase in Y* will cause an increase in X and cause the NX line to shift up by the change in X.
• An increase in ε will cause X to decrease and IM to increase and NX will fall (assuming the Marshall-Lerner condition holds) at each level of Y. The NX line will shift down.
• A change in Y does NOT cause a shift of the NX line, only a movement along it.

(3) The multiplier

An increase in Y causes an increase in demand (the ZZ line is upward sloping).

- In a closed economy, all of the increase in Y falls on domestic goods.
- In an open economy, some of the increase in Y falls on foreign goods (IM). The ZZ line is, therefore, flatter.
- The flatter ZZ line corresponds to a smaller multiplier.

4. CHANGES IN DEMAND AND THEIR EFFECTS ON Y AND NX

(1) Changes in demand

Changes in demand represent changes in C, I, and/or G that fall entirely on domestic goods.

- Any change of this type will cause the ZZ line to shift.
- The size of the shift equals the initial change in demand.
- Equilibrium will occur at the point where Y = Z.
- As Y changes, IM will change as we move along the NX line; therefore, NX will change.
- For example, a decrease in ZZ will cause lower Y, lower IM, and an increase in NX (either a trade surplus increases or a trade deficit falls).

Learning Tip

- You must understand that changes in domestic demand do not cause shifts in the NX line.
- Changes in Y cause movements along the NX line and cause the trade balance to change.
- Exports will not change since Y* and ε have not changed.
- The multiplier is smaller here (compared to a closed economy) because some of the change in demand now also goes to foreign goods.

(2) Changes in foreign demand (ΔY^*)

Changes in foreign demand represent changes in X and/or IM [I will review the effects of changes in the real exchange rate in the next section]. An increase in Y* will cause an increase in exports (X). The increase in X has two effects: (1) ZZ shifts up by the change in X; and (2) the NX line shifts up by the change in X.

- The effects of the change in X are the same as those described above.
- The new equilibrium again occurs where Y = Z.
- The change in Y equals the change in X times the multiplier.
- As Y increases, IM will rise.
- The increase in IM is, however, smaller than the increase in X.
- NX, therefore, increase as X increases (the trade balance improves).

Learning Tip

Make sure you understand the discussion that accompanies Figure 19-4.

- Any increase in X will cause Y and IM to increase. Despite the income-induced increase in imports, the trade balance will improve when X increases.
- Any reduction in X will cause Y and IM to fall. Despite the income-induced reduction in imports, the trade balance will deteriorate when exports fall.

5. THE REAL EXCHANGE RATE, NET EXPORTS, AND OUTPUT

The real exchange rate, ε, is the relative price of domestic goods in terms of foreign goods. A reduction in ε (a real depreciation) will cause:
(1) an increase in X as domestic goods are relatively cheaper;
(2) a reduction in the quantity of imports (IM) as foreign goods are relatively more expensive; and
(3) an increase in the price of imports and, therefore, an increase in the import bill. The same quantity of imports now costs more to buy.

For a depreciation to cause an increase in NX, the combined effects of (1) and (2) must exceed the effects of (3). The condition for which a depreciation causes NX to increase is called the Marshall-Lerner condition.

Learning Tip

If the Marshall-Lerner condition does NOT hold, a depreciation would cause NX to fall. Why? The effects of (3) would dominate the combined effects of (1) and (2).

Assuming the Marshall-Lerner condition holds, a reduction in the real exchange rate will cause an increase in X, a decrease in IM, and an increase in NX. As NX increases, the ZZ line shifts up by the change in NX, and the NX line shifts up by the change in NX.

The effects of a reduction in the real exchange rate on Y and on the trade balance are the same as the effects of a change in Y*:

- Y increases
- as Y increases, IM increases but not enough to offset the initial increase in NX
- the trade balance improves

6. EXCHANGE RATE POLICY AND FISCAL POLICY

By now, you should recognize the following:

(1) increases in G cause Y to increase and NX to fall
(2) reductions in G cause Y to fall and NX to increase
(3) reductions in ε (depreciations) cause Y to increase and NX to increase
(4) increases in ε (appreciations) cause Y to fall and NX to fall

Therefore,

- To raise Y, governments can: (1) increase G; and/or (2) reduce ε.
- To improve the trade balance, governments can: (1) reduce G; and/or (2) reduce ε.

Learning Tip

- Different situations can exist causing governments to pursue a variety of combinations of exchange rate and fiscal policies.
- You should review Table 19-1 ("Exchange-Rate and Fiscal Policy Combinations").

7. THE J-CURVE

(1) Introduction and review

First, you should review the material in #5. If the Marshall-Lerner condition does NOT hold, a depreciation (reduction in ε) will cause NX to fall. For example, suppose the real exchange rate decreases by 8%. This 8% depreciation causes the price of imports to increase by 8%. Further assume that the quantity of exports increases by 2% and that the quantity of imports falls by 3%.
• In this case, the depreciation has a relatively greater effect on the price of imports than on the quantities of X and IM.
• This depreciation will also cause a deterioration of the trade balance (NX falls).

(2) Graphical depiction of this adjustment

• Over time, the quantities of X and IM will respond to the change in the real exchange rate.
• Eventually, this depreciation will cause the trade balance to improve.
• The graphical representation of this adjustment is called the J-curve.

Learning Tip

• If the Marshall-Lerner condition does NOT initially hold, a depreciation will cause NX to fall and have a negative effect on domestic output.
• The existence of the J-curve effect can also explain the lagged response of U.S. net exports to real depreciations and appreciations during the 1980s.

8. SAVING, INVESTMENT, AND NET EXPORTS

You must become familiar with the implications of the following equilibrium condition:

$NX = S + (T - G) - I.$

(1) Trade balance

• If NX > 0, total saving exceeds investment (and, therefore, a current account surplus and capital account deficit exist).
• If NX < 0, total saving is less than investment and the country must borrow the difference.

(2) Budget deficit

An increase in the budget deficit will result in: (1) an increase in S; (2) reduction in I; or (3) a reduction in NX.

(3) Saving

An increase in total saving will cause: (1) an increase in I; or (2) an increase in NX.

SELF-TEST QUESTIONS

1. What are the components of domestic demand for goods (1)?

2. What are the components of demand for domestic goods (1)?

3. Why must we divide IM by ε to obtain the value of imports (1)?

4. What are the two determinants of imports? Briefly explain how an increase in each affects imports (1).

5. What are the two determinants of exports? Briefly explain how an increase in each affects exports (1).

6. Why is the NX line downward sloping (1)?

7. What happens to the size of the multiplier after introducing net exports (3)?

8. What effect does an increase in G have on demand, the ZZ line, imports, exports and net exports (3)?

9. An increase in Y* causes an increase in exports, an increase in income (Y) and an increase in imports (as Y increases). Given that both exports and imports increase, what happens to the trade balance as Y* increases (3)?

10. What effect will an increase in ε have on the quantities of imports and exports (4)?

11. What effect will an increase in ε have on the cost of imports (4)?

12. Briefly explain what is meant by the Marshall-Lerner condition (4)?

13. If the Marshall-Lerner condition holds, what effect will an increase in ε have on the NX relation (4)?

14. Suppose policy makers want to reduce a trade deficit while leaving Y unchanged. What type of exchange rate and/or fiscal policy can they pursue (4)?

15. Suppose the Marshall-Lerner condition does NOT hold. A 12% depreciation will have what effect on the quantities of imports, exports and on the trade balance (5)?

16. What does the J-curve represent (5)?

17. In 2006, the United States had a trade deficit. What does this suggest about the relation among private saving, public saving, and investment (6)?

18. What are the possible effects of a country increasing its saving (private or public) (6)?

REVIEW PROBLEMS

1. Suppose you are given the following information about an economy: C = 1200; I = 300; G = 500; X = 450; and IM = 400. Further assume that all variables are expressed in terms of domestic goods.

a. Calculate the level of "domestic demand for goods," the level of "demand for domestic goods" and net exports. What is the difference between the demand for domestic goods and the domestic demand for goods? Compare this with the trade balance.

b. Repeat the analysis in part a. This time, however, assume IM = 500 and that all other variables are the same.

c. Repeat the analysis in a. This time, however, assume that X = 400. Use the original values of the variables.

d. Based on your analysis in parts a, b and c, under what condition will the demand for domestic goods be greater than, less than or equal to the domestic demand for goods?

2. Suppose the goods market is represented by the following behavioral equations.

$C = 500 + .5Y_D$ $\quad$ $I = 500 - 2000r + .1Y$ $\quad$ $G = 500$

$X = .1Y^* - 100\varepsilon$ $\quad$ $IM = .1Y + 100\varepsilon$ $\quad$ $T = 400$

$Y^* = 2000$ $\quad$ $r = .05$ (5%) $\quad$ $\varepsilon = 1$

$Z = C + I + G + X - IM/\varepsilon$ $\quad$ $Y = Z$ in equilibrium

a. Calculate equilibrium GDP (Y).

b. Given your answer in a, calculate C, I, X and IM.

c. At this level of output, is the economy experiencing a trade surplus or deficit?

d. Suppose G increases by 100 (to 600). Calculate the new equilibrium level of output. What is the size of the multiplier?

e. Based on your answer to d, calculate the new level of IM. Calculate the change in net exports caused by this increase in G.

3. Repeat the analysis in #2 (parts a - d). This time, however, assume that the marginal propensity to import is .2. That is, $IM = .2Y + 100/\varepsilon$. Assume all other variables are the same.

4. This question refers to your analysis in #2 and #3. Compare the changes in Y caused by the increase in G in #2 and #3. What happened to the size of the multiplier as the marginal propensity to import increases?

5. For each of the following events, assume that the goods market is initially in equilibrium and that a trade surplus exists (NX > 0) at the initial level of output. Explain what effect each event will have on the demand for domestic goods, the ZZ line, equilibrium output, exports, imports, the trade balance and the NX line.

a. tax cut

b. reduction in G

c. decrease in Y*

d. increase in ε

e. a simultaneous reduction in ε and increase in G

6. Suppose the domestic economy is initially experiencing a trade deficit. Further assume that government officials would like to eliminate the trade deficit.

a. What type of (domestic) policy could be pursued to eliminate the trade deficit? What effect would this policy have on output? Explain.

b. What type of exchange rate policy could be pursued to eliminate the trade deficit? What effect would this policy have on output? Explain.

c. Suppose domestic policy makers can put pressure on foreign policy makers to alter their fiscal policy. What type of foreign fiscal policy could be implemented to eliminate the trade deficit? What effect would this policy have on domestic and foreign output? Explain.

7. Assume that trade is balanced ($NX = 0$) at the initial level of output. Further assume that the government wants to increase Y while leaving trade in balance. Discuss and explain what type of policies could be implemented to achieve this goal.

8. Assume that $NX < 0$ and that the government wants to increase Y and simultaneously eliminate the trade deficit at the new equilibrium level of output. Discuss and explain what type of policies could be implemented to achieve this goal.

9. Assume that Y is too high and that $NX > 0$. Further assume that the government wants to reduce Y without changing the trade surplus. Discuss and explain what type of policies could be implemented to achieve this goal.

10. For this question, assume the Marshall-Lerner condition does NOT hold. Further assume that there is a trade deficit at the initial level of output. Now suppose that a real depreciation occurs.

a. Discuss and explain what effect this depreciation will have on X, IM, NX, the NX line, the ZZ line and domestic output. In the graph below, illustrate the effects of this depreciation. Clearly illustrate in the graph, the new equilibrium.

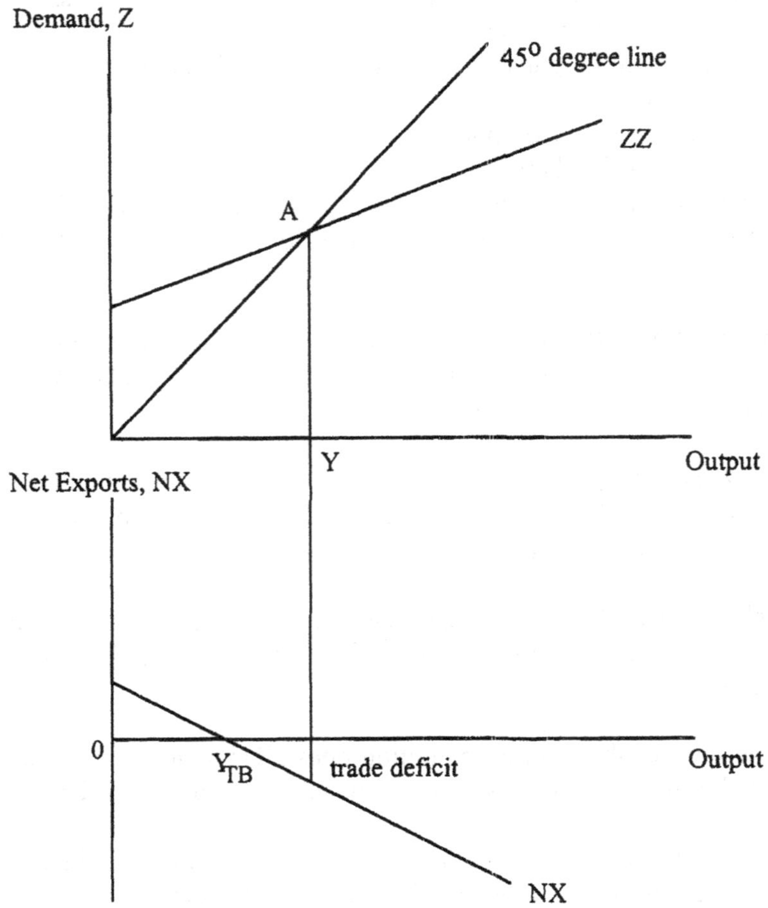

b. Based on your analysis in a, what type of exchange rate policy should be pursued in the short run (when the Marshall-Lerner condition does not hold) to increase economic activity? Explain.

11. Suppose the real exchange rate depreciates by 12%. For each of the following cases, briefly explain whether the Marshall-Lerner condition holds and explain what effect the 12% real depreciation will have on NX and Y.

a. X increases by 4%, IM falls by 6%
b. X increases by 7%, IM falls by 4%
c. X increases by 7%, IM falls by 6%
d. X increases by 6%, IM falls by 7%
e. X increases by 5%, IM falls by 9%

12. Assume the Marshall-Lerner condition holds. Use the equation provided below to answer the following question.

$$NX = S + (T - G) - I.$$

For each of the following events, explain what happens to net exports, output, and to each of the variables on the right-hand side of the above equation.

a. decrease in Y^*

b. decrease in T

c. increase in ε

d. decrease in G

e. simultaneous decrease in G and decrease in Y^*

MULTIPLE CHOICE QUESTIONS

NOTE: Unless specified otherwise, assume the Marshall-Lerner condition holds.

Use the information provided below to answer questions 1 and 2. Assume the domestic economy is in equilibrium and that:

C = 1000   I = 200 G = 400   Exports = 300   Imports = 350

All of the above variables are measured in terms of domestic goods.

1. The level of "demand for domestic goods" is:

a. 1550
b. 1600
c. 1900
d. 2250

2. The level of "domestic demand for goods" is:

a. 1550
b. 1600
c. 1900
d. 2250

3. Which of the following expressions represents the "demand for domestic goods"?

a. C + I + G
b. C + I + G + X
c. C + I + G + X/ε - IM
d. all of the above
e. none of the above

4. Which of the following expressions represents net exports (NX)?

a. X - IM
b. IM - X
c. IM - εX
d. X - IM/ε

5. Which of the following events would cause a reduction in exports?

a. reduction in ε
b. increase in Y
c. reduction in Y*
d. all of the above

6. Which of the following events would cause a reduction in imports?

a. increase in Y*
b. decrease in Y*
c. reduction in ε
d. an increase in Y

7. The net export line is downward sloping because of the effects of:

a. Y on IM
b. Y* on X
c. ε on X
d. ε on IM

8. In the model presented in this chapter, a reduction in G will cause:

a. both the ZZ line and NX line to shift down by the change in G
b. a reduction in Y and a reduction in imports
c. an increase in exports and an increase in net exports
d. an increase in net exports and the net export line to shift up

9. Which of the following events will cause both Y and NX to increase?

a. reduction in ε
b. reduction in Y*
c. increase in G
d. reduction in T

10. An increase in the marginal propensity to import will cause:

a. the ZZ line to become flatter and a given change in G to have a smaller effect on output
b. the ZZ line to become flatter and a given change in G to have a larger effect on output
c. the ZZ line to become steeper and a given change in G to have a smaller effect on output
d. the ZZ line to become steeper and a given change in G to have a larger effect on output

11. Assume the Marshall-Lerner condition holds. A real appreciation will cause:

a. the NX line to shift up
b. a reduction in NX
c. an increase in Y
d. all of the above

12. A reduction in Y* will tend to cause:

a. the ZZ line to shift down
b. the NX line to shift down
c. a reduction in Y
d. a reduction in NX
e. all of the above
f. none of the above

13. Suppose a government wishes to increase Y and leave NX unchanged. The government, therefore, should:

a. increase G
b. reduce T
c. increase G and reduce ε
d. reduce ε

14. Suppose a government wishes to reduce Y and increase NX. Which of the following policies would most likely achieve this?

a. reduce ε
b. reduce G
c. increase G and reduce ε
d. increase ε

15. Suppose the Marshall-Lerner condition does NOT hold. A real depreciation will tend to cause:

a. a reduction in NX and a reduction in Y
b. an increase in NX and a reduction in Y
c. an increase in NX and an increase in Y
d. a reduction in NX and an increase in Y

16. The J-curve illustrates the effects of:

a. Y on NX
b. Y* on exports
c. a real depreciation on NX
d. Y on imports

17. The goods market is in equilibrium when:

a. NX = 0
b. Y equals the demand for domestic goods
c. Y equals domestic demand for goods
d. domestic demand equals demand for domestic goods

18. In the model presented in this chapter, a reduction in the budget deficit could cause:

a. an increase in NX
b. and increase in I
c. a reduction in saving
d. all of the above

19. In the model presented in this chapter, a trade surplus (NX > 0) indicates that:

a. public plus private saving > investment
b. a budget deficit exists
c. there exists a budget surplus
d. the economy is in equilibrium

CHAPTER 20.
OUTPUT, THE INTEREST RATE, AND THE EXCHANGE RATE

OBJECTIVES, REVIEW, AND TUTORIAL

After working through the chapter and the following material , you should be able to:

(1) Understand what is meant by equilibrium in the goods and financial markets (review).

(2) Become familiar with the assumptions and simplifications in this chapter.

(3) Understand the interest parity condition and what it implies about the relation between the interest rate and the exchange rate.

(4) Understand the open-economy version of the IS-LM model.

(5) Explain the effects of fiscal and monetary policy in the open economy under flexible exchange rates.

(6) Discuss the role of monetary policy under fixed exchange rates.

(7) Examine the effects of fiscal policy under fixed exchange rates.

(8) Understand how changes in capital mobility alter the ability of monetary policy to affect domestic output under fixed exchange rates.

1. A REVIEW OF THE GOODS AND FINANCIAL MARKETS EQUILIBRIUM

(1) Assumptions

In this chapter, we assume:
- The Marshall-Lerner condition holds.
- The aggregate price level (both domestic and foreign) is constant.
- The expected future exchange rate ($\overline{E}^e$) is given (i.e., does not change).

Learning Tip
• The first assumption implies that a reduction in the real exchange rate (a depreciation) will cause an increase in NX.
• The second assumption implies that inflation is zero and, therefore, that $i = r$.
• The second assumption also implies that $\varepsilon = E$.

(2) Goods market

The goods market is in equilibrium when output equals demand. This condition is represented graphically by the IS relation. You should understand that:

- An increase in the interest rate (i) will cause a reduction in I, a reduction in demand, and a reduction in output
- A reduction in E (depreciation) will cause an increase in NX, an increase in demand, and an increase in output.

(3) Financial market (money versus bonds)

Financial market equilibrium occurs when the supply of money equals the demand for money. This condition is represented graphically by the LM relation.

Learning Tip

- The demand for domestic money is assumed to be determined solely by domestic residents. That is, we assume that Germans do not hold dollars.
- An increase in Y causes an increase in money demand and an increase in i.
- An increase in the money supply causes a reduction in i.

2. THE INTEREST PARITY CONDITION AND THE DETERMINANTS OF THE EXCHANGE RATE

The interest parity condition indicates that the domestic interest rate must equal the foreign interest rate plus the expected rate of depreciation of the domestic currency. The interest parity condition can be rearranged to obtain the following:

$$E = \{(1+i)/(1+i^*)\} \overline{E}^e.$$

This implies a positive relation between E and i. Why? Suppose the interest parity condition holds and that i increases.

- The increase in i makes domestic bonds relatively more attractive.
- Financial investors will switch out of foreign bonds and into domestic bonds.
- To buy domestic bonds, investors must first obtain dollars. This causes an increase in the demand for the dollar.
- The increase in the demand for the dollar causes an increase in the price of the dollar. The dollar appreciates (E increases).
- Hence, an increase in i causes an appreciation (an increase) in E.
- The interest parity (IP) relation illustrates this positive relation between i and E (given i^* and $\overline{E}^e$).

Learning Tip

You must understand the above discussion which implies that E is a decreasing function of i.
- An increase in i causes an appreciation and an increase in E.
- A reduction in i causes a depreciation and a reduction in E.

You must also understand how much E must change given $\overline{E}^e$. Suppose i increases by 2%.
- This will cause the dollar to appreciate by 2% today.
- With $\overline{E}^e$ unchanged, the dollar is now expected to depreciate by 2% over the coming year.
- This expected 2% depreciation of the dollar corresponds to a 2% appreciation of the pound.
- In fact, the pound must be expected to appreciate by 2% to compensate for the 2% increase in i.

3. THE OPEN ECONOMY VERSION OF THE IS-LM MODEL

Y, i, and E will be determined simultaneously given the IS, LM, and IP relations.

(1) The IS relation

Output depends on i, E, and the other factors (i.e., T, G, Y*, i*, and $\overline{E}^e$) included in the equilibrium condition. An increase in i now has two effects on Y:
- I falls, demand falls, and output falls
- Given the IP relation, the increase in i causes an appreciation, a reduction in NX, a reduction in demand, and a reduction in output.

These changes in I and NX will have a multiplier effect on Y.

(2) The LM relation

It is the same as before.

(3) The IP relation

It is the same as above.

Learning Tip

Make sure you can explain why the IP relation is upward sloping.

You may also be required to understand how changes in i* and $\overline{E}^e$ affect the position of the IP curve.

(1) The foreign interest rate
- An increase in the foreign interest rate will make foreign bonds more attractive.
- The demand for the foreign currency will increase, and the demand for the domestic currency will decrease.
- Therefore, the domestic currency will depreciate (E falls).
- This increase in i* and subsequent reduction in E is represented as a leftward shift in the IP curve.

• How much does E decrease? Enough to cause an expected appreciation of the domestic currency to offset the rise in i*.

(2) Changes in $\overline{E}^e$

• For simplicity, assume that E initially is equal to $\overline{E}^e$.

• An increase in the expected future exchange rate will cause individuals to expect an appreciation of the domestic currency.
• The expected rate of return on foreign bonds is now lower.
• The demand for the foreign currency will fall and the demand for the domestic currency will increase.
• Therefore, the domestic currency will appreciate (E increases).
• This increase in $\overline{E}^e$ and subsequent increase in E is represented as a rightward shift in the IP curve.

(3) Warning
• Changes in either i* or $\overline{E}^e$ will cause shifts in the IP curve AND will cause changes in the exchange rate.
• These changes in the exchange rate will also cause changes in net exports and cause SHIFTS of the IS curve.
• If your instructor emphasizes these points, make sure you understand them.

(4) Equilibrium

The IS and LM curves determine Y and i. The equilibrium value of E is found by looking at the IP relation, given i. Specifically, E adjusts to maintain the interest parity condition.

Learning Tip

You should now realize that any shift in the IS and LM curves which causes:
• an increase in i will cause, as we move along the IP relation, an increase in E (an appreciation)
• a reduction in i will cause, as we move along the IP relation, a reduction in E (a depreciation).

4. FISCAL AND MONETARY POLICY UNDER FLEXIBLE EXCHANGE RATES

Learning Tip

This is a good place to check your understanding of what has been discussed in class and in the text. Make sure you understand what the IS, LM, and IP relations represent.
• Can you define them?
• Can you explain why each has its particular shape?
• Can you explain what causes the IS and LM curves to shift?

(1) Fiscal policy

An increase in G will cause:

- An increase in demand and a rightward shift in the IS curve.
- As output increases, transactions increase, and, therefore, money demand increases.
- To maintain equilibrium in the financial markets, i must rise (we move along the LM curve).
- As i rises, U.S. bonds are more attractive.
- Financial investors switch from foreign bonds to U.S. bonds.
- This switch corresponds to an increase in the demand for the dollar and an appreciation of the dollar (E rises as we move along the IP relation).
- The higher i causes a reduction in I and a reduction in NX.
- FINAL RESULT: Y increases, i increases, and E increases.

Learning Tip

- The fiscal expansion causes a deterioration of the trade balance for two reasons: (1) as Y increases, imports rise; and (2) the appreciation also reduces NX.
- An increase in G will cause an increase in both the budget deficit and trade deficit (twin deficits).
- The effects on I are still ambiguous since Y and i both increase.

(2) Monetary policy

A reduction in the money supply will cause:

- an increase in i to maintain financial market equilibrium causing the LM curve to shift up.
- The higher i has two negative effects on demand: (1) investment falls; and (2) the appreciation of the dollar (U.S. bonds are more attractive) causes NX to fall.
- The drop in I and NX has a multiplier effect on Y.
- FINAL RESULT: Y falls, i increases and E increases.

Learning Tip

Make sure you can discuss and explain the effects of an increase in the money supply and the effects of a reduction in government spending.

5. FIXED EXCHANGE RATES

(1) Introduction

In this case, the central bank: (1) chooses to peg the exchange rate at some level $\bar{E}$; and (2) takes actions (i.e., changes the money supply) so that $\bar{E}$ occurs. It is assumed that financial and foreign exchange markets believe that the exchange rate will remain pegged at $\bar{E}$.

Learning Tip

There are several important implications of the above assumptions:

- First, given that the expected exchange rate equals $\overline{E}$, $i = i^*$.
- Second, financial market equilibrium can be represented as $M/P = YL(i^*)$.
- Third, the central bank must change the money supply to keep $i = i^*$.
- And finally, the central bank gives up monetary policy as a policy instrument to maintain the pegged exchange rate.

(2) Monetary policy

Suppose $i = i^*$ and that the central bank reduces M so that $i > i^*$.

- In a closed economy, the higher i causes a reduction in I and reduction in Y.
- In the open economy, the increase in i will cause the dollar to appreciate.
- To prevent the appreciation, the central bank must increase M to bring i back to i^*.
- FINAL RESULT: i returns to i^*, M returns to its original level (to keep $i = i^*$ and to prevent the change in E) and Y does not change. Hence, monetary policy cannot be used to change output under fixed exchange rates.

(3) Fiscal policy

An increase in G causes:

- An increase in demand and an increase in Y.
- As Y increases, money demand increases and i tends to increase.
- The increase in i will tend to cause an appreciation of the dollar.
- The central bank, given its commitment to a pegged exchange rate, will prevent the appreciation by maintaining $i = i^*$.
- To keep $i = i^*$, the central bank "accommodates" the increase in money demand by increasing the money supply
- As the IS curve shifts to the right, the LM curve shifts down to keep $i = i^*$.
- FINAL RESULT: Y increases, i and E do not change.

Learning Tip

- Make sure you can explain the opposite of this example.
- Make sure you can explain why fiscal policy is more powerful under fixed exchange rates than under flexible exchange rates.
- You should review the reasons why countries choose to fix their exchange rates.

6. CAPITAL MOBILITY AND FIXED EXCHANGE RATES

Recall that the monetary base represents the central bank's liabilities. The central bank has two assets: (1) bonds; and (2) foreign exchange reserves. I will review an increase in the central bank's purchase of bonds in two situations.

(1) Perfect capital mobility

- The central bank purchase of bonds ($\Delta B > 0$) causes an increase in the money supply.
- This increase in M causes i to fall below i*.
- With no intervention, E falls and a depreciation occurs.
- Given its commitment to peg E, the central must intervene and buy dollars with its holdings of foreign exchange reserves. This causes i to increase.
- The central bank keeps buying the domestic currency (and loses foreign exchange reserves) until i = i*.
- With perfect capital mobility, the above events happen very quickly.
- In sum, the central bank cannot permanently affect i.

(2) Imperfect capital mobility

With imperfect capital mobility, it takes time for investors to shift between domestic and foreign bonds.

- The central bank again buys bonds ($\Delta B > 0$), M increases and i falls below i*.
- With imperfect capital mobility, only some investors move into foreign bonds and, therefore, sell domestic currency.
- The central bank will again intervene by buying domestic currency with its foreign exchange reserves.
- This time, however, the intervention will be small, only partially offsetting the initial bond purchase.
- In short, the central bank will lose some foreign exchange reserves; however, i may remain below i* for a sufficient amount of time for Y to increase as I increases.

Learning Tip

As capital becomes increasingly mobile, the ability of a central bank to use open-market operations (purchase and sale of bonds) to affect Y will diminish. Why? When i < i*, a more rapid response by investors will require a larger central bank intervention and a greater loss of foreign exchange reserves.

SELF-TEST QUESTIONS

1. What are the determinants of consumption (1)?

2. What are the determinants of investment (1)?

3. What are the determinants of net exports (1)?

4. Briefly discuss the interest parity condition (1).

5. An increase in the interest rate will have what effect on the exchange rate (2)?

6. Briefly explain the relation between i and E (2).

7. Suppose $i < i^*$ and that the interest parity condition holds. What is expected to happen to the value of the domestic and foreign currencies over the next year (2)?

8. In the goods market, changes in the interest rate now have two effects on output. What are they (3)?

9. What effect does an increase in G have on Y, i, E, and NX under flexible exchange rates (3)?

10. What effect does a reduction in M have on Y, i, E, and NX under flexible exchange rates (4)?

11. Briefly discuss the difference between fixed exchange rates and a crawling peg (5).

12. Briefly discuss the difference between a devaluation and a revaluation (5).

13. Under fixed exchange rates with perfect capital mobility, the central bank must do what to peg the currency (5)?

14. Under fixed exchange rates, an increase in government spending will have what effect on Y, i and E (5)?

15. How does the central bank respond to the increase in G in #14 (5)?

REVIEW PROBLEMS

1. Suppose the expected exchange rate between the dollar and pound in one year is 1.25 (1.25 pounds buy one dollar). Now suppose that the U.S. one-year interest rate is 5% (i = .05) and is 7% in the United Kingdom (i* = .07). Assume that interest parity holds. Use equation (18.4) to help answer this question.
a. Calculate the current exchange rate given the above information.
b. Calculate the current exchange rate if i increases to 6%.
c. Calculate the current exchange rate if i increases to 7%.
d. Calculate the current exchange rate if i increases to 8%.
e. Based on your analysis in a - d, what happens to E as i increases? Does the dollar appreciate or depreciate as i increases?
f. What happens to the value of the pound as i increases?

2. Assume the interest parity condition holds.
a. What happens to the expected rate of depreciation or appreciation of the dollar as i increases? Explain.
b. What happens to the expected rate of return on U.K. bonds as i increases?

3. For given values of $\overline{E}^e$ and i*, why is the interest parity relation upward sloping?

4. Assume interest parity holds and that i = 6%, i* = 6% and $\overline{E}^e = .9$.
a. What is the current exchange rate?
b. What is the expected rate of appreciation or depreciation?
c. What is the expected rate of return on U.K. bonds?
d. Based on your analysis, if i = i*, what do financial and foreign exchange markets expect will happen to the exchange rate during the next year? Explain.

5. Suppose an economy is initially closed. Now assume the country becomes "open" under flexible exchange rates. What happens to the slope of the IS curve as the economy becomes open under flexible exchange rates? Explain.

6. a. In the graph provided below, illustrate the effects of a reduction in G under flexible exchange rates. Initially assume that NX = 0.

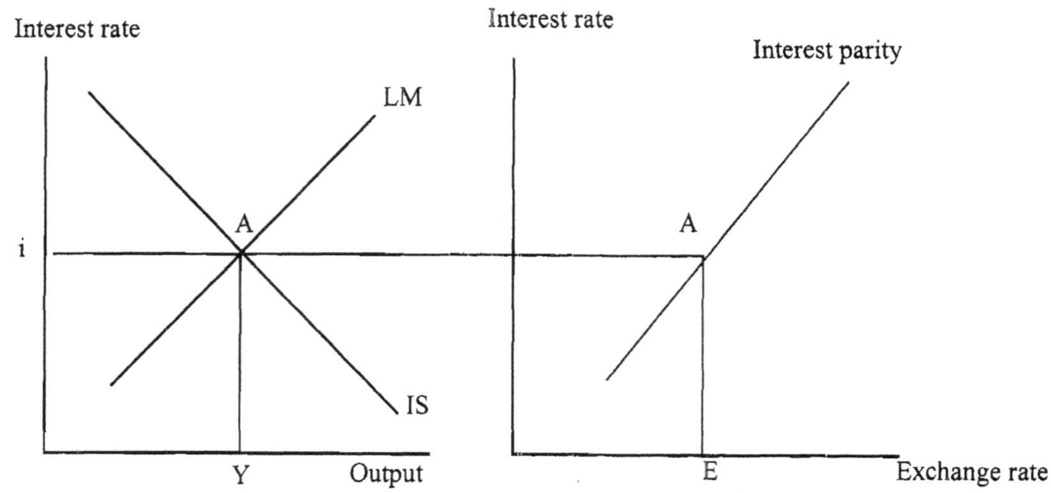

b. Explain what effect the decrease in G has on i, Y and E.
c. Explain what happens to C, I, and NX.

7. Based on your analysis in #6, what do you think would happen to the U.S. trade deficit if G were reduced (or T increased) to cut the budget deficit? Explain.

8. The text includes an example where M falls under flexible exchange rates. Suppose NX was initially zero prior to the decrease in M.
a. Discuss what effect this decrease in M has on C and I.
b. What effect does this decrease in M have on E and Y? Why does E change?
c. What effect does this decrease in M have on NX? Explain.

9. a. In the graph provided below, illustrate the effects of an increase in M under flexible exchange rates. Initially assume that NX = 0.

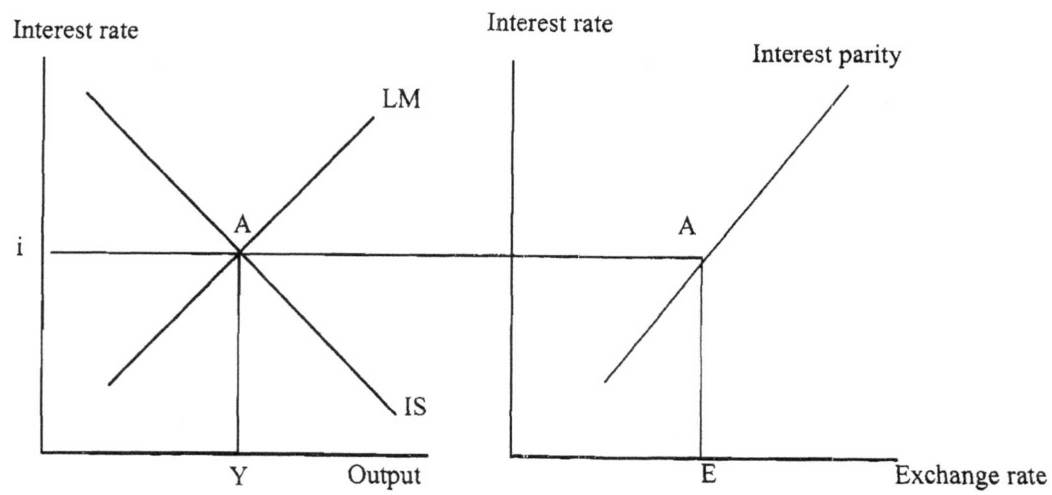

b. Explain what effect the increase in M will have on i, Y and E.
c. Why does E change?

d. What happens to the expected rate of return on foreign bonds as a result of the increase in M? What happens to i*?
e. What happens to C and I as a result of the increase in M?
f. Explain what happens to NX as a result of the increase in M.

10. Use the graph provided below to answer this question. Assume the economy is initially operating at the level of output Y_0 and that NX = 0.

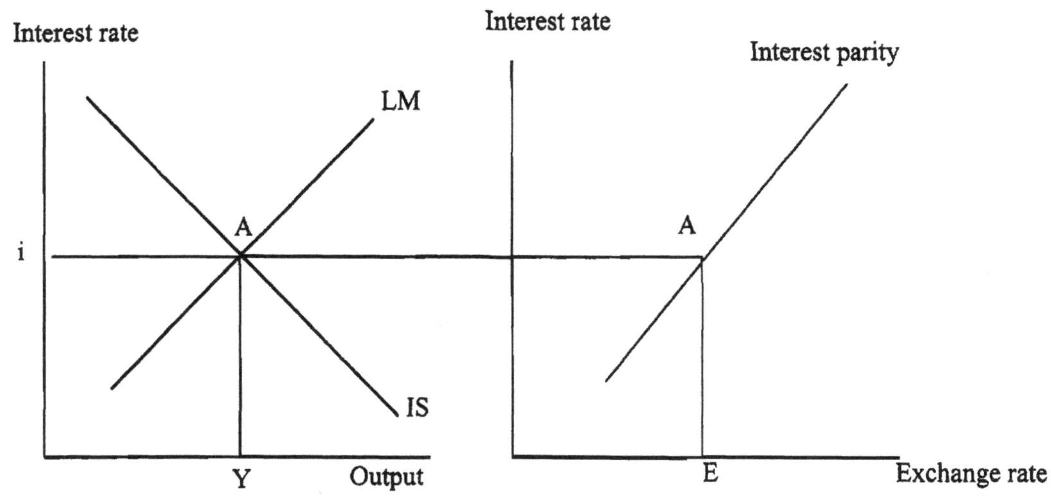

a. Suppose G increases. Further assume that the central bank wants to maintain output at the initial level of output. What type of policy must the central bank pursue to keep Y at the original level? Explain and show this in your graph.
b. What happens to i and E as a result of this combined monetary and fiscal policy?
c. Discuss what happens to the components of demand as a result of this combined policy action.

11. The chapter includes an example where G increases under fixed exchange rates.
a. What happens to C and I in this example?
b. What happens to the exchange rate in this example?
c. What happens to net exports in this example (assume the NX was initially negative, a trade deficit exists)?

12. Use the IS-LM graph provided below to answer this question. Suppose government spending decreases under fixed exchange rates.

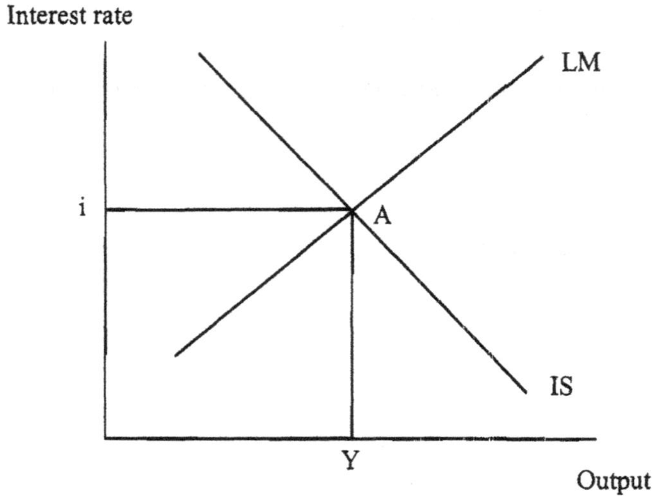

a. Graphically illustrate what will happen to the economy as a result of this reduction in G.
b. What must the central bank do to maintain the pegged exchange rate? What happens to the money supply?
c. What happens to C and I?
d. What happens to net exports? Initially assume that NX < 0.

13. Suppose there are two countries (A and B) that are <u>identical</u> in every way with the following exception: A operates under a fixed exchange rate regime and B operates under flexible exchange rates. Suppose G falls by the same amount in both countries.
a. In which of the two countries will the change in Y be the greatest? Explain.
b. Based on your analysis in a, what effect will the choice of fixed versus flexible exchange rates have on the output effects of fiscal policy? Explain.

14. Under fixed exchange rates, what effect will an increase in i* have on the model? Explain.

15. Under fixed exchange rates with perfect capital mobility, what effect will a monetary contraction have on Y, i and the composition of the central bank's balance sheet?

16. Under fixed exchange rates with imperfect capital mobility, can the central bank pursue a policy to reduce Y? Explain.

MULTIPLE CHOICE QUESTIONS

Unless specified otherwise, assume that the Marshall-Lerner condition holds.

1. Investment does NOT depend on which of the following variables?

a. Y
b. r
c. r*
d. all of the above

2. Which of the following events will cause an increase in net exports?

a. increase in Y
b. decrease in Y
c. decrease in Y*
d. an increase in E

3. If both the domestic and foreign price levels are fixed (do not change), we know that:

a. Y = Y*
b. r = i
c. NX = 0
d. E > 1

4. The interest parity condition indicates that the exchange rate (E) is a function of which set of variables?

a. $\overline{E}^e$, i, i*
b. i, i*, Y
c. i, i*, Y*
d. none of the above

5. Assume the interest parity condition holds and that i = 8% and i* = 6%. This implies that:

a. the dollar is expected to appreciate by 2%
b. the dollar is expected to depreciate by 2%
c. the foreign currency is expected to depreciate by 2%
d. the expected return (measured in dollars) on foreign bonds is less than the expected return on U.S. bonds

6. Assume the interest parity condition holds. An increase in i will cause:

a. a reduction in E
b. an increase in E
c. an increase in i*
d. a reduction in i*

7. Assume the interest parity condition holds. A reduction in i will cause:

a. the dollar to be expected to appreciate over the next year
b. the dollar to be expected to depreciate over the next year
c. an increase in E
d. a reduction in i*

8. In the open economy model, the IS relation indicates that an increase in i now has effects on which components of demand?

a. I and NX
b. C and NX
c. NX and G
d. only I

9. An increase in G under flexible exchange rates will cause:

a. an increase in E
b. a depreciation of the domestic currency
c. an increase in Y and an increase in NX
d. all of the above

10. A reduction in G under flexible exchange rates will cause:

a. an increase in NX
b. a reduction in E
c. a reduction in Y
d. all of the above

11. A monetary expansion under flexible exchange rates will cause:

a. a reduction in i, increase in E, and increase in Y
b. a reduction in E and an increase in Y
c. ambiguous effects on I since i falls and Y increases
d. a reduction in i* and increase in E

12. A monetary contraction under flexible exchange rates will cause:

a. a reduction in I and a reduction in Y
b. a reduction in E
c. an increase in i and a leftward shift in the IS curve
d. a depreciation of the domestic currency and a reduction in Y

13. Suppose there is a simultaneous reduction in G and increase in M under flexible exchange rates. Given this information, we know with certainty that:

a. E decreases
b. E increases
c. Y increases
d. Y decreases

14. In a fixed exchange rate regime, we know that:

a. $i = i^*$
b. $i > i^*$
c. $i < i^*$
d. $E = 1$

15. Under fixed exchange rates, the central bank must act to keep:

a. $Y = Y^*$
b. $NX = 0$
c. $i = i^*$
d. the money supply constant

16. Under a fixed exchange rate regime, an increase in G will cause:

a. an increase in Y
b. an increase in M
c. no change in the domestic interest rate
d. all of the above

17. An increase in G will tend to have the greatest effect on Y in which of the following cases?

a. fixed exchange rates, all else fixed
b. flexible exchange rates, all else fixed
c. flexible exchange rates in which the central bank simultaneously reduces the money supply
d. flexible exchange rates in which the central bank does not accommodate the increase in G

18. With fixed exchange rates and imperfect capital mobility, a central bank's attempt to increase output will result in:

a. an increase in foreign exchange holdings
b. a reduction in foreign exchange holdings
c. a reduction in bond holdings
d. an increase in i

CHAPTER 21. EXCHANGE RATE REGIMES

OBJECTIVES, REVIEW, AND TUTORIAL

After working through the chapter and the following material, you should be able to:

(1) Be familiar with the model of aggregate demand and aggregate supply for the open economy.

(2) Explain the short-run and medium-run effects of a devaluation on P, Y, the real exchange rate, and net exports.

(3) Explain what is meant by an "overvaluation," and explain under what circumstances a devaluation can eliminate an overvaluation.

(4) Discuss the arguments for and against devaluations.

(5) Understand that the expected return on domestic and foreign bonds must be equal.

(6) Explain in detail the exchange rate movements under flexible exchange rates.

(7) Re-examine the effects of monetary policy on interest rates and exchange rates, and understand the importance of expectations.

(8) Explain the advantages and disadvantages of fixed and flexible exchange rate regimes.

(9) Understand the difference among a hard peg, a currency board, and a dollarization.

(10) Understand what role expectations play under fixed exchange rates, and explain how exchange rate crises can occur.

1. FIXED EXCHANGE RATES, AD, AND AS

(1) Review

Under fixed exchange rates:

• the government fixes the price of domestic currency (in terms of the foreign currency) at some rate, $\overline{E}$.

• $E = E^e = \overline{E}$, so $i = i^*$.

• Since $i = i^*$, the central bank no longer can choose the money supply.

Learning Tip

• A reduction in $\overline{E}$ is called a devaluation.

• An increase in $\overline{E}$ is called a revaluation.

• A reduction in the real exchange rate (a real depreciation) causes an increase in net exports.

• An increase in the real exchange rate has the opposite effects.

(2) AD in the open economy

- Goods market equilibrium occurs when $Y = C + I + G + NX$.
- An increase in P will cause a real appreciation, a reduction in net exports, and a reduction in output.
- The AD curve is, therefore, downward sloping.
- Increases in P* and G and reductions in T and $\overline{E}$ will cause rightward shifts in the AD curve.

(3) AS and equilibrium

- The AS curve is essentially the same as previously presented.
- All other properties of the model are the same: (1) Y will return to Y_n; and (2) P will change, and the AS curve will shift when Y does not equal Y_n.

2. DEVALUATIONS

(1) Short-run analysis

A devaluation (reduction in $\overline{E}$) will cause:

- a real depreciation, increase in net exports, an increase in Y, and a rightward shift in the AD curve.
- As Y increases above Y_n, P will increase but not enough to offset the reduction in $\overline{E}$

(2) The dynamics and medium-run analysis

- With Y above Y_n, the AS keeps shifting and P increasing until $Y = Y_n$.
- As P increases, the effects of the devaluation on the real exchange rate disappear.
- In the medium run, $Y = Y_n$, and P is higher.
- The increase in P completely offsets the initial devaluation, leaving the real exchange rate unchanged.
- In the medium run, the level of $\overline{E}$ is neutral; it has no real effect on the real exchange rate, net exports, and Y.

Learning Tip
Make sure you can explain the effects of a revaluation.

3. OVERVALUATIONS

An overvalued real exchange rate makes a country's goods too expensive and will cause a trade deficit. There are two cases to consider.

(1) Overvaluation with a recession

With Y less than Y_n, the economy will adjust by itself. AS shifts down and P falls. As P falls (we move along the AD curve):

- a real depreciation occurs and net exports increase
- as net exports increase, Y returns to Y_n
- this adjustment, however, will take time

A devaluation can solve this problem. A reduction in $\overline{E}$ will cause a real depreciation. This real depreciation will cause an increase in net exports and an increase in AD. The increase in AD will cause Y to return to Y_n.

Learning Tip

In theory, the devaluation is preferred because the adjustment most likely occurs more quickly (when compared to the case where the economy adjusts by itself). The other approach will require more time as AS shifts down over time.

(2) Overvaluations without a recession

A devaluation cannot permanently affect the real exchange rate when $Y = Y_n$. To permanently change net exports, the government must increase public or private saving or reduce investment.

For example, a reduction in government spending will, in the medium run, leave Y unchanged. The lower P, however, will cause a real depreciation and an increase in net exports. Specifically, the drop in government spending will be completely offset by an equal increase in net exports. You should note that Y will fall in the short run.

To prevent the recession, the government could combine a cut in G with a devaluation leaving AD unchanged. The drop in G will be exactly offset by the devaluation-induced increase in net exports.

Learning Tip

You might want to examine the effects (both short-run and medium-run) of other events in the economy (e.g. increase in G, a change in P*, etc.).

4. FIXED EXCHANGE RATES AND EXCHANGE RATE CRISES

Under fixed exchange rates, $i = i^*$ since $\overline{E} = E^e$. An exchange rate crisis can occur if financial market participants, for whatever reason, expect a devaluation (i.e., a reduction in $\overline{E}$).

(1) An Example

Suppose individuals are certain there will be a 5% devaluation during the coming month. What are the effects?
• The expected devaluation of the domestic currency causes foreign bonds to be more attractive and causes capital outflows.
• The demand for the domestic currency will drop, and there will be pressure for the currency to depreciate.
• To prevent the depreciation, the central bank can buy its domestic currency with foreign exchange reserves. However, it will quickly lose its reserves.

(2) Other Possible Responses

• Raise interest rates. The increase in the interest rate must be enough to offset the expected devaluation. In the above example, the monthly rate would have to increase by 5% (60% higher at an annual rate).
• Devalue. Unless the central bank wants to accept the higher interest rate (which would have negative effects on demand), it will eventually have to devalue.

Learning Tip

• The belief that a devaluation will occur can cause a devaluation to occur.
• Review the EMS example in the chapter. This event was triggered by the increase in interest rates in Germany.

5. DEVALUATIONS

(1) Arguments for devaluations

• They can be used to correct overvaluations and avoid recessions.
• The cost of not devaluing (an exchange rate crisis, high domestic interest rates, etc.) may be too high.

(2) Arguments against devaluations

• Without devaluations, the economy will adjust by itself to a simultaneous overvaluation and recession.
• They defeat the purpose of fixed exchange rates and, by changing the exchange rate, reintroduce risk.
• Frequent devaluations may lead to expectations of future devaluations and, therefore, cause exchange rate crises.

(3) Effects of expected devaluations (exchange rate crises)

As long as $E = E^e = \overline{E}$, $i = i^*$. If, however, foreign exchange markets expect a devaluation, they expect E to decrease in the future. To maintain interest parity, one of two events will occur:

- i must rise to offset the effects of the expected devaluation
- the government will be forced to devalue

If the domestic interest rate rises, demand for domestic goods will fall, and aggregate demand will drop.

6. MOVEMENTS IN E IN A FLEXIBLE EXCHANGE RATE REGIME

The interest parity condition requires that the expected return from holding U.S. bonds must equal the expected return from holding foreign bonds. This is represented, as presented in previous chapters, by the following:

$(1 + i_t) = (E_t)(1 + i^*_t)/E^e_{t+1}$.

There are two interpretations of this equation that we can review.

(1) Simple case: E^e_{t+1} constant

In the simple case, E^e_{t+1} is treated as exogenous. In this case, the exchange rate will change whenever the domestic interest rate, foreign interest rate, or future expected exchange rate changes. If, as was the case in the previous chapters, we assume that the future expected exchange rate is constant, changes in E will be caused by changes in domestic and foreign rates.

(2) More realistic case: E^e_{t+1} not constant

Rearranging the above equation yields: $E_t = [(1 + i_t)/(1 + i^*_t)]\, E^e_{t+1}$. As noted in the book, the expression for the future expected exchange rate follows from this equation where it would depend on the domestic and foreign interest rate in period t+1 and the future expected exchange rate in period t+2. This can be done repeatedly to show that the current exchange rate will depend on the current domestic and foreign interest rates, future expected domestic and foreign interest rates, and some future expected exchange rate, say E^e_{t+n}.

(3) Implications of more realistic case.

E_t will change when:

- even if current domestic and foreign interest rates do not change.
- expectations of future domestic interest rates and, therefore, future macro policy change.
- the future expected exchange rate changes (this would be a one-for-one relationship).

(4) Determinants of E^e_{t+n}

One can think of E^e_{t+n} as the future exchange rate that must occur to achieve a current account balance. Therefore, it will change whenever individuals believe that, for example, a depreciation is required to eliminate a current account deficit.

Learning Tip

The relationship between current domestic interest rates and, therefore, current macro policy is not as simple as was initially presented.

- Changes in the current interest rate may not have as great an effect on the exchange rate if future expected interest rates do not change.
- The effect of current policy on the exchange rate will depend crucially on how it alters, if at all, expectations of future policy and future interest rates.
- Because of the above, current exchange rates might experience significant fluctuations in a flexible exchange rate regime.

7. THE CHOICE OF FIXED VS. FLEXIBLE EXCHANGE RATE REGIMES

The choice between these two regimes is based on a comparison of the following:

(1) In a fixed exchange rate regime, one gives up the ability to manipulate the interest rate and nominal exchange rate.

(2) In a fixed exchange rate regime, exchange rate crises can occur forcing a devaluation.

(3) In a flexible exchange rate regime, the exchange rate might experience significant volatility.

8. HARD PEGS, CURRENCY BOARDS, AND DOLLARIZATIONS

It is important for you to know the differences among hard pegs, currency boards, and dollarizations. Therefore, review this material in the chapter.

It is also important for you to understand the requirements for a common currency:

- Countries must experience similar shocks.
- If countries experience different shocks, there must be a high degree of factor mobility.

SELF-TEST QUESTIONS

1. Discuss what happens to the nominal exchange rate when a devaluation and revaluation occur (1).

2. What does the interest parity condition suggest occurs when exchange rates are fixed (1)?

3. Explain what effect an increase in the price level (P) has on the real exchange rate, net exports, demand and output (1).

4. What are the short-run effects of a devaluation on the real exchange rate, net exports, aggregate demand, the price level and output (1)?

5. When Y is above Y_n, what happens over time to the aggregate supply curve and to the price level (1)?

6. An increase in the price level has what effect on the real exchange rate (1)?

7. What are the medium-run effects of a devaluation on the real exchange rate, net exports, aggregate demand, the price level and output (1)?

8. What is meant by an overvalued real exchange rate (1)?

9. What effect will an overvalued real exchange rate have on net exports and on output (1)?

10. Suppose $Y = Y_n$ and that a trade deficit exists. Can a devaluation by itself eliminate this trade deficit? Explain (1).

11. Suppose foreign exchange markets expect a devaluation. What must happen to the domestic interest rate to maintain the interest parity condition (2)?

12. What are the two costs a country faces if it resists a devaluation (2)?

13. What are the three arguments against a devaluation (2)?

14. What is the interest parity condition (3)?

15. When the future expected exchange rate is not assumed constant, what variables determine the current exchange rate (3)?

16. What are the advantages of a fixed exchange rate regime (4)?

17. What are the advantages of a flexible exchange rate regime (4)?

18. What are the conditions for an optimal currency area (4)?

19. What is a currency board (4)?

20. What is a hard peg (4)?

21. What is a dollarization and why will one occur (4)?

REVIEW PROBLEMS

1. a. Briefly explain what effect a reduction in P will have on the real exchange rate, net exports, demand, and output.
b. Based on (a), does a reduction in P cause the AD curve to shift? Explain.

2. a. Briefly discuss what effect a revaluation has on $\overline{E}$, the real exchange rate, and net exports.
b. Based on (a), what effect does a revaluation have on the AD curve? Briefly explain.

3. "A real depreciation of the domestic currency will cause a rightward shift in the AD curve." Is this statement true, false or uncertain? Explain.

4. In the open economy version of the aggregate supply and aggregate demand model, why is the AD curve downward sloping? Explain.

5. Initially assume that $Y = Y_n$.
a. Briefly discuss the medium-run effect of a 5% devaluation on the real exchange rate, P and Y.
b. Given (a), what are the medium-run effects of a 5% devaluation on net exports? Briefly explain.
c. Devaluations are said to be neutral in the medium run. Explain.

6. Suppose the economy is initially operating at the natural level of output. Now suppose the government revalues the domestic currency by 10%. Discuss and explain the short-run and medium-run effects of this revaluation on the real exchange rate, P, net exports, and output. Use the graph provided below to illustrate the dynamic effects of the revaluation.

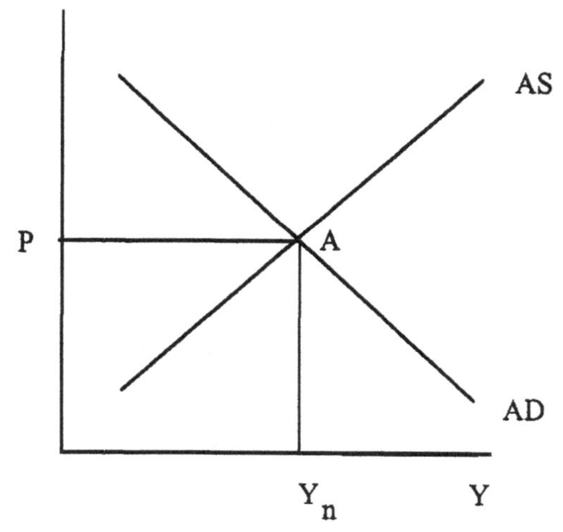

7. Suppose the economy is initially operating at the natural level of output. Now suppose the government increases government spending. Discuss and explain the short-run and medium-run effects of this increase in G on the real exchange rate, P, net exports and output. On a separate piece of paper, illustrate the dynamic effects of the revaluation.

8. Suppose $Y > Y_n$.

a. If the government allows the economy to adjust to this situation by itself, discuss what will happen to the price level (P), the real exchange rate, net exports and output.

b. If the government wants to change $\overline{E}$ to reach Y_n (when $Y > Y_n$), what should the government do? Briefly explain.

9. Suppose the economy is initially operating at the natural level of output. Now suppose the government reduces government spending.

a. Discuss and explain the short-run and medium-run effects of this decrease in G on the real exchange rate, P, net exports and output.

b. Does this decrease in G have a permanent effect on the trade deficit? Briefly explain.

c. To prevent any short-run change in output when G is reduced, should the government increase $\overline{E}$, decrease $\overline{E}$, or leave $\overline{E}$ fixed at its current level? Explain.

10. Assume (initially) that $E = E^e = \overline{E}$ and that $i = i^* = 5\%$. Let i and i* be the interest rate on one-year (domestic and foreign) bonds.

a. Suppose foreign exchange markets expect a 5% devaluation over the next year. Calculate what must happen to i to maintain the interest parity condition.

b. Based on your answer in (a), what will happen to aggregate demand and output? Explain.

c. To prevent the change in i, what must the government do in response to this expected devaluation? Explain.

11. Suppose the Dollar-Mexican peso exchange rate is fixed and that financial market participants suddenly expect a devaluation of the peso. Assume that there is now believed to be a 50% chance of a 10% devaluation over the next month and a 50% chance of no devaluation.

a. How much must the Mexican central bank raise the monthly interest rate to maintain interest parity? How much does the interest rate increase when expressed at an annual rate?

b. Repeat the analysis in (a). This time, however, assume that the expected devaluation is 20%. What happens to the required increase in i as the size of the expected devaluation increases? Briefly explain.

c. Repeat the analysis in (a). This time, however, assume that the chance of a devaluation is greater and is now equal to 75%. What happens to the required increase in i as the chance of the expected devaluation increases? Briefly explain.

d. As the interest rate changes in (a), (b), and (c), what happens to the demand for goods in Mexico? Briefly explain.

12. a. When financial market participants expect a devaluation and the central bank does not raise the interest rate, what happens to the relative attractiveness of domestic bonds? Briefly explain.

b. What will the central bank have to do to maintain the current exchange rate if it does not raise the interest rate? How long will this last?

13. Why is an increase in the interest rate in response to an expected devaluation viewed as an unpleasant option?

MULTIPLE CHOICE QUESTIONS

1. A devaluation represents:

a. a reduction in $\overline{E}$
b. an increase in $\overline{E}$
c. an increase in P
d. a reduction in the real exchange rate

2. A revaluation represents:

a. a reduction in $\overline{E}$
b. a reduction in P
c. an increase in P*
d. none of the above

3. The open economy version of the AD curve is downward sloping because:

a. a decrease in P causes an increase in M/P, a drop in r and an increase in investment
b. a reduction in $\overline{E}$ causes an increase in net exports
c. an increase in P causes a real appreciation and a decrease the demand for domestic goods
d. an increase in Y causes an increase in nominal wages and an increase in P

4. Which of the following events will NOT cause a real depreciation of the domestic currency?

a. a decrease in P
b. a reduction in $\overline{E}$
c. an increase in P*
d. none of the above

5. Which of the following events will NOT cause a rightward shift in the AD curve?

a. a decrease in P
b. a reduction in $\overline{E}$
c. an increase in P*
d. a reduction in T

6. Under fixed exchange rates, we would expect:

a. net exports to be zero
b. $i = i^*$
c. $i > i^*$
d. net exports to be negative (i.e., a trade deficit)

7. A 5% devaluation:

a. represents a 5% reduction in $\overline{E}$
b. will cause P to increase by 5% in the medium run
c. will cause no change in the real exchange rate in the long run
d. all of the above
e. none of the above

8. In the short run, a 10% devaluation will cause:

a. an increase in net exports
b. P to increase by less than 10%
c. a real depreciation
d. all of the above
e. none of the above

9. Initially assume that $Y = Y_n$. In the medium run, a devaluation will have:

a. no effect on Y
b. no effect on P
c. no effect on net exports
d. all of the above
e. both a and c

10. Suppose the country has an overvalued real exchange rate and that $Y < Y_n$. In this situation, we would expect that:

a. P will increase over time until $Y = Y_n$
b. as the economy adjusts by itself, net exports will increase as a real depreciation occurs
c. an increase in $\overline{E}$ will cause a rightward shift in the AD curve and an increase in output
d. domestic goods will become less competitive as the economy adjusts by itself

11. Suppose the country has an overvalued real exchange rate and that $Y = Y_n$. Which of the following events will cause a permanent increase in net exports?

a. an increase in $\overline{E}$
b. a reduction in $\overline{E}$
c. an increase in government spending
d. a reduction in government spending

12. Suppose the country has an overvalued real exchange rate and that $Y = Y_n$. Which of the following combination of policies will most likely reduce a trade deficit without causing a change in output?

a. an increase in government spending (G) and a reduction in $\bar{E}$

b. an increase in G and an increase in $\bar{E}$

c. a reduction in G and a reduction in $\bar{E}$

d. a reduction in G and an increase in $\bar{E}$

13. Initially assume that $Y = Y_n$. A 5% revaluation will cause:

a. a 5% increase in P in the medium run
b. a 5% reduction in P in the medium run
c. a permanent increase in net exports
d. a permanent reduction in net exports

14. Suppose foreign exchange markets expect a devaluation. Which of the following actions would help maintain the interest parity condition?

a. an increase in i
b. a reduction in i
c. an increase in $\bar{E}$
d. none of the above

15. Suppose the financial market participants expect a devaluation. Which of the following might occur as a result of the government's or central bank's actions (in response to the expected devaluation)?

a. increase in interest rates
b. loss of foreign exchange reserves
c. devaluation
d. all of the above

16. Suppose the financial market participants expect a devaluation. Further assume that the government and central bank do not want to implement a policy that might result in a loss of output. Given this information, which of the following actions will most likely be taken?

a. increase in interest rates
b. devaluation
c. revaluation
d. none of the above

CHAPTER 22. DEPRESSIONS AND SLUMPS

OBJECTIVES, REVIEW, AND TUTORIAL

After working through the chapter and the following material, you should be able to:

(1) Understand how the economy adjusts over time when output is below the natural level of output.

(2) Understand the effect of a reduction in inflation on the LM curve and the effect of a reduction in expected inflation on the IS curve.

(3) Explain what the liquidity trap is and how it can affect how the economy responds to changes in the money supply and changes in inflation.

(4) Explain the effects of a deflation in the IS-LM model.

(5) Understand the causes of the Great Depression.

(6) Understand the factors that contributed to the recovery from the Great Depression.

(7) Discuss what factors caused the Japanese slump and its recent recovery.

(8) Explain why monetary and fiscal policy have not been able to correct the Japanese slump.

1. DISINFLATION AND DEFLATION

(1) Short-run adjustment to the natural level of output

When the economy is operating below the natural level of output, the economy will adjust so that output returns to the natural level of output. You should already know this based on your understanding of the AD/AD model presented earlier. To review, when output is below the natural level of output, we will observe the following:

- Inflation will decrease.
- Lower inflation causes an increase in real money growth.
- An increase in real money growth, causes a downward shift in the LM curve and an increase in output over time.

(2) Brief review of the IS and LM curves.

It is important to remember the following:

• Money demand and, therefore, financial market equilibrium depends on the nominal interest rate.
• Investment and, therefore, the demand for goods depend on the real interest rate.
• Changes in expected inflation, given i, will cause changes in the real interest rate and shifts in the IS curve.
• Changes in expected inflation will not affect the position of the LM curve (when i is on the vertical axis).

(3) Macro effects of disinflation and deflation

When inflation decreases, we will observe the increased money growth and, as discussed above, the tendency for the economy to return to the natural level of output.

There is, however, a potentially contractionary effect of this drop in inflation (i.e., disinflation) or deflation.

• As inflation falls, the expected inflation rate might fall.
• As this occurs, the real interest rate, all else fixed, increases causing a reduction in investment.
• The drop in investment will cause a leftward shift in the IS curve and, all else fixed, a drop in output.

(4) Summary of the effects of disinflation

• If the effects of the disinflation on the LM curve dominate the effects of the disinflation on the IS curve, output will increase.
• However, if the effects of the disinflation on the LM curve dominate the effects of the disinflation on the IS curve, output will increase.

2. THE LIQUIDITY TRAP

The ability of monetary policy to increase output and, similarly, the ability of disinflations to return the economy to the natural level of output are greatly reduced when a liquidity trap exists. A liquidity trap occurs when the nominal interest rate equals zero.

(1) Characteristics of a liquidity trap

• Recall that as the nominal interest rate falls, individuals will increase their money holdings and reduce their bond holdings. Hence, money demand is downward sloping.
• When i = 0, however, money demand becomes horizontal at the zero interest rate.
• When money demand becomes horizontal, any increase in the money supply will simply be held by individuals and the interest rate will not fall.
• The LM curve also becomes horizontal at the zero nominal interest rate.

(2) Implications of the liquidity trap

When a liquidity trap exists, we now know that:

• an increase in the nominal money supply will have no effect on the interest rate and cause no shift in the LM curve; therefore, Y will not change.
• an increase in the real money supply caused by a reduction in inflation will have no effect on i, cause no shift in the LM curve, and have no effect on output.

(3) Combined effects of disinflations and the liquidity trap

When a disinflation occurs in the presence of a liquidity trap, we observe the following:

• there is no drop in the nominal interest rate and no shift in the LM curve.
• the reduction in expected inflation causes an increase in the real interest rate, a reduction in investment, a leftward shift in the IS curve, and a drop in output.

3. FACTORS CONTRIBUTING TO THE GREAT DEPRESSION

(1) The fall in spending

The stock market crash caused a decline in consumer wealth and an increase in uncertainty.

• The decline in wealth and increase in uncertainty caused a decrease in consumption.
• The increase in uncertainty also caused firms to reduce investment.
• The drop in consumption and investment caused the IS curve to shift left and, all else fixed, caused Y and r to fall.

Learning Tip

• Recall that the crash occurred after the Great Depression had begun.
• The crash was most likely the result of the end of a speculative bubble, not caused by news about the Great Depression.

(2) The drop in the nominal money supply

The bank failures between 1929 and 1933 caused individuals to increase their currency holdings.

• The increase in the ratio of currency to deposits caused a reduction in the money multiplier and a reduction in the nominal money supply.
• The decline in M was not caused by a reduction in the monetary base (H); H actually increased during the period.
• The drop in M was largely offset by an equal drop in P.
• Since M/P did not change, the LM curve did not shift down with the drop in P.

(3) Deflation

As reviewed above, changes in expected inflation cause the IS curve to shift. The expected deflation in the early 1930s caused the IS curve to shift to the left, i to fall, r to increase, and Y to fall even further.

4. THE RECOVERY FROM THE GREAT DEPRESSION

The recovery was caused by:

(1) an increase in nominal money growth (the LM curve shifts down);
(2) the end of deflation (the IS curve shifts to the right); and
(3) possibly as a result of programs included in the New Deal.

Learning Tip

- You should review the features of the New Deal discussed in the text.
- The simultaneous high unemployment and high output growth can be easily explained by Okun's law. A long period of high growth was needed to reduce the high unemployment.

5. THE JAPANESE SLUMP AND RECOVERY

(1) Cause of the slump

- The primary cause of the slump was the significant drop in stock prices in Japan.
- The drop in stock prices had a significant effect on wealth and on the demand for goods.
- Stock prices fell because of the end of a speculative bubble.
- Output has also likely decreased (or growth remained sluggish) because of the contractionary effects of disinflation and deflation.

(2) Failure of macro policy

- Monetary policy failed because it was used too late and when finally implemented was not effective because of the existence of a liquidity trap.
- Fiscal policy has not been that effective because much of the spending has been on public work projects of 'doubtful usefulness.'

(3) Possible solutions

- Create inflation and inflation expectations to eliminate the deflation problem.
- Restructure the banking system.

(4) The Recovery

Output growth in Japan since 2003 suggests that a recovery will continue. This recovery is believed to be the result of:

- A regime change in monetary policy
- The cleanup of the banking system.

SELF-TEST QUESTIONS

1. Explain the difference between deflation and disinflation (1).

2. Explain how the economy adjusts when output is below the natural level of output (1).

3. What interest rate matters for money demand and what interest rate matters for spending decisions? (1)

4. What effect does a reduction in inflation have on the LM curve? (1)

5. What effect does a drop in expected inflation have on the IS curve? (1)

6. What is a liquidity trap? (1)

7. What does the money demand curve look like when a liquidity trap exists? (1)

8. What does the LM curve look like when a liquidity trap exists? (1)

9. To what extent can changes in M affect Y when a liquidity trap exists? (1)

10. What are the combined effects of a liquidity trap and deflation? (1)

11. What is a depression? (2)

12. Did the stock market crash occur before the beginning of the Great Depression? (2)

13. What was the primary cause of the stock market crash? (2)

14. List the two effects of the crash on individuals. (2)

15. What effect did the crash have on the IS curve? (2)

16. Why did M1 fall between 1929 and 1933? (2)

17. What happened to M/P between 1929 and 1933? (2)

18. What was the "New Deal"? (2)

19. What was the cause of the Japanese slump? (3)

20. Why did stock prices fall in Japan? (3)

21. What is the Japanese banking problem? (3)

REVIEW PROBLEMS

1. Explain what effect each of the following events will have on the IS curve, LM curve, real interest rate, and output.
a. reduction in consumer wealth
b. increase in uncertainty (i.e., reduction in confidence) of consumers
c. increase in uncertainty (i.e., reduction in confidence) of firms
d. a reduction in the nominal supply of money

2. When expected inflation is negative (i.e., $\pi^e < 0$), what do individuals expect will happen to the price level over time? Briefly explain.

3. Suppose the nominal interest rate (i) is 5%.
a. Calculate the real interest rate for each of the following rates of expected inflation (or deflation): 3%, 2%, 1%, 0, -1% and -3%.
b. As expected inflation falls from 3% to 0, what happens to r?
c. As expected inflation goes from 0 to -3% (i.e., an expected deflation), what happens to r?

4. Use the IS and LM model to answer this question. Suppose expected inflation is 3%.
a. Now suppose expected inflation falls to 0. What effect will this have on the position of the IS and LM curves? Briefly explain. What effect will this have on Y, i, and r? Briefly explain.
b. Now suppose individuals expect a deflation of 3% (i.e., $\pi^e = -3\%$). What effect will this expected deflation have on the position of the IS and LM curves? Briefly explain. What effect will this expected deflation have on Y, i, and r? Briefly explain.

5. Use the IS and LM model (and graph found below) to answer this question. Assume individuals currently expect a deflation of 3% (i.e., $\pi^e = -3\%$). Now suppose that individuals no longer expect the price level to fall so that $\pi^e = 0$. What effect will the end of the deflation have on the position of the IS and LM curves? Briefly explain. What effect will the end of the expected deflation have on i, r, and Y? Briefly explain.

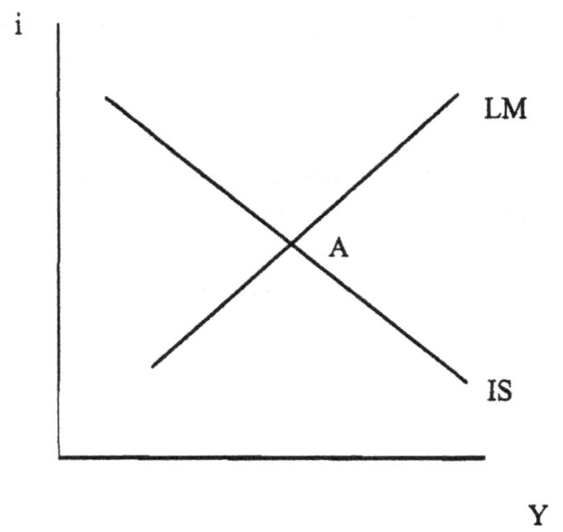

6. Explain the effects of an increase in the proportion of money held as currency on the following variables: the monetary base, the money multiplier, the nominal money supply, and the LM curve.

7. Between 1929 and 1933, the nominal money supply fell by 27%. The real money supply remained approximately the same during this period. Given this information, what must have happened to leave the real money supply unchanged? Briefly explain.

8. Between 1929 and 1933, three <u>simultaneous</u> events occurred: (1) consumer wealth fell; (2) uncertainty increased; and (3) deflation. Use the graph provided below (where A represents the initial equilibrium) to explain how these three simultaneous shocks could cause the real interest rate (r) to: (1) increase; (2) decrease; or (3) remain constant.

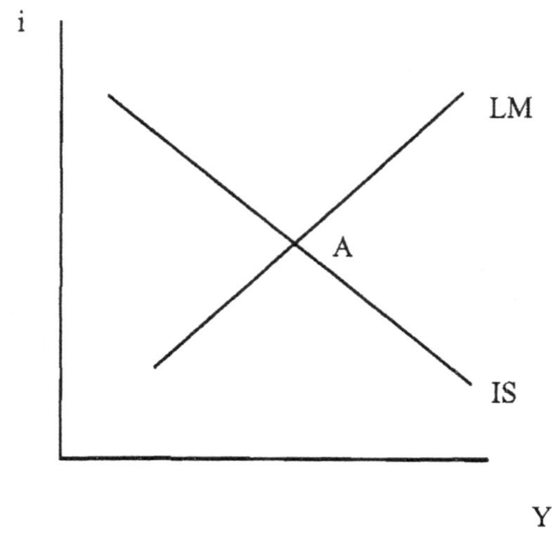

9. a. Based on your understanding of the IS-LM model, what type of fiscal policy do think could have been implemented in the early 1930s to help offset the effects of the Great Depression on output? Briefly explain.
b. Based on your understanding of the IS-LM model, what type of monetary policy do think could have been implemented in the early 1930s to help offset the effects of the Great Depression on output? Briefly explain.

10. Between 1933 and 1941, both the average growth rate (of output) and unemployment rate were high. Are these facts inconsistent with Okun's law? Briefly explain.

11. How did the deflation contribute to the Great Depression? Briefly explain.

MULTIPLE CHOICE QUESTIONS

1. Between 1929 and 1932, which of the following occurred in the United States?

a. the average annual growth rate was negative
b. the price level fell
c. the nominal money supply fell
d. all of the above
e. both a and b

2. The stock market crash in 1929 occurred:

a. before the beginning of the Great Depression
b. after the start of the Great Depression
c. at the same time that the Great Depression began
d. as a result of news about the Great Depression

3. The stock market crash had which of the following effects?

a. a reduction in consumer wealth
b. a reduction in the purchase of durable goods
c. a reduction in the purchase of investment goods
d. all of the above

4. Based on the IS-LM model, the stock market crash caused:

a. a leftward shift in the IS curve
b. a lower interest rate (r) and a rightward shift in the IS curve
c. a shift down in the LM curve
d. a reduction in Y and an increase in r

5. The decrease in the nominal money supply between 1929 and 1933 was caused by:

a. a reduction in the money multiplier
b. a reduction in the monetary base
c. a reduction in the price level
d. an increase in the price level

6. Between 1929 and 1933, the fall in the nominal money supply:

a. was significantly greater than the drop in the price level (P)
b. was significantly smaller than the drop in P
c. was approximately equal to the drop in P
d. caused the LM curve to shift down

7. An increase in the rate of deflation will cause:

a. an increase in the real interest rate (r)
b. a reduction in r
c. no change in r
d. the IS curve to shift to the right

8. If the rate of deflation goes from 3% to 10%, we know that the IS curve will shift:

a. down by 7%
b. down by 10%
c. up by 7%
d. up by 10%

9. An increase in the rate of expected deflation will cause:

a. an increase in r and a decrease in Y
b. a reduction in r and an increase in Y
c. an increase in Y and an increase in r
d. a reduction in Y and a reduction in r

CHAPTER 23.
HIGH INFLATION

OBJECTIVES, REVIEW, AND TUTORIAL

After working through the chapter and the following material, you should be able to:

(1) Understand the relation between budget deficits and money creation.

(2) Define seignorage and explain the determinants of seignorage.

(3) Explain the effects of inflation on real money balances.

(4) Explain the relation among budget deficits, seignorage, and inflation when money growth is constant.

(5) Explain the relation among budget deficits, seignorage, and inflation when money growth is not constant.

(6) Discuss both orthodox and heterodox stabilization programs, and explain how they can be used to end hyperinflations.

1. INTRODUCTION TO HYPERINFLATION

There are several concepts that you must understand.

(1) Ingredients of a hyperinflation

- High inflation is associated with high money growth.
- Money growth is high because the budget deficit is high.
- The budget deficit is high because of a major shock (economic or political) which affects spending or taxes.

(2) Financing of deficits

The government can finance a budget deficit by:

- borrowing (issuing bonds)
- creating money (debt monetization)

Learning Tip

In both instances, the government issues bonds.
- With debt monetization, the central bank buys the bonds, causing an increase in the monetary base and money supply.
- In the first case, the bonds are NOT bought by the central bank. M does not change in this case.

(3) Seignorage

• When the deficit is financed entirely by money creation, we observe that ΔM = \$Deficit (all measured in nominal terms and on a monthly basis).
• Seignorage are the revenues (in real terms) from money creation: $\Delta M/P$.
• Rearranging, we observe that Seignorage = $\Delta M/P = (\Delta M/M)(M/P)$.

Seignorage is greater:

• the higher is money growth, for given real money balances
• the higher are real money balances, for a given rate of money growth.

Learning Tip
• Be careful with the above interpretation. Faster money growth, for given real money balances, will increase seignorage. However, M/P will not remain constant when money growth changes (see below). • Make sure you understand how equations (23.2) and (23.3) are obtained.

(4) Inflation and real money balances

Real money balances are given by:

$M/P = YL(i) = YL(r + \pi^e)$.

As expected inflation increases, i increases and the opportunity cost of holding money increases.
• People reduce their real money balances.
• With hyperinflation, two other effects occur which cause individuals to reduce their real money balances: (1) barter; and (2) dollarization.

2. THE RELATION AMONG DEFICITS, SEIGNORAGE AND INFLATION

There are two cases to consider.

(1) Case 1: Constant money growth

In the long run, we can assume that:

• Y and r are constant
• $\Delta M/M = \pi = \pi^e$
• Therefore, seignorage = $(\Delta M/M)[\overline{Y}\, L(\overline{r} + \Delta M/M)]$.

An increase in money growth has an ambiguous effect on seignorage. Why?

- As money growth increases, the first term increases, causing seignorage to increase.
- As money growth increases, however, real money balances (the second term) declines, causing seignorage to fall.
- The effects of money growth on seignorage are, therefore, ambiguous.
- Empirical evidence indicates the following relation between money growth and seignorage:

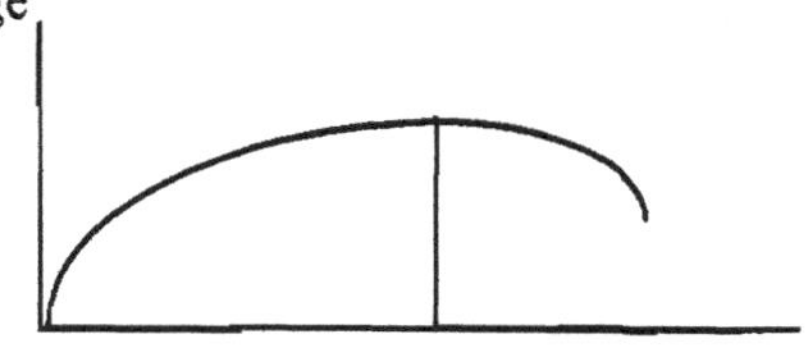

Learning Tip

- There is a seignorage-maximizing rate of money growth (see point A).
- If to the right of A, increases in money growth will cause reductions in seignorage.
- If to the left of A, increases in money growth will cause increases in seignorage.
- This analysis indicates that, in the long run, there is a maximum level of seignorage; this occurs at A.

(2) Case 2: Dynamics

In the short run, increases in money growth lead to little change in real money balances. Why?

- It may take time for π and π^e to adjust to the change in money growth.
- Increases in money growth, with real money balances relatively constant in the short run, can yield increases in seignorage above the level shown in the above graph.
- As expected inflation adjusts and M/P falls, the government will have to continue to increase the rate of money growth to achieve these temporarily high levels of seignorage.
- Result: we will observe continually increasing rates of money growth and inflation.

3. RELATED ISSUES

(1) Inflation tax

The inflation tax = $\pi(M/P)$ where π is the tax rate and M/P is the tax base.

Seignorage = $(\Delta M/M)(M/P)$

The inflation tax will equal seignorage only when $\pi = \Delta M/M$.

(2) Hyperinflation and economic activity

In the short run, a hyperinflation may increase economic activity.

In the long run, a hyperinflation will reduce economic activity. Why?

- The exchange system is less efficient.
- Price signals are less useful.
- Borrowing at a nominal interest rate is more of a gamble, causing investment to fall.

4. END OF HYPERINFLATIONS: STABILIZATION PROGRAMS

(1) Elements of a stabilization program

- fiscal reform and credible reductions in the budget deficit
- a credible central bank commitment to refrain from debt monetization
- incomes policies (e.g. wage and price controls)

(2) Types of stabilization programs

- Orthodox stabilization programs rely only on fiscal and monetary policies.

- Heterodox stabilization programs rely on fiscal and monetary policies AND incomes policies.

Learning Tip

You should review the discussion about the Bolivian hyperinflation.

SELF-TEST QUESTIONS

1. Define hyperinflation (Introduction).

2. What are the two ways a government can finance a budget deficit (1)?

3. What is meant by debt monetization (1)?

4. How does one interpret the following equation: $\Delta M = \$Deficit$ (1)?

5. Define seignorage (1).

6. Seignorage is equal to the product of what two variables (1)?

7. What are the three determinants of real money balances (2)?

8. An increase in inflation has what effect on real money balances (2)?

9. Define barter (2).

10. Define dollarization (2).

11. When nominal money growth is constant forever, what is the relation between actual inflation and expected inflation (2)?

12. What does the relation between seignorage and money growth look like (2)?

13. What is the expression for the inflation tax (2)?

14. What must happen to money growth for seignorage to continue to increase in the short run (2)?

15. What does the Tanzi-Olivera effect represent (2)?

16. What effect does hyperinflation have on economic activity in the short run and in the long run (2)?

17. What are the three possible elements of a stabilization program (3)?

18. What is the difference between orthodox and heterodox stabilization programs (3)?

19. What were the three main features of the (successful) September, 1985 Bolivian stabilization program (3)?

REVIEW PROBLEMS

1. For each of the following (constant) monthly rates of inflation, calculate the percentage rise in the price level over 12 months. Assume that the price level is 1 at the beginning of the period. Hint: refer to footnote 2 in the chapter.
a. 0.1% b. 0.2% c. 1% d. 9% e. 20% f. 40%

2. Suppose government spending increases by $200 billion which results in a $200 billion increase in the deficit. This government has two options to finance this deficit: (1) borrow; or (2) debt monetization.
a. Briefly discuss what effect this increase in G has on the IS and LM curves when the government pursues option 1.
b. Briefly discuss what effect this increase in G has on the IS and LM curves when the government pursues option 2.

3. In 1995, the real money supply in the United States (measured at 1982-84 dollars) was $737 billion; M1 = $1123 billion and the CPI for 1995 was 152.4. For this question, assume that real money balances remain constant.
a. Calculate seignorage for each of the following rates of money growth: 1% (.01), 5% (.05) and 10% (.10).
b. What happens to seignorage as money growth increases?
c. Realistically, will real money balances remain constant as money growth increases? Explain.

4. Suppose money growth is 5% (.05).
a. Calculate seignorage for each of the following levels of real money balances (measured in billions): 800, 600 and 400.
b. What happens to seignorage as real money balances decrease? Explain.

5. Explain what effect an increase in each of the following variables will have on real money balances (Note: make sure you <u>explain</u> why real money balances changes):
a. Y
b. π^e

6. For this question, assume that r and Y are constant.
a. Given M/P, what happens to seignorage as money growth increases? Briefly explain.
b. What happens to π^e in the long run when money growth increases? Briefly explain.
c. What happens to real money balances when π^e increases? Briefly explain.
d. Based on your answers to (a) - (c), what will happen to seignorage in the long run when money growth increases to some permanently higher level? Briefly explain.

7. Suppose the rate of money growth which maximizes seignorage in the long run is 10%.
a. If money growth is now 5%, what happens to seignorage in the long run if the government increases money growth? Explain.
b. If money growth is now 15%, what happens to seignorage in the long run if the government increases money growth? Explain.

8. Suppose π = 10% and that real money balances (M/P) are 500.
a. Calculate the inflation tax.
b. Given π and M/P, under what conditions will the inflation tax be equal to seignorage?
c. Given π and M/P, under what conditions will the inflation tax be greater than seignorage?
d. Given π and M/P, under what conditions will the inflation tax be less than seignorage?

9. Assume that the demand for real balances is represented by the following: $M/P = Y[.5 - (r + \pi^e)]$, where Y = 2000 and r = .05 (5%). Initially assume that π^e = .10 (10%) and does not change in the short run.
a. Given the above information, calculate seignorage for the following rates of money growth: .01 (1%), .10 (10%), .25 (25%) and .30 (30%).
b. What happens to seignorage in (a) as money growth increases?
c. Now assume that π^e equals the rate of money growth in the long run. Calculate seignorage that occurs in the long run for each of the following rates of money growth: .01 (1%), .10 (10%), .25 (25%) and .30 (30%).
d. In (c), as money growth increases from .01 to .25, what happens to seignorage?
e. In (c), as money growth increases from .25 to .30, what happens to seignorage? Can you explain why this occurs?
f. Why does seignorage always increase in (a) but not always increase in (c)?

10. Which of the following policies would be included in (a): (1) orthodox stabilization program; and (2) heterodox stabilization program?
a. monetary contraction
b. the adoption of fixed exchange rates
c. decrease in G
d. rules which limit the extent to which wages can increase
e. restrictions of firms' pricing policies

11. Briefly explain what effect a hyperinflation can have on economic activity in the short run and in the long run.

MULTIPLE CHOICE

1. Suppose the monthly rate of inflation is .05 (5%). What is the annual rate of inflation assuming this monthly rate of inflation does not change?

a. 5%
b. 50%
c. 60%
d. 79.6%

2. Which of the following is generally associated with hyperinflation?

a. money growth is high
b. the budget deficit is high
c. the economy is affected by a major shock
d. all of the above

3. When the government finances its deficit through debt monetization, we know that:

a. M increases
b. M decreases
c. there is no change in M
d. none of the above

4. When the government finances its budget deficit entirely by money creation, the real budget deficit equals:

a. M/P
b. $\Delta M/M$
c. $\Delta M/P$
d. $\Delta M/\Delta P$

5. Seignorage represents:

a. revenues from money creation
b. the Tanzi-Olivera effect
c. real money balances
d. none of the above

6. Which of the following expressions represents seignorage?

a. $(\Delta M/M)(M/P)$
b. $\Delta M/M$
c. $YL(i)/P$
d. none of the above

7. Which of the following events will cause an <u>increase</u> in the real money balances that people want to hold?

a. decrease in Y
b. increase in r
c. increase in π
d. none of the above

8. Assume real money balances is constant. Seignorage will increase when:

a. money growth decreases
b. money growth increases
c. an increase in money growth can have a positive or negative effect on seignorage in this case
d. none of the above

9. Assume money growth is constant. A reduction in real money balances will:

a. cause seignorage to increase
b. cause seignorage to fall
c. have no effect on seignorage
d. have uncertain effects on seignorage

10. During a hyperinflation, we might expect:

a. barter to occur
b. dollarization to occur
c. debt monetization to occur
d. all of the above

11. In the long run, an increase in inflation will tend to cause:

a. real money balances to increase
b. real money balances to decrease
c. no effect on real money balances
d. a decrease in the opportunity cost of holding money

12. Assume output growth is zero. If money growth is constant forever, which of the following will occur?

a. $\pi = \pi^e$
b. $\Delta M/M = \pi$
c. $\Delta M/M = \pi^e$
d. all of the above

13. Suppose money growth increases to some permanently higher rate. In the long run, we know that:

a. seignorage will increase
b. seignorage will fall
c. seignorage will not change
d. the effects on seignorage are ambiguous

As the proportion (λ) of labor contracts which are indexed increases, changes in unemployment will have a greater effect on inflation. Why?

- When u falls, wages increase.
- As wages increase, prices increase.
- With wage indexation, some wages will increase within the same period as prices rise.
- This indexation-induced increase in wages causes a second increase in prices within the same period.
- Therefore, the same drop in u causes a greater increase in π.

(2) Differences in u_n across countries

The natural rate of unemployment is given by the following expression:

$u_n = (\mu + z)/\alpha$.

Therefore, differences in μ, z, and/or α will cause u_n to vary across countries.

(3) European Unemployment

Critics argue that "labor market rigidities" cause high unemployment in Europe. Several possible explanations for these labor market rigidities exist:

- Generous unemployment insurance
- A high degree of employment protection
- Relatively high minimum wages
- Bargaining rules that increase bargaining power.

Learning Tip

- While each of the above factors would cause an increase in unemployment, a number of European countries have low unemployment.
- The explanation for the varying unemployment rates across Europe requires a deeper understanding of a possible relationship between institutions and shocks and how these different "rigidities" affect labor markets in each country.

(4) Differences in u_n over time

The natural rate of unemployment in the United States increased during the 1950-1989 period. During the 1990s, this trend appears to have changed. There are several possible causes of the simultaneous drop in unemployment and drop in inflation in the United States during this period:

- a reduction in benefits paid to workers;
- the drop in the price of imports caused by an appreciation of the dollar; and
- the drop in the price of raw materials (e.g. oil).

SELF-TEST QUESTIONS

1. What are the determinants of inflation (1)?

2. Given the original Phillips curve, why is there a negative relation between inflation and the unemployment rate (1)?

3. What is meant by the "wage-price spiral" (2)?

4. Give the two reasons why the original Phillips curve vanished (2).

5. How does the original Phillips curve differ from the modified Phillips curve (2)?

6. What happens to inflation when the unemployment rate is low (2)?

7. Define the natural rate of unemployment (2).

8. List the determinants of u_n (2).

9. What happens to inflation when $u > u_n$? What happens to inflation when $u < u_n$ (2)?

10. What is the level of u_n today in the United States (2)?

11. What does wage indexation represent (3)?

12. What effect does an increase in wage indexation have on the relation between the unemployment rate and changes in inflation (3)?

13. Explain the labor market rigidities that affect European labor markets (3).

14. What has happened to u_n in the United States since the 1960s (3)?

CHAPTER 24.
SHOULD POLICYMAKERS BE RESTRAINED?

OBJECTIVES, REVIEW, AND TUTORIAL

After working through the chapter and the following material, you should be able to:

(1) Explain why the effects of policy on output are uncertain.

(2) Recognize that this uncertainty should lead policymakes to be more cautious.

(3) Understand how game theory can be used to examine policy.

(4) Discuss what is meant by the time inconsistency of optimal policy and its implications for restraints on policymakers.

(5) Discuss the games between policymakers and voters and the games between policymakers.

(6) Explain the cases for and against a balanced-budget Amendment.

(7) Discuss any other possible restraints that can be imposed on fiscal policymakers.

1. UNCERTAINTY OF MACRO POLICY

(1) Explanation of uncertainty

The effects of changes in the money supply are uncertain because we do not know:
• how much short-term and long-term interest rates will change
• how much stock prices will change
• how long it will take for changes in the above variables to affect investment and consumption
• how long it will take for the J-curve effects to disappear (i.e., for NX to increase in response to a depreciation).

There is also uncertainty because:
• the policy may affect the economy after it is needed (e.g. after the recession is over)
• an increase in unemployment may reflect either a deviation from u_n or an increase in u_n.

(2) Implications of uncertainty

The uncertainty of policy (caused by, for example, a range of possible values of Okun's coefficient or the parameter α in the Phillips curve relation) leads policymakers to be more cautious. Why?
• The more active is policy (both monetary and fiscal), the wider the range of possible outcomes (the more uncertain the effects).
• For example, an increase in money growth could push Y well above Y_n and cause an increase in inflation.

2. GAME THEORY AND THE TIME INCONSISTENCY OF OPTIMAL POLICY

(1) Game theory

Economists use game theory to explain the implementation and effects of macro policy. This explains the strategic interactions between the policymakers and people and firms (the players).
• The effects of policy depend on the expectations of people and firms.
• Policymakers determine policy based on how the economy is doing (as determined by people and firms).

(2) Time inconsistency of optimal policy

This occurs when incentives exist to cause policymakers to deviate from announced policies.
• In terms of the Fed, the Fed has an incentive to deviate from a stated policy of zero inflation once people and firms have responded to this announced policy. Why?
• Once people and firms respond to the stated policy, an increase in money growth will cause an increase in output above Y_n AND an increase in inflation (above zero).

Learning Tip

You should review the hijacking discussion to understand the time inconsistency problem.

3. ESTABLISHING CENTRAL BANK CREDIBILITY

To establish central bank credibility, the central bank can give up some (or all!) of its policy-making power.

(1) Suggested changes to deal with time inconsistency
• make the central bank independent
• choose conservative central bankers

(2) Restraints on policymakers

Tight restraints on macro policy (e.g. fixed-money-growth rules) will deal with time inconsistency. However, they also may have large costs.

Learning Tip

Think about the following example. Suppose there is a large drop in output below Y_n.
• What type of monetary and fiscal policy do you think should be implemented?
• If tight rules were imposed on policymakers, could your policies be implemented?
• If these policies cannot be implemented, what happens to the economy?

4. THE GAMES PEOPLE (POLICYMAKERS) PLAY

(1) Policymakers and voters

To please voters and get re-elected, policymakers might pursue expansionary macro policy prior to elections; this would cause political business cycles. There is little evidence of this.

(2) Policymakers and policymakers

• Deficit reduction: Democrats are more open to tax increases, while Republicans prefer cuts in spending. Each side holds out (a war of attrition), and little progress is made on deficit reduction.

• Preferences about inflation and unemployment: Democrats are more concerned about unemployment, while Republicans are more concerned about inflation. RESULT: Growth tends to be higher in the first half of Democratic administrations compared to growth in the first half of Republican administrations.

5. THE BALANCED-BUDGET AMENDMENT

(1) The case against

• It eliminates the use of fiscal policy as a policy instrument.

(2) The case for

• Deficits during recessions may have negative effects on the economy.
• Existence of lags limits the effectiveness of fiscal policy.
• The amendment is the only way to reduce the deficit.

Learning Tip

• A balanced-budget amendment may also make the economy more unstable. See review problem #13.
• Make sure you can explain each of the following:
  a. The Growth and Stability Pact
  b. Spending caps
  c. PAYGO rule

SELF-TEST QUESTIONS

1. Arguments for restraints on policymakers fall into what two categories (1)?

2. List some of the questions that indicate why the effects of changes in the money supply on output are uncertain (1).

3. What is meant by the baseline case (1)?

4. Does uncertainty about the effects of macro policy suggest that policymakers should be more or less active (1)?

5. Explain what is meant by fine tuning (1).

6. What is the "optimal control" approach to macro policy (2)?

7. What is game theory (2)?

8. Who are the "players" in the context of macro policy (2)?

9. Briefly explain what is meant by the time inconsistency of optimal policy (2).

10. What would be a government's best policy toward hijackings (2)?

11. Describe an "independent central bank" (2).

12. What is the relation between central bank independence and inflation (2)?

13. Would you characterize Alan Blinder as a conservative central banker (2)?

14. Explain what the political business cycle suggests will happen to the growth of output (3).

15. Does the evaluation of the ratio of U.S. debt to GDP support the existence of political business cycles (3)?

16. How do "wars of attrition" help explain the debate about deficit reduction (3)?

17. Democrats and Republicans typically have different preferences of inflation and unemployment. What are they (3)?

18. What is the primary argument against a balanced-budget amendment (3)?

19. Why do some economists support a balanced-budget amendment (3)?

20. What is the Growth and Stability Pact (3)?

21. Explain how a PAYGO rule works (3).

REVIEW PROBLEMS

1. List the reasons why a given change in the money supply will have uncertain effects on output.

2. When the economy is operating at the baseline case, what are unemployment and the rate of growth of output?

3. Refer to Figure 24-2.
a. By 1986, which model predicted the largest increase in output?
b. By 1986, which model predicted the smallest increase in output?
c. By 1990, which model predicted the largest increase in output?
d. By 1990, which model predicted the smallest increase in output?

4. Explain the difference between self restraints by policymakers and restraints on policymakers.

5. Given the uncertainty about the effects of macro policy, what are the advantages and disadvantages of a policy that tries to achieve constant unemployment?

6. Briefly comment on how effective each of the following policies/strategies would be in dealing with hijacking:
a. Stated policy of NO negotiations. If a hijacking occurs, the government does negotiate.
b. Stated policy of NO negotiations. If a hijacking occurs, the government does NOT negotiate.
c. Stated policy of negotiations. If a hijacking occurs, the government does negotiate.
d. Stated policy of negotiations. If a hijacking occurs, the government does NOT negotiate.

7. Suppose the Fed increases the money supply by, say, 10%.
a. Discuss what happens to the effect on unemployment as the range of possible values of Okun's coefficient increases.
b. For a given value of Okun's coefficient, discuss what happens to the effects on inflation as the range of possible values of the parameter α increases.
c. Discuss what happens to the effects on inflation as the range of possible values of the parameter α increases AND the range of possible values of Okun's coefficient simultaneously increases.

8. Suppose the Fed announces a policy of zero inflation. Further assume that individuals and firms believe the Fed is credible.
a. Why is there an incentive for the Fed to deviate from the above stated policy?
b. Would its actions, if the Fed were to deviate, be consistent with the goals of the policy?
c. What would happen over time to Fed credibility?
d. To what extent does your analysis in parts (a), (b) and (c) illustrate the time inconsistency of optimal policy?

9. What are the problems associated with a constant-money-growth rule?

10. What type of relation do you think exists between central bank independence and average money growth? Explain.

11. a. Assuming that political business cycles exist, discuss what most likely happens to each of the following variables during the periods prior to an election: government spending, taxes, unemployment, and the growth of output.
b. Is the average rate of growth of output during the years of Democratic administrations consistent with political business cycles? Explain.

12. Given preferences about inflation and unemployment, what do you think a comparison of the average money growth during Republican and Democratic administrations would reveal? Explain.

13. Taxes are affected by the level of economic activity: When output increases, tax revenues typically increase, when output falls, tax revenues fall. Suppose a balanced-budget amendment is passed which requires that the budget always be in balance (i.e., G must always equal T). Further assume that the economy is initially operating at the natural level of output and that the budget is currently in balance.
a. Suppose consumer confidence suddenly drops. What effect will this have on the IS curve, the AD curve, output, tax revenues and on the budget?
b. Given the existence of the balanced-budget amendment, what will policymakers have to do in this situation?
c. Based on (a) and (b), what effect does the existence of a balanced-budget amendment have on the output effects of any shock to aggregate demand?
d. Based on your analysis in (c), what happens to the fluctuations in output caused by shocks to aggregate demand in the presence of a balanced-budget amendment?

MULTIPLE CHOICE QUESTIONS

1. The effects of changes in the money supply on output are uncertain because policymakers do not know how much :

a. short-term interest rates will change
b. long-term interest rates will change
c. stock prices will change
d. all of the above

2. The baseline case refers to the situation where:

a. inflation is zero
b. unemployment is equal to the natural rate of unemployment rate
c. output growth is zero
d. all of the above

3. The 12 models discussed in the chapter illustrate that changes in money growth will have:

a. identical output effects in all 12 models
b. no effect on output after three years in all 12 models
c. a different effect on output depending on the model
d. none of the above

4. Uncertainty about the effects of policy on output should cause policymakers to use:

a. more active policies
b. less active policies
c. fine tuning
d. both a and c

5. Which of the following policies toward hijackings would you recommend to a government?

a. State policy of NO negotiations. If a hijacking occurs, the government does negotiate.
b. State policy of NO negotiations. If a hijacking occurs, the government does NOT negotiate.
c. State policy of negotiations. If a hijacking occurs, the government does negotiate.
d. State policy of negotiations. If a hijacking occurs, the government does NOT negotiate.

6. The time inconsistency of optimal policy refers to:

a. fine tuning
b. optimal control theory
c. a situation where there is an incentive for policymakers to deviate from an announced policy
d. wars of attrition

7. Which of the following actions do you think would better deal with time inconsistency? Circle all that apply.

a. appoint central bankers for longer terms
b. choose conservative central bankers
c. appoint central bankers for shorter terms
d. choose liberal central bankers

8. Alan Blinder's statement that the Fed had a responsibility to use monetary policy to help the economy from a recession had which of the following effects?

a. bond prices increased
b. interest rates fell
c. interest rates increased
d. none of the above

9. The more independent the central bank, we would expect:

a. higher inflation
b. lower inflation
c. higher money growth
d. both a and c

10. If a political business cycle exists, we would expect increases in growth of output:

a. in the first year of an administration
b. in the second year of an administration
c. just after an election
d. just prior to an election

11. Between the end of World War II and the end of the 1970s, the ratio of U.S. Debt to GDP:

a. increased
b. decreased
c. remained constant
d. supports the existence of a political business cycle

12. Since 1948, growth has been highest on average in which year of an administration?

a. the first
b. the second
c. the third
d. the fourth

13. When comparing growth rate for Democratic and Republican administrations, what do we observe?

a. the growth rate in the first half of Democratic administrations > the growth rate in the first half of Republican administrations
b. the growth rate in the first half of Democratic administrations = the growth rate in the first half of Republican administrations
c. the growth rate in the first half of Democratic administrations < the growth rate in the first half of Republican administrations
d. the growth rate in the first half of Democratic administrations < the growth rate in the second half of Democratic administrations

14. Which of the following helps explain why some economists favor a balanced-budget amendment?

a. deficits during recessions may have negative effects on the economy
b. because of lags in the legislative process
c. because of skepticism of any rules Congress imposes on itself
d. all of the above

CHAPTER 25. MONETARY POLICY: A SUMMING UP.

OBJECTIVES, REVIEW, AND TUTORIAL

After working through the chapter and the following material, you should be able to:

(1) Summarize what we have learned about monetary policy.

(2) Understand the costs and benefits of inflation.

(3) Briefly discuss the current debate about the optimal inflation rate.

(4) Distinguish between money and other liquid assets.

(5) Discuss the effects of and proper response of the Fed to changes in the demand for M1.

(6) Become familiar with the organization and instruments of the Fed.

(7) Discuss the practice of monetary policy.

1. THE COSTS OF INFLATION

There are four types of costs of inflation.

(1) Shoe-leather costs

- Increases in inflation cause increases in the nominal interest rate.
- As i increases, individuals reduce their holdings of real money balances.
- Individuals, therefore, make more trips to the bank.
- These "trips" reduce leisure and/or time spent working.

(2) Tax distortions

- Increases in inflation can increase the effective tax rate on capital gains (even though the real value of the asset did not change).
- Increases in inflation, prior to the early 1980s, pushed individuals into higher income tax brackets as their nominal income increased (bracket creep). This would occur even if their real income did not change.

(3) Money illusion

- Certain computations become more difficult when there is inflation.
- Evidence exists which indicates that some people make incorrect decisions as a result of money illusion.

(4) Inflation variability

• Inflation generally becomes more variable as inflation increases.
• Bonds, therefore, become riskier.

2. THE BENEFITS OF INFLATION

(1) Seignorage

• The ultimate source of inflation is money creation.
• The money creation can finance some government spending that allows for less borrowing or lower taxes.

(2) Option of negative real interest rate

• The nominal interest rate cannot be negative.
• A positive rate of inflation, therefore, can cause a negative real interest rate.
• This negative real interest rate can make investment very attractive.
• If inflation were zero, the real interest rate would always be positive.

(3) Money illusion

• The existence of money illusion can make it easier for individuals to accept reductions in the real wage.
• Suppose a reduction in the real wage is needed. Individuals are more likely to accept a fixed nominal wage when inflation occurs rather than accept a reduction in the nominal wage when there is no inflation.

3. THE OPTIMAL RATE OF INFLATION

• One's views about the optimal rate of inflation depend on one's views of the costs and benefits of inflation.
• Those who argue for some inflation note that going from a low rate of inflation (say 4%) to 0% is likely to increase the unemployment rate for some time.
• This would result in "transition" costs not discussed above.

4. MONETARY AGGREGATES: M1 and M2

Learning Tip

• Make sure you understand the components of M1 and M2.
• Also make sure you understand the difference among the components of M1 and M2.

5. CHANGES IN THE DEMAND FOR M1 AND THE IMPLICATIONS FOR MONETARY POLICY

• The demand for M1 depends on how attractive the components of M1 are in comparison to other liquid assets.
• If other liquid assets become more attractive, the demand for M1 will fall.
• This decrease in the demand for M1 will cause the LM curve to shift down, i to fall, and Y to increase.

Learning Tip

- If the Fed keeps M1 constant, these shifts in the demand for M1 can cause changes in output (via the effects on i).
- To prevent any change in output, the Fed should:
    - increase the supply of M1 when the demand for M1 increases
    - reduce the supply of M1 when the demand for M1 falls
    - these responses keep the LM curve from shifting and i from changing
- These shifts in the demand for M1 can also cause the price level to change (via the effects on the aggregate demand curve).
- This last result can explain why there is not a perfect relation between the monetary aggregates and inflation.

6. THE TAYLOR RULE AND INFLATION TARGETING

The Taylor rule is given by the following: $i = i^* + a(\pi - \pi^*) - b(u - u_n)$ where:

- i^* is the target nominal interest rate = the nominal interest rate associated with the target rate of inflation in the medium run (i.e., $i^* = r_n + \pi^*$ where r_n is the natural real interest rate);
- π^* is the target rate of inflation;
- u_n is the natural unemployment rate; and
- a and b are parameters.

The rule indicates the following actions to be taken by the central bank:

(1) if inflation is greater than π^*, the central bank should raise the nominal interest rate; and

(2) if $u > u_n$, the central bank should reduce the nominal interest rate.

The parameters a and b indicate the extent to which the central bank will raise (or lower) the nominal interest rate when inflation and unemployment deviate from target.

7. ORGANIZATION AND INSTRUMENTS OF THE FED

(1) Organization

You should become familiar with:
- the Federal Reserve Districts
- the Board of Governors
- the Federal Open Market Committee (FOMC)

(2) Instruments

The Fed has three policy instruments:
- Reserve requirements
- Lending to banks (discount policy)
- Open market operations (purchase and sale of bonds)

Learning Tip
• Reserve requirements affect the money supply by affecting the money multiplier. • An increase in reserve requirements would reduce the size of the money multiplier. • The Fed primarily uses open market operations to conduct monetary policy. • Changes in the discount rate are primarily used as a signal of Fed actions.

7. PRACTICE OF POLICY

The Fed sets target ranges for monetary aggregates for two reasons:

- to serve as a signal of the Fed's intentions
- to serve as a benchmark for judging the Fed's behavior

SELF-TEST QUESTIONS

1. What happens to the nominal interest rate, opportunity cost of holding money and real money balances when inflation increases (1)?

2. What are shoe-leather costs (1)?

3. Describe bracket creep (1).

4. What tends to happen to inflation variability as inflation increases (1)?

5. Do bonds become more or less risky as inflation increases (1)?

6. What is an indexed bond (1)?

7. List the three benefits of inflation (1).

8. Can the real or nominal interest rate be negative (1)?

9. What are the components of M1 and M2 (2)?

10. What are money market mutual fund shares and money market deposit accounts (2)?

11. What is broad money (2)?

12. What is narrow money (2)?

13. Which monetary aggregate has the stronger relation with inflation, M1 or M2 (2)?

14. What are the three target variables included in the Taylor rule (2)?

15. Briefly summarize the requirements of the Humphrey-Hawkins Act (3).

16. Briefly describe each of the following: the Board of Governors, the Federal Open Market Committee (FOMC) and the Open Market Desk (3).

17. List the three instruments of monetary policy (3).

18. What is the discount rate (3)?

19. What is the federal funds market and federal funds rate (3)?

REVIEW PROBLEMS

1. Suppose an individual bought a house for $100,000 in 1991 and sold it five years later. For simplicity, assume that: (1) the value of the house increases by the rate of inflation during each year; and (2) the capital gains tax is 25%.

a. Calculate the effective tax rate on the sale of the house for each of the following rates of inflation: 0%, 3%, 6%. Assume that the rate of inflation is constant at that rate for each of the five years.

b. What happens to the real value of the house over the five years for each of the rates of inflation?

c. When inflation is zero, how much tax is owed? Briefly explain.

d. What happens to the effective tax rate as the rate of inflation increases?

2. List the costs of inflation.

3. a. List the benefits of inflation.

b. What determines the optimal rate of inflation?

4. Can the nominal interest rate on a bond be negative? Explain.

5. Suppose the nominal interest rate is 1%.

a. Calculate the real interest rate when inflation equals: -2%, -1%, 0%, 1%, 2%, 3% and 5%.

b. What happens to the real interest rate as inflation increases.

c. What do you think happens to investment in this example as inflation increases?

d. Why might policymakers want a negative real interest rate?

6. Is M1 larger than M2? Explain.

7. a. List the components of M1.

b. List the components of M2.

c. What is the least liquid asset in M2?

8. Use the graph provided below to answer this question.

a. In the mid-1970s, what effect did the introduction of NOW accounts have on the demand for M1?

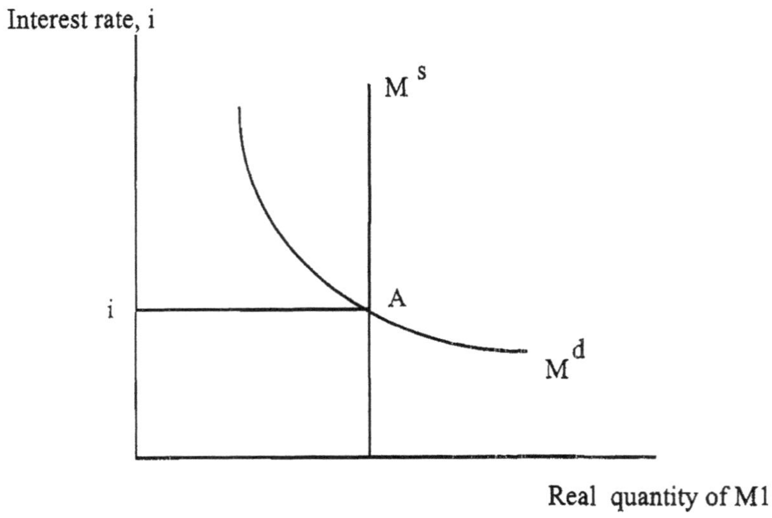

b. Discuss what effect this event had on the interest rate.

9. Use the graph provided below to answer this question.

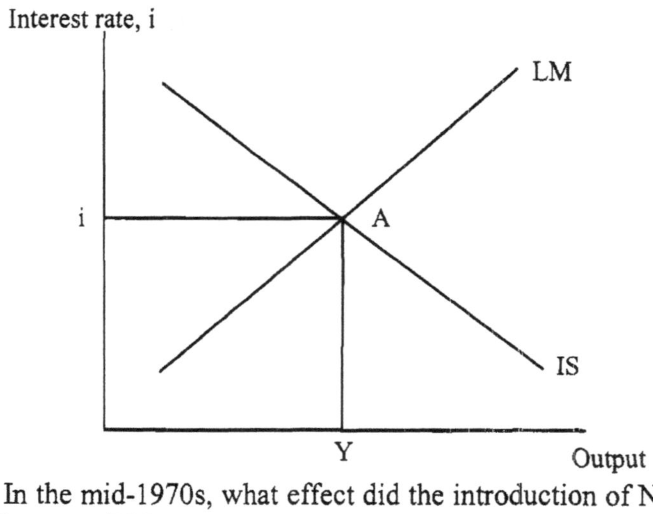

a. In the mid-1970s, what effect did the introduction of NOW accounts have on the LM curve, i, and output (Y)?

b. Based on your analysis in (a), what happened to aggregate demand and the price level?

c. Did this change in the price level occur as a result of a change in the quantity of M1?

10. Assume that output is initially at the natural level of output. Now suppose that individuals decide to switch their assets holdings from M1 to stock mutual funds.

a. What effect will this have on the demand for M1 and M2?

b. What effect will this have on aggregate demand and on the price level?

c. If the Fed is concerned about increases in the price level, should it keep the supply of M1 fixed? Explain.

11. What does your analysis in #9 and #10 suggest about the relation between the monetary aggregates and inflation?

12. Assume the central bank follows the Taylor rule discussed in the chapter.

a. Suppose a central bank is confronted with the following situation: $\pi > \pi^*$ and $u > u_n$. In such a situation, what should the central bank do, given that its actions are based on the Taylor rule? Explain.

b. Some economists believe that the Fed should be concerned only with achieving price stability. Suppose the Fed adopted such a strategy. Given this, briefly discuss the relative magnitude of the parameters a and b.

13. a. How many Federal Reserve Districts are there?

b. How many members are on the Board of Governors? How long are their terms?

c. How many members are on the FMC?

14. a. List the three instruments of monetary policy.

b. Briefly describe how each of the three instruments can be used to increase the money supply.

15. Why does the Fed announce ranges for monetary aggregates?

MULTIPLE CHOICE QUESTIONS

1. Which of the following is a function of money?

a. store of value
b. unit of account
c. medium of exchange
d. all of the above

2. An increase in inflation has which of the following effects?

a. increase in the nominal interest rate
b. increase in the opportunity cost of holding money
c. reduction in real money balances
d. all of the above
e. both a and b

3. As inflation increases, the effective tax rate on capital gains:

a. increases
b. decreases
c. becomes negative
d. remains constant if the real value of the asset does not change

4. Which of the following is a cost of inflation?

a. tax distortions
b. inflation variability
c. money illusion
d. all of the above

5. Bracket creep refers to:

a. the effects of inflation on the effective tax on capital gains
b. money illusion
c. the fact that, prior to the early 1980s, inflation could push individuals into higher income tax brackets
d. none of the above

6. Higher inflation generally causes:

a. inflation variability to increase
b. inflation variability to decrease
c. no effect on inflation variability
d. an increase in individuals' demand for real money balances

7. Which of the following is a benefit of inflation? Circle all that apply.

a. seignorage
b. the possibility of negative real interest rates
c. money illusion and real wage adjustments
d. tax distortions

8. Which of the following cannot occur?

a. $r = 0$
b. $r < 0$
c. $i < 0$
d. $i > r$

9. Which of the following is NOT a component of M1?

a. travelers checks
b. currency
c. time deposits
d. checkable deposits

10. Which of the following is a component of M2 but not a component of M1?

a. travelers checks
b. savings deposits
c. currency
d. checkable deposits

11. Which of the following is the least liquid of the assets in M2?

a. travelers checks
b. money market mutual fund shares
c. money market deposit accounts
d. time deposits

12. Narrow money refers to:

a. the monetary base
b. M1
c. M2
d. M3

13. Broad money refers to:

a. the monetary base
b. M1
c. M2
d. M3

14. Tighter restrictions on check writing on money market mutual funds would have which of the following effects?

a. demand for M1 falls
b. the LM curve shifts down
c. the interest rate decreases
d. all of the above
e. none of the above

15. The introduction of NOW accounts in the mid-1970s most likely caused (all else fixed):

a. i to increase
b. Y to fall
c. the LM curve to shift down
d. an increase in the demand for M1

16. Suppose the Fed wishes to keep Y constant. Now, assume that individuals switch some of their assets from M1 to stock funds. Which of the following actions should the Fed take to achieve its goal?

a. increase the supply of M1
b. decrease the supply of M1
c. leave M1 constant
d. buy bonds

17. Which of the following monetary aggregates has the strongest relation with inflation?

a. M1
b. M2
c. the currency equivalent index
d. none of the above

18. How many districts banks are included in the Federal Reserve system?

a. 5
b. 7
c. 12
d. 14

19. How many members are on the Board of Governors?

a. 4
b. 7
c. 12
d. 14

20. How many members are on the FOMC?

a. 4
b. 7
c. 12
d. 14

21. How long (measured in years) are the terms of members on the Board of Governors?

a. 4
b. 7
c. 12
d. 14

22. An increase in the reserve requirements has which of the following effects?

a. reduces the money multiplier
b. increases the money multiplier
c. decreases H (the monetary base)
d. increases the money supply

23. An increase in the discount rate is viewed as a signal that:

a. the Fed is going to follow an expansionary policy
b. the Fed is going to follow a contractionary policy
c. the Fed is going to increase its purchase of bonds
d. the Fed is going to reduce the reserve requirements

24. Which of the following explains why the Fed announces target ranges for monetary aggregates? Circle all that apply.

a. so it can miss them
b. to serve as a signal of Fed policy
c. to serve as a benchmark for its behavior
d. to guarantee that the growth in the monetary aggregates will fall in the target range

CHAPTER 26. FISCAL POLICY: A SUMMING-UP

OBJECTIVES, REVIEW, AND TUTORIAL

After working through the chapter and the following material, you should be able to:

(1) Understand the government budget constraint.

(2) Understand the relation between the change in debt, the initial level of debt and current government spending and taxes.

(3) Know the implications of tax cuts on the path of debt and future taxes.

(4) Explain the determinants of changes in the debt-to-GDP ratio.

(5) Understand the Ricardian equivalence proposition.

(6) Discuss the other three fiscal policy issues (i.e., stabilization, wars, and the dangers of high debt).

(7) Discuss the current state of the U.S. budget deficit.

1. THE GOVERNMENT BUDGET CONSTRAINT

There are several issues you need to understand.

(1) Deficit measures

The correct measure of the deficit (all variables in real terms) is:

Deficit = $rB_{t-1} + G_t - T_t$ where

- rB_{t-1} are the interest payments on the debt
- $G_t - T_t$ is the primary deficit.

The official measure of the deficit is:

Official deficit = $iB_{t-1} + G_t - T_t$.

Learning Tip
• The correct measure is also called the inflation-adjusted deficit. • The official measure overstates the correct measure by πB_{t-1}. • A primary surplus occurs if $T_t > G_t$.

(2) The government budget constraint

This simply states that the change in government debt during t equals the deficit in t.

$B_t - B_{t-1}$ = Deficit = $rB_{t-1} + G_t - T_t$.

Or, $B_t = (1 + r)B_{t-1} + G_t - T_t$.

Note: Increases in B_{t-1}, r, and G_t and reductions in T_t cause B_t to increase.

2. IMPLICATIONS OF TAX CUTS ON THE PATH OF DEBT AND ON FUTURE TAXES

There are two cases to consider.

(1) Full repayment in year 1

Prior to year 0, assume the government has balanced its budget (G = T = 500) and that $B_0 = 0$. Also assume that G does not change. Suppose the government cuts T by 100 in year 0 and decides to repay the debt in year 1.

Implications:
- Debt at the end of 0 is now 100.
- Debt at the end of 1 is $B_1 = (1 + r)100 + G_1 - T_1 = (1 + r)100 + 500 - T_1$.
- $B_1 = 0$ since the government repays the debt.
- To repay the debt, the government must raise T_1 and run a primary surplus. What is T_1?
- Set $B_1 = 0$ and solve for T_1. $0 = (1 + r)100 + 500 - T_1$; $T_1 - 500 = (1 + r)100$.
- The government must run a primary surplus equal to (1 + r)100. Equivalently, T_1 must increase by (1 + r)100 above G_1.
- This tax increase will pay off the debt and interest payments.

(2) Full repayment in year t

Assume the same initial situation as described above.

Implications:
- Prior to the repayment of the debt, the primary deficit is zero for each year.
- Since G = T, the debt increases each year by the size of the interest payments (they accumulate over time).
- By year t-1, $B_{t-1} = 100(1 + r)^{t-1}$.
- Since $B_t = 0$, we see that $0 = 100(1 + r)(1 + r)^{t-1} + G_t - T_t$.
- So, $T_t - G_t = 100(1 + r)^t$.

Learning Tip

- The future tax increase to repay the debt is larger:
  - the larger the initial tax cut
  - the higher is r
  - the longer the government waits to repay the debt
- If the primary deficit is 0, the debt increases each year by the size of the interest payments.
- To keep the debt constant, a primary surplus equal to the interest payments must occur each year.

3. THE DEBT-TO-GDP RATIO

The change in the debt ratio is given by the following:

$(B_t/Y_t) - (B_{t-1}/Y_{t-1}) = (r - g)(B_{t-1}/Y_{t-1}) + (G_t - T_t)/Y_t.$

There are two cases to consider.

(1) Case 1: primary deficit is 0

The debt ratio increases if $r > g$; it decreases if $r < g$; and it remains constant if $r = g$. For example, suppose $r > g > 0$. Here, Y is growing over time. However, the effects of the interest payments on the debt dominate ($r > g$) causing the ratio to increase.

(2) Case 2: $r = g$

Here, the debt ratio increases or decreases depending on the ratio of the primary deficit to GDP. If $G > T$, the debt ratio will increase over time. If $G < T$, the debt ratio will shrink.

Learning Tip

- Make sure you understand how the above ratio was obtained.
- Assuming $G = T$, the relative size of r and g will determine whether the debt ratio increases.
- Also make sure you can explain the changes in the Belgian Debt Ratio since 1970 as shown in Figure 26-2.

4. THE RICARDIAN EQUIVALENCE PROPOSITION

The Ricardian proposition works as follows:

- Suppose the government cuts T by 100 in t announcing it will increase T in t+1 to repay the debt.
- Taxes will increase by $100(1 + r)$ in t+1.
- The present value of the future tax increase is $100(1 + r)/(1 + r) = 100$.
- Summary: Taxes are cut by 100 today, and the present value of the future tax increase is 100.
- The present value of after-tax income is, therefore, constant.
- Individuals do not change consumption when taxes are cut today because human wealth does not change.

Implications:
(1) The tax cut does not change consumption; the IS curve does not shift to the right; Y and r do not change.
(2) What do people do with the tax cut? They save it!
(3) Private saving increases one for one with the deficit.

Learning Tip

The evidence suggests that increases in deficits are not met with an equal increase in private saving.

5. OTHER FISCAL POLICY ISSUES

(1) The cyclically adjusted deficit

This measure of the deficit is what the deficit would be, given existing tax (T) and spending (G) rules, if $Y = Y_n$.

Learning Tip

- Changes in G, T and, by the way, Y_n will cause changes in the cyclically adjusted deficit.
- Changes in Y caused by other factors (e.g. consumer confidence) have no effect on the cyclically adjusted deficit.

(2) Wars and deficits

Governments may use deficits to finance wars in order to: (1) pass on the burden of the debt; and (2) smooth taxes.

Learning Tip

- If governments did not rely on deficits, the current generation would be solely responsible for "financing" (via a tax increase) the increase in G.
- Tax rates would change over time to "pay for" the changes in G.
- These changes in tax rates would affect worker-leisure decisions, untaxed activities, etc.

(3) Dangers of high debt

If financial market participants require a risk premium to hold domestic bonds, r will increase. This increase in r will have two effects:

- the debt ratio increases faster (assuming $r > g$)
- Y could fall as r increases (this would cause g to fall).

What can high debt ratio countries do?

- They could reduce debt ratios by pursuing policies that increase g and/or construct budgets that call for primary surpluses.
- They could also use debt repudiation; this is an extreme action which would make it very difficult to borrow in the future.

6. THE U.S. BUDGET DEFICIT

Learning Tip

- You should review this section of the chapter.
- Make sure you understand the differences between the government budget numbers and the NIPA numbers.
- And finally, be sure you can explain each of the following: (1) entitlement programs; (2) Social Security Trust Fund; and (3) current projections of future budgets.

SELF-TEST QUESTIONS

1. What equation represents the budget deficit in year t (1)

2. What is the inflation-adjusted deficit (1)?

3. The change in the government debt in period t is determined by what (1)?

4. The change in the government debt can be decomposed into two parts. What are they (1)?

5. What is the primary deficit (1)?

6. What is the expression that represents the official measure of the deficit in year t (1)?

7. Official measures of the deficit overstate the correct measure by what amount (1)?

8. Suppose the debt is now positive and that the primary deficit is zero and will remain so in the future. What will happen, if anything, to the debt over time (1)?

9. To keep the debt from changing, what must happen to the primary deficit (1)?

10. What determines whether the debt ratio increases or decreases over time (1)?

11. What is the Ricardian equivalence proposition (2)?

12. What is the cyclically adjusted deficit (2)?

13. The deficit can serve as an automatic stabilizer. Explain (2).

14. What are the two reasons for relying on deficits to finance wars (2)?

15. What is meant by tax smoothing (2)?

16. What is meant by debt repudiation (2)?

17. How do the national income and product accounts (NIPA) treat on-budget and off-budget items (3)?

18. What is the difference between gross federal debt and net federal debt (3)?

19. What are entitlement programs (3)?

REVIEW PROBLEMS

1. Use the information provided below to answer this question. Assume that B, G, and T are measured in real terms (and in billions of dollars).

$B_{t-1} = 900$ $G_t = 200$ $T_t = 190$ $i_t = .10$ $\pi_t = .05$

a. Calculate the official measure of the deficit in year t.
b. Calculate the correct (i.e., inflation-adjusted) measure of the deficit in year t.
c. Calculate the primary deficit in year t.
d. Discuss what happens to the primary deficit in year t if the nominal interest rate in year t increases to 15%.
e. To what extent does the official measure of the deficit overstate the correct measure?
f. Given the above information, what will happen to the level of the debt between years t-1 and t? Explain.

2. Use the information provided in #1 to answer this question.
a. What must happen to taxes in year t for the primary deficit to be zero?
b. What must happen to taxes in year t for the debt to remain constant between t-1 and t?
c. What must happen to taxes in year t for the debt to be fully repaid in t?

3. Use the information provided in #1 to answer this question.
a. Calculate the official measure of the deficit for each of the following rates of inflation (assume that all other variables are the same): .02, .04, .06 and .10.
b. Calculate the correct measure of the deficit for the following rates of inflation: .02, .04, .06 and .10.
c. To what extent does the official measure of the deficit overstate the correct measure for each of the following rates of inflation: .02, .04, .06 and .10?
d. What happens to the difference between the two measures of the deficit as inflation becomes higher? Explain.

4. Use the information provided below to answer this question: $B_{t-1} = 0$; $G_{t-1} = 400$; $T_{t-1} = 400$; and $r = .05$ Assume in year t that the government cuts taxes by 50 (for one year). Assume r and G do not change.
a. Calculate the debt at the end of t.
b. Suppose the government decides to repay the debt fully in year t + 1. What will the debt be at the end of t + 1? What must happen to taxes in period t + 1 to repay the debt fully in year t + 1? How much must they change?

5. Use the information provided in #4 to answer this question. Assume in year t that the government cuts taxes by 50 (for one year). Assume r and G do not change. Suppose the government decides to repay fully the debt in year t + 3. What is the level of the debt at the end of t + 3? What must happen to taxes in period t + 3 to repay fully the debt? How much must they change?

6. If spending is unchanged, a reduction in taxes must eventually be offset by an increase in taxes in the future.
a. What will happen to the size of the future tax increase as the government waits longer to increase taxes? Explain.
b. What will happen to the size of the future tax increase as r increases? Explain.

7. To keep the debt from increasing over time, what must happen to the primary deficit? To keep the debt from increasing over time, what must happen to the inflation-adjusted deficit? Explain.

8. Use the information provided below to answer this question; B, G and T are all measured in real terms; $G_t = 500$; $T_t = 400$; $Y_t = 2000$; $B_{t-1} = 1000$; $Y_{t-1} = 2000$; $r = .05$; and $g = 0$.

a. Calculate the debt ratio at the end of years t-1 and t.

b. Did the debt ratio increase, decrease or remain constant? Explain why any change might have occurred.

9. Suppose $r = .04$ and that the primary deficit is zero. Discuss what will happen to the debt ratio for each of the following values of g: 0, .02, .04, .06.

10. Suppose $g = .02$ and that the primary deficit is zero. Discuss what will happen to the debt ratio for each of the following values of r: .01, .02, .03., .04.

11. Discuss what factors could cause the debt ratio to decrease over time.

12. Assume the Ricardian equivalence proposition holds. Suppose the government cuts taxes by $100 billion in period t and announces it will increase taxes in period t+1 to repay the debt.

a. How much will taxes increase in period t+1?

b. Explain what effect this tax cut in period t will have on consumption, private saving, total saving, the IS curve, the interest rate, investment and output in period t?

c. In this case, to what extent did this tax cut increase output?

13. Discuss what effect each of the following events will have on the cyclically adjusted deficit.

a. increase in consumer confidence that causes an increase in consumption

b. reduction in taxes

c. reduction in government spending

d. reduction in business confidence that causes a reduction in investment

14. What are the two reasons why governments rely on deficits to finance wars?

15. a. Discuss what effect a reduction in r will have on the debt ratio.

b. Discuss what effect a reduction in g will have on the debt ratio.

c. To keep the debt ratio from changing in (a) and (b), what would have to happen to the primary deficit? What effect would this change in the primary deficit have on output growth (g) in the short run? Explain.

16. Do you see any long-run consequences of debt repudiation? Explain.

MULTIPLE CHOICE QUESTIONS

1. Which of the following represents the correct measure of the deficit in year t (in real terms)?

a. $G_t - T_t$
b. $rB_{t-1} + G_t - T_t$
c. $G_t - T_t - \pi_t B_{t-1}$
d. $rB_t + G_t - T_t$

2. The government budget constraint is represented by:

a. $B_t - B_{t-1} = \text{Deficit}$
b. $B_t - B_{t-1} = rB_t + G_t - T_t$
c. all of the above
d. none of the above

3. The official measure of the deficit overstates the correct measure by:

a. iB
b. rB
c. πB
d. $(i - \pi)B$

4. An increase in which of the following variables will cause an increase in the level of debt in period t (B_t)?

a. r
b. G_t
c. B_{t-1}
d. all of the above

5. The primary deficit is represented by what?

a. $G_t - T_t$
b. $(1 + r)B_{t-1} + G_t - T_t$
c. $rB_{t-1} + G_t - T_t$
d. $iB_{t-1} + G_t - T_t$

6. Which of the following events would cause the official measure of the deficit to be more inaccurate? Circle all that apply.

a. an increase in inflation
b. an increase in G
c. an increase in r
d. an increase in the level of the debt

7. To keep the debt level constant, which of the following must occur?

a. primary deficit must equal zero
b. the official deficit must equal zero
c. the primary surplus must equal zero
d. the primary surplus must equal the interest payments

8. Assume r = .05. Suppose the government cuts taxes by $100 billion in period t and will repay the debt in full in year t + 1. How much must taxes increase in year t + 1?

a. $5 billion
b. $100 billion
c. $105 billion
d. none of the above

9. Assume r = .05 and that B_t = 500. What must occur in the next period to repay the debt in full?

a. a primary surplus of $25 billion
b. a primary surplus of $500 billion
c. a primary surplus of $525 billion
d. a primary surplus of zero

10. Assume government spending does not change. Suppose the government cuts taxes in year t. The future tax increase to repay this debt will be higher:

a. the longer the government waits to raise taxes
b. the higher is the interest rate (r)
c. the lower is the interest rate (r)
d. both a and b

11. Which of the following conditions will cause a reduction in the level of debt over time?

a. primary surplus > real interest payments on the debt
b. primary surplus < real interest payments on the debt
c. primary deficit > real interest payments on the debt
d. primary deficit < real interest payments on the debt

12. Which of the following events will cause the debt ratio to increase?

a. reduction in r
b. reduction in g
c. a reduction in the primary deficit
d. all of the above

13. Which of the following events will cause the debt ratio to decrease?

a. an increase in r
b. an increase in the primary deficit
c. an increase in g
d. all of the above
e. none of the above

14. Since 1970, the Belgian debt ratio:

a. has steadily increased
b. has remained roughly constant
c. has steadily decreased
d. none of the above

15. The most recent reduction in the Belgian debt ratio is the result of which of the following?

a. lower growth
b. lower interest rates
c. primary deficits
d. all of the above

16. Suppose the government cuts taxes in period t and announces it will increase taxes in t + 1. According to the Ricardian equivalence proposition, this tax cut in year t will have which of the following effects in year t?

a. no change in consumption
b. an equal increase in private saving
c. no change in investment
d. no change in output
e. all of the above

17. According to the Ricardian equivalence proposition,

a. private saving increases one for one with the deficit
b. total saving increases as the deficit increases
c. total saving decreases as the deficit increases
d. investment increases one for one with the deficit

18. The empirical evidence from the 1980s and 1990s for the United States suggests that the increase in the deficits during the early 1980s was associated with:

a. a one for one increase in private saving
b. a less than one for one increase in private saving
c. no change in private saving
d. a decrease in private saving

19. Which of the following will cause an increase in the cyclically adjusted deficit?

a. increase in G
b. reduction in taxes
c. a reduction in consumer confidence that causes a recession
d. all of the above
e. both a and b

20. Countries tend to rely on deficits to finance wars in order to:

a. pass on the burden of the debt
b. use the deficit as an automatic stabilizer
c. smooth taxes
d. all of the above
e. both a and c

21. Debt repudiation occurs when:

a. when the government runs a primary deficit
b. the primary deficit is zero
c. when the government repays the debt in full
d. the government cancels its debt

22. Which of the following are characteristics of the national income and product account (NIPA) measure of the deficit?

a. the NIPA numbers are based on a calendar year
b. the NIPA numbers do not distinguish between on-budget and off-budget items
c. the NIPA numbers do not count the sale of assets as revenue
d. all of the above

CHAPTER 27. EPILOGUE: THE STORY OF MACROECONOMICS

OBJECTIVES, REVIEW, AND TUTORIAL

After working through the chapter and the following material, you should be able to:

(1) Discuss the building blocks of modern macroeconomics introduced by Keynes.

(2) Discuss the progress made on the neoclassical synthesis.

(3) Understand the debate about monetary versus fiscal policy.

(4) Understand the debate about the Phillips curve.

(5) Discuss the three implications of rational expectations.

(6) Become familiar with the integration of rational expectations and its implications.

(7) Know the current developments in macroeconomics.

(8) Understand the basic propositions of the core (i.e., common beliefs) of macroeconomics.

1. BUILDING BLOCKS OF MODERN MACROECONOMICS INTRODUCED BY KEYNES

Keynes argued that changes in effective demand (what we now call aggregate demand) determined output in the short run. In developing effective demand, Keynes introduced:

- the multiplier
- the notion of liquidity preference (demand for money)
- the importance of expectations in affecting consumption and investment
- the idea that expectations can cause changes in demand and output

2. PROGRESS MADE DURING THE NEOCLASSICAL SYNTHESIS

Much progress was made during this period. For example,

- The IS-LM model was developed.
- The theories of consumption, investment, and money demand were developed.
- Macroeconometric models were constructed to make predictions about economic activity.

Learning Tip
You might want to review which economists were responsible for which developments.

3. EARLY AREAS OF DEBATE

There were several areas of debate during this period.

(1) Monetary versus fiscal policy

• Keynes emphasized fiscal rather than monetary policy.
• Later, others argued that the IS curve was relatively steep, making fiscal policy the more effective policy tool.
• Friedman and Schwartz challenged this by arguing that the Great Depression was caused by a reduction in the money supply.

(2) The Phillips curve

• In the 1960s, many Keynesian economists believed that there was a tradeoff between inflation and unemployment in the medium run.
• Friedman and Phelps, however, argued that there was no medium-run tradeoff.

(3) Role of policy

• Some argued for the use of fine tuning, while others (e.g. Friedman) argued that policy makers should use simple rules.

4. IMPLICATIONS OF RATIONAL EXPECTATIONS

Lucas and Sargent argued that Keynesian economics ignored the full implications of expectations on behavior. Rational expectations had three implications.

(1) Lucas critique

Since individuals' expectations and, therefore, behavior would adjust to policy changes, macroeconometric models would not predict well what would occur as a result of policy changes.
• The macroeconometric models were based on backward-looking behavior and expectations.
• Under rational expectations, however, behavioral equations would change as policy changes; the models did not take this into account.

(2) The Phillips curve

• When rational expectations was introduced in Keynesian models, deviations in output from the natural level were short-lived.
• Anticipated changes in the money supply, under rational expectations, had no effects on output even in the short run.
• Unanticipated changes in the money supply, under rational expectations, would cause changes in output.

(3) Policy

The theory of policy now needed to take into account the strategic interactions among the players (policy makers, firms, and people): game theory (rather than optimal control theory).

Learning Tip

You should review the discussion in the text about:

- the random walk of consumption
- the staggering of wage and price decisions

5. CURRENT DEVELOPMENTS

There are three groups of current research.

(1) New Classicals

- These economists generally assume competitive markets and flexible wages and prices.
- Early work focused on real business cycle models where output always equals the natural level of output and changes in output are caused by changes in technological progress (or regress).

(2) New Keynesians

These economists have focused on:

- efficiency wages
- nominal rigidities
- menu costs
- imperfects in credit markets

(3) New Growth Theory

These economists, led by Romer and Lucas, have explored:

- the determinants of technological progress
- the possibility of increasing returns to scale

6. THE CORE (COMMON BELIEFS)

Learning Tip

You should simply review this short section of the chapter.

SELF-TEST QUESTIONS

1. What was business cycle theory (1)?

2. What is meant by effective demand (1)?

3. What does liquidity preference represent (1)?

4. What are "animal" spirits (1)?

5. The neoclassical synthesis refers to what (2)?

6. Who developed the IS-LM model (2)?

7. Which economist helped develop the theory of investment AND money demand (2)?

8. What type of policy did Keynes argue should be used to fight recessions (2)?

9. Friedman and Schwartz concluded that the Great Depression was caused by what (2)?

10. In the 1960s, most economists believed what about the relation between unemployment and inflation in the medium run (2)?

11. What is stagflation (3)?

12. What was Lucas and Sargent's main argument about Keynesian economics (3)?

13. What does the Lucas critique represent (3)?

14. Rational expectations suggests that anticipated changes in the money supply will have what effect on output (3)?

15. Does rational expectations suggest that policy should be based on optimal control theory or on game theory (3)?

16. What is meant by the random walk of consumption (3)?

17. Who developed the overshooting model of exchange rates and what does this model predict (3)?

18. In real business cycle models, output always equals what (4)?

19. What does the staggering of wage and price decisions represent (3)?

20. Prescott argued that fluctuations in output in real business cycle models were caused by what (4)?

21. Describe menu costs (4).

REVIEW PROBLEMS

In addition to the following problems, make sure you can answer the questions included in the Self-Test section.

1. List the building blocks of modern macroeconomics introduced by Keynes.

2. List the economists responsible for each of the following developments/theories:

a. IS-LM model
b. consumption
c. investment
d. money demand
e. growth theory
f. rational expectations
g. real business cycle
h. new growth theory

3. As the IS curve becomes steeper, what happens to the output effects of a given change in the money supply? Explain.

4. Suppose the Fed wishes to reduce aggregate prices and assume that output initially equals the natural level of output. Based on rational expectations, should the Fed announce its policy in advance of the policy's implementation? Explain.

5. Assume: (1) individuals have rational expectations; (2) individuals believe the Fed will increase the money supply by 4%; and (3) the economy is initially operating at the natural level of output. Given this information, explain what happens to output for the following cases: (a) the money supply increases by 6%; (b) the money supply increases by 4%; and (c) the money supply increases by 2%.

6. Can output slowly return to the natural level with rational expectations? Briefly explain.

7. What are the characteristics of markets in rational expectations and real business cycle models?

8. In the real business cycle model developed by Prescott, what must happen for output to change (i.e., increase and decrease)? Explain.

9. List the areas of research in New Keynesian economics.

10. Briefly describe the basic set of propositions that represent the core of macroeconomics.

MULTIPLE CHOICE QUESTIONS

1. Which of the following is a building block of modern macroeconomics introduced by Keynes? Circle all that apply.

a. the multiplier
b. liquidity preference
c. rational expectations
d. technological regress

2. Liquidity preference refers to the theory of what?

a. consumption
b. investment
c. money demand
d. exchange rates

3. Who wrote *The General Theory*?

a. Solow
b. Keynes
c. Friedman
d. Lucas

4. By which decade had the neoclassical synthesis occurred?

a. 1930s
b. 1940s
c. 1950s
c. 1960s

5. Which of the following economists was (were) responsible for the theory of consumption? Circle all that apply.

a. Keynes
b. Modigliani
c. Friedman
d. Tobin
e. Lucas
f. Solow

6. Which of the following economists was (were) responsible for the theory of investment? Circle all that apply.

a. Keynes
b. Modigliani
c. Friedman
d. Tobin
e. Lucas
f. Solow

7. Which of the following economists was (were) responsible for the theory of money demand? Circle all that apply.

a. Keynes
b. Modigliani
c. Friedman
d. Tobin
e. Lucas
f. Solow

8. Which of the following economists was (were) responsible for the theory of growth? Circle all that apply.

a. Keynes
b. Modigliani
c. Friedman
d. Tobin
e. Lucas
f. Solow

9. When the IS curve is steep,

a. changes in the interest rate will have a greater effect on demand and output
b. monetary policy will work very well
c. fiscal policy can affect output faster and more reliably than monetary policy
d. fiscal policy will NOT work very well

10. The work by Friedman and Phelps indicates that:

a. there is a medium-run tradeoff between inflation and unemployment
b. there is NO medium-run tradeoff between inflation and unemployment
c. there is NO short-run tradeoff between inflation and unemployment
d. none of the above

11. The Lucas critique refers to:

a. the debate about monetary and fiscal policy
b. the criticism of the use of macroeconometric models
c. stagflation
d. technological regress

12. Lucas' work on rational expectations suggests that:

a. only unanticipated changes in the money supply affect output
b. only anticipated changes in the money supply affect output
c. both anticipated and unanticipated changes in the money supply affect output
d. neither anticipated nor unanticipated changes in the money supply will affect output

13. Rational expectations suggests that policy should be based on:

a. game theory
b. optimal control theory
c. business cycle theory
d. backward-looking expectations

14. Which of the following statements is true about real business cycle theory?

a. Y is always above the natural level
b. Y is always below the natural level
c. Y always equals the natural level
d. Y is sometimes above, below or equal to the natural level

15. The work by Robert Hall suggests that the best forecast of consumption next year:

a. is last year's consumption
b. is this year's consumption
c. equals last year's level of disposable income
d. equals this year's level of disposable income

16. Which of the following is a characteristic of the New Classical model?

a. menu costs
b. efficiency wages
c. nominal rigidities
d. competitive markets with flexible wages and prices

17. Imperfections in credit markets indicate that:

a. individuals can borrow freely at the quoted interest rate
b. firms can borrow freely at the quoted interest rate
c. banks turn down potential customers at the quoted interest rate
d. both a and b

18. Which of the following is an area of research in New Keynesian economics? Circle all that apply.

a. menu costs
b. efficiency wages
c. the determination of technological progress
d. nominal rigidities

19. Which of the following is NOT one of the basic propositions of the core of macroeconomics?

a. changes in aggregate demand affect output in the short run
b. monetary policy affects output in the short run and medium run
c. output always equals the natural level
d. fiscal policy affects output in both the short run and medium run

20. Those economists who believe that the economy adjusts slowly over time believe that:

a. there is a need for active stabilization policy
b. Y never returns to the natural level
c. tight rules should be imposed on monetary and fiscal policy
d. Y always equals the natural level

APPENDIX.
THE GOODS MARKET: DYNAMICS [OPTIONAL]

Learning Tip

• The material in this optional appendix will help you understand the behavior in the goods market when firms hold inventory.

• This material will also help you understand the dynamic effects discussed in Chapter 5.

• Obviously, this material is optional. If your instructor does not cover this, you can skip this. However, if your instructor does discuss dynamics in any detail (in Chapter 3 and/or 5), you should work through these problems.

OBJECTIVES, REVIEW AND TUTORIAL

After working through the following material, you should be able to:

(1) Recognize that firms and consumers may not immediately adjust their production and consumption.

(2) Explain the relationship among production, sales, and inventory investment.

(3) Discuss and explain what is meant by and solve for equilibrium output in this dynamic model.

(4) Explain how production, consumption, and sales respond over time to changes in autonomous spending.

(5) Interpret a consumption equation which includes lagged values of disposable income.

(6) Explain the simulated effects of a change in autonomous spending on sales, production and consumption in an economy in which the consumption equation includes lagged values of disposable income.

1. NEW ASSUMPTIONS AND DYNAMIC PROPERTIES OF THE MODEL

In Chapter 3, we assumed that:

(1) Firms responded to a change in demand with an instantaneous and equal change in production;
(2) Inventory investment was always equal to zero; and
(3) Changes in disposable income in period t affect consumption only in period t.

In this appendix, the above assumptions will be relaxed so that we now assume that:

(1) Firms do not respond instantaneously to a change in demand;
(2) Inventory investment can be positive, negative or equal to zero;
(3) Firms set production at the beginning of each period before they know demand (i.e., sales);
(4) Firms set production in period t equal to the level of expected sales for period t;
(5) Expected sales in period t equal the actual level of sales in the previous period (i.e., expected sales for period t equal Z_{t-1});
(6) Assumptions (4) and (5) imply that production in period t+1 will be set equal to demand in period t: $Y_{t+1} = Z_t$;
(7) Each period lasts three months (i.e., one quarter); and
(8) Investment, government purchases and taxes are constant over time.

Learning Tip

- Inventory investment can now be positive or negative. Why? Once production has been set at the beginning of t, an increase in demand during the period will be satisfied by firms drawing down their inventories. In this case, demand exceeds production and inventory investment is negative.
- Here is an alternative explanation. In period t, firms set $Y_t = Z_{t-1}$. Why? Firms expect sales in period t to be equal to last period's sales. Three cases can occur:

  (1) If $Z_t = Z_{t-1}$, $Y_t = Z_t$ and inventory investment is zero;
  (2) If $Z_t > Z_{t-1}$, $Y_t < Z_t$ and inventory investment is negative (i.e., firms respond to the increase in Z by reducing their inventory stock); and
  (3) If $Z_t < Z_{t-1}$, $Y_t > Z_t$ and inventory investment is positive (i.e., firms respond to the decrease in Z by allowing their inventory stock to rise).
- Make sure you understand the notation introduced in this chapter (i.e., t refers to the current period, t-1 refers to the last period, and so on).

2. EQUILIBRIUM OUTPUT

(1) Demand (Z_t): As we saw in the text, demand at time t is given by:

$$Z_t = c_1 Y_t + [c_0 + \overline{I} + G - c_1 T].$$

Learning Tip

- For now, we assume that consumption in period t depends on current disposable income. As you know, this will not always be the case since consumption in period t may depend on current and lagged values of disposable income.
- c_1 is the slope of ZZ.
- The expression in brackets represents autonomous spending.
- G, $\overline{I}$ and T are constant through time; hence, they do not require time subscripts.

(2) Production and sales: Firms set production in period t+1 equal to sales in period t. That is,

$$Y_{t+1} = c_1 Y_t + [c_0 + \overline{I} + G - c_1 T].$$

Learning Tip

Make sure you understand the above equation. Y_{t+1} depends on current demand. Current demand, Z_t, depends on current output, Y_t. Hence, production in period t+1, Y_{t+1}, depends on production in the current period, Y_t.

(3) Equilibrium output: The economy achieves equilibrium when output is constant. If output is constant, $Y_{t+1} = Y_t$. Let Y represent this constant, equilibrium level of output (i.e., $Y = Y_{t+1} = Y_t$). Equilibrium output, as derived in the chapter, is represented by:

$$Y = (1/(1 - c_1))[c_0 + \overline{I} + G - c_1 T].$$

Learning Tip

- The above equation is identical to the one obtained in Chapter 3.
- The term $1/(1 - c_1)$ represents the multiplier.
- WARNING: When autonomous spending changes, output no longer adjusts immediately to the change in demand.

3. DYNAMIC EFFECTS OF CHANGES IN AUTONOMOUS SPENDING

If you can explain what the following geometric series represents, you understand the dynamic effects of a change in autonomous spending on output, sales and consumption:

$$1 + c_1 + c_1^2 + c_1^3 + \ldots\ldots + c_1^n.$$

Let's quickly review the example in the chapter. Suppose government purchases increase by $1 billion in period t. What happens to demand, output and consumption over time?

(1) Demand effects. Demand increases by $1 billion in period t (the 1 in the above expression represents this). After firms respond (in t+1) by increasing output by $1 billion, consumption will now rise in period t+1 by c_1 times the $1 billion increase in income (c_1 in the above expression represents this "second round" increase in demand). Firms again respond (now in period t+2) to this second increase in demand, ... and so on. Each subsequent term represents the next period's increase in demand.

(2) Output effects. In period t, there will be no change in output. In period t+1, firms respond by increasing output by $1 billion. As income increases, consumption and demand will rise. In period t+2, firms respond to this increase in demand. The process continues as described above. Each subsequent term represents the next period's change in output.

(3) Consumption effects. This has already been described above. In short, each time income rises, consumption will rise by c_1 times the change in income.

Learning Tip

- For a given value of the marginal propensity to consume (c_1), the above expression represents the total change in demand and the total change in output caused by, for example, a given change in government purchases.
- As n increases, the above geometric series is given by $1/(1 - c_1)$ which is the multiplier you have already studied.
- Does the above process ever stop? Yes! Each subsequent increase in output gets smaller and smaller over time. The process eventually stops when $Y = Z$ at the new equilibrium level of output.

4. CONSUMPTION EQUATIONS WHICH INCLUDE LAGGED VALUES OF Y_D

Consumption in period t may be a function of both current disposable income and lagged disposable income. Such behavior would be represented by the following equation (regression):

$$(\Delta C_t - \overline{\Delta C}) = 0.30(\Delta Y_{Dt} - \overline{\Delta Y_D}) + 0.19(\Delta Y_{Dt-1} - \overline{\Delta Y_D}) + 0.08(\Delta Y_{Dt-2} - \overline{\Delta Y_D}) + \text{residual}.$$

You must be able to do two things here: (1) explain what this equation means; and (2) given these results, calculate and explain what the marginal propensity to consume is.

(1) Interpretation of results

These results indicate that:

- A \$1 billion increase in disposable income (above its mean) in period t will cause a \$0.30 billion increase in consumption (above its mean) in period t. Note: I will omit the phrase "above its mean" below; however, you should understand that this is how you interpret these types of equations.
- A \$1 billion increase in disposable income last period (i.e., in period t-1) will cause a \$0.19 billion increase in consumption in period t.
- A \$1 billion increase in disposable income two periods ago (i.e., in period t-2) will cause a \$0.08 billion increase in consumption in period t.

(2) Alternative interpretation and derivation of the marginal propensity to consume

Say disposable income increases by \$1 billion in period t. This will cause:

- Consumption to rise by \$0.30 billion in period t;
- Consumption to rise by \$0.19 billion in period t+1; and
- Consumption to rise by \$0.08 billion in period t+2.

The total effect on consumption of this \$1 billion increase in disposable income is \$0.57 billion (i.e., \$0.30 + \$0.19 + \$0.08 = \$0.57). The marginal propensity to consume is 0.57.

5. DYNAMIC EFFECTS IN THE PRESENCE OF LAGS

Suppose the consumption function is represented by the following equation

$$C_t = c_0 + 0.30Y_{Dt} + 0.19Y_{Dt-1} + 0.08Y_{Dt-2}.$$

Suppose that government purchases (G) increases by $1 billion in period t. Here are several questions that you must be able to answer. Think about the questions and try to answer them before looking at the explanations found below.

- Questions:

(1) How much does output change in period t in response to this period t change in government purchases?

(2) What is the marginal propensity to consume? What is the size of the multiplier? How much will output eventually change?

(3) Will this change in G cause output to change more rapidly in an economy represented by the above consumption function or in an economy represented by the model presented in Chapter 3 (in an economy that has the same marginal propensity to consume)?

- Answers:

(1) Output will not change in period t. Why? Firms have already set production in period t to the level of demand which occurred in period t-1.

(2) $\Delta Y = [1/(1 - 0.52)]100 = (2.08)100 = 208$. The eventual change is $208 billion. The marginal propensity to consume is 0.52. The multiplier is 2.08.

(3) The adjustment is slower. Why? In Chapter 3, we assumed that firms change output immediately and by the same amount in response to a change in demand. Here, both output and consumption respond with a lag to changes in demand and Y_D, respectively. This means that output will respond more slowly over time to any change in demand.

Learning Tip

In Chapter 3, a $100 billion change in disposable income caused consumption to change fully in period t. The above equation indicates that it takes more time for a change in disposable income to affect consumption.

- How many periods will it take for the initial change in disposable income to affect consumption? Three (t, t+1 and t+2).
- You should note that once output begins to change in response to the change in demand, "other" changes in disposable income will occur.

REVIEW PROBLEMS

1. Suppose demand in period t-1 was 2000 and that the consumption function is represented by the following equation: $C_t = c_0 + 0.8Y_{Dt}$. Further assume that production is set so that $Y_{t+1} = Z_t$. Answer the following questions given this information.

a. At what level of output will firms set production at the beginning of period t? Why? Briefly explain.
b. Suppose government purchases (G) increases by $75 billion in period t. Briefly explain what effect this increase in G will have on the following variables in period t:

(1) production;
(2) sales (demand);
(3) inventory investment; and
(4) consumption.

c. What effect will this period t increase in G have on production and consumption in period t+1?

2. Suppose the economy is represented by the following dynamic model:

$Y_{t+1} = Z_t$	$C_t = c_0 + c_1 Y_{Dt}$	$Z_t = C_t + I_t + G_t$	$G_t = G$
$I_t = \overline{I}$	$T_t = T$	$Y_{Dt} = Y_t - T$	

In this dynamic model, production in period t+1 depends on production in period t. Briefly explain why this is so.

3. Suppose the economy is represented by the following dynamic model:

$Y_{t+1} = Z_t$	$C_t = c_0 + c_1 Y_{Dt}$	$Z_t = C_t + I_t + G_t$	$G_t = G$
$I_t = \overline{I}$	$T_t = T$	$Y_{Dt} = Y_t - T$	

Suppose $Y = Y_0$ in period t. Now assume that government purchases (G) are <u>reduced</u> by $150 billion in period t. Use the graph included below to answer the following questions. Suppose $Y = Y_0$ at t. Now suppose that G is cut by $150 billion in period t.

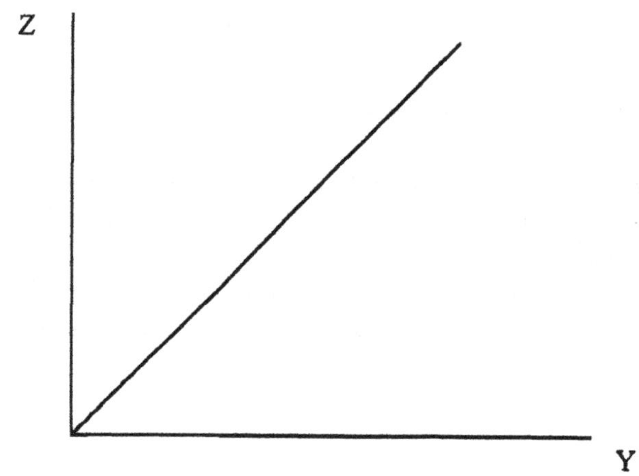

a. Graphically illustrate the effects of this cut in G on ZZ.
b. In your graph, illustrate the level of output, sales and inventory investment that occur in period t.
c. What happens to output in period t+1? Why? Show this level of output in your graph and illustrate the level of demand and any inventory investment which occur in period t+1.
d. What will eventually happen to output in this economy? Show this level of output in your graph.
e. Given this cut in G of $150 billion, what determines how much output will eventually change? Briefly explain.

4. The purpose of this problem is to verify the relation between the following geometric series and the multiplier.

a. Given the following series (note: I have omitted the values of $(c_1)^j$ where $j > 10$), what is the value of the expression when: (1) $c_1 = .5$; and (2) $c_1 = .9$?

$$1 + c_1 + (c_1)^2 + (c_1)^3 + (c_1)^4 + (c_1)^5 + (c_1)^6 + (c_1)^7 + (c_1)^8 + (c_1)^9 + (c_1)^{10}.$$

b. What number does the above expression approach when: (1) $c_1 = .5$; and (2) $c_1 = .9$?
c. What does the expression $1/(1 - c_1)$ represent?
d. What does the expression $1/(1 - c_1)$ equal when: (1) $c_1 = .5$; and (2) $c_1 = .9$?
e. Do your calculations in (d) verify your conclusions in (b) for each value of c_1?

5. Suppose the economy is represented by the following equations:

$Y_{t+1} = Z_t$	$C_t = c_0 + c_1 Y_{Dt}$	$Z_t = C_t + I_t + G_t$	$G_t = G$
$I_t = \bar{I}$	$T_t = T$	$Y_{Dt} = Y_t - T$	

a. Which of these equations represent behavioral equations?
b. Which of these equations represent identities?
c. Which of these equations represent equilibrium conditions?

6. Suppose the economy is represented by the following equations:

$Y_{t+1} = Z_t$	$C_t = c_0 + c_1 Y_{Dt}$	$Z_t = C_t + I_t + G_t$	$G_t = G$
$I_t = \bar{I}$	$T_t = T$	$Y_{Dt} = Y_t - T$	$c_1 = 0.6$

Suppose there is a $50 billion <u>increase</u> in government purchases in 1997:1.

a. Based on your understanding of the dynamic model, calculate the quarter-to-quarter changes in production, government purchases, consumption and sales for 1997:1, 1997:2, 1997:3 and 1997:4. Place your answers in the table found below.
b. Calculate the cumulative changes in production, government purchases, consumption and sales for 1997:1, 1997:2, 1997:3 and 1997:4. Place your answers in the table found below.

c. What will be the eventual cumulative change in Y after the economy reaches its new equilibrium, under the assumption that Y is constant in equilibrium? How do you know?

Quarter	Production	Government Spending	Consumption	Sales
		Quarter-to-quarter increases		
1997:1				
1997:2				
1997:3				
1997:4				
		Cumulative increases		
1997:1				
1997:2				
1997:3				
1997:4				

7. Suppose the economy is represented by the following equations:

$Y_{t+1} = Z_t$ $\quad C_t = c_0 + c_1 Y_{Dt}$ $\quad Z_t = C_t + I_t + G_t$ $\quad G_t = G$

$I_t = \overline{I}$ $\quad T_t = T$ $\quad Y_{Dt} = Y_t - T$ $\quad c_1 = 0.75$

Suppose there is a \$100 billion <u>reduction</u> in government purchases in 1997:1.

a. Based on your understanding of the dynamic model, calculate the quarter-to-quarter changes in production, government purchases, consumption and sales for 1997:1, 1997:2, 1997:3 and 1997:4. Place your answers in the table found below.

b. Calculate the cumulative changes in production, government purchases, consumption and sales for 1997:1, 1997:2, 1997:3 and 1997:4. Place your answers in the table found below.

c. What will be the eventual cumulative change in Y after the economy reaches its new equilibrium, under the assumption that Y is constant? How do you know?

Quarter	Production	Government Spending	Consumption	Sales
		Quarter-to-quarter changes		
1997:1				
1997:2				
1997:3				
1997:4				
		Cumulative changes		
1997:1				
1997:2				
1997:3				
1997:4				

8. Suppose the economy is represented by the following equations:

$Y_{t+1} = Z_t$	$C_t = c_0 + c_1 Y_{Dt}$	$Z_t = C_t + I_t + G_t$	$G_t = 600$	
$c_0 = 100$	$\overline{I} = 200$	$T_t = 400$	$Y_{Dt} = Y_t - T$	$c_1 = 0.5$

a. Solve for the equilibrium level of GDP, under the assumption that GDP is constant in equilibrium.
b. At this level of output, what is the value of inventory investment? Explain.
c. Suppose that G increases by 100 in period t. In the space below, graphically illustrate the effects of this increase in G on the ZZ line.

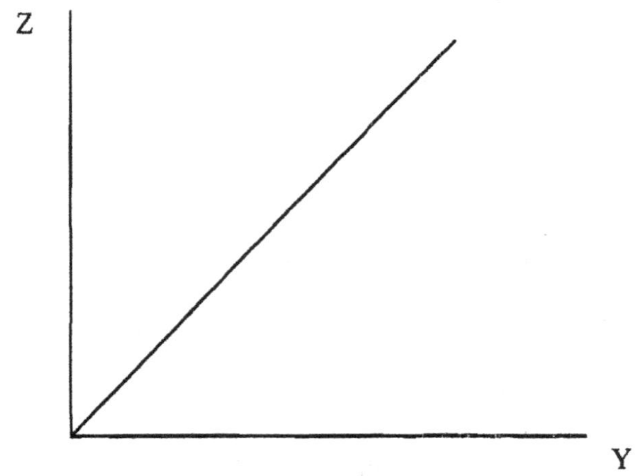

d. What happens to production, demand, and consumption in period t as a result of this period t increase in G? Briefly explain.
e. After the increase in G in period t, what is the value of inventory investment in period t?
f. What will be the final level of output which occurs as a result of this increase in G?

9. Suppose the economy is represented by the following equations:

$Y_{t+1} = Z_t$	$C_t = c_0 + c_1 Y_{Dt}$	$Z_t = C_t + I_t + G_t$	$G = 1000$	$c_0 = 200$
$\overline{I} = 200$	$T = 800$	$Y_{Dt} = Y_t - T$	$c_1 = 0.5$	

a. Solve for the equilibrium level of GDP, under the assumption that GDP is constant in equilibrium.
b. Suppose that T is <u>cut</u> by 100 in period t. What happens to production, demand, and consumption in period t as a result of this period t reduction in T? Briefly explain.
c. After the reduction in T in period t, what is the value of inventory investment in period t?
d. What will be the final level of output which occurs as a result of this reduction in T?

10. Suppose the economy is represented by the following equations:

$Y_{t+1} = Z_t$ $\quad Z_t = C_t + I_t + G_t$ $\quad G = 600$ $\quad c_0 = 100$

$\bar{I} = 200$ $\quad T_t = 400$ $\quad Y_{Dt} = Y_t - T$

$C_t = c_0 + 0.30Y_{Dt} + 0.19Y_{Dt-1} + 0.11Y_{Dt-2}$

a. What is the marginal propensity to consume in this economy?
b. Solve for the equilibrium level of GDP, under the assumption that GDP is constant.
c. Suppose G increases by 100 in period t+1. What happens to production, sales, consumption and inventory investment in period t+1?
d. At what level of output will the economy settle in response to this increase in G? What is the size of the multiplier?

11. Suppose economy A and economy B are identical in every way with the following exception:

Consumption equation in economy A: $C_t = 100 + 0.28Y_{Dt} + 0.14Y_{Dt-1} + 0.08Y_{Dt-2}$

Consumption equation in economy B: $C_t = 100 + 0.50Y_{Dt}$

a. What is the marginal propensity to consume in economy A and B?
b. What is the multiplier in economy A and B?
c. Suppose both economy A and B are operating at their respective equilibrium levels of GDP, under the assumption that GDP is constant in equilibrium. Compare the levels of GDP in the two economies. In which economy is production highest?
d. Suppose G increases by 100 in each country in period t+1. How much will production and consumption change in each country in period t+1?
e. How much will production and consumption change in A and B in period t+2 in response to the period t+1 increase in G?
f. Given your answer in part (e), in which of these two economies will this increase in G have a more rapid effect on GDP? Explain.
g. GDP will increase in both of these economies as a result of the increase in G. In which of these two economies will the eventual change in GDP be greatest? Explain.

MULTIPLE CHOICE QUESTIONS

1. Which of the following is NOT an assumption of the dynamic model of the goods market?

a. inventory investment is always equal to zero
b. firms do not respond instantaneously to a change in demand
c. firms set production at the beginning of each period before they know demand (i.e., sales)
d. expected sales in period t equal the actual level of sales in the previous period (i.e., expected sales for period t equal Z_{t-1})

2. Suppose government purchases increase by 200 in period t and assume that firms set production at the beginning of each period equal to expected demand (i.e., $Y_{t+1} = Z_t$). We know that this period t increase in G will cause:

a. no change in production in period t
b. production in period t to increase by 200
c. production in period t to increase by less than 200
d. production in period t+1 to increase by more than 200

3. Suppose government purchases increases by \$1 billion and that this causes a series of increases in output equal to the following geometric series:

$1 + 0.9 + 0.81 + \ldots\ldots$

This suggests that the total change in production caused by this \$1 billion increase in government purchases will be:

a. \$20 billion
b. \$10 billion
c. \$5 billion
d. \$3 billion

4. Suppose $Y_t = Z_t$ in period t. This suggests that:

a. inventory investment is positive in period t
b. inventory investment is negative in period t
c. inventory investment is equal to zero in period t
d. production will increase in period t+1

5. Assume the consumption equation is given by the following: $C_t = c_0 + 0.5Y_D$. If $Z_{t-1} = 2500$ and government purchases are reduced by 200 in period t, production in period t will be:

a. 2500
b. 2400
c. 2300
d. 2100

6. Which of the following variables in the dynamic model presented in Chapter 4 is generally assumed to be constant over time?

a. disposable income
b. production
c. consumption
d. investment

The following five questions rely on the information provided below:

$Y_{t+1} = Z_t$ $\quad C_t = c_0 + c_1 Y_{Dt} Z_t = C_t + I_t + G_t G = 200$ $\quad c_0 = 180$

$\overline{I} = 200$ $\quad T = 100$ $\quad Y_{Dt} = Y_t - T$ $\quad c_1 = 0.8$

7. Under the assumption that GDP is constant, equilibrium output will be:

a. 500
b. 2000
c. 2400
d. 2500

8. Suppose G increases by 50 in period t. We know that:

a. Y will rise by 40 in period t
b. C will rise by 40 in period t
c. Y will rise by 40 in period t+1
d. C will rise by 40 in period t+1

9. The period t increase in G will cause:

a. inventory investment in period t to be +50
b. inventory investment in period t to be -50
c. inventory investment in period t to be zero
d. none of the above

10. This increase in G in period t will cause:

a. Y to increase by 40 in period t
b. Y to increase by 40 in period t+1
c. Y to increase by 50 in period t
d. Y to increase by 50 in period t+1

11. When the economy eventually reaches its new, constant level of output, we know that:

a. inventory investment will be zero at this level of output
b. output will be equal to the multiplier times autonomous spending
c. output will have increased by 100
d. all of the above
e. both (a) and (b)

Answer the following four questions using the information provided below: Assume that firms do hold inventory in the following two economies. Suppose economy A and economy B are identical in every way with the following exception:

Consumption equation in economy A: $C_t = 100 + 0.40Y_{Dt} + 0.25Y_{Dt-1} + 0.15Y_{Dt-2}$

Consumption equation in economy B: $C_t = 100 + 0.75Y_{Dt}$

12. The estimated coefficient, 0.25, in the consumption equation for economy A indicates that a $1 billion increase in disposable income in period t will cause:

a. a $0.25 billion increase in consumption in period t
b. a $0.25 billion increase in consumption in period t-1
c. a $4 billion increase in consumption in period t
d. a $0.25 billion increase in consumption in period t+1

13. The marginal propensity to consume for economy A is:

a. 5
b. 4
c. 1/(1-0.4) = 1.67
d. 0.8

14. Suppose G increases by 100 in both economies in period t.

a. the increase in Y in period t+1 in response to this period t increase in G will be greater in A than in B
b. the increase in Y in period t+1 in response to this period t increase in G will be greater in B than in A
c. the increase in Y in period t+1 in response to this period t increase in G will be the same in A and B
d. the increase in Y in period t in response to this period t increase in G will be greater in A than in B
e. the increase in Y in period t in response to this period t increase in G will be greater in B than in A

15. This period t increase in G will cause:

a. the eventual change in Y to be greater in A than in B
b. the eventual change in Y to be greater in B than in A
c. the same change in Y in A and B
d. none of the above

SOLUTIONS

TO REVIEW PROBLEMS

AND

ANSWERS

TO MULTIPLE CHOICE

QUESTIONS

CHAPTER 1

REVIEW PROBLEMS

1. Macroeconomics is the study of aggregate economic variables (e.g. aggregate output, inflation, and the unemployment rate).

2. This list could vary: inflation, employment, unemployment, output, interest rates, the budget deficit and money growth.

3. Unlike in the "hard" sciences (e.g. physics and chemistry), macroeconomists generally cannot study the effects of a change in one particular variable while holding all other factors constant. In the macroeconomy, often many variables are changing simultaneously which makes the analysis of certain issues and hypotheses both difficult and exciting.

4. This can be broken into two parts. First, labor market rigidities (minimum wage, unemployment benefits, and worker protection) might have caused the high unemployment. Second, others will argue that significant increases in wages and inadequate macro policies have caused the high unemployment.

5. There are several potential benefits of the adoption of the Euro: (1) the symbolic importance of common currency for these countries; (2) the elimination of exchange rate uncertainty; and (3) the creation of one of the largest economic powers in the world.

6. When a country buys more goods and services from abroad than it sells, its spending exceeds its income. To finance this trade deficit, a country must borrow from the rest of the world. If foreigners suddenly decide no longer to lend to the United States, this would force the United States to suddenly eliminate its trade deficit and experience a crisis similar to the one experience by Thailand.

7. The rapid economic growth in China has been caused by capital accumulation and increases in technological progress.

MULTIPLE CHOICE QUESTIONS

1. B 2. C 3. D 4. A 5. D 6. B 7. C 8. B

CHAPTER 2

REVIEW PROBLEMS

1. a. \$Y in 1995 is \$2.8(10) + \$.70(10) + \$4.0(8) = \$67
\$Y in 2005 = \$3.1(7) + \$.85(13) + \$4.5(11) = \$82.25
b. Y in 1995 equals \$Y in 1995 since 1995 is the base year: \$67.
Y in 2005 is \$2.8(7) + \$.70(13) + \$4(11) = \$72.70.
c. The GDP deflator in 1995 = (\$Y in 1995/Y in 1995) = \$67/\$67 = 1.
The GDP deflator in 2005 = (\$Y in 2005/Y in 2005) = \$82.25/\$72.70 = 1.13.
d. The percentage change in Y is 8.5%. The percentage change in the GDP deflator is 13%.

2. Nominal GDP and real GDP in 1995 are the same since we use the same prices to calculate both figures. The prices in 1995 are the same prices used to obtain real GDP since 1995 is the base year.

3. a. The final product of steel is 0 since steel is not a final good. The final product of the lobster company is \$200 and the final product of the car company is \$1000. GDP = \$200 + \$1000 = \$1200.
b. Value added for steel is \$400. Value added for the lobster company is \$200. Value added for the car company is \$1000 - \$400 = \$600. GDP is \$400 + \$200 + \$600 = \$1200.
c. Total wages are \$1000. Total profits are \$200. GDP is (again!) \$1200.
d. As discussed in the chapter, all three approaches to GDP yield the SAME value of total output.
e. Labor's share is 83%; profit's share is 17%.

4. Without more information, we can say nothing about inflation and real GDP. Nominal GDP can increase because of changes in the price level and/or changes in real output.

5. a. \$Y in 1985 = .94(4296.5) = 4038.7. The GDP deflator in 1992 = (6020.2/4979.5) = 1.209.
b. To obtain the following values, simply divide nominal GDP by the GDP deflator: 4150.8, 4405.2, 4539.9, 4716.5, 4839.4, 4895.1, 4868, 5136.3. Real GDP fell in 1991. This indicates that aggregate output was lower in 1991 compared to 1990.
c. Prior to 1987, the real GDP figure is always greater than the nominal GDP figure because prices in the base year (1987) are higher than prices in these years. After 1987, the real GDP figure is always less than the nominal GDP figure because prices in the base year (1987) are less than prices in these years.
d. Nominal GDP can change simply because the price level is changing. Economists are concerned about changes in aggregate output. Real GDP measures changes in aggregate output.

6. If the increase in the price level is greater (in a proportionate sense) than the reduction in real output, nominal GDP will increase.

7. The price of potatoes would not change since their quality is most likely the same. Cars now offer more services/characteristics (e.g. air bags). The increase in the price of cars would be reduced to reflect the fact that some of the increase in the price is due to improvements in the quality of cars. Personal computers also now offer greater characteristics (more memory, more features, etc.). Hedonic pricing would indicate that the price of computers actually fell.

8. a. Number unemployed = 10; number employed = 50; therefore, the labor force = 60. u = 10/60 = 16.7%. The participation rate = 60/100 = 60%.
b. The labor force drops to 55. u = 5/55 = 9.1%. The participation rate falls to 55/100 = 55%. Both rates fell. As fewer people search, the number of unemployed (and u) falls and the participation rate falls.
c. The number of employed = 52; the number of unemployed = 8; therefore, the labor force remains constant at 60. u falls to 8/60 = 13.3%. The participation rate does not change.
d. The size of the labor force would increase (to 70). The number of employed individuals would not change. The number of unemployed individuals would increase (to 20). The unemployment rate would increase to 28.6% and the participation rate would increase to 70%.

MULTIPLE CHOICE QUESTIONS

1. C 2. D 3. B 4. A 5. C 6. C 7. D 8. C 9. A 10. B 11. D 12. B 13. D 14. C 15. B 16. C 17. A

APPENDIX 1:
AN INTRODUCTION TO NATIONAL INCOME AND PRODUCT ACCOUNTS

REVIEW PROBLEMS

1. GNP is the market value of all final goods and services produced by factors of production supplied by U.S. residents.

2. Consumption, investment, government purchases, net exports and changes in business inventories.

3. National income includes several items that are not included in personal income: corporate profits retained by firms, and net interest payments paid by firms not received by households. National income also does not include transfer payments which are included in personal income.

4. Personal disposable income is personal income minus taxes. If taxes are greater than 0, personal disposable income is less than personal income.

5. Nonresidential investment and residential investment.

6. Durable goods, nondurable goods and services.

7. Yes, if imports exceed exports.

8. a. If receipts of factor income from the rest of the world [which represent income from U.S. capital or U.S. residents abroad] exceed payments of factor income to the rest of the world [which represent income received by foreign capital or foreign labor in the United States], GNP is greater than GDP.
b. If receipts of factor income from the rest of the world are less than payments of factor income to the rest of the world, GNP is less than GDP.

MULTIPLE CHOICE QUESTIONS

1. C 2. B 3. D 4. A 5. F 6. A 7. A 8. D

CHAPTER 3

REVIEW PROBLEMS

1. a. Y in 1993: 5136. Y in 1994: 5343. Rate of growth: 4%. The level of economic activity increased; that is, real aggregate output increased.
b. Rates of growth: C (3.5%), I (12.2%), G (-1%), X (8.6%), IM (13.8%), I_S (247%). Fastest: inventory investment (though this is a bit misleading since it is the smallest component of Y). Slowest: government spending fell! Components' shares in 1993: C (67%), I (16%), G (18%), X (12%), IM (13%), I_S (0.3%). Components' shares in 1994: C (67%), I (17%), G (17%), X (12%), IM (14%), I_S (1%). G's share fell, while Q's share increased. Inventory investment's share also increased.
c. The trade deficit (IM > X) increased from 73 to 114. While X increased between the two years, IM increased even more.

2. Call the alternative measure which excludes inventory investment Yalt. Yalt > Y when I_S is negative. When inventories fall, firms have sold goods that were produced in a previous period. Y adjusts C, I, G and X for any sales that come from inventory. Yalt < Y when I_S is positive. Here, firms have increased inventories during the period. These goods represent production. If we excluded them from the output numbers, we would obtain a measure that understates the "true" level of aggregate output. It is important to include I_S since some goods are produced and not sold in a year (I_S >) and in other cases some goods that are purchased were produced in a previous period ($I_S < 0$).

3. Call the alternative measure which excludes net exports (NX) Yalt. Yalt > Y when NX is negative (a trade deficit). Yalt does not take into account the fact that some goods are sold abroad (X) and some goods purchased by domestic residents (firms and governments) were produced abroad (Q). Yalt < Y when NX is positive. In this case, Yalt understates the level of output since it ignores the fact that the country is selling more goods to foreigners than it is importing. The correct measure of Y should adjust purchases by recognizing that some of C, I, and G are imports and that some goods produced at home are sold abroad.

4. a. 200. They draw down their savings accounts or borrow.
b. C = 700. C increases by 50 to 750. Disposable income increased by 100 and C increased by 50; the marginal propensity to consume (mpc) is .5.
c. $S = -200 + .5Y_D$. S = -200. This represents the dissaving that would occur to pay for the consumption that occurs when disposable income is 0. The marginal propensity to save is .5; it is 1 - mpc.

5. a.

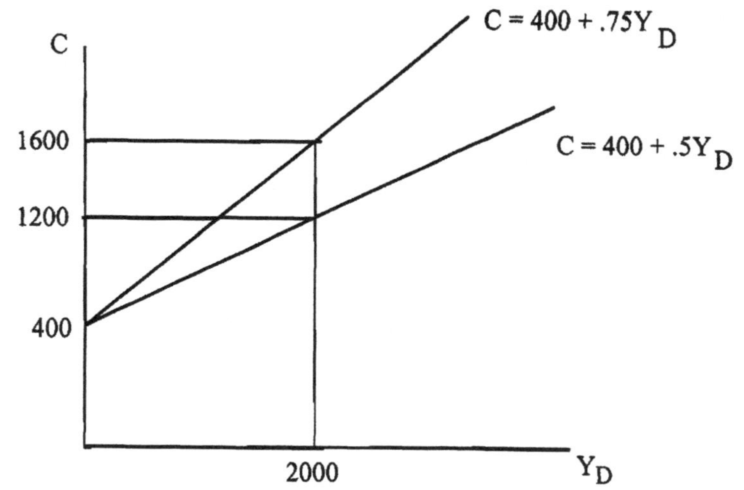

The vertical intercept is 400, autonomous consumption. The slope is .75, the mpc. C = 1600.
b. A reduction in the mpc will cause C to fall and the consumption function to become flatter. C falls to 1200.

6. a. The mpc is .5. The marginal propensity to save is 1 - .5 = .5.
b. Z = 1200 + .5(Y - 400) = 1000 + .5Y. Z is 1000 when Y is 0. This is the level of autonomous expenditures. If Y increases by 1, Z rises by .5. This is the mpc.
c. When Y is 1600, Z is 1800; when Y is 1800, Z is 1900; when Y is 2000, Z is 2000; when Y is 2200, Z is 2100; when Y is 2400, Z is 2200. Equilibrium occurs when Y is 2000 since Y = Z at that level of Y.
d. When Y is 1600, Z > Y. Firms set production equal to demand. Since demand exceeds Y, firms will increase Y over time. When Y is 2400, Y > Z. Production exceeds demand and firms will cut back on production.

7. a. Y = 1500 + .5(Y - 400) = 1300 + .5Y. Solve for Y: Y = 1300/.5 = 2600.

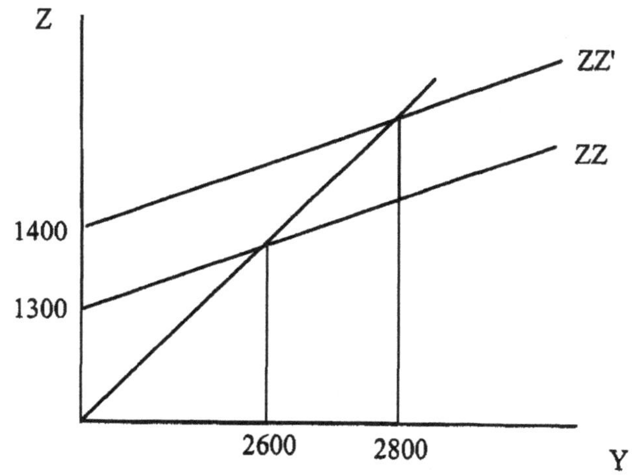

b. Plug in the numbers and you get: Y = 1400 + .5Y; Y = 2800. Output increases by 200. The multiplier is 2 (every 1-dollar change in C causes a 2-dollar change in Y).
c. See graph.

d. As demand increases by 100, firms respond by increasing production. The higher production also represents higher income. As income rises, consumption rises again, causing firms to increases Y yet again. This is the multiplier process at work.

8. a. $Y = 1500 + .8(Y - 400) = 1500 - 320 + .8Y$; $Y = 1180/.8 = 5900$.
b. $Y = 1280 + .8Y$; $Y = 1280/.8 = 6400$. Y rises 500 given the increase in C of 100; the multiplier is 5.
c. The ZZ line became steeper; the slope is greater. A change in Y now has a greater effect on Z (via C).
d. The change in output and the multiplier both increased. Any change in Y now causes an even greater increase in C and a greater subsequent increase in Y.
e. ZZ becomes steeper (see ZZ').

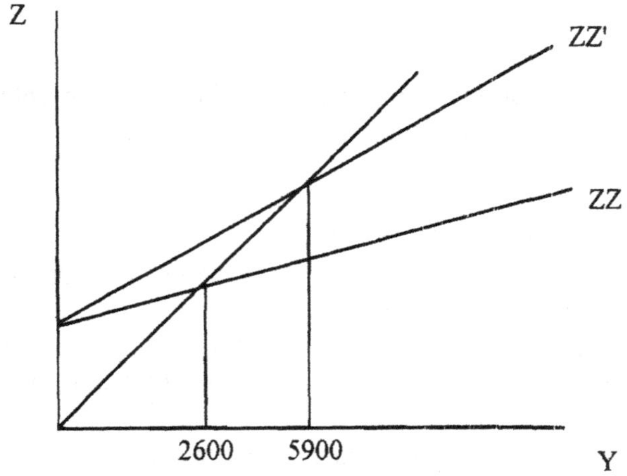

9. a. OA is autonomous spending. OA will decrease when G, I or autonomous consumption decrease, or when T increases.
b. OY_1 is production, Y_1E is demand, Y_1F is production. The economy is not in equilibrium since production is greater than demand.
c. OY_2 is production, Y_2B is production, Y_2C is demand. No, the economy is not in equilibrium since demand is greater than production.
d. Equilibrium output occurs at the level of Y where Y = Z. This occurs at the point where ZZ crosses the 45-degree line.

10. a. The multipliers will be ($1/(1-c_1)$): 1.7, 2, 2.5, 5, and 10. The multiplier increases as the mpc increases.
b. As the mpc increases, the ZZ line becomes steeper causing a higher level of equilibrium output.
c. How much should G increase to achieve this change in Y? The required change in G = 1000/(the multiplier). Plug in the numbers and you get: 588, 500, 400, 200 and 100.

11. a. Autonomous expenditures are greater in B, while the mpc is greater in A.
b. The level of autonomous expenditures in both countries will increase the SAME amount (100). Both curves will shift up by the exact same amount.

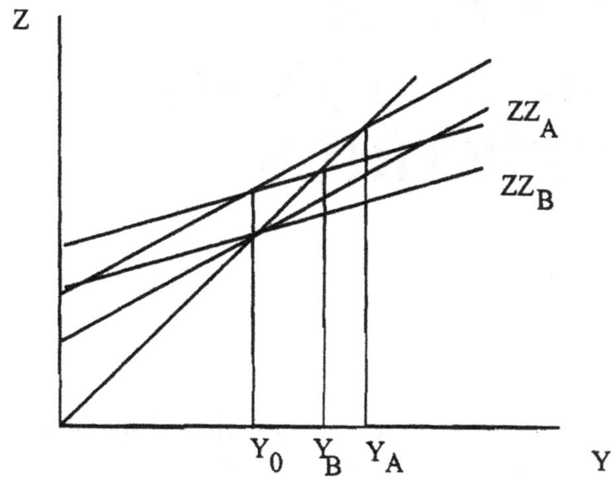

c. Output will increase more in A than in B, even though G increased by the same amount. Why? The multiplier is greater in A than in B.

12. a. Y = 300 + .9(Y - 1000) + 200 + 2000 = 1600 + .9Y; Y = 16000.
b. C = 300 + .9(16000 - 1000) = 13800.
c. S = -300 + .1(Y - T). Plug in the numbers: S = 1200.
d. Y = 1500 + .9Y; Y = 15000. Y falls as individuals increase their desire to save. This increased desire to save reflects a reduction in C and a reduction in demand. The drop in demand causes a drop in Y.
e. Be careful here! S = - 200 + .1(15000 - 1000) = 1210. When the new equilibrium is reached, S returns to its original level. This represents the paradox of thrift.

13. a. autonomous expenditures and Y both fall; the slope of ZZ and the multiplier do not change
b. autonomous expenditures and Y both increase; the slope of ZZ and the multiplier do not change
c. autonomous expenditures and Y both fall; the slope of ZZ and the multiplier do not change
d. autonomous expenditures do not change, Y increases, the slope of ZZ and the multiplier also increase.
e. autonomous expenditures do not change, Y decreases, the slope of ZZ and the multiplier also decrease.

MULTIPLE CHOICE QUESTIONS

1. D 2. D 3. A 4. B 5. D 6. A 7. C 8. D 9. C 10. D 11. C 12. B 13. D 14. E 15. C 16. C 17. C 18. D 19. A 20. C

APPENDIX 3: AN INTRODUCTION TO ECONOMETRICS

REVIEW PROBLEMS

1. a. 152.
b. 151.
c. It indicates how much consumption will increase above normal when disposable income increases by one unit above normal. It is the marginal propensity to consume.
d. Quite confident since the t-statistic is greater than 2.
e. The measure of fit.
f. Not great.
g. The slope of the line (which happens to be the marginal propensity to consume).

2. a. .6, the multiplier is 2.5.
b. .5, the multiplier is 2.
c. $(\Delta Y_{Dt} - \overline{\Delta Y_D})$
d. $(\Delta C_t - \overline{\Delta C})$
e. The results for Canada are slightly better given the higher $\overline{R}^2$.

MULTIPLE CHOICE QUESTIONS

1. A 2. B 3. D 4. A

CHAPTER 4

REVIEW PROBLEMS

1. a. Yes. Recall that wealth represents assets minus liabilities. An individual could have saved in earlier periods and accumulated a large quantity of wealth. Even though her income today could be low (or even 0), she could have a sizable quantity of wealth.
b. Yes. The answer is similar to a. If the individual saved in earlier periods, she will have accumulated assets. Even if saving is 0 today, the individual can still have wealth.
c. Yes. This can occur if one's liabilities exceed one's assets.

2. a. Flow variables: saving, investment, income
b. Stock variables: wealth, business inventories, the money supply and capital. Note: the <u>change</u> in business inventories is a flow variable.

3. As nominal income falls, transactions fall. As transactions fall, the individual will reduce her nominal money demand.

4. a. Nominal money demand increases by 10% and there is no change in the money supply.
b. Nominal money demand increases and there is no change in the money supply.
d. Bond demand increases (via the actions of the central bank), the money supply increases, and there is no change in money demand.

5. a. Velocity = $Y/M. Therefore, 1964: 4.04; 1974: 5.32; 1984: 6.84; and 1994: 5.87. Between 1964 and 1984, velocity increased. Between 1984 and 1994, velocity fell.
b. Yes. As i increased between 1964 and 1984, we would expect that individuals would reduce their money holdings for a given level of income. This would cause velocity to increase (as it did). When i falls, the opposite occurs and velocity should decrease. This also occurred between 1984 and 1994.
c. Changes in wealth should have no effect on money demand. Only $Y and the interest rate affect money demand.

6. a. See the graph included below. At i", individuals demand M" while the supply of money equals M; there is an excess supply of money. M represents the amount of money that actually exists.

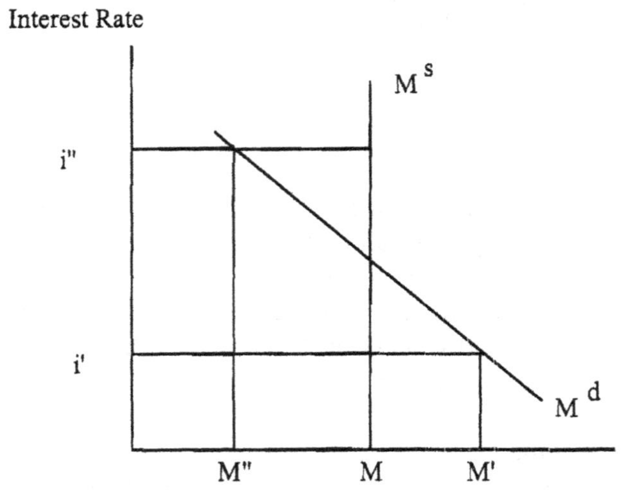

b. i must fall to restore equilibrium. As i falls, the supply of money does NOT change. As i falls, however, the demand for money increases.
c. At i', money demand exceeds money supply. Individuals want to hold M' while only M exists.
d. i must increase to restore equilibrium. As i increases, money supply does not change while money demand falls.

7. a. See the graph below. Individuals hold M.
b. The reduction in \$Y will cause a reduction in money demand to $M^{d'}$. i will fall to i'.

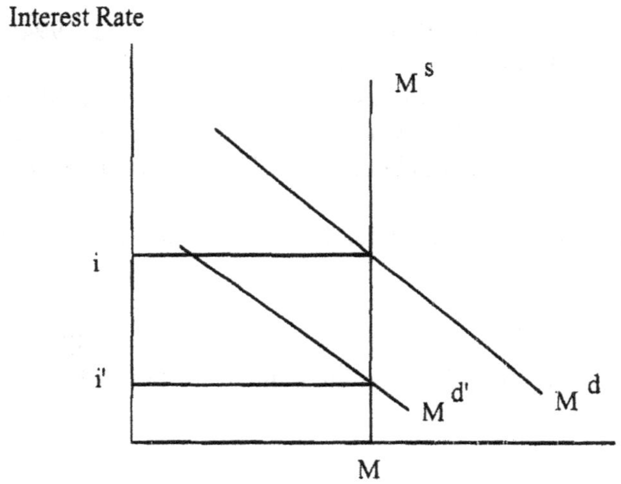

c. At i, money demand is lower so money supply exceeds money demand.
d. i must fall.
e. As i falls, money demand increases.
f. At i', individuals now hold M again. This is the same quantity that was held in part a.

8. a. See the graph. They hold M at the initial interest rate.
b. This will cause the money supply curve to shift to the left. i will rise.

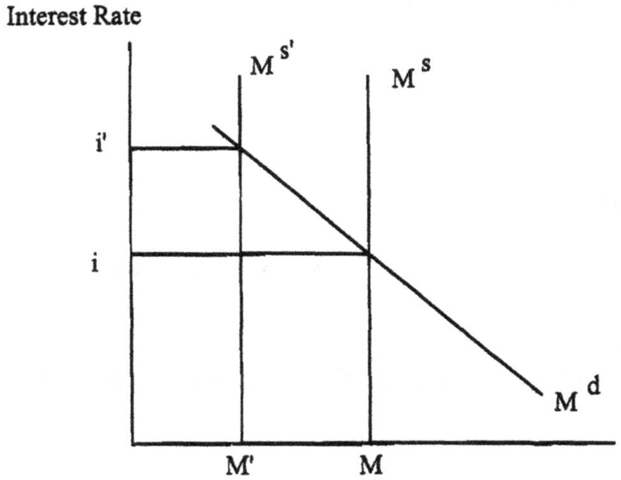

c. The actual quantity of money has decreased.
d. i must increase to restore equilibrium (to reduce money demand so that money supply and money demand are again equal).
e. As i increases, money demand falls.
f. They now hold M'. M' is less than the original quantity of money held.

9. Use the following equation to answer these questions: $i = (\$200 - \$P_B)/\$P_B$. Simply plug in the numbers.
a. 33.3%
b. 25%
c. 11.1%
d. 2.6%
e. As expected, i increases as the price of the bond falls.

10. Use the following formula to calculate the price of the bond: $\$P_B = \$1000/(1 + i)$. Simply plug in the numbers.
a. $952.38
b. $909.09
c. $869.57
d. The price of the bond falls.

11. a. The Fed's holding of bonds (assets) increases by $10 million.
b. The Fed's liabilities (currency) increases by the same amount.
c. Bond prices increase.
d. The interest rate will fall.
e. The money demand curve does NOT shift.
f. Central bank money increases by $10 million.
g. The money supply also increases by $10 million.

12. a. The Fed's holding of bonds (assets) decreases by $20 million.
b. The Fed's liabilities (currency) fall by the same amount.
c. Bond prices fall.
d. The interest rate will increase.
e. The money demand curve does NOT shift.
f. Central bank money falls by $20 million.
g. The money supply also decreases by $20 million.

13. When CU = 0, M = D, H = R, and the money multiplier is $1/\theta$. All numbers are in millions of dollars.
a. The monetary base, H, will equal 500.
b. Given the reserve ratio, every $1 of reserves can support $5 of deposits, so D = 2500 (5 x 500).
c. The money supply is given by M = CU + D = 0 + 2500 = 2500.
d. The money multiplier is $1/\theta = 1/.2 = 5$.

14. a. The monetary base increases by 50 to 550.
b. Since no currency is held, reserves also increase by 50 to 550.
c. Each additional $1 of reserves supports $5 of deposits. So, deposits will increase by 250.
d. The money supply will also increase by 250.

15. a. The monetary base decreases by 10.
b. The amount of reserves will fall by 10.
c. For reasons given in #14, the deposits will fall by 50.
d. The money supply will also fall by 50.

16. a. Plugging in the numbers, we get: 10, 5, 3.33, 2.5, and 2.
b. It decreases.
c. We can illustrate this relation using a simple example. Suppose a bank has 100 additional reserves (from a new deposit of 100). When the reserve ratio is .1, the bank can increase loans by 90 (or increase bond holdings by 90); 10 must be held as reserves. If the reserve ratio were .5, the bank could only increase loans by 50 (or increase bond holdings by 50); it must hold 50 as reserves. The higher reserve ratio limits the extent to which banks can create money. Alternatively, when the ratio is .1, the 100 of new reserves can support 1000 of new deposits. When the ratio is .5, the 100 of new reserves can support "only" 200 of new deposits.

17. a. 50/500 = .10
b. c = CU/M = 250/750 = .33.
c. H = CU + R = 50 + 250 = 300.
d. M = D + CU = 250 + 500 = 750.
e. There are two ways to do this: (1) M/H = 750/300 = 2.5; (2) $1/[c + \theta(1-c)] = 2.5$.
f.

Banks' Balance Sheet

Assets	Liabilities
R 50	D 500
Bond Holdings 450	

Central Bank Balance Sheet

Assets	Liabilities
Bond Holdings 300	CU 250
	R 50

18. All numbers in millions.
a. It should buy bonds. Given that the multiplier is 2.5, the Fed should by $40 worth of bonds (100/2.5 = 40).
b. The increase in bond demand will increase the price of bonds.
c. It should sell bonds. It should sell $16 worth of bonds (-40/2.5 = -16).
d. The increase in supply will cause bond prices to fall.

19. The money multiplier is $1/[c + \theta(1-c)]$.
a. Plugging in the numbers yields 3.57, 2.78 and 1.67.
b. It decreases.
c. See the answer to part (c) of #16.

20. a. Plugging in the numbers, we get: 5.27, 3.57 and 1.82.
b. It falls.
c. As c increases, a greater portion of money is held in the form of currency. CU is a "leakage" from the banking system. The more currency is held, banks cannot use this portion of H to create money. Hence, the money supply is smaller.

21. a. The supply of central bank money decreases causing i to rise. The effects are the same.

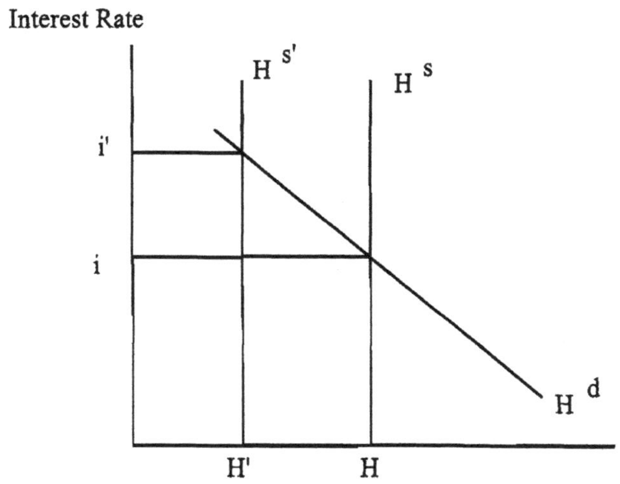

b. To save space, I will not repeat the graphs, but simply describe in words what happens. The decrease in income causes a reduction in money demand, a reduction in currency demand and a reduction in reserve demand. We also observe a reduction in the demand for central bank money. This leftward shift in H^d will cause a reduction in the interest rate. The results are the same.
c. The increase in the reserve ratio will cause an increase in the demand for reserves and a subsequent increase in the demand for central bank money. This will cause an increase in i. The results are the same. In the money market model, the higher reserve ratio will cause a reduction in the money supply and an increase in i.

MULTIPLE CHOICE QUESTIONS

1. C 2. A. 3. D 4. D 5. C 6. A 7. B 8. C 9. B 10. B 11. A 12. A 13. D 14. B 15. C 16. B 17. C 18. C 19. B 20. A

CHAPTER 5

REVIEW PROBLEMS

1. a. Plugging in the numbers, we get: I = 600 when i = 5; I = 500 when i = 10; and I = 400 when i = 15. As expected, I falls when i increases.
b. Plugging in the numbers, we get: 650, 700 and 750. Again, as expected, I increases as Y increases.

2. a. Y = 180 + .7(Y - 400) + 100 - 18i + .1Y + 400. This yields:
Y = 400 + .8Y - 18i. Subtract .8Y from both sides and then divide by .2. This gives us the following: Y = 2000 - 90i. This is the IS equation.
b. Using the above equation and plugging in the numbers for i yields: 1550, 1100, 650, and 200. Your plot should be downward sloping; it represents the IS curve.
c. The higher i causes a reduction in investment which causes a reduction in demand and output. The lower output/income causes a reduction in both consumption and saving.
d. Y = 2000 - 90(8) = 1280. WARNING: Y does not just increase by 100; there is a multiplier effect here. Replace G with 500 and we get: Y = 500 + .8Y - 18i. Solving for Y and letting i = 8 yields: Y = 2500 - 90(8) = 1780. The 100 increase in G causes Y to increase by 500. The multiplier must be 5.
e. An increase in G causes the IS curve to shift to the right by 500 (i.e., the size of the shift equals the increase in G times the multiplier).

3. a. A lower interest rate causes an increase in I and an increase in Y; this explains the slope of the IS curve and represents a movement along the IS curve. The IS curve does NOT shift as i falls.
b. The exact opposite of a. This will cause a movement along the IS curve (no shift).
c. This reduction in consumption will cause the IS curve to shift to the left; the equilibrium level of output is now lower (at each i) because of this drop in demand.
d. This will cause a reduction in consumption and a leftward shift in the IS curve.

4. a. 3 x \$1 = \$3. Her (daily) nominal money demand is \$3.
b. 3 x \$1.20 = \$3.60. As the price of the good increases, the individual will increase her nominal money demand so that she can continue to purchase the same real quantity of goods and services (in this case, her favorite beverage).
c. To convert her nominal money demand to real money demand, we simply divide her nominal money demand by the price deflator. Her initial real money demand was: \$3/1 = \$3. Her final real money demand is \$3.60/1.2 = \$3. Her real money demand did NOT change. She simply increased her nominal money demand proportionately as the price of the good increased.
d. As income increases, the demand for goods and, therefore, transactions increases. She probably will increase her consumption of her favorite beverage. To purchase these goods, she will increase her nominal money demand and, since P is assumed to be constant, real money demand.

5. a. The drop in Y will cause a drop in transactions and, therefore, a drop in money demand. Money demand falls to $M^{d'}$. At the initial interest rate, there is now an excess supply of money. Individuals hold more money than they would like.
b. For the financial market to be in equilibrium, i must fall to restore equilibrium. The new equilibrium is given by point A'. See the graph.

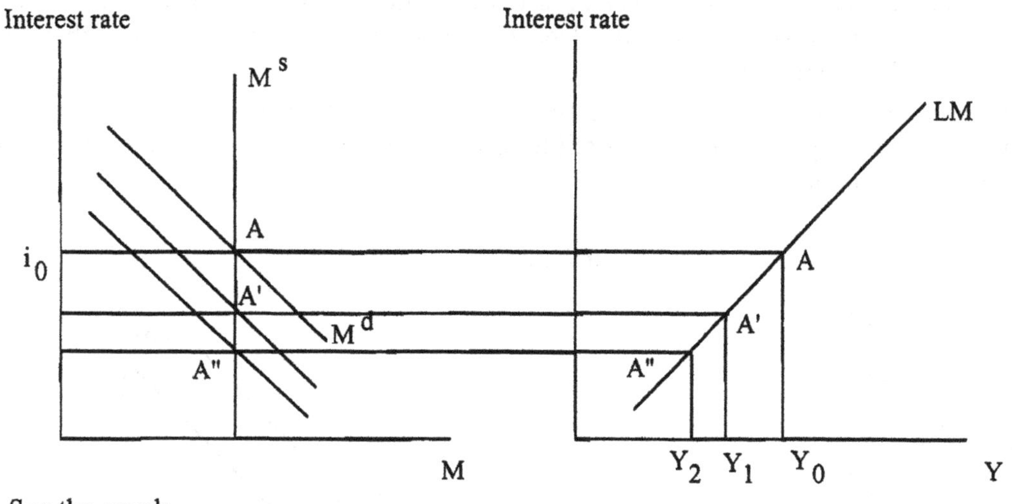

c. See the graph.
d. The combinations of i and Y which maintain equilibrium in the financial market is the LM curve.

6. a. See the graph. At the initial i, money demand exceeds money supply.

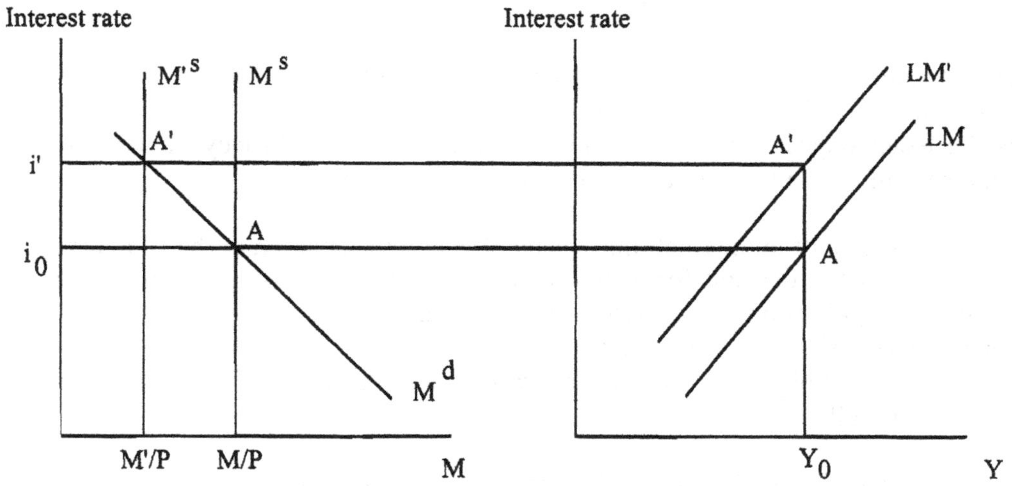

b. i must increase to i'. As i increases, money demand falls resulting in a new equilibrium at point A'.
c. The LM curve must shift up to reflect the higher interest rate which is required to maintain equilibrium in the financial market. The LM curve shifts up to LM'.

7. a. 5400 = 6Y - 120i. So, 120i = 6Y - 5400. Dividing by 120 yields: i = .05Y - 45. This is the LM relation.
b. Plugging in the numbers yields: 5%, 10% and 15%. Plotting the i - Y combinations should (?!) yield an upward sloping line. This is the LM curve.
c. i = .05(1400) - 45 = 25%. Return to the original equation included in a. Replace 5400 with 5000 and solve for i when Y = 1400. Plugging in the numbers yields: i = 28.33%. i increases by 3.33%.
d. The LM curve must shift up (by 3.33%) to reflect this higher interest rate. i must be higher at each level of Y to maintain equilibrium when the money supply falls.

8. a. The increased use of credit cards has caused a reduction in money demand. This causes the money demand curve to shift to the left. People can consolidate their payments each month; hence, they can hold/demand less money.
b. See the graph. The money demand curve shifts to $M^{d'}$. At the original interest rate, money supply now exceeds money demand. i must fall to restore equilibrium (as i falls, money demand increases). The new equilibrium is at A'.

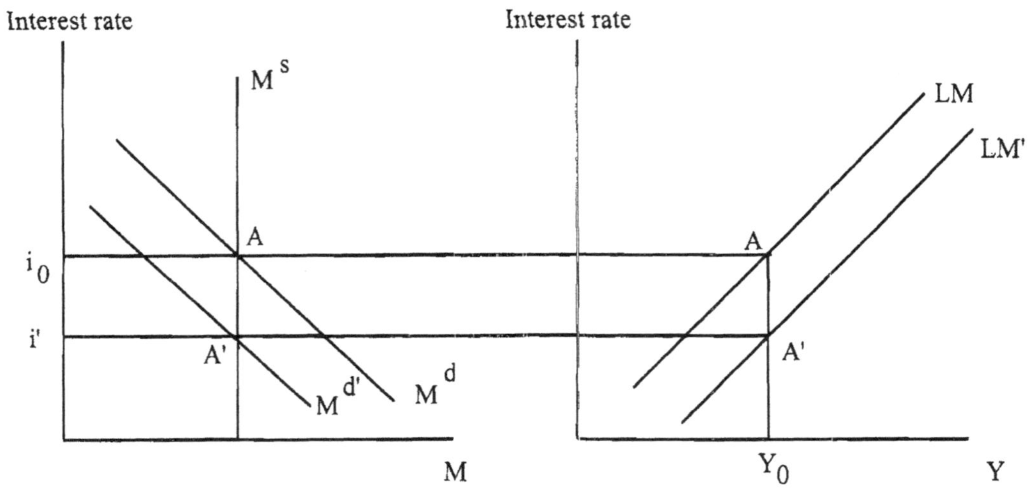

c. The interest rate must now be lower (at each Y) to maintain equilibrium in the financial market. This implies that the LM curve must shift down to LM'.
d. This is the exact opposite of the example we just examined. Money demand increases causing an increase in i. The LM curve would shift up in this case.

9. a. The IS curve will shift to the right; this has no effect on the position of the LM curve.
b. Y will increase as the demand for goods increases. As Y increases, money demand will increase causing the equilibrium interest rate to increase; i increases.
c. Both C and S increase because Y increases.
d. The effects on I are ambiguous. The higher Y will tend to increase I. The higher i, however, will tend to cause I to fall.

10. a. This has no effect on the IS curve. The LM curve will shift up.
b. The reduction in the money supply will cause i to increase. As i increases, I will fall. The reduction in I causes a reduction in demand and firms respond by reducing output.
c. The lower Y causes both C and S to fall.
d. I unambiguously falls because Y is lower and i is higher; both of these events cause I to fall.

11. a. A fiscal expansion will cause the IS curve to shift to the right and cause Y and i to increase. The higher Y will cause I to increase. The higher i will cause I to fall. Without knowing the exact magnitudes of these effects, we do not know whether I will increase or decrease.
b. Yes. The output effects must dominate the interest effects.
c. Yes. The effects of the lower i on I must dominate the effects of the lower Y on I.

12. a. $Y = C + I + G$. Substitute in the equations for C and I and we have: $Y = 180 + .7(Y - 400) + 100 - 18i + .1Y + 400$. Collecting terms yields: $Y = .8Y + 400 - 18i$. Solve for Y: $.2Y = 400 - 18i$. Divide both sides by .2 and we get the IS equation: $Y = 2000 - 90i$.

b. 5400 = 6Y - 120i. Solving for i yields: 120i = 6Y - 5400. Dividing both sides by 120 yields the LM equation: i = .05Y - 45.
c. Y = 2000 - 90[.05Y - 45] = 2000 - 4.5Y + 4050. Adding 4.5Y to both sides yields: 5.5Y = 6050. Dividing by 5.5 gives us the overall equilibrium level of Y: Y = 6050/5.5 = 1100.
d. i = .05(1100) - 45 = 55 - 45 = 10 (10%).
e. C = 180 + .7(1100 - 400) = 670. I = 100 - 18(10) + .1(1100) = 30.
f. Be careful here. You must change G in the original equation included in a. Y = .8Y + 410 - 18i. So, .2Y = 410 - 18i. Y = 2050 - 90i.
Calculation of Y: Y = 2050 - 90(.05Y - 45). Solving for Y, we get: Y = 1109.1.
Calculation of i: i = .05(1109.1) - 45 = 55.46 - 45 = 10.46 (10.46%).
Calculation of C: C = 180 + .7(1109.1 - 400) = 676.4.
Calculation of I: I = 100 - 18(10.46) + .1(1109.1) = 22.6 (I fell). The negative effects of the higher i must have offset the positive effects of the higher Y.
g. Return to the original LM equation and replace 5400 with 5600. 5600 = 6Y - 120i. Solving for i yields: i = .05Y - 46.67. Substituting this into the original IS equation, we get: Y = 2000 - 90[.05Y - 46.67] = 2000 - 4.5Y + 4200.3. Solving for Y: Y = 1127.3.
Calculation of i: i = .05(1127.3) - 46.67 = 9.7 (9.7%).
Calculation of C: C = 180 + .7(1127.3 - 400) = 689.1.
Calculation of I: I = 100 -18(9.7) + .1(1127.3) = 38.1.
I increases as M increases for two reasons: (1) i is lower; and (2) Y is higher.

13. a. The IS curve shifts to the right.
b. To keep i at the initial level, the Fed must increase the money supply as money demand increases. This will shift the LM curve down; see the graph. The final equilibrium is at point A'.

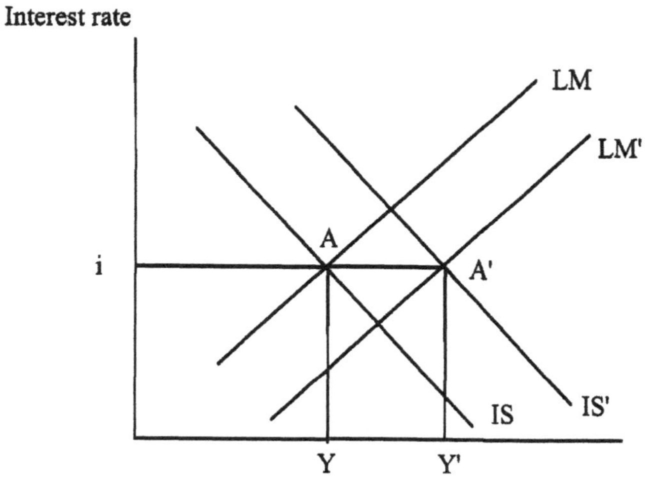

c. C and S both increase because Y increase. I also increases because Y increases (there is no offsetting effect of higher i here).

14. a. The IS curve shifts to the right.
b. To keep Y constant, the Fed will have to pursue contractionary monetary policy and reduce the money supply. This will cause the LM curve to shift up. The final equilibrium will be point A'. See the graph.

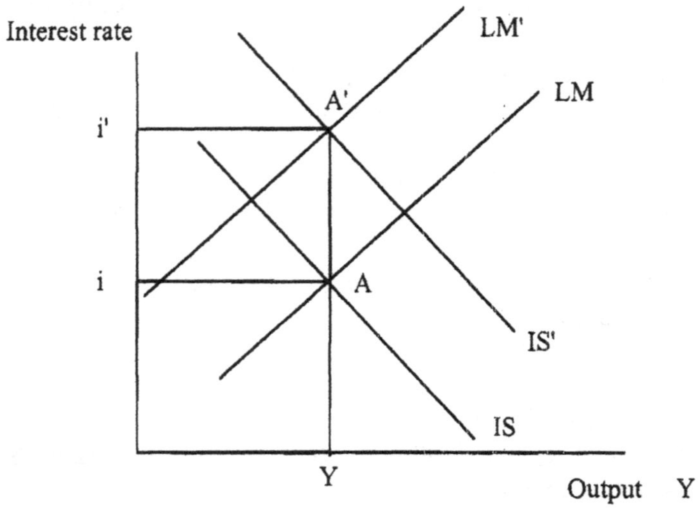

c. The effects on C and S are a bit subtle here. Y does not change. However, T is lower. So, at A', disposable income is higher; therefore, C and S are higher. In fact, it is the tax cut that stimulates C which causes the IS curve to shift to the right. Investment falls because of the higher i (there is no change in Y to offset this). In fact, the drop in I completely offsets the increase in C.

15. a. IS to right, move along the LM curve, Y increases, i increases, consumption increases, ambiguous effects on I (Y is higher, i is higher).
b. The exact opposite of a.
c. LM shifts down, move along the IS curve, i is lower, Y is higher, I is higher and C is higher.

16. a. The IS curve shifts to the left. The increase in T causes a reduction in disposable income. This causes a reduction in C and a reduction in demand.
b. See the graph. IS shifts to the left. As Y falls, money demand falls causing i to fall. The economy moves from point A along the LM curve to point A'.

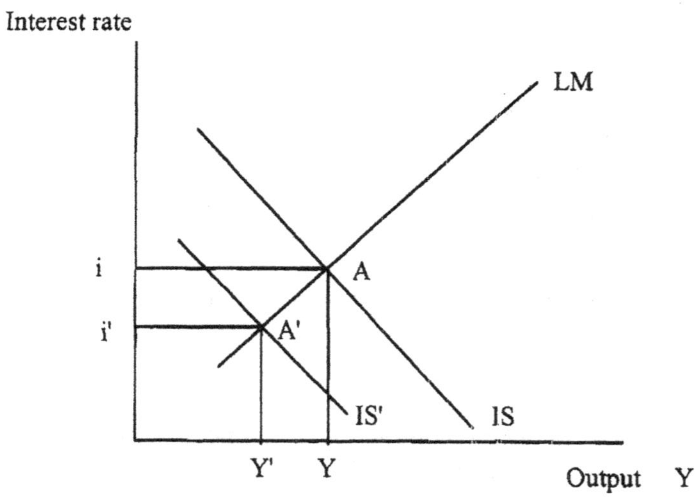

c. Consumption falls as Y falls. i falls as money demand falls. The effects on investment are ambiguous since i falls and Y falls.

17. a. The LM curve shifts down to LM'.

b. See the graph. The financial market is always assumed to be in equilibrium so the economy moves from point A to point B on the LM curve. The lower i causes an increase in I. As demand increases, Y increases. As Y increases, money demand increases causing i to increase and the economy moves along the LM curve until it reaches the new overall equilibrium at point A'

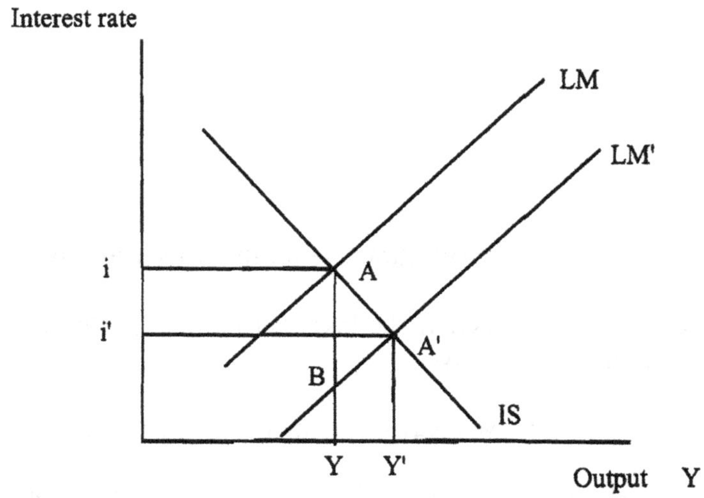

c. C increases during the adjustment as Y increases. The interest rate initially falls to the point indicated by point B. As money demand increases, however, we move from B to A' and the interest rate rises to its final (lower) level. I increases because of the increase in Y and drop in i.

18. a. A lower i would have no effect on demand. Therefore, equilibrium output in the goods market would be independent of the interest rate. In this case, the IS curve would be vertical.

b. An increase in M would cause a lower i. The lower i, however, would have no effect on I and on demand. Y would not increase.

c. Increases in G would cause Y to increase. In this case, Y would increase even further. The higher i would have no negative effect on I. None of the increase in G would be offset by an increase in i.

MULTIPLE CHOICE QUESTIONS

1. D 2. B 3. A 4. B 5. A 6. D 7. D 8. C 9. A 10. B 11. B 12. A 13. A 14. D 15. C 16. B 17. A 18. B 19. C

CHAPTER 6

REVIEW PROBLEMS

1. a. 150 + 12 = 162
b. 250 - 162 = 88
c. 162/250 = 64.8%
d. 12/162 = 7.4%
e. 100/250 = 40%

2. a. An increase in the wage makes it financially more attractive for the worker to stay with the firm, thus reducing quits.
b. A higher wage makes it more costly to the worker if she loses her job due to shirking. The worker will, therefore, shirk less and be more productive.

3. It will increase if the proportion of the unemployed leaving unemployment decreases.

4. An increase in the unemployment rate will increase the chances of one losing his job. This will cause the separation rate to increase.

5. Primary labor market: jobs are good, wages are high and turnover is low. Secondary labor market: jobs are poor, wages are low and turnover is high.

6. a. The nominal wage is set based on the expected price level since workers care about the real wage. A reduction in the expected price level will cause a proportionate reduction in W.
b. This increases bargaining power. As bargaining power increases, W will increase.
c. The prospects of being unemployed are more distressing. Workers will be willing to accept lower wages, so W falls.

7. a. The markup increases. Given W, P will increase.
b. The markup decreases. Given W, P will fall.
c. Since firms set P as a markup over cost, a reduction in W will cause a reduction in P.

8. a. As u falls, workers have more bargaining power thus increasing W. Given P, W/P will increase.
b. See explanation in part a! A reduction in u causes an increase in W/P.
c. The prospects of being unemployed are more distressing. Workers will be willing to accept lower wages so W falls. Given P, W/P will fall. So, at each u, W/P is lower. This represents a shift down in the WS relation.
d. At a given u, the chances of getting a job are higher as structural change increases. u is less of a threat to workers so bargaining power increases. This increases W; given P, W/P increases. So, at each u, W/P is higher. This represents a shift up in the WS relation.
e. An increase in P will cause a proportionate increase in W. The WS relation does NOT shift.

9. a. Simply plug the numbers into the equation $W/P = 1/(1 + \mu)$: .91, .83, .77 and .71.
b. It decreases.
c. As the markup increases, firms set P even further above W. Given W, this higher P causes the real wage to fall.

10. a. In perfectly competitive markets, firms set prices equal to costs. So, the markup is 0.
b. Since P = W when the markup is 0, W/P = 1.

11. a. As described previously, this causes the WS relation to shift down. This will cause an increase in the natural unemployment rate and no change in W/P.
b. As described above, this will cause an increase in W/P in the WS relation. The WS relation shifts up causing the natural unemployment rate to increase with no change in W/P.
c. This will raise the markup of price over cost. Firms will raise P given W. This will reduce W/P in the PS relation. The PS relation shifts down causing an increase in the natural rate of unemployment and a reduction in the real wage.
d. This will cause the WS relation to shift up, the natural rate of unemployment to increase and no change in the real wage.

12. a. Since u_n increased, N and Y will both fall.
b. Since u_n increased, N and Y will both fall.
c. Since u_n increased, N and Y will both fall.
d. Since u_n increased, N and Y will both fall.
Note: If u_n falls, both N and Y will increase.

MULTIPLE CHOICE QUESTIONS

1. B 2. B 3. D 4. A 5. A 6. E 7. D 8. B 9. B 10. A 11. B 12. C 13. D 14. D 15. A 16. B 17. A 18. B 19. C

CHAPTER 7

REVIEW PROBLEMS

1. a. The nominal wage will increase by 5% and firms will increase P by 5%.
b. The nominal wage will fall by 2% and firms will reduce P by 2%.
c. Firms will increase the markup over cost. Given W, this indicates that P will increase.
d. Firms will reduce the markup over cost. Given W, this indicates that P will fall.
e. An increase in Y corresponds to an increase in employment and reduction in u. As u falls, bargaining power increases causing W to increase. As W increases, firms increase P.
f. A reduction in Y corresponds to a reduction in employment and increase in u. As u increases, bargaining power falls causing W to fall. As W falls, firms reduce P.

2. An increase in Y corresponds to an increase in employment and reduction in u. As u falls, bargaining power increases causing W to increase. As W increases, firms increase P. Therefore, an increase in Y corresponds to an increase in P. The AS curve is upward sloping.

3. The lower P has no effect on M. As P falls, however, M/P increases causing the LM curve to shift down. As the LM curve shifts down, i falls. The reduction in i causes an increase in I and an increase in Y. We move from point A to point B.

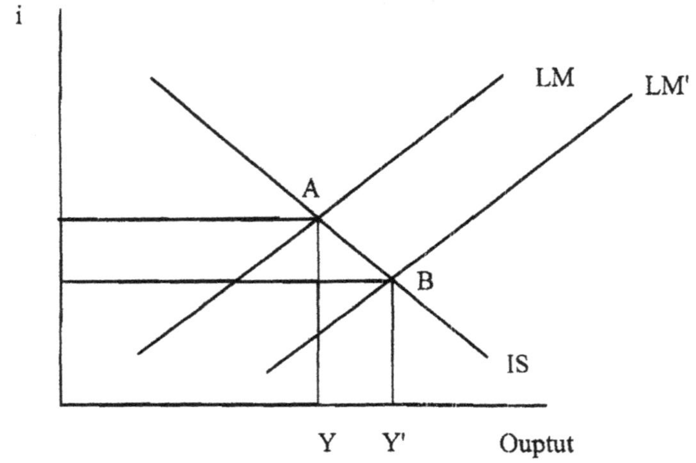

4. A reduction in P causes an increase in M/P. The increase in M/P causes the LM curve to shift down. This shift in the LM curve causes i to fall. Alternatively, a lower P causes a reduction in nominal money demand. As i falls, I increases and Y increases (we move along the IS curve). Therefore, a reduction in P causes an increase in Y in the goods market; the AD curve is downward sloping.

5. Note: if the curve is not listed, it does not shift.
a. IS to right and AD to right
b. IS to left and AD to left
c. LM down and AD to right
d. LM up and AD to left
e. IS to right and AD to right
f. IS to left and AD to left
g. IS to left and AD to left
h. IS to right and AD to right
i. LM up and the AD curve does NOT shift (move along it)
j. LM down and the AD curve does NOT shift (move along it)

6. a. u is below u_n, N above N_n and P above P^e.
b. The expected price level will increase.
c. The nominal wage will increase (because of b).
d. The AS curve will shift up.

7. a. u is above u_n, N below N_n and P below P^e.
b. The expected price level will fall.
c. The nominal wage will fall (because of b).
d. The AS curve will shift down.

8. a. As the AS curve shifts up, the price level will increase. The higher P has no effect on M. M/P will fall. As M/P falls, i increases causing I to fall. As I falls, Y falls. This describes the movement along the AD curve.
b. As the AS curve shifts down, the price level will fall.. The lower P has no effect on M. M/P will rise. As M/P rises, i falls causing I to increase. As I increases, Y increases. This describes the movement along the AD curve.

9. a. The economy goes from A to B to C and, after several more adjustments, to the final equilibrium, D.

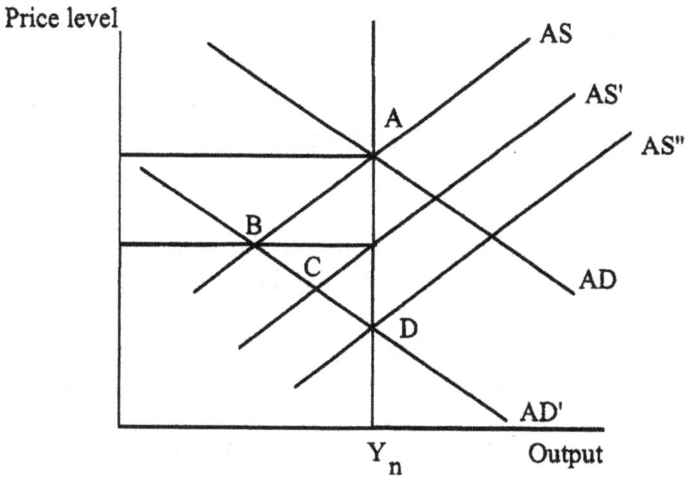

b. The initial effects are: (1) P falls; (2) M/P falls (M falls more than P initially); (3) i increases; (4) I falls; and (5) Y falls.
c. Initially, u increases above u_n and Y falls below Y_n. During the adjustment, u and Y return to their natural levels. In the medium run, u and Y equal their natural levels.

d. The AS curve shifts down as the expected price level falls.
e. P falls; M/P increases; i falls; I increases; and Y increases.
f. P falls proportionately so that M/P does not change in the medium run. i, I and Y return to their initial levels.
g. Yes. P will equal P^e in the medium run.

10. a. 6%.
b. No.
c. The nominal wage will fall by 6% leaving the real wage unchanged in the medium run.

11. a. The economy goes from A to B to C and, after several more adjustments, to the final equilibrium, D.

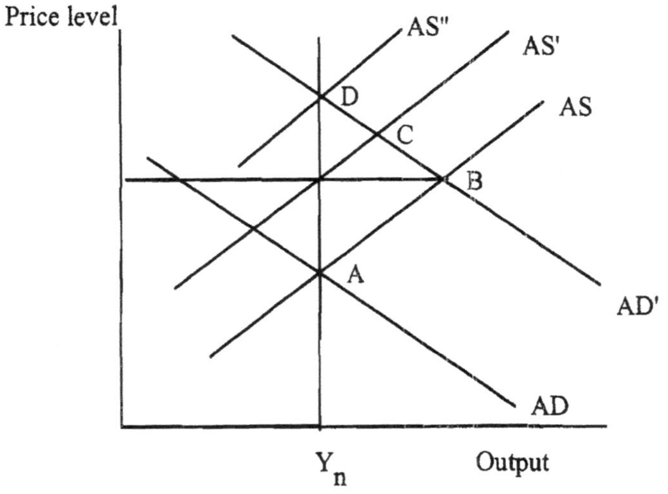

b. P is higher; M/P falls; i increases; effects on I are ambiguous (Y is higher and i is higher); and Y increases.
c. Short-run: u is below u_n, Y is above Y_n. Dynamic adjustment: u returns to u_n, Y returns to Y_n. Medium run: u and Y return to their natural levels.
d. AS shifts up because the expected price level increases.
e. P increases; M/P falls; i increases; I now falls; Y falls.
f. P is higher; M/P is permanently lower; i is permanently higher; I is permanently lower; and Y returns to original. NOTE: the change in G equals the size of the reduction in I.
f. Yes. P will equal P^e in the medium run.

12. Yes. i was higher and I was lower. The IS curve has shifted to the right while the LM curve has shifted up. All of the increase in G is completely offset by the reduction in I.

13. a. The higher price level causes the M/P to fall and the LM curve to shift up. As the interest rate increases output falls. The graph should include an upward shift in the LM curve with no shift in the IS curve.
b. C falls because Y is lower. I falls because i is higher AND because Y is lower.

14. The drop in the price of oil will cause a reduction in the markup over cost. This will cause the PS relation to shift up to PS'; the economy moves from point A to point B. As this happens, the real wage will increase and u will fall.

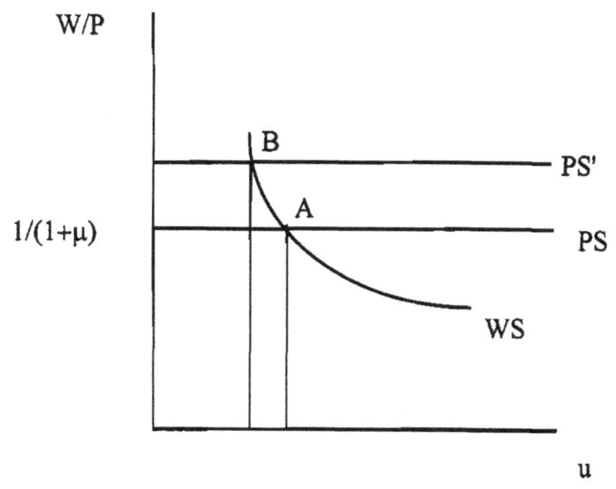

15. The lower price of oil causes an increase in the natural level of output. This causes the AS curve to shift down (the horizontal distance between AS and AS' is the increase in the natural level of output to Y_n'). The final equilibrium occurs at point D. In the short run: P decreases; Y rises, i falls; I rises (i is lower and Y is higher); the real wage is higher; and u is lower. In the medium run: P is lower; Y is higher; i is lower; I is higher; W/P is higher; and u is lower.

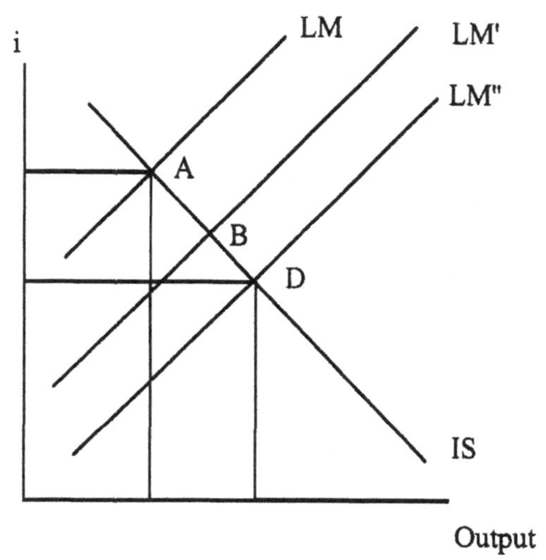

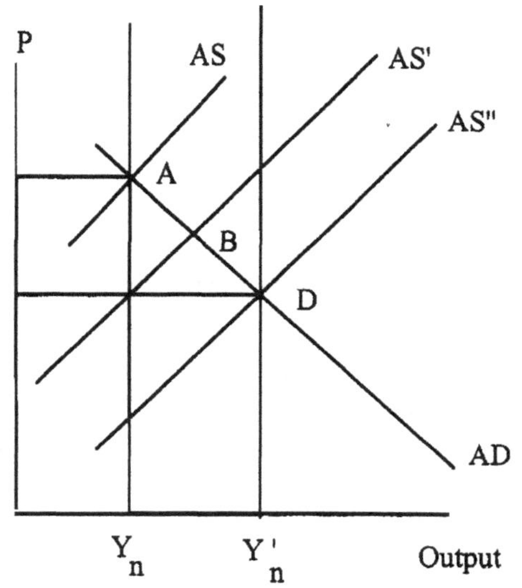

16. The reduction in unemployment benefits represents a reduction in z. The WS relation shifts down causing a reduction in u_n. The real wage will not change here because the PS relation does not shift. The effects on the IS-LM and AS-AD graphs are the same as those included in #15. Y increases, P falls, i falls, I increases and u falls. Note: the IS and AD curves do not shift here.

MULTIPLE CHOICE QUESTIONS

1. D 2. C 3. B 4. C 5. B 6. C 7. D 8. B 9. D 10. A 11. B 12. D 13. E 14. B 15. B 16. C 17. D 18. E 19. A

CHAPTER 8

REVIEW PROBLEMS

1. a. A reduction in expected inflation will cause a reduction in inflation. Why? As expected inflation falls, wage growth falls. Since firms base price increases as a markup over costs, if wage growth declines, the increase in prices (inflation) will decline.
b. A reduction in the markup over costs will cause firms to reduce the size of any increase in prices. This will cause inflation to fall.
c. Any factor which reduces wages will, given the markup, allow firms to decrease the size of any price increase. This will reduce the inflation rate.

2. a. Any policy which reduces u will increase the bargaining power of workers and cause wages to increase. The increase in wages will cause a higher rate of inflation.
b. u must increase. As u increases, bargaining power falls and wages fall. As wages fall, inflation will fall.

3. a. Plug in the numbers and you get: (in %) 4, 6, 8, and 10.
b. Expected inflation is higher because individuals expect a greater portion of last period's inflation to persist.

4. Note: actual and expected inflation must be equal for u to be equal to the natural rate.
a. $u_n = .10/2 = .05$.
b. $u_n = .10/2 = .05$.
c. How expectations are formed will not affect the natural rate of unemployment.

5. a. Simply plug in the numbers: 7%.
b. 3%. Inflation falls by 4%. As unemployment increases, wage growth declines causing inflation to decline.
c. Nothing. Expected inflation in t is based on last period's inflation rate.

6. The following equation is used to calculate inflation in period t: $\pi_t = \pi_{t-1} - 1.5(u_t - u_n)$.
a. Plug in the numbers and we get .025 = 2.5% inflation. Inflation in t is less than inflation in t-1 (4%). You should know this by simply comparing unemployment in t with the natural rate of unemployment.
b. Plugging in the numbers yields: 1%, -0.5% and -2%.
c. Each 1% increase in unemployment causes the inflation rate to fall by 1.5%.
d. As u falls, the inflation rate is falling.

7. a. Using the equation included in the answer to #6, we obtain a 5.5% inflation rate. It is greater than the inflation rate in the previous period. This should not be surprising since u this period is below the natural rate.
b. We get (in %): 7, 8.5 and 10.
c. Each 1% drop in u causes the inflation rate to increase by 1.5%.
d. As u falls, the inflation rate increases. As u increases, the inflation rate will decrease.

8. This should be an easy question!
a. Since u is at the natural rate, we know that the inflation rate will neither increase or decrease. So, inflation in t will be the same as it was in t-1 which was 4%.

b. If inflation in t-1 was 3%, it will be 3% in period t. If inflation in t-1 was 6%, it will be 6% in period t.
c. When u is at the natural rate, inflation will not change; consequently, inflation in t will equal inflation in t-1.

9. a. If inflation is rising, u must be below the natural rate. When u is below the natural rate, there is pressure for wages to increase. As wages increase, inflation will increase above expected.
b. If inflation is falling, u must be above the natural rate. When u is above the natural rate, there is pressure for wages to decrease. As wages decrease, inflation will decrease below expected.
c. When inflation is constant, we know that u is at the natural rate. The labor market is in equilibrium.

10. a. Without information about the natural rates of unemployment in the two countries, we can say nothing about what will happen to the inflation rate in the two countries. The extent to which the inflation rate will change depends on a comparison of u with the natural rate.
b. If the inflation rate in A is falling, this implies that u is above the natural rate in A.
c. If the inflation rate in B is rising, this implies that u is below the natural rate in B.

11. If u is kept below the natural rate, inflation will increase over time.
b. If u is kept above the natural rate, inflation will fall over time.

12. A given reduction in the unemployment rate will now have a smaller effect on inflation in that period. When u falls below the natural rate, inflation falls. If some contracts are indexed, wages will fall within the period in response to the drop in inflation. As wages fall, firms reduce prices even further. If there are fewer contracts that are indexed, the indexation-induced reduction in inflation will be that much smaller. The drop in inflation will be smaller.

13. This reduction represents a reduction in costs. This can be examined in much the same way a change in oil prices has been examined. The drop in benefits represents a reduction in nonwage costs. This will cause a reduction in the markup. As the markup falls, the PS curve shifts up. This will cause a reduction in the natural rate of unemployment and an increase in the equilibrium real wage.

14. An increase in oil prices will cause an increase in the markup and cause the PS curve to shift down. This will cause an increase in the unemployment rate and a reduction in the equilibrium real wage. Equilibrium employment will also fall causing a reduction in the natural level of output. If, however, workers accept the drop in the wage without any increase in unemployment, we will observe a downward shift in the WS curve; this would be represented formally as a drop in the catchall variable z. In this case, the equilibrium real wage still falls. There will, however, be no change in the natural rate of unemployment, no change in N and no change in the natural level of output. The equilibrium real wage does fall.

MULTIPLE CHOICE QUESTIONS

1. D 2. C 3. B 4. C 5. B 6. D 7. C 8. C 9. C 10. A 11. C 12. B 13. B 14. B 15. A 16. A 17. A 18. C

CHAPTER 9

REVIEW PROBLEMS

1. a. Output growth must be (in %): 2, 3, 4, and 5.
b. The normal growth rate must increase. As the labor force grows more quickly, employment will rise at a faster rate. To keep u constant, output will have to grow at a faster rate too.
c. Output growth must be (in %): 1, 2, 3, and 4.
d. If the labor force is more productive, output growth will have to increase to keep u constant.

2. a. (all in %): -.4, -.8, and -1.2. Each 1% increase in output growth causes u to fall by .4 percentage points.
b. (all in %): +.4, +.8, and +1.2. Each 1% decrease in output growth causes u to increase by .4 percentage points.
c. Unemployment does not change. Output growth must be 3% to keep u constant.

3. As output growth falls, there are two reasons why u will increase by less than 1%. First, firms will hoard labor (work them less intensively, rather than lay them off). Second, the prospects for employment are less favorable. Consequently, some workers leave the labor force. The 1% drop in output growth will cause u to increase by less than 1%.

4. Yes. A given deviation of output growth from the normal rate will now have a greater effect on the change in u.

5. a. (all in %) 4, 2, 0, and -2. The growth rate falls.
b. (all in %) 0, 2, and 4. Output growth increases.

6. a. Output growth will be 2% and u will equal 6%. In the medium run, we know that u must be constant. For u to be constant, output growth must equal the normal rate. We also know that inflation must be constant. If inflation is constant, we know that u must be at the natural level.
b. In the medium run, the rate of inflation and the adjusted money growth will be the same: 5% = 7% - 2%.

7. a. Money growth is neutral in the medium run; it will have no effect on these two variables.
b. In the medium run, the rate of inflation and the adjusted money growth will be the same: 1% = 3% - 2%.

8. Again, output growth and unemployment will not be affected by this in the medium run. Inflation will increase by 3% in the medium run.

9. To calculate this, simply multiply 2 by the number of years: 2, 4, 6, 8, and 10. The number of point-years of excess unemployment increases the longer u remains above the natural level.

10. The number of point-years of excess u will be given by $u - u_n = 8/\alpha$. Plug in the numbers and we get: 5.3, 5.7, 7, and 8.
b. They increase. α tells us how sensitive inflation is to changes in u. As this parameter decreases in size, we will need a greater change in u to decrease inflation by 8%.

11. a. Using the equation in the answer to #10 (after replacing 8 with 9), we get: 7.8.
b. The central bank has no control over this. This is determined by the parameter α.
c. Yes: (1) u could be 7.8% above the natural level for just one year; (2) u could be 3.9% above the natural level for two years; and (3) u could be 2.6% above the natural level for three years. There are many other combinations.

12. a. $-2 = -.5(g_{yt} - 2)$. Solving for the growth rate, we get 6%.
b. $-3 = -.5(g_{yt} - 2)$. Solving for the growth rate, we get 8%.

13. a. The sacrifice ratio is the point-years of excess unemployment needed to reduce inflation by 1%. The sacrifice ratio is equal to $1/\alpha$.
b. .67, .77, .87, 1, and 1.1.
c. It increases. α tells us how sensitive inflation is to changes in u. As this parameter decreases in size, we will need a greater change in u to decrease inflation by 1%.

14. a. $-8 = -1(u_t - 6)$. Solving for unemployment, we get 14%; that is, u must be 8% above the natural level.
b. $8 = -.5(g_{yt} - 3)$. Solving for g_{yt}, we get -13%.

15. Note: all numbers are in percentage terms.
a.

Year	0	1	2	3	4	5	6	7	8
Inflation	18	15	12	9	6	3	3	3	3
Unemployment	6	9	9	9	9	9	6	6	6
Output growth	3	-3	3	3	3	3	9	3	3
Money growth	21	12	15	12	9	6	12	6	6

Note: Money growth in the above table refers to nominal money growth.

b. First, we determine the path of inflation. Once this is specified, we determine from the Phillips curve, what u must be each year to reduce inflation by 3% each year; u must be 3% above the natural level. Once inflation is at the desired level, u can return to the natural level. Once the path of u is determined, we can determine (from Okun's law) what output growth must be each year. First, output growth must fall to cause the increase in u. Once u remains constant at 9%, output growth returns to normal. To reduce u in year 6, output growth must increase. And finally, output growth settles at the normal rate in years 7 and on. The required path of money growth is obtained by adding inflation and output growth for each year. Money growth first must fall to cause a reduction in output growth and increase in u. In year 2, money growth must increase to get output growth back to normal. Money growth then follows the path of inflation to keep output growth constant. Money growth increases in year 6 to push u back to the natural level (via its effects on output growth).

16. Yes!!! By announcing such a policy, expectations can adjust. Individuals will expect lower inflation. Nominal wages will fall as inflation falls. If actual and expected inflation both fall at the same time, there can be a disinflation without any increase in u.

17. The sacrifice ratios for these three years are not consistent with the traditional approach. The sacrifice ratio for the traditional approach is 1; all three in the table exceed 1. The sacrifice ratios for these three years are not consistent with the Lucas critique. The sacrifice ratio for the Lucas critique is zero; all three in the table exceed 1 and, therefore (!), are greater than 0.

MULTIPLE CHOICE QUESTIONS

1. C 2. A 3. B 4. E 5. C 6. C 7. D 8. B 9. D 10. C 11. D 12. A 13. A 14. B 15. A 16. D 17. A 18. D 19. B

CHAPTER 10

REVIEW PROBLEMS

1. a. Plug the numbers into the following equation $1000(1 + i)^{40}$: \$2388, \$1963, \$1611 and \$1322.
b. The dollar amount drops as i falls.

2. a. $\$17{,}945(1 + .012)^{40} = \$28{,}918$.
b. $\$17{,}945(1 + .022)^{40} = \$42{,}853$.
c. The increase in the standard of living drops as the rate of growth declines.

3. The two conclusions are: (1) growth has been strong (i.e., there have been significant increases in the standard of living); and (2) the levels of output per capita have converged over time.

4. The evidence suggests there is a negative relation between the initial level of Y/N and the rate of growth in Y/N. This indicates, all else fixed, that the country with the highest level of Y/N in 2004 (the United States) will experience the slowest growth rate in Y/N while the country with the lowest level of Y/N in 2004 (Japan) will experience the fastest growth rate.

5. a. $\$11{,}233(1.046)^{54} = \$127{,}411$.
b. The difference is \$91,313, a nontrivial amount!

6. a. \$2(4000) + \$4(8000) = \$40,000
b. (2 pesos times 2000) + (20 pesos times 1000) = 24,000 pesos.
c. (24,000 pesos) times .10 = \$2400. Relative consumption is 2400/40000 = .06 (6%).
d. \$2(2000) + \$4(1000) = \$8000. Relative consumption using the purchasing power parity method is 8000/40000 = .20 (20%).
e. The method used can have a significant effect on a comparison of relative consumption and relative standards of living. Simply compare the 6% and 20% figures.

7. a. 141
b. 282. N, K and Y all increase by 100%.
c. 155.6. N, K and Y all increase by 10%.
d. Yes. If you double the inputs, Y also doubles.
e. Easy answer. 2.7%. Why? Constant returns to scale.

8. a. $Y/N = (K^{1/2})(N^{1/2})/N = (K/N)^{1/2}$. Y/N is determined by the level of K/N.

b. $Y/N = (200/100)^{1/2} = 1.41$. $K/N = 2$.

c. 1.41, 1.73 and 2. Y/N increases at a decreasing rate which is consistent with decreasing returns to capital.

d.

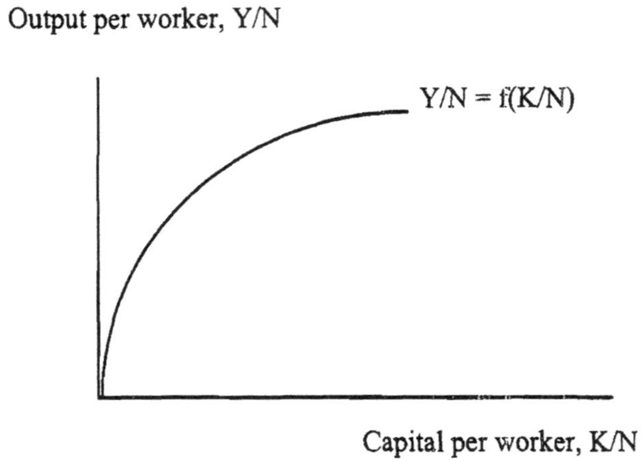

9. a. Y/N increases over time in this country.

b. An increase in K/N will cause the curve to shift up. A higher K/N will yield a higher level of Y/N at each point in time.

c. A decrease in K/N will cause the curve to shift down. A lower K/N will yield a lower level of Y/N at each point in time.

d. The slope represents the annual rate of growth in output per worker. It represents the rate of technological progress.

e. The slope would increase if the rate of technological progress increased.

f. Since growth did not occur during this period, the line would be horizontal.

10. a. Country B

b. Country A

c. Country A

d. Country A

MULTIPLE CHOICE QUESTIONS

1. D 2. B 3. E 4. B 5. A 6. B 7. A, C 8. C 9. D 10. B 11. D 12. B 13. C 14. C 15. A 16. C 17. D

CHAPTER 11

REVIEW PROBLEMS

1. Rearrange equation (11.2) to answer this question.
a. 4.4
b. 4.8. The capital stock increases as s increases; there will be more investment as saving increases.
c. 4. The capital stock decreases as δ increases; a greater portion of the capital stock depreciates.

2. Uncertain. Assuming that depreciation occurs, the capital stock will increase only when investment exceeds depreciation. Investment could be positive and the capital stock can fall if I < depreciation.

3. a. If the capital stock is increasing, I must exceed depreciation; therefore, saving per worker must exceed depreciation.
b. If the capital stock is decreasing, I must be less than depreciation; therefore, saving per worker must be less than depreciation.
c. If the capital stock is constant, I must equal depreciation; therefore, saving per worker must equal depreciation.

4. a. Depreciation per worker equals: .2, .3, .4, and .5.
b. Depreciation increases at a constant rate.

5. Note: I have omitted per worker below to save space.
a. AB is depreciation; AC is investment; AD is output; CB is the change in capital; and CD is consumption.
b. Investment exceeds depreciation so K/N will increase. As K/N rises, Y/N will increase as well.
c. No.
d. It is determined by the level of K/N where the investment line intersects the depreciation line.

6. Note: I have omitted per worker below to save space.
a. EF is investment; EG is depreciation; EH is output; FG is the change in capital; and FH is consumption.
b. K/N and Y/N will decrease over time.
c. No.
d. It is determined by the level of K/N where the investment line intersects the depreciation line.

7. a.

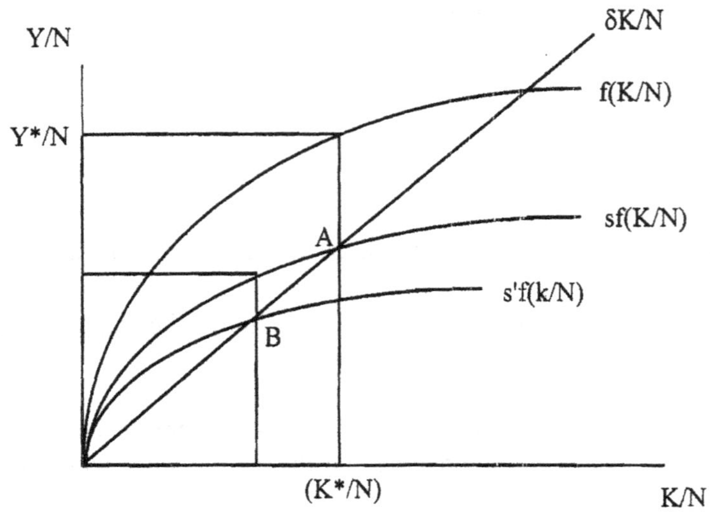

b. The lower s causes a reduction in saving and an increase in consumption. It takes one period for the change in saving/investment to affect capital; consequently, K/N and, therefore, Y/N do not change in period t.
c. At the initial K/N, investment is now less than depreciation. K/N and Y/N will fall over time.
d. In the short run, the lower s causes a reduction in Y/N. Hence, the rate of growth in Y/N is negative.
e. Once the new steady state is reached, Y/N remains constant. The lower s has no long-run effect on the growth of Y/N.
f. It permanently reduces the level of Y/N.

8. a. A reduction in δ will reduce the slope of the depreciation line. The line will become flatter.
b. At the initial level of K/N, the decline in the depreciation rate will cause investment to exceed depreciation. This situation will cause K/N and Y/N to increase over time. In short, the drop in the depreciation rate will cause a new steady state level of Y/N and K/N (both increase).

9. a. Increases in the saving rate cause increases in K/N and Y/N. To maximize Y/N, the saving rate must be one (s = 1).
b. Such a policy would cause consumption to be zero. All income would be going to saving to support this high level of K/N. Individuals most likely (!) would not like this since they care about consumption, not production.

10. a. The higher s causes an increase in saving and a reduction in consumption. It takes one period for the change in saving/investment to affect capital; consequently, K/N and Y/N will not change in period t.
b. The higher s will cause K/N and Y/N to increase in the long run. The effects of the higher s on consumption in the long run depend on where the economy is prior to the increase in s. If capital is above the golden rule, the higher s will cause a reduction in consumption. If capital is below the golden rule, the higher s will cause higher consumption (up to a point).

11. a. See answer to part (b) of #7.
b. The lower s will cause K/N and Y/N to decrease in the long run. The effects of the lower s on consumption in the long run depend on where the economy is prior to the increase in s. If capital is above the golden rule, the lower s will cause an increase in consumption up to a point. If capital is below the golden rule, the lower s will cause lower consumption.

12. a. Plugging in the numbers, we get: 1, 1.41, 1.73, 2, and 2.24.
b. It increases at a decreasing rate.
c. Yes. If you double both N and K, Y will double.

13. Use the following equations to answer this question: $K/N = (s/\delta)^2$; $Y/N = s/\delta$; C/N in the steady state equals $s(1-s)/\delta$.
a. K/N will be: 4, 36, 100, 196 and 324. Y/N will be: 2, 6, 10, 14 and 18.
b. The steady state levels of C/N will be: 1.8, 4.2, 5, 4.2 and 1.8.
c. Capital is below the golden rule and C/N increases.
d. Capital is above the golden rule and C/N falls.
e. K/N is 100; C/N is 5; s is .5.

14. a. The government must raise the saving rate. To do this, it must either reduce the budget deficit or increase the budget surplus.
b. Any increase in s in the short run will reduce C/N.
c. C/N will increase.

15. a. 4.
b. Yes it does. Try doubling K, N and H. Y will also double. Alternatively, Y/N will not change when K, N and H all double.
c. Yes it does. Try increasing K from 400 to 450 to 500. Y will increase at a decreasing rate.
d. Yes it does. Try increasing H from 400 to 450 to 500. Y will increase at a decreasing rate.

16. a. K and H. Increases in K/N will cause increases in Y/N because workers will have more capital with which to produce goods. Increases in H/N will also cause increases in Y/N because workers have a better set of skills to produce goods.
b. The saving rate must increase.
c. Increased education spending or increases in on-the-job training; these will increase H/N.

17. At low saving rates ($s < s_G$), an increase in the saving rate will cause an increase in K/N, an increase in Y/N, and an increase in depreciation per worker (I/N). Depreciation per worker (I/N) increases at a constant rate (i.e., at the rate of depreciation). In this case, the increase in Y/N exceeds the increase in I/N. In this case, if the change in Y/N exceeds the change in I/N, C/N must increase. So, an increase in the saving rate will cause an increase in C/N. Graphically, we observe that the slope of the production function is greater than the slope of the depreciation line. At saving rates above s_G, an increase in the saving rate will cause a reduction in C/N for similar reasons.

MULTIPLE CHOICE QUESTIONS

1. C 2. A 3. A 4. C 5. C 6. D 7. A 8. B 9. D 10. B 11. D 12. D 13. B 14. D 15. D 16. B 17. C 18. D 19. B 20. D 21. C 22. C

CHAPTER 12

REVIEW PROBLEMS

1. Patents will have no effect on the fertility of research. Patents will increase the appropriability of research.

2. If patent protection is poor, firms may not be able to profit from their own new products (that are the result of the R&D). Thus, R&D spending will fall and technological progress will likely decrease.

3. a. 100, 110, 120, 130 and 150.
b. NA increases as A increases.

4. a. 100
b. 200. If you double all inputs, output doubles. Yes.
c. Y equals 100, 122.5 and 141.4. Yes. The increase in Y gets smaller with each additional increase in K.
d. Y equals 100, 118.3 and 134.2. Yes. The increase in Y gets smaller with each additional increase in NA.

5. The level of output is determined by K and NA (or N and A). An increase in any two (three) of these variables will cause Y to increase.

6. a. Multiply .15 by each level of I. 15, 16.5, 18 and 19.5.
b. This level of investment increases at a constant rate.

7. a. Multiply .20 by each level of I/NA. 2, 4, 6 and 8.
b. Required investment increases at a constant rate.

8. a. As g_N increases, required investment rises. Since N is growing at a faster rate, more investment will be needed to maintain K/NA.
b. As g_A increases, required investment rises. Since NA (via A) is growing at a faster rate, more investment is needed to maintain K/NA.
c. An increase in δ will cause required investment to increase. Since K is depreciating at a faster rate, more investment will be needed to offset this depreciation.

9. a. 1.5
b. I/NA exceeds the amount needed to keep K/NA constant. K/NA will increase over time.
c. I/NA is less than required investment. K/NA will decrease over time.
d. I/NA must be 1.5 to keep K/NA constant.

10. a. I/NA is greater than the required level. K/NA will increase over time. As K/NA increases, Y/NA will also increase.
b. I/NA is less than the required level. K/NA will fall over time. As K/NA falls, Y/NA will fall.
c. Yes. I/NA equals the required level of investment per NA.

11. a. Since both are constant, the rate of growth is zero!
b. They both grow at 5%.
c. 3%
d. 2%
e. 2%

12. a. The rate of growth of Y in the steady state is determined by the rate of growth in NA. The rate of growth in NA is determined by the rate of growth in the population and rate of technological progress. An increase in either of these will cause the rate of growth in Y to increase.
b. The rate of growth in Y/N equals the rate of technological progress. Increases in the rate of technological progress will cause an increase in the rate of growth in Y/N.

13. a. See the graph.

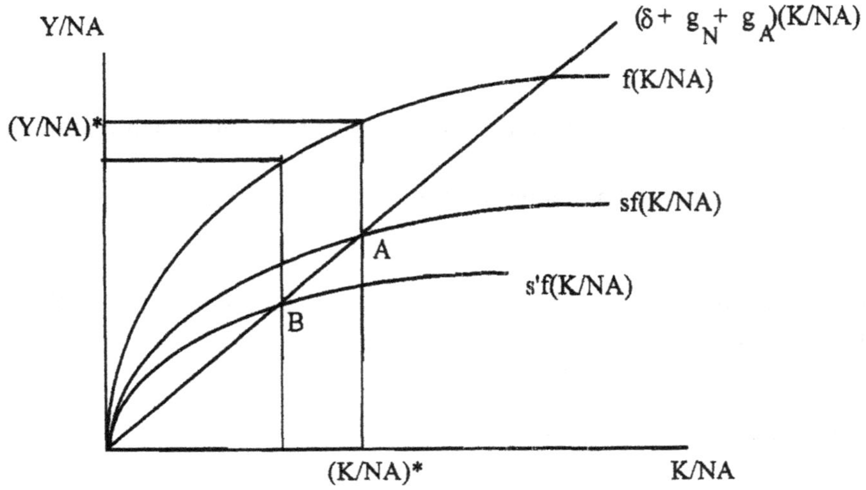

b. The lower saving rate causes the investment curve to shift down. I/NA is now less than required investment. K/NA and Y/NA will fall over time until the new steady state is reached at point B.
c. Y/NA and K/NA will be permanently lower.
d. Output per worker grew at the rate of growth in technological progress.
e. During the adjustment, the growth rate of Y/N declines.
f. Once the new steady state is reached, Y/N grows at the same long-run rate: the rate of technological progress, g_A.

14. False. As discussed in #13 and in the text, changes in the saving rate affect the rate of growth of Y/N only in the short run. In the long run, Y/N grows at g_A which is independent of the saving rate.

15. Since Y/NA and K/NA are constant, Y and K grow at the same rate as NA ($g_N + g_A$). Y/N and K/N grow at g_A.

16. In the steady state, we know that Y/N grows at g_A. An increase in g_A will, therefore, cause the long-run rate of growth of Y/N to increase permanently.

17. An increase in s will K/NA to increase in the short run. Once the new steady state is reached, K/NA will be constant at some permanently higher level. In the short run, Y/NA will increase to some permanently higher level. As Y/NA is rising, Y/N will be growing at a rate about g_A. Once the new steady state is reached, however, Y/N will grow at g_A.

18. a. No. The economy is in steady state when the rate of growth of Y/N equals g_A.
b. This high growth must be caused by capital accumulation.

19. a. No. The economy is in steady state when the rate of growth of Y/N equals g_A.
b. This low growth must be caused by a reduction in capital accumulation.

20. a. Yes. The economy is in steady state when the rate of growth of Y/N equals g_A.
b. The growth in Y/N is caused by balanced growth, the rate of technological progress.

21. The slowdown has been caused by a slowdown in the rate of technological progress. The rate of growth in Y/N has coincided with a decline in the rate of growth in technological progress.

MULTIPLE CHOICE QUESTIONS

1. A 2. B 3. D 4. C 5. D 6. D 7. B 8. C 9. C 10. A 11. A 12. C 13. C 14. E 15. A 16. B 17. D 18. A 19. D 20. D 21. E 22. A 23. C 24. D 25. B 26. A

CHAPTER 13

REVIEW PROBLEMS

1. a. Y will equal 100, 120, 140 and 160.
b. Labor productivity increases. As A increases, each worker now produces even more output; therefore, labor is more productive.

2. a. N will equal 2000, 1600, 1333.3, and 1000.
b. As A increases, N falls. As labor becomes more productive, firms need less labor to produce the same quantity of output.

3. a. N will equal 2, 1.33, 1, and .67.
b. As A increases, the firm will need less workers to produce one more unit of output.
c. The cost of one unit is W/A. As A increases, the firms needs fewer workers so the cost of producing the one unit falls.

4. a. The percentage change in N equals the percentage change in Y minus the percentage change in A. So, N falls by 3%, falls by 1%, remains constant, increases by 1% and increases by 2%.
b. N falls if the percentage change in Y < the percentage change in A.
c. N increases if the percentage change in Y > the percentage change in A.
d. N remains constant if the percentage change in Y = the percentage change in A.

5. An increase in A reduces the cost of producing output. Since firms set the price as a markup over cost, the reduction in the cost will cause firms to reduce the price at any level of output. Hence, the AS curve shifts down.

6. Productivity coming from the widespread use of new technologies may cause consumers to raise their expectations of future income and firms to raise their expectations of future profits. Individuals will increase consumption and firms will increase investment. The increase in C and I will cause an increase in aggregate demand.

7. Productivity coming from a more efficient use of existing technology may cause firms to cut costs and eliminate jobs. Such reorganization may increase uncertainty about job security and cause consumption to fall. The drop in C will cause a reduction in aggregate demand.

8. In all likelihood, this statement is true. The empirical evidence also supports this statement. You should understand, however, that a sharp reduction in AD could (at least theoretically) more than offset the positive effects of the higher A on the AS curve. We will ignore this case.

9. This statement will not always be true. If AD increases sufficiently, P could increase. See the graph below for several possible cases. Point B represents this initial equilibrium.

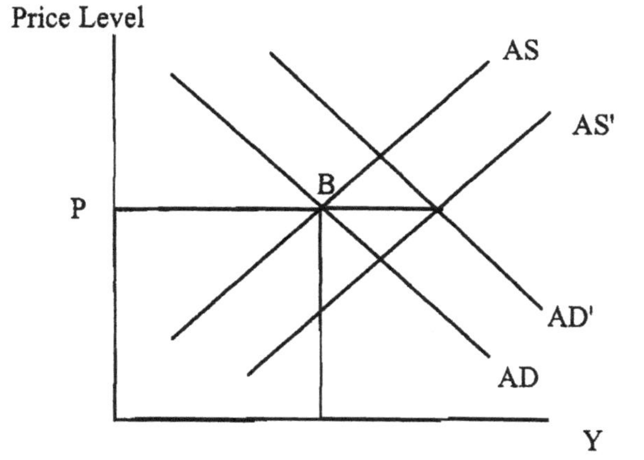

If the AD curve shifts beyond AD', P increases. If the AD curve shifts out to AD', P does not change. If the AD curve shifts to some point below AD' (or if the AD curve shifts left), P will fall.

10. a. The real wage will be: .45, .68, .91 and 1.36.
b. As A increases, the real wage increases. The increase in A reduces firms' costs. They respond by lowering the price. As P falls, given W, the real wage increases.
c. Increases in A cause an increase in the real wage and cause the PS relation to shift up by the size of the change in A.
d. The real wage will increase by 7%.

11. a. The real wage will be: .48, .71, .95, and 1.43.
b. Increases in A cause an increase in the real wage. Why? Wage setters will set the nominal wage based on productivity gains. As A increases, the nominal wage increases. Given P, an increase in W causes an increase in W/P.
c. The WS relation shifts up the size of the change in A.
d. The real wage will increase by 7%.

12. The PS and WS relations both shift up by 3%. Since both relations shift up by the same amount, the new equilibrium (call it B') occurs directly above B at the same natural rate of unemployment. The real wage increases by 3% while u_n does not change.

13. The analysis here is exactly the opposite of the analysis in #12. When A falls (and expectations are correct), both the WS and PS relations shift down by the change in A. Since the shifts in the two relations are the same, the natural rate of unemployment does not change. The real wage, however, will fall (the drop equals the drop in A).

14. a. The PS relation will shift up by just 3%. The WS relation, however, continues to shift up by 7% since wage setters have not yet adjusted their expectations of productivity growth. The real wage increases by 3% while the natural rate of unemployment increases (see point B').

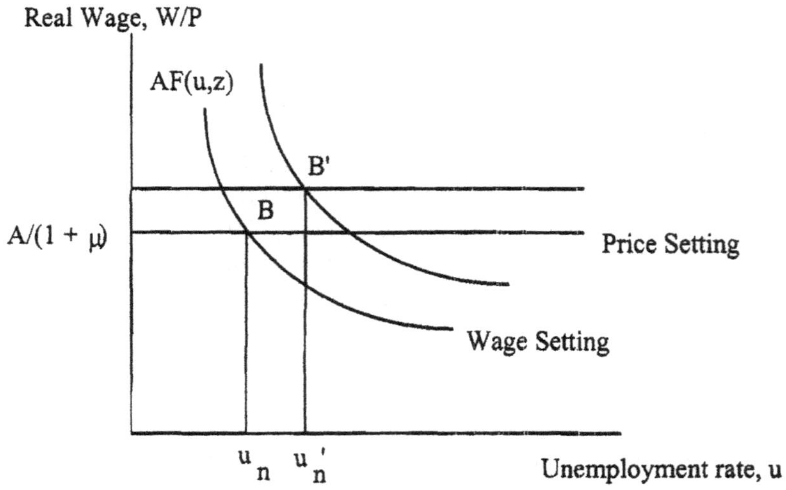

b. Over time, expectations of productivity growth will adjust to the productivity slowdown. Once this occurs, the PS and WS relations will shift by the same amount each year (3%). The real wage will increase by 3% each year and the natural rate of unemployment will not change since the WS and PS shifts are the same.

15. a. The PS relation will continue to shift by the actual change in productivity. As expectations of productivity growth adjust, the WS relation will also (eventually) shift by the actual change in A.
b. Once this occurs, the real wage will increase at the rate of productivity growth and the unemployment rate will be unaffected by changes in A.

16. There are two reasons why the CPI increased faster than the GDP deflator: (1) the steady decline in the relative price of investment goods relative to consumption goods (investment goods are not included in the CPI and are included in the GDP deflator); and (2) an increase in the relative price of foreign goods (these will be included in the CPI).

17. All else fixed, an increase in the relative demand for skilled workers would increase the relative wage of skilled workers. This did not happen during this period because there was a simultaneous increase in the supply of skilled workers to match the increase in demand. This increase in supply offset the relative wage effects of the increase in demand.

MULTIPLE CHOICE QUESTIONS

1. D 2. B 3. B 4. C 5. B 6. C 7. B 8. A 9. D 10. D 11. C 12. C 13. B 14. B 15. A 16. A 17. B 18. A 19. B 20. A 21. B 22. C

CHAPTER 14

REVIEW PROBLEMS

1. Expected inflation = $(P^e_{t+1} - P_t)/P_t$. The exact definition of the real rate is $[(1+i)/(1+\pi^e)] - 1$. In the answers below, the first number is expected inflation and the second number is r (all in %).
a. 0, 10
b. 3, 6.8
c. 5, 4.8
d. 7, 2.8
e. 10, 0
f. The nominal rate equals the real rate only when expected inflation is 0 (part a).
g. $i > r$ when expected inflation is positive (parts b-d).
h. $r = 0$ when expected inflation equals the nominal interest rate (part e).

2. a. 10 b. 7 c. 5 d. 3 e. 0

3. a. See the answers below.

i	π^e	r^I	r^{II}
2%	0	2%	2%
5%	3%	1.94%	2%
10%	8%	1.85%	2%
15%	13%	1.77%	2%
20%	18%	1.7%	2%
50%	48%	1.35%	2%
100%	98%	1.0%	2%

b. As inflation increases, the approximate definition's ability to measure accurately the real interest rate declines. This is obvious by looking at the numbers.

4. $r = i - \pi^e$. r will increase if i increases. r will increase if, for a given i, π^e falls.

5. Yes. Look at the definition of r in #4. A reduction in i, given expected inflation, would cause r to fall. However, if expected inflation falls more than the reduction in i, the real interest rate will increase.

6. The discount factors are: $1/(1+i)$ for one year and $1/(1+i)^2$ for two years.
a. When the interest rate is zero the discount factors equal 1; we can simply add the sum of future payments. \$200,000.
b. \$100,000/1.04 + \$100,000/1.0816 = \$188,610.
c. \$100,000/1.08 + \$100,000/1.1664 = \$178,327.
d. The higher is the interest rates, the lower is the present value. As i increases, the discount factor increases; the weights on the future sums are smaller.

7. a. Individual B receives the larger present value. Each receives a three-year stream of $50,000 payments. However, B receives one today. $1 today is worth more than $1 received a year from now. Since B receives her payments one year sooner than A, the present value is larger.
b. They will be equal only if the interest rate is zero. See the answer to #6, part a.

8. a. $100,000/1.1 = $90,909.
b. $100,000/1.21 = $82,645.
c. $100,000/1.331 = $75,131.
d. As the payment occurs further into the future, the present value falls. The weight gets smaller (the discount factor gets larger).

9. a. Using the (what should now be familiar) equation: present value of the first year payment, $20,000; present value of the second year payment, $20,000; present value of the third year payment, $20,661; present value of the fourth year payment, $21,037.
b. The present value of the 4-year payment option is (add the numbers in a): $81,698. This also represents the highest one-year payment the student should make. If the college's one year price is below this, you should recommend the one-time payment. If the college's one year price is above this, you should recommend the four-year payment plan.

10. Use the following equation to obtain the future value of the $100,000: $100,000(1 + i_t)(1 + i_{t+1})(1 + i_{t+2}).
a. Plugging in the numbers, we get: Case 1, $100,000; Case 2, $140,448; Case 3, $125,928.
b. Case 2 yields the highest future value because the interest rates are higher in this case. Alternatively, with i higher in case 2, you would need to receive a greater future sum to yield a present value of $100,000.

11. a. The opportunity cost of holding money is the nominal interest rate, 9%. All figures are in percentages (%).
b. Real return on bonds, 9. Real return on money, 0.
c. Real return on bonds ($r = i - \pi^e$): 8, 6, 2, and 0.
Real return on money ($0 - \pi^e$): -1, -3, -7, and -9.
d. Nothing. It remains fixed at 9%.
e. The opportunity cost measured in real terms = real return on bonds minus real return on money: 8 - (-1) = 9; 6 - (-3) = 9; 2 - (-7) = 9; and 0 - (-9) = 9. Nothing happens to the opportunity cost of holding money (measured in real terms) as expected inflation increases.
f. Nothing. What will determine the opportunity cost of holding money is the nominal interest rate. Changes in expected inflation do not affect the opportunity cost of holding money because they affect the real return on money and bonds equally.

12. a. 10%.
b. The increase in expected inflation will have no effect on money demand (the curve does NOT shift). The real interest rate consistent with financial market equilibrium is 8%.
c. No effect on money demand. The real interest rate consistent with equilibrium falls to 5%.

13. Let's begin with the medium-run effects of a reduction in money growth. In the medium run, this change in money growth will have no effect on output. That is, Y will return to the natural level of output. The real interest rate will also return to the natural real interest rate. With output growth unchanged in the medium run, we know that inflation will drop by an amount equal to the reduction in money growth. With inflation lower and the real interest rate unchanged, we know that the nominal interest rate will fall as well (the Fisher effect also applies when there are reductions in inflation). In the short run, the reduction in money growth will cause an increase in the nominal interest rate and an increase in the real interest rate. This increase in r will cause a reduction in investment and a reduction in output (Y falls below the natural level). With Y below the natural level, the Phillips curve suggests that expected inflation will fall over time. It is this adjustment in expected inflation that will cause Y and r to return to their initial levels and i to fall below its initial level.

14. a. A drop in G will cause a leftward shift in the IS curve. At the initial natural level of output, the real interest rate consistent with goods market equilibrium is lower. Hence, r_n falls.
b. A drop in T will cause a rightward shift in the IS curve. At the initial natural level of output, the real interest rate consistent with goods market equilibrium is higher. Hence, r_n increases.
c. A reduction in the price of oil will cause a reduction in the price level and an increase in the natural level of output. Assuming that the change in the price of oil does not affect the demand for goods, r_n will fall as the economy moves along the fixed IS curve.

15. a. 2%.
b. See the graph. The drop in expected inflation, given i, causes the equilibrium real interest rate to increase to 5%. Investment decreases and the IS curve shifts to the left. Note: the vertical distance between the two IS curves represents the reduction in expected inflation. The drop in expected inflation is represented by the distance between points A and B in the graph.

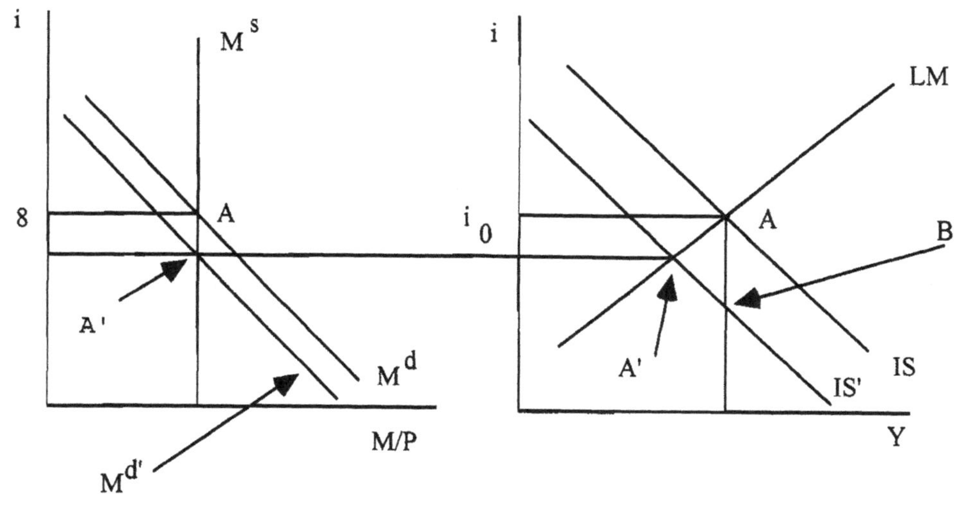

c. The drop in expected inflation causes an initial increase in r. As r increases, I falls causing a reduction in demand and a leftward shift in the IS curve. Y will fall causing a reduction in money demand and a reduction in the nominal interest rate. As Y falls, C falls as well.

d. The 3% reduction in expected inflation causes the real interest rate to increase, but by less than 3%. Why? As Y falls, nominal money demand falls, causing the nominal interest rate to fall. So, some of the reduction in expected inflation is offset by a reduction in i. Where would point A' be in the money supply-money demand graph? Money demand falls as Y falls. So, point A' is below A.

MULTIPLE CHOICE QUESTIONS

1. C 2. D 3. B 4. C 5. B 6. C 7. C 8. A 9. C 10. D 11. D 12. C 13. C 14. B 15. C 16. C 17. D 18. B 19. C 20. A 21. D 22. D 23. A 24. B 25. C 26. E

CHAPTER 15

REVIEW PROBLEMS

1. a. 100/1000 = 10%
b. 100/900 = 11.1%

2. As the rating increases, the bond is viewed as less risky (the probability of a default is perceived to be lower). This will cause the risk premium on the bond to fall. As the risk premium falls, the interest rate falls.

3. If a sufficient number of financial market participants believed that the probability of default increased, they might require a (higher) risk premium on bonds issued by the U.S. government. This would have raised the interest rate on these bonds.

4. a. $1000/1.1 = $909.09
b. $1000/[(1.1)(1.08)] = $841.75
c. In one year, this two-year bond is a one-year bond: $1000/(1.08) = $925.93

5. a. $1000/1.08 = $925.93
b. $1000[(.108)(1.06)] = $873.52
c. $1000/1.06 = $943.40
In each case, the price of the bonds increases as the interest rates fall. This is what you should expect!!

6. Recall that the two-year rate is (approximately) a simple average of the current one-year rate and expected future one-year rate. Plugging in the numbers, we get:
a. 7% b. 5.5% c. 6%

7. a. It increases by .5% to 7.5%. The yield curve becomes steeper.
b. It falls to 5%. The yield curve becomes steeper (it is still downward sloping).

8. a. 6%. Upward sloping.
b. Two-year rate increases to 6.5%. The two-year rate changes by less than the change in the current one-year rate because the expected future one-year rate did not change.
c. Two-year rate increases to 6.75%. The two-year rate still changes by less than the change in the current one-year rate because the expected future one-year rate changed by less than the current one-year rate.
d. Two-year rate increases to 7%. The two-year rate changes by the same amount as the change in the current one-year rate because the expected future one-year rate also changed by the same amount as the change in the current one-year rate.
e. The two-year rate increased by the same amount as the current one-year rate in the last case where the current and expected future one-year rates increased by the same amount. This is the condition which is needed for the two-year rate to increase by the same amount as the current one-year rate.

9. a. The expected future one-year rate must increase (or, the current one-year rate must fall).
b. The expected future one-year rate must drop so that it equals the current one-year rate (or, the current one-year rate must increase so that it equals the expected future one-year rate).
c. The expected future one-year rate must drop so that it falls below the current one-year rate (or, the current one-year rate must increase so that it increases above the expected future one-year rate).

10. a. The expected future one-year rate will fall causing the yield curve to become flatter.
b. The expected future one-year rate will fall causing the yield curve to become flatter.
c. The expected future one-year rate will fall causing the yield curve to become flatter.
d. The expected future one-year rate will increase causing the yield curve to become steeper.

11. a. This will cause the expected future interest rate to fall and expected output to increase. The expected increase in Y will raise expectations of future profits. The reduction in the expected future interest rate will increase the present value of future profits. Both of these results will cause stock prices to rise.
b. This will reduce future output. Expectations of future profits will be lower causing stock prices to fall. This answer assumes that expectations of interest rates remain constant.

12. a. No effect. The expectation of the increase in Y is already built into expectations of future profits. Thus, stock prices do not change.
b. No effect. The effects of the expected Fed contraction (higher future interest rates and lower future Y) are, again, already built into expectations of future profits. Thus, stock prices do not change.

13. a. This event will raise i^e and cause Y^e to fall. The higher expected interest rate (as described in previous answers) will cause stock prices to fall. The reduction in expected output will (as described in previous answers) cause stock prices to fall. Therefore, stock prices will fall.
b. This event will cause i^e to fall and cause Y^e to fall. The lower expected interest rate (as described in previous answers) will cause stock prices to rise. The reduction in expected output, however, will (as described in previous answers) cause stock prices to fall. Therefore, the effects of this event on stock prices are ambiguous.
c. This event will cause Y^e to increase with no change in the interest rate. Here, stock prices will increase.

14. a. Unexpected changes in monetary policy will cause: (1) the interest to fall and output to increase; or (2) the interest rate to increase and output to fall. In case 1, both effects cause stock prices to increase. In case 2, both effects cause stock prices to fall. In short, the effects work together here to affect stock prices.
b. Unexpected changes in fiscal policy will cause: (1) the interest to fall and output to fall; or (2) the interest rate to increase and output to increase. In case 1, the lower future i would increase stock prices, while the lower future Y would reduce stock prices. The opposite happens in case 2. Conclusion: we do not know which effect will dominate so the effects are ambiguous.

15. a. As described #14, part b, the effects will be ambiguous.
b. The Fed acts to keep the interest rate fixed at its original level. To do so, the Fed would have to pursue contractionary monetary policy; reduce the money supply to shift the LM curve up so it intersects the new IS curve at point C.
c. The Fed acts to keep Y fixed at its original level. To do so, the Fed would have to pursue expansionary monetary policy; increase the money supply to shift the LM curve down so it intersects the new IS curve at point D.
d. Stock prices will fall. The lower output will cause individuals to revise down their expectations of future profits. There is no interest rate effect here to offset this.
e. Stock prices will increase. The lower interest rate will increase the present value of future profits. There is no output effect to offset this.

MULTIPLE CHOICE QUESTIONS

1. B 2. C 3. C 4. A 5. B 6. D 7. C 8. D 9. C 10. A 11. A 12. B 13. D 14. C 15. C 16. C 17. A 18. D 19. A 20. D

CHAPTER 16

REVIEW PROBLEMS

1. a. $1,600,000
b. Divide total wealth by 40: $40,000.
c. The individual will have to borrow $15,000 to achieve her desired level of consumption: $40,000 - $25,000 (current disposable income) = $15,000.
d. Total wealth will increase by $10,000. Divide this sum by 40 to determine how much consumption can increase each year: $10,000/40 = $250. Or, you could divide her new level of total wealth ($1,610,000) by 40 to get: $40,250.
e. Without knowing the future real interest rates, we cannot calculate the new level of human wealth. We do know, however, that this permanent increase in income will have a greater effect on total wealth than does the one time increase in part d. She will, therefore, increase her consumption more as a result of this event than in response to the event in part d.

2. a. This will reduce housing wealth.
b. This will reduce financial wealth.
c. This will reduce current disposable income and reduce human wealth.
d. This will reduce human wealth.

3. a. $10,000/1.05 = $9523.81.
b. (1-.1)($12,000)/(1.05)(1.07) = $9612.82.
c. Sum the values in a and b to get: $19,136.63.
d. $10,000/1.06 = $9433.96 (1-.1)($12,000)/(1.06)(1.08) = 9433.96
Adding the two figures yields: $18,867.92
e. Changing the numbers and using the same approach as that included above yields: $20,890.08.
f. Changing the numbers and using the same approach as that included above yields: $19,350.25.
g. The highest price the firm is willing to pay is the present value of the profits from the machine: in c, $19,136.63; in d, $18,867.92; in e, $20,890.08; and in f, $19,350.25.
h. An increase in r will cause the present value to fall. An increase in expected future profits will increase the present value. A reduction in the rate of depreciation will cause an increase in present value.

4. I will use equation (8.5) to calculate the present values here.
a. Plugging in the numbers yields: $10,000/.15 = $66,666.67. This is also the highest price the firm is willing to pay. The user cost of capital is .15.
b. Plugging in the numbers yields: $10,000/.14 = $71,428.57. This is also the highest price the firm is willing to pay. The user cost of capital is .14; it falls as r falls.
c. Plugging in the numbers yields: $10,000/.17 = $58,823.53. This is also the highest price the firm is willing to pay. The user cost of capital is .17; it increases as the depreciation rate increases.
d. Plugging in the numbers yields: $9,000/.15 = $60,000. This is also the highest price the firm is willing to pay. The user cost of capital does not change when expected profits change.
e. In b, investment will increase; in c, investment will decrease; in d, investment will fall.

5. The rental cost of capital is r + δ. An increase in r and an increase in δ will cause the rental cost of capital to increase. A higher interest rate will reduce the present value of expected profits. Firms will tend to reduce investment when this occurs. When δ increases, the capital wears out more quickly, thus reducing the amount of profits received from each unit of capital over time.

6. a. Firm A is unaffected by this increase in the price of oil so its investment will not change. As the price of oil increases, profits from oil exploration will rise. The increase in profits represents an increase in cash flows for firm B. With additional cash flows, firm B will likely increase investment in both of its operations.
b. Again, firm A will not be affected by this. If only profitability matters, there is no reason for firm B to increase investment in its steel operation (the profitability of steel has not changed). The profitability of oil has increased so we would likely see an increase in investment for firm B in oil exploration.

7. a. This will decrease profits, decrease profit per unit of capital and, therefore, reduce investment.
b. This will increase sales and increase profits. Profit per unit of capital will increase causing an increase in investment.
c. Given sales, the lower is capital, the higher is profit per unit of capital. Investment will increase.

8. a. To maintain the ratio of capital to sales of 4, this $20 million permanent increase in sales (and output) will cause firms to increase investment by $80 million to achieve the needed increase in investment to maintain the capital-to-sales ratio. In short, I will increase by $80 million in t. Consumption, on the other hand, will increase at most by $20 million (given that the change is perceived to be permanent). If the change in sales/income is believed to be partially temporary, consumption will increase less than $20 million. I changes more than C.
b. The capital stock will increase by $80 million.
c. The initial increase in sales increased profit per unit of capital. As the capital stock increases, however, profit per unit of capital (given the higher sales) will decline to its normal level.

9. Sales will fall. Profit per unit of capital will fall; therefore, investment will fall. The drop in investment will cause the capital stock to fall.

MULTIPLE CHOICE QUESTIONS

1. D 2. B 3. D 4. D 5. B 6. C 7. E 8. D 9. B 10. A 11. B 12. C 13. A 14 D 15. A 16. D 17. C 18. C

CHAPTER 17

REVIEW PROBLEMS

1. Note: If the curve or variable is not listed, it does not change.
a. reduces nonhuman wealth; causes a reduction in consumption; causes a leftward shift in the IS curve
b. increases the present value of after-tax profits; increases investment; causes a rightward shift in the IS curve
c. increases human wealth; increases consumption; causes a rightward shift in the IS curve
d. reduces investment; causes a leftward shift in the IS curve
e. LM shifts down
f. increases nonhuman wealth; increases present value of after-tax profits; increases investment; increases consumption; causes a rightward shift in the IS curve
g. decreases human wealth and, therefore, consumption; decreases expectations of future profits and, therefore, investment; IS shifts to left
h. IS shifts to the right

2. a. future LM curve shifts up causing Y'^e to fall and r'^e to increase
b. future IS curve shifts to the right causing Y'^e to increase and r'^e to increase
c. future IS curve shifts to the right causing Y'^e to increase and r'^e to increase

3. a. The size of the multiplier depends on the size of the effect of a change in current income on current spending.
b. A change in current income, with expectations of future income unchanged, is unlikely to have a large effect on current spending. This causes a small multiplier to exist.

4. a. The present value of human wealth falls causing a reduction in consumption. Also, the present value of profits falls causing a reduction in investment.
b. Given expectations of future interest rates, changes in the current interest rate are likely to have small effects on the present value of human wealth and small effects on the present value of profits. Thus, the effects of changes in the current interest rate on current spending are likely smaller.

5. a. The IS curve is steeper for two reasons. First, the effects of changes in the current interest rate on consumption and investment are now smaller. Second, given any change in current spending, the multiplier is also smaller. For these two reasons, a given reduction in the current interest rate will have a smaller effect on output (the IS curve is steeper).
b. No effect!

6. I will not include the graphs here.
a. This event causes C and I to increase resulting in a rightward shift in the IS curve; there is no shift in the LM curve. The shift in the current IS curve causes Y and r to increase.
b. The exact opposite of a.
c. Consumption will increase because of the increase in human wealth. Firms may also increase investment as they revise upwards their expectations of future profits (caused by the increase in Y'^e). The increase in C and I causes a rightward shift in the IS curve. Y and r both increase; the LM curve does not shift.
d. The exact opposite of c.

7. I will not include the graphs here. Hint: you must first examine how each event affects the future r and Y.

a. This will cause r'^e to fall and Y'^e to increase. The lower future r will cause current C and I to increase. The higher future Y will have the same effect. The increase in C and I will cause the IS curve to shift to the right and r and Y will increase.

b. This will cause both r'^e and Y'^e to increase. The higher future Y will cause current C and current I to increase. The increase in C and I will cause the IS curve to shift to the right. However, the higher future r will cause current C and current I to fall. This will tend to cause the IS curve to shift to the left. The effects on the position of the current IS curve are ambiguous. If the combined effects cause the IS curve to shift to the right, Y and r increase. If the combined effects cause the IS curve to shift to the left, Y and r decrease.

c. This is the opposite of b. This event will cause both r'^e and Y'^e to fall. The remainder of the analysis is the exact opposite of that included in b.

8. a. The future IS curve shifts to the right as future G increases. The future r will not change because of the Fed policy. Future output will be higher.

b. The increase in future Y (caused by the increase in G and Fed response) will cause an increase in both current consumption and current investment. This will cause the IS curve to shift to the right (there is no shift in the LM curve), Y to increase and r to increase.

9. a. The future IS curve shifts to the right as future G increases. The Fed, to keep Y constant, will reduce the future money supply which shifts the LM curve up. The final (future) result: no change in future Y and an increase in the future r.

b. An increase in the future r will cause a reduction in both current C and current I. This causes a leftward shift in the current IS curve (with no shift in the LM curve). Both the current interest rate and current level of output fall.

10. a. The future IS curve shifts to the right as future G increases. There is no Fed response so the expected future r increases as future Y increases.

b. The results in this case are ambiguous. The increase in future Y would cause an increase in C and I and a rightward shift in the current IS curve. However, the higher future r has the opposite effect. Current output could increase, decrease or remain constant.

11. a. Current output will increase the most in #9 for two reasons: (1) future output increases the most in this case; and (2) there is no (offsetting) increase in the future interest rate in this case.

b. As seen in #8-#10, the effects on current output depend crucially on what individuals expect the Fed to do. In one case, current output falls; in another case, current output rises; and in the final case, the effects on current Y are ambiguous. The Fed response can affect future Y and future r, variables which also affect current economic behavior.

12. a. The increase in future taxes will cause the expected future interest rate to fall. As this occurs, the current long-term interest rate falls, causing the yield curve to become flatter.
b. The increase in future taxes will cause future output to fall. Note: Both the future r and future Y fall. The drop in the future r will cause the current IS curve to shift to the right. The drop in future Y will cause the current IS curve to shift to the left.
c. If the future interest rate effects just offset the future income effects plus the effects of this future tax increase in human wealth, there will be no change in current output since the current IS curve does not shift.
d. If the future interest rate effects dominate the future income effects plus the effects of this future tax increase in human wealth, the current IS curve will shift to the right and current Y increases.
e. If the future interest rate effects are less than the future income effects plus the effects of this future tax increase in human wealth, the current IS curve will shift to the left and current Y decreases.

13. a. The increase in current taxes will cause the current IS curve to shift to the left and cause current Y to fall. The expected future tax increase will have (as described in #12) ambiguous effects on current spending and current output.
b. If the expectation of an increase in future taxes would have caused current Y to increase, output will fall even further if financial markets do not expect T to increase in the future. If the expectation of an increase in future taxes would have caused current Y to fall, output will fall less if financial markets do not expect T to increase in the future.

14. a. The increase in future government spending will cause an increase in the expected future interest rate, a reduction in investment, a reduction in the capital stock, and, therefore, a reduction in future output.
b. There are three effects that you must consider. The increase in current G will cause the current IS curve to shift right; this would cause current Y to increase. The reduction in future expected income will cause reductions in both current C and current I; this would cause the current IS curve to shift left. And finally, the increase in the expected future interest rate will cause reductions in both current C and current I; this would cause the current IS curve to shift left. The final position of the IS curve depends on the relative magnitude of these three effects (it could shift left, right, or remain unchanged).
c. Yes, it could be recessionary. If the future r and future Y effects dominate the effects of the increase in current G, the IS curve would shift left causing current output to fall.

15. a. The increase in future government spending will cause an increase in the expected future interest rate, a reduction in investment, no change in the capital stock, and, therefore, no change in future output.
b. There are two effects that you must consider. The increase in current G will cause the current IS curve to shift right; this would cause current Y to increase. The increase in the expected future interest rate will cause reductions in both current C and current I; this would cause the current IS curve to shift left. The final position of the IS curve depends on the relative magnitude of these two effects (it could shift left, right, or remain unchanged).
c. Yes, it could be recessionary. If the future r effects dominate the effects of the increase in current G, the IS curve would shift left causing current output to fall.

MULTIPLE CHOICE QUESTIONS

1. C 2. A 3. A 4. B 5. D 6. D 7. D 8. A 9. C 10. C 11. C 12. A 13. A 14. E 15. A 16. B 17. D 18. D 19. C 20. A 21. B 22. D 23. A

CHAPTER 18

REVIEW PROBLEMS

1. a. It now costs 1.6 pounds to buy one dollar. The price of domestic currency has, therefore, increased.
b. On Monday, 1.5 pounds. On Friday, 1.6 pounds.
c. The value of the dollar has increased. By Friday, one dollar now buys more pounds (or, it takes fewer dollars to buy one pound).
d. Appreciated.
e. E increased.

2. a. It declines.
b. The value of the dollar has decreased.
c. A depreciation.

3. E = 1.5 one week ago. If the currency depreciates, E falls. If the currency appreciates, E increases.
a. E decreased by 10% to 1.35.
b. E decreased by 20% to 1.2.
c. E increased by 10% to 1.65.
d. E increased by 20% to 1.8.

4. Use the equation $\varepsilon = EP/P^*$ to calculate the ratio.
a. Plugging in the numbers, we get: 12/30 = .4 , 14/30 = .467 , and 16/30 = . 533.
b. It increases.
c. It will decrease.

5. Use the definition of the real exchange rate included in the answer to #4 here.
a. Plugging in the numbers, we get: .825, .9626, and 1.1.
b and c. It increases. Given P and P*, as the dollar appreciates (E increases), it takes more pounds to obtain the same number of dollars. With P* constant, the pound cost of U.S. goods will be relatively higher.
d. Real appreciation (all else fixed).

6. a. The real exchange rate is 1996 is (1.5)(1.5)/1.2 = 1.875. The real exchange rate in 1997 is (1.6)(1.65)/1.25 = 2.112.
b. 12.6%. The real exchange rate increased: a real appreciation.
c. The percentage change in E = 6.7%. A nominal appreciation.
d. The percentage change in P was 10%. The percentage change in P* was 4.2%.
e. The nominal appreciation was less than the real appreciation. P increased more than P* so the effects of the nominal appreciation on the real exchange rate were magnified by the relatively greater increase in the price (in dollars) of domestic goods.

7. E decreases by 5% and P and P* are both increasing.
a. If the real exchange rate appreciates (increases) while the nominal exchange rate depreciates (falls), this implies that P must be increasing at a rate at least 5% above the rate of increase in P*. The more than 5% higher rate of inflation in the domestic economy more than offsets the nominal depreciation.
b. Not clear. There are two cases. Case 1: Foreign country is experiencing the higher rate of inflation. This would cause the real depreciation to be even greater. Case 2: Inflation in the domestic economy is greater than in the foreign country; however, the differential must be less than 5% to prevent a real appreciation.
c. The nominal depreciation of 5% would cause, all else fixed, a 5% real depreciation; however, both P and P* are increasing AND the real exchange rate does not change. What is happening? The rate of inflation in the domestic economy must be exactly 5% lower than in the foreign country to offset the increase in P* AND the nominal depreciation.

8. Use the following equation: $i = i^* - (E^e - E)/E$.
a. $i = .10 - (1.4 – 1.5)/1.5 = .167$ (or, 16.7%).
b. No, $i > i^*$. Despite this, the bonds offer the same expected return. When you buy U.K. bonds, you will receive pounds that will appreciate over the course of the year. The expected depreciation of the dollar (appreciation of the pound) offsets the interest rate differential.

9. Use the equation included in the answer to #8.
a. They expect an appreciation. The expected appreciation is 2% (E is expected to rise by 2%). i must be .06 - .02 = 4%.
b. Appreciate. The expected appreciation is 3.3% (E will rise by 3.3%). i must be .06 - .033 = 2.7%.
c. They expect a depreciation. The expected depreciation is 3.3%. i must be .06 + .033 = 9.3%.

10. i is greater than i*. The expected depreciation of the dollar (appreciation of the mark) offsets the interest rate differential to satisfy the arbitrage relation.

11. i is less than i*. The expected appreciation of the dollar (depreciation of the mark) offsets the interest rate differential to satisfy the arbitrage relation.

12. a. foreign b. foreign c. foreign d. foreign e. they both offer the same expected returns f. foreign g. foreign h. domestic i. domestic j. they both offer the same expected returns

MULTIPLE CHOICE QUESTIONS

1. D 2. D 3. C 4. A 5. D 6. A 7. B 8. C 9. E 10. A 11. B 12. B 13. C 14. D 15. A 16. C 17. C 18. D 19. B 20. D 21. B 22. F 23. E

CHAPTER 19

REVIEW PROBLEMS

1. a. domestic demand = C + I + G = 2000; demand for domestic goods = C + I + G + (X – IM/ε) = 2050. The difference is 50. X - IM = 50. They are the same.
b. Domestic demand does not change: 2000; demand for domestic goods = 1950. The difference is -50. X - IM = -50. They are the same.
c. Domestic demand does not change: 2000; demand for domestic goods = 2000. There is no difference. X - IM = 0.
d. The demand for domestic goods is greater than domestic demand when X > IM (a trade surplus). The demand for domestic goods is less than domestic demand when X < IM (a trade deficit). The demand for domestic goods equals domestic demand when X = IM (a trade balance).

2. Simply plug in the numbers (given the equilibrium condition) and solve.
a. Y = Z = 1200/.5 = 2400.
b. C = 500 + .5(2400 - 400) = 1500
I = 500 - 100 + .1(2400) = 640
X = 100
IM = .1(2400) + 100 = 340
c. NX = -240, a trade deficit.
d. Jumping some steps, we have Y = 1300 + .5Y; Y = 1300/.5 = 2600. Y increases by 200 given the 100 increase in G; so, the multiplier is 2.
e. IM = .1(2600) + 100 = 360. X does not change; therefore, there is now a larger trade deficit (NX = -260).

3. a. Again, jumping some steps, we have: Y = 1200 + .5Y + .1Y - .2Y. So, Y = 1200 + .4Y; Y = 1200/.6 = 2000.
b. C = 1300
I = 600
X = 100
IM = 500
c. A trade deficit of 400 now exists (IM - X = 400).
d. Y = 1300/.6 = 2166.7. The increase in G causes Y to increase by 166.7. Every one dollar increase in G causes Y to increase by 1.667.

4. The change in Y is smaller in #3 because the marginal propensity to import is higher. As the marginal propensity to import increases, a greater portion of any given change in Y will fall on foreign goods, thus reducing the effects on Y.

5. a. Demand for domestic goods rises; ZZ shifts up; Y increases; X does not change; IM increases; NX falls; we move along the NX line (no shift).

b. Demand for domestic goods falls; ZZ shifts down; Y falls; X does not change; IM falls; NX increases; we move along the NX line (no shift).

c. X falls so the demand for domestic goods falls; ZZ shifts down; Y falls; X falls; IM falls with Y; NX falls; NX line shifts down.

d. X decreases and IM rises so the demand for domestic goods falls; ZZ shifts down; Y falls; NX falls; the NX line shifts down.

e. The reduction in the real exchange rate causes an increase in NX. The increase in NX combined with the increase in G causes the demand for domestic goods to increase; ZZ shifts up; Y increases; the depreciation causes the NX line to shift up; X increases because of the depreciation; IM falls because of the depreciation (all else fixed); the final effects on NX are ambiguous since the depreciation and increase in G have competing effects.

6. a. A reduction in G or increase in T will cause Y to fall and IM will fall. This will reduce the trade deficit.

b. A depreciation will make domestic goods relatively cheaper. NX will increase and the trade deficit will shrink. Y will increase.

c. Expansionary fiscal policy. For example, if foreign governments were to increase G or cut T, Y* would increase. As Y* increases, X increases. Y will increase.

7. An increase in G by itself will increase Y. However, IM will increase causing a trade deficit. A depreciation by itself will raise output but cause a trade surplus. So, the government will have to combine a fiscal expansion with a depreciation.

8. Depreciate the currency. This stimulates Y AND increases NX. If the depreciation cannot be used to achieve the exact level of output with trade balance, a depreciation combined with a change in fiscal policy will be needed.

9. An appreciation will cause the drop in Y but it will reduce the trade surplus. A cut in G will cause Y to fall but it will cause the trade surplus to increase (as IM falls). So, a combination of the two will be needed: contractionary fiscal policy and appreciation of the currency.

10. a. See the graph. The economy moves from point A to B. Since the Marshall-Lerner condition does NOT hold, a depreciation will cause NX to fall, the NX line to shift down and the ZZ line to shift down (the size of the shifts in ZZ and NX will be the same). Such a policy will cause Y to fall to Y'. At the new level of output, the trade deficit has increased.

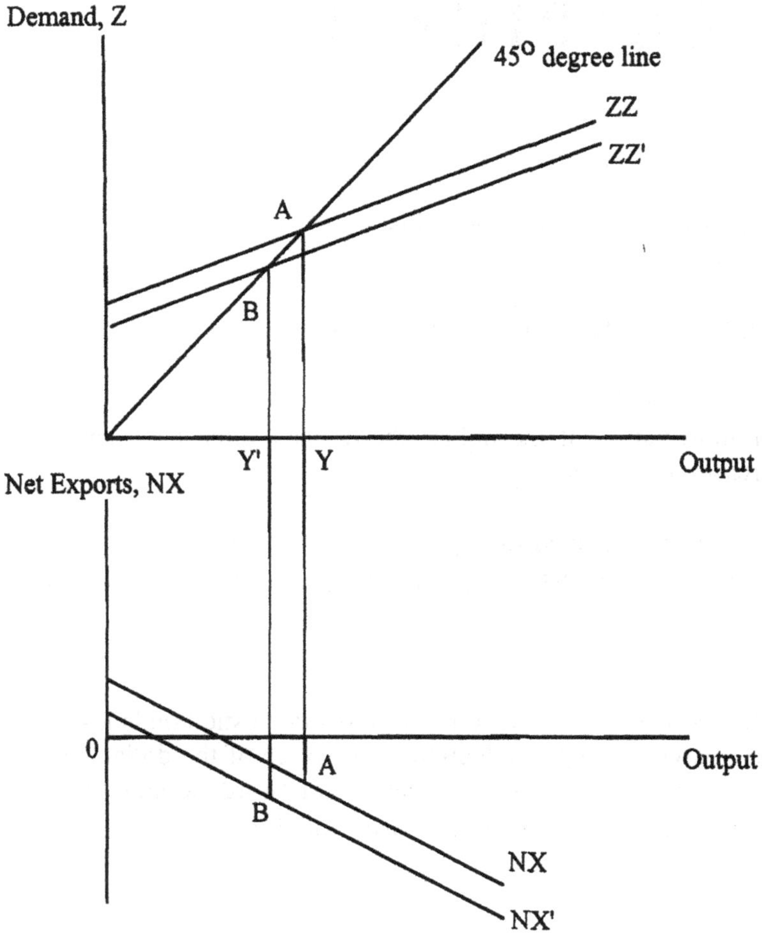

b. An appreciation would cause an increase in Y. Even though the quantities of X and IM would fall, the price effects would dominate causing an increase in NX and, therefore, an increase in ZZ and Y.

11. a. No. The price effect dominates the quantity effect.
b. No. The price effect dominates the quantity effect.
c. Yes. The quantity effect dominates the price effect.
d. Yes. The quantity effect dominates the price effect.
e. Yes. The quantity effect dominates the price effect.

12. a. NX falls; Y falls; S falls (as Y falls); I falls (as Y falls).
b. Y increases; S increases; NX falls (as IM increases); I increases.
c. NX falls; Y falls; S falls (as Y falls); I falls (as Y falls).
d. Y falls; S falls; I falls; and NX increases (as IM falls).
e. NX falls as a result of the drop in Y* (all else fixed); but, Y falls because of the drop in G; this drop in Y will cause IM to fall and NX to increase; total effects on NX are ambiguous; S falls (as Y falls); I falls (as Y falls).

MULTIPLE CHOICE QUESTIONS

1. A 2. B 3. E 4. D 5. C 6. C 7. A 8. B 9. A 10. A 11. B 12. E 13. C 14. B 15. A 16. C 17. B 18. D 19. A

CHAPTER 20

REVIEW PROBLEMS

1. Use the following interest parity condition to answer this: $i = i^* - (E^e - E)/E$.
a. Plug in the numbers and we get: 1.225.
b. E = 1.238.
c. This should (?!) be easy. If $i = i^*$, we know that $E = E^e = 1.25$.
d. E = 1.263.
e. As i increases, E will rise (appreciate).
f. The higher E reflects an appreciation of the dollar; the dollar's value has increased. The pound's value, therefore, decreases as i increases.

2. a. Suppose $i < i^*$. The dollar is expected to appreciate. If i increases, E rises today and, therefore, does not have to rise as far given E^e. Therefore, the size of the expected appreciation decreases as i increases.
b. It increases.

3. Assume interest parity initially holds. A reduction in i makes domestic bonds less attractive. The demand for the dollar decreases causing a reduction in the price of the dollar. The dollar, therefore, depreciates and E decreases. Hence, the IP relation is upward sloping. The dollar is now expected to appreciate (which maintains the interest parity condition given E^e).

4. Easy question!
a. .9
b. 0
c. 6%
d. Nothing. Since $i = i^*$, the expected rate of depreciation must be zero to maintain the interest parity condition (equate the expected returns on the two bonds).

5. The IS curve becomes flatter since there are now two effects of a change in i on the demand for goods. In the closed economy, the lower i stimulated investment which had a multiplier effect on Y. In an open economy the lower i still causes an increase in investment. There is now a second, additional effect on the demand for goods. As i falls, the dollar will depreciate causing net exports to increase. Thus, a lower i causes I and NX to increase. The effects of the lower i on Y will, therefore, be greater in an open economy.

6. a. The economy moves from point A to B.

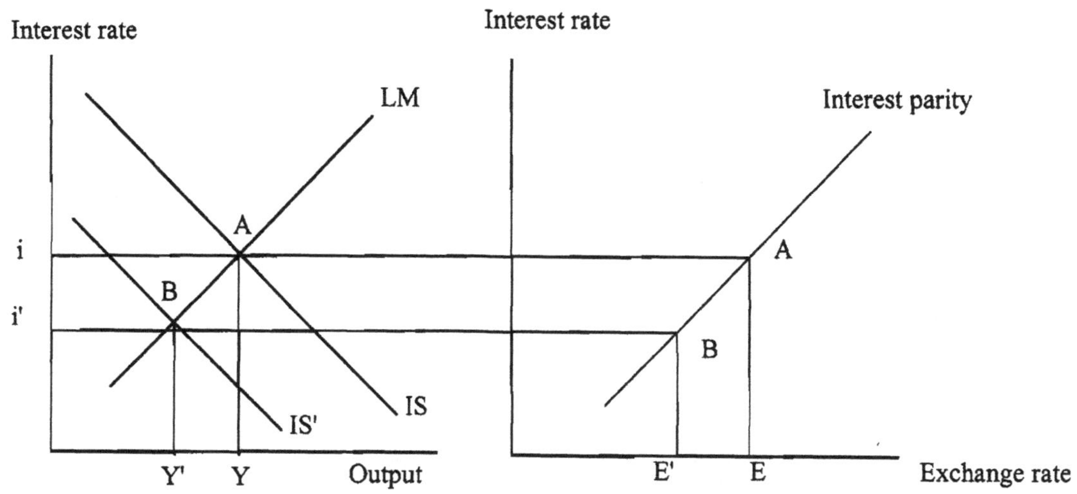

b. The IS curve shifts to IS' and i falls to i'. The decrease in G causes a reduction in Y. The lower i causes, via the IP relation, a reduction in E; the currency depreciates.
c. C will fall as Y is lower. The effects on I are ambiguous since i is lower but Y is lower, too. NX increases for two reasons: (1) Y is lower causing IM to fall; and (2) the depreciation causes NX to increase.

7. A reduction in the budget deficit (caused by either a reduction in G or an increase in T) as shown in #6 will cause lower Y and, most importantly, an increase in E; NX will increase. Therefore, a reduction in the budget deficit will cause (if NX is initially negative) a reduction in the trade deficit. This is the twin deficit issue.

8. a. The decrease in M causes an increase in i and lower Y. C will fall as Y falls. I also falls since Y is lower and i is higher.
b. Y falls. E will increase as i increases (the currency appreciates). E must rise to maintain the interest parity condition. In particular, as i increases, domestic bonds are more attractive which causes an increase in the demand for the dollar. This causes an increase in the price of the dollar (E rises).
c. Ambiguous! The lower Y (brought about by the effects of i on I) will cause IM to fall and NX to increase. The increase in E (the appreciation) will cause NX to fall. These two effects compete with one another! This is an issue not discussed in the text.

9. a. See the graph. The economy moves from point A to B.

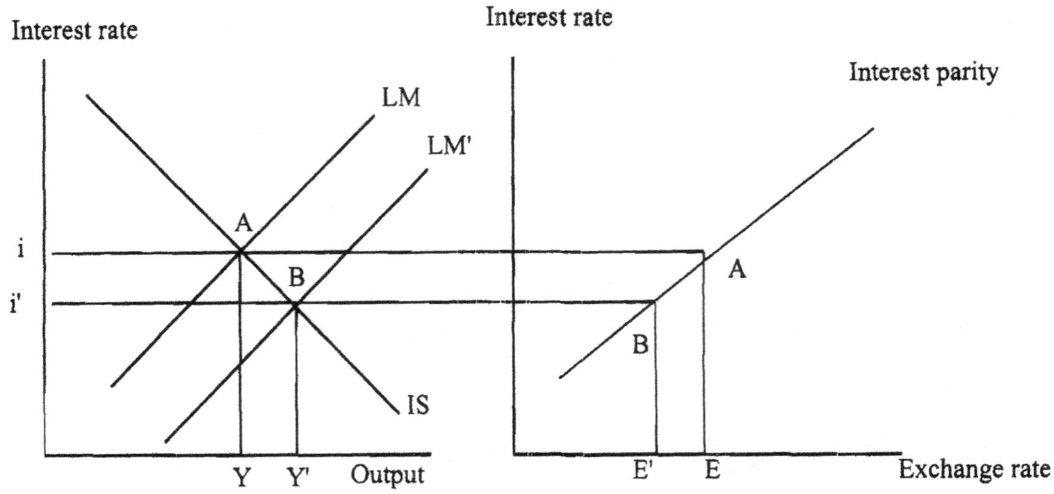

b. To maintain equilibrium in financial markets, i will fall. As i falls, the currency will depreciate (E falls). The depreciation causes NX to increase. As i falls, I increases. The increase in NX and I causes Y to increase to Y'.

c. Same old story! E will fall as investors move away from domestic bonds. This reduction in E is also required to maintain the interest parity condition.

d. The decrease in E, given E^e, will reduce the size of any expected depreciation. The drop in i causes a reduction in the expected return on the foreign bond. i*, however, does not change.

e. C increases as Y increases. I increases as i falls and as Y increases.

f. Again, ambiguous. The higher Y caused by the increase in I will cause an increase in IM. The depreciation will cause an increase in NX.

10. a. See the graph. The economy will move from point A to B.

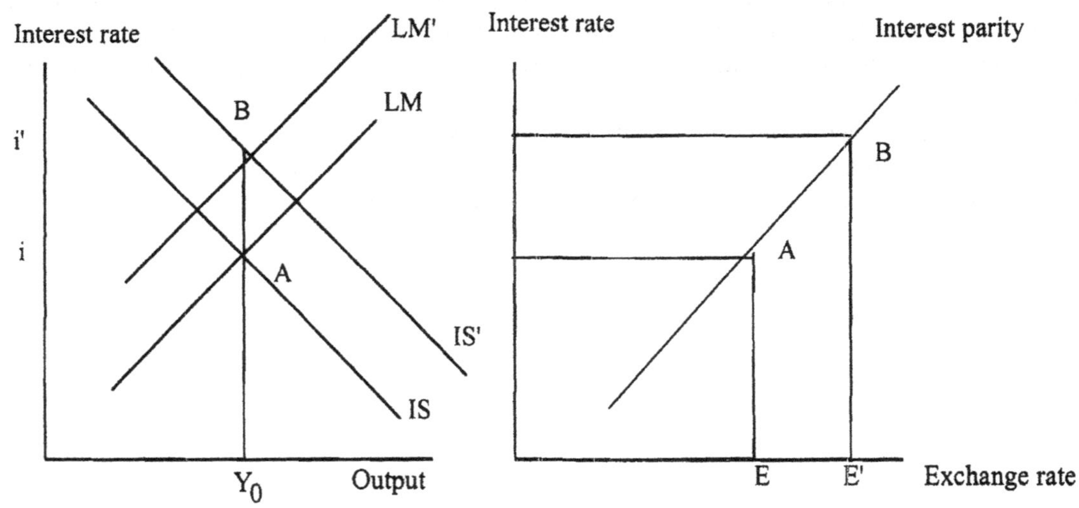

To keep Y at Y_0, the Fed will have to pursue contractionary monetary policy to completely offset the effect of the higher G on Y. The LM curve shifts left to LM'. All of the higher G must be offset (see below).
b. i increases and E increases (an appreciation).
c. G is higher. Both I (via i) and NX (via higher E) are lower. In fact, the increase in G is completely offset by the combined reduction in I and NX.

11. a. C is higher as Y rises. I is unambiguously higher since Y is higher. i cannot rise under fixed exchange rates so there is no offsetting effect of higher i under fixed exchange rates.
b. Nothing (it is fixed).
c. It gets worse, not because E changes (it does not), but because the higher Y causes an increase in imports and a further increase in the trade deficit.

12. a. See the graph. The economy will move from point A to B.

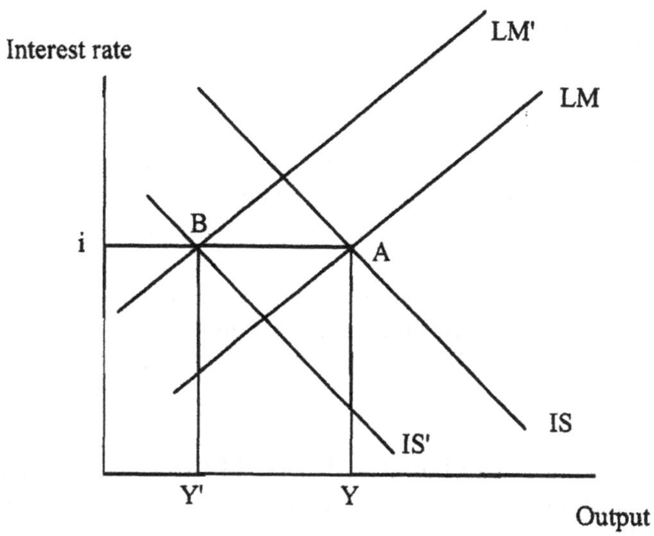

b. The central bank cannot allow i to fall below i* as the IS curve shifts to IS'. The central bank, therefore, reduces the money supply as money demand falls. The decrease in the money supply causes the LM curve to shift up to LM' leaving i fixed at its original level (which equals the fixed i*).
c. C falls as Y falls. I falls as Y falls.
d. The trade deficit will shrink (not because E has changed, it has not) because IM will fall as Y falls.

13. a. See the graph. Country A will move to point F (as described in #12). Country B will move to point G; i will be allowed to fall in a flexible exchange rate regime causing I and NX to increase and, therefore, partially offsetting the effects of the cut in G on Y.

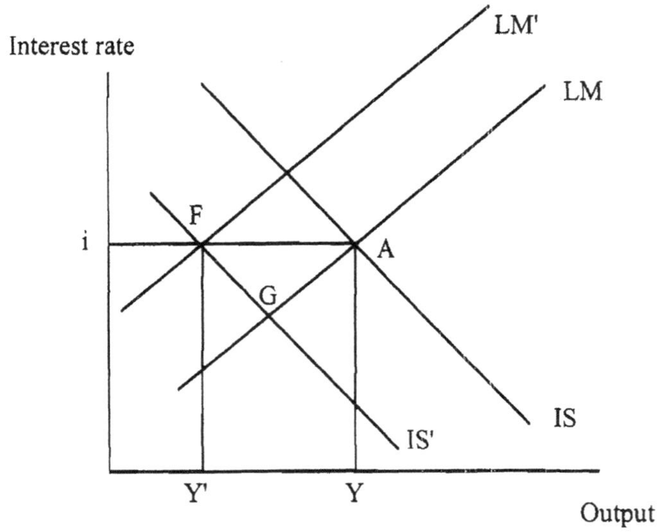

b. The choice matters! Under fixed exchange rates, Y changes more since i and E will not be allowed to change. Under flexible exchange rates, i and E will change partially offsetting the effects of G on Y.

14. Under fixed exchange rates, i must equal i*. If i* increases, the central bank will have to pursue policy to raise i. The central bank will, therefore, have to reduce M, causing the LM curve to shift up and raise i. This will cause I to fall and Y to fall. The IS curve does not shift here.

15. Y and i will not change. The central bank sale of bonds will cause M to fall and i to increase above i*. The demand for the dollar will increase since domestic bonds are more attractive. The central bank will be forced to "sell" dollars and buy foreign exchange to prevent the appreciation. It will continue to do this as long as i > i*. As it buys foreign currency with domestic currency, the monetary base and money supply increase causing i to fall back to i*. There will be no change in Y. The central bank has reduced its holdings of domestic bonds and increased its holdings of foreign currency.

16. Yes. Investors will not respond as quickly to the higher i (described in #15). As long as i is above i*, investment will fall causing Y to fall.

MULTIPLE CHOICE QUESTIONS

1. C 2. B 3. B 4. A 5. B 6. B 7. A 8. A 9. A 10. D 11. B 12. A 13. A 14. A 15. C 16. D 17. A 18. B

CHAPTER 21

REVIEW PROBLEMS

1. a. A reduction in P causes the real exchange rate to decrease. This real depreciation will make domestic goods more attractive so NX increases. The demand for goods will increase causing output to increase as well.
b. A lower P causes only a movement along the AD curve (the curve DOES not shift).

2. a. A revaluation causes $\overline{E}$ to rise and the real exchange rate to increase. This increase in the real exchange rate will cause NX to fall.
b. A revaluation causes the AD curve to shift to the left as the demand for goods falls.

3. Uncertain. If the real depreciation is caused by a change in $\overline{E}$, the AD curve does shift. If, however, the real depreciation is caused by a reduction in P, we observe only a movement along the AD curve.

4. A reduction in P causes a real depreciation, given $\overline{E}$. This real depreciation makes domestic goods more attractive. The increase in NX causes the IS curve to shift to the right and the equilibrium level of output in the goods market to increase. A lower P, therefore, causes an increase in Y.

5. a. A 5% devaluation will have no long-run effect on output. The price level will increase by 5%, thus completely offsetting the effects of the devaluation on the real exchange rate.
b. There are no long-run effects on NX. Output has not changed and the real exchange rate returns to its original level.
c. Devaluations have no effect on real variables in the long run. They will affect only the price level, leaving the real exchange rate, output, employment, NX etc. unchanged. It is for this reason that devaluations are said to be neutral.

6. See the graph.

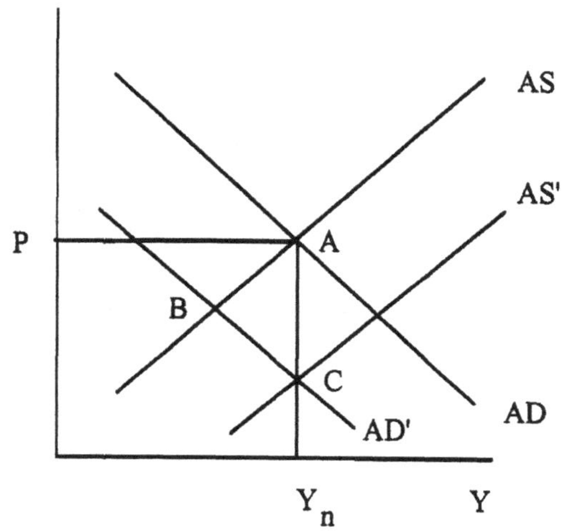

The revaluation will cause the real exchange rate to increase in the short run. This will cause NX and AD to fall; the economy will move to point B. P will fall in the short run, but not enough to prevent the real exchange rate from falling. With Y below the natural level, the AS curve will shift down over time. As this occurs, P falls causing the real exchange rate to decrease. Eventually, the economy returns to the natural level at point C. All of the effects of the revaluation have been offset by the lower P. Net exports and Y will return to their original levels.

7. This will increase AD and cause P and Y to increase. As P increases, the real exchange rate increases (i.e., a real appreciation). NX falls in the short run because Y is higher and the real exchange rate has increased. With Y above Y_n, the AS curve will shift up causing P to rise over time. P will increase and the AS curve will shift up until Y returns to the natural level. At the final equilibrium, Y equals Yn and G is higher. This increase in G has caused a one-for-one reduction in NX. Why? The permanently higher P causes a real appreciation which causes the reduction in NX.

8. a. P will rise over time as the AS curve shifts up. As P increases, the real exchange rate increases causing NX to fall. As NX falls, Y will also fall.
b. The government would have to reduce AD. To reduce AD (to bring Y back to Y_n), the government would have to revalue the domestic currency. This increase in $\overline{E}$ would cause a drop in AD and bring Y back to the natural level.

9. a. If you examine this graphically, your graph should be identical to the one included in the answer to #6. In the short run, Y and P fall. As P falls, the real exchange rate falls causing a real depreciation. As the AS curve shifts down over time, P continues to fall. As P falls, the real exchange rate continues to fall. In the long run, Y returns to the natural level and P is lower. All of the drop in G is completely offset by a real depreciation: NX increases.
b. The lower G permanently reduces the trade deficit through its effects on the real exchange rate.
c. The government should devalue the currency. This will keep AD constant and prevent the drop in Y.

10. a. i must rise to 10% to offset the 5% expected devaluation (and to maintain the interest parity condition).
b. The increase in i will cause a drop in investment. As aggregate demand falls, output will fall.
c. The government must either convince markets that it will not devalue (a very difficult task) or simply devalue.

11. a. The expected devaluation equals .5(0) + .5(10%) = 5%. To maintain interest parity, the monthly interest rate must increase by 5%. The annual rate is 12 x 5% = 60%.
b. The expected devaluation equals .5(0) + .5(20%) = 10%. To maintain interest parity, the monthly interest rate must increase by 10%. The annual rate is 12 x 10% = 120%. It gets larger because the expected devaluation is now greater.
c. The expected devaluation equals .25(0) + .75(10%) = 7.5%. To maintain interest parity, the monthly interest rate must increase by 7.5%. The annual rate is 12 x 7.5% = 90%. It gets larger because the expected devaluation is now greater.
d. It falls because investment falls.

12. a. It decreases. The expected devaluation, given the equal i and i*, causes the expected return on foreign bonds to increase.
b. It must buy its currency to prevent the depreciation as investors sell dollars to buy foreign bonds. It can do this only as long as it has foreign exchange reserves (they will be lost quickly with perfect capital mobility).

13. The higher interest rate depresses aggregate demand and causes Y to fall.

MULTIPLE CHOICE QUESTIONS

1. A 2. D 3. C 4. D 5. A 6. B 7. D 8. D 9. E 10. B 11. D 12. C 13. B 14. A 15. D 16. B

CHAPTER 22

REVIEW PROBLEMS

1. a. Consumption decreases, the IS curve shifts left, Y falls and r falls. LM does not shift.
b. Consumption decreases, the IS curve shifts left, Y falls and r falls. LM does not shift.
c. Investment decreases, the IS curve shifts left, Y falls and r falls. LM does not shift.
d. The LM curve shifts up, r increases and Y falls. IS does not shift.

2. They expect the price level to fall over time.

3. a. The real interest rate is simply i minus the expected inflation rate. The values of r will be: 2%, 3%, 4%, 5%, 6% and 8%.
b. r increases.
c. r increases.

4. a. The IS curve shifts to the left; the vertical distance between the two IS curves represents the drop in expected inflation. The LM curve does not shift. i will decrease, r will increase and Y will fall as the demand for goods falls.
b. The expected deflation causes the IS curve to shift left even further since the real rate must be higher. The LM curve does not shift. i will fall and r will continue to increase; Y will fall as the demand for goods falls.

5. If individuals no longer expect deflation, the real rate will decrease causing an increase in investment. The IS curve shifts to the right; again, the vertical distance represents the change in expected inflation. The economy moves from point A to B. i will increase and r will fall; Y will increase as the demand for goods increases. The LM curve does not shift. See the graph.

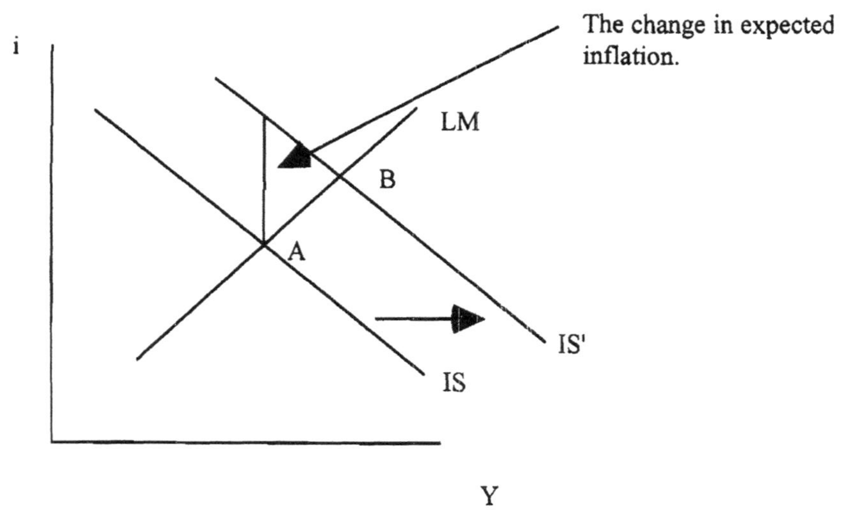

6. An increase in the proportion of money held in the form of currency: (1) has no effect on the monetary base; (2) will cause the money multiplier to fall; (3) will cause the money supply to fall; and (4) will cause the LM curve to shift up.

7. The real money supply is M/P. If M fell and M/P did not change, there must have been a proportionate drop in P.

8. The deflation causes the IS curve to shift to the left. The reduction in consumer wealth and increase in uncertainty also cause the IS curve to shift to the left. The effects on r depend on the size of the shifts in the IS curve. If the new equilibrium occurs at B, r does not change because i has fallen as much as expected deflation. This is the situation that I have depicted. This, however, will not necessarily occur. The final equilibrium depends on where that final IS curve (IS") occurs.

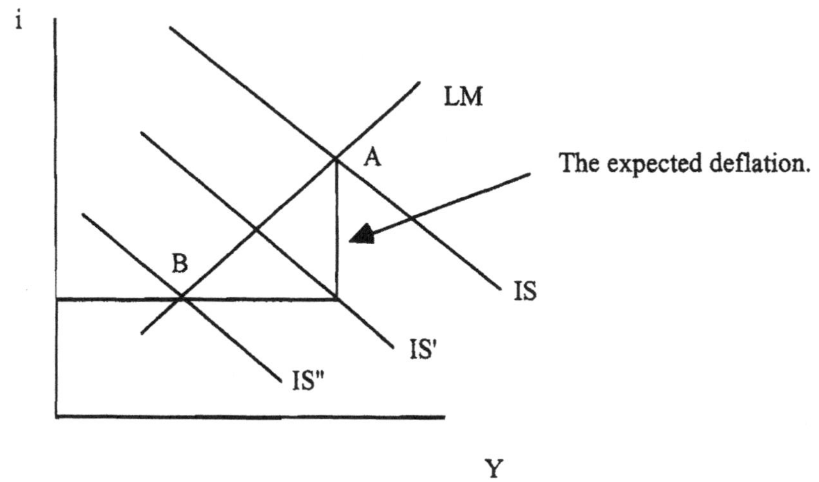

9. a. Expansionary fiscal policy (via a cut in T and/or an increase in G) would have caused the IS curve to shift to the right. If sufficient, the shift in the IS curve could have prevented the drop in Y.
b. Expansionary monetary policy would have shifted the LM curve down and caused r to fall. This could have prevented the drop in Y.

10. Yes. High growth rates were needed to bring down the high unemployment rate.

11. The deflation caused the real interest rate to increase. This caused the IS curve to shift left. The increase in r caused a reduction in the demand for goods.

MULTIPLE CHOICE QUESTIONS

1. D 2. B 3. D 4. A 5. A 6. C 7. A 8. A 9. A

CHAPTER 23

REVIEW PROBLEMS

1. Assume that the price index at the beginning of the first month is 1. The price index at the end of the 12 months will be $(1 + \text{monthly rate of inflation})^{12}$.

a. $(1 + .001)^{12} = 1.012$; $(1.012 - 1)/1 = .012$ -- a 1.2% annual rate.

b. $(1 + .002)^{12} = 1.024$; $(1.024 - 1)/1 = .024$ -- a 2.4% annual rate.

c. $(1 + .01)^{12} = 1.127$; $(1.127 - 1)/1 = .127$ -- a 12.7% annual rate.

d. $(1 + .09)^{12} = 2.813$; $(2.813 - 1)/1 = 1.813$ -- a 181.3% annual rate.

e. $(1 + .20)^{12} = 8.916$; $(8.916 - 1)/1 = 7.916$ -- a 791.6% annual rate.

f. $(1 + .40)^{12} = 56.694$; $(56.694 - 1)/1 = 55.694$ -- a 5569.4% annual rate.

2. Note: in both cases, the IS curve shifts to the right as G increases.

a. In option 1, we assume that the bonds are bought by individuals other than the Fed. This bond sale by the government, therefore, has no effect on the money supply. The IS curve shifts right and the LM curve does not shift. The interest rate increases and output increases.

b. In option 2, the Fed buys the bonds causing an increase in the monetary base and an increase in the money supply. The IS curve shifts to the right and the LM curve shifts down because of the debt monetization. Interest rates may not increase at all as a result of this. Output again increases (more than it will in option 1).

3. a. To calculate seignorage, simply multiply money growth and real money balances (which are constant). .01(737) = 7.37 billion; .05(737) = 36.85 billion; and .10(737) = 73.7 billion.

b. Seignorage increases as money growth increases.

c. No. In the long run, the higher money growth will cause higher inflation. The increase in inflation will cause nominal interest rates to increase. As nominal interest rates increase, individuals will reduce their real money balances. That is, M/P will not remain constant at 737 as money growth increases.

4. Use the same approach here as described in #3 to calculate seignorage.

a. When M/P is 800, seignorage is 40. When M/P is 600, seignorage is 30. When M/P is 400, seignorage is 20.

b. Seignorage decreases as real money balances fall. Seignorage is the product of money growth and the level of real money balances. All else fixed, as real money balances fall, seignorage will also fall.

5. a. As Y increases, individuals are making more transactions. To facilitate the purchase of these goods and services, they will demand more money. So, as Y increases, real money balances also increase.

b. As expected inflation increases, given the real interest rate, the nominal interest rate will increase. As nominal interest rates increase, individuals will reduce their real money balances.

6. a. Seignorage will increase. Since M/P is assumed to be constant, any increase in money growth will cause an increase in seignorage since seignorage is the product of money growth and the level of real money balances.
b. From previous chapters, we know that increases in money growth cause a 1-for-1 increase in expected (and actual) inflation in the long run. So, an increase in money growth will cause an increase in expected inflation.
c. As expected inflation increases, the nominal interest rate will also increase. As nominal interest rates increase, individuals will reduce their real money balances. So, an increase in expected inflation will cause M/P to fall in the long run.
d. The effects are ambiguous. On the one hand, the higher money growth will tend to cause increases in seignorage. On the other hand, as money growth increases, the higher nominal interest rates (caused by the higher expected inflation) will cause reductions in real money balances. This reduction in real money balances tends to cause seignorage to fall. So, the effects are ambiguous.

7. a. As long as money growth does not exceed 10%, the higher money growth (as shown in the figure in the text and in this study guide) will cause an increase in seignorage. The effects of higher money growth on seignorage offset the effects of the lower real money balances on seignorage.
b. We are past the seignorage-maximizing rate of money growth. Any increases in money growth will cause reductions in seignorage.

8. The inflation tax is simply the inflation rate times the level of real money balances.
a. The inflation tax is .10(500) = 50.
b. Seignorage is money growth times the level of real money balances. The inflation tax and seignorage will be equal only when money growth and inflation are equal.
c. The inflation tax will be greater when inflation exceeds the rate of money growth.
d. The inflation tax will be less than seignorage when money growth exceeds the rate of inflation.

9. a. M/P = 2000[.5 - (.05 + .10)] = 700. To calculate seignorage, simply multiply 700 by each of the rates of money growth: .01(700) = 7; .10(700) = 70; .25(700) = 175; and .30(700) = 210.
b. Seignorage increases as money growth increases.
c. Note: as money growth increases, expected inflation and the nominal interest rate increase. M/P will then decline as money growth increases. When money growth is .01, we have M/P = 2000[.5 - (.05 + .01)] = 880 and seignorage is 8.8. Using a similar approach, when money growth is .10, M/P is 700 and seignorage is 70. When money growth is .25, M/P is 400 and seignorage is 100. When money growth is .30, M/P is 300 and seignorage is 90.
d. Seignorage increases.
e. Seignorage falls. The negative effects of higher money growth on M/P now dominate the positive effects of higher money growth on seignorage.
f. Seignorage always increased in (a) because we assumed (unrealistically) that M/P would not change as money growth increases. If M/P is constant, higher money growth will always result in higher seignorage. M/P, however, will fall as money growth increases. At some point, seignorage will fall as money growth increases.

10. Orthodox include: a, b and c
Heterodox include a, b, c, d, and e.

11. In the short run, prior to any adjustment in expectations of inflation, a hyperinflation may cause an increase in economic activity. In the long run, however, hyperinflations will likely cause economic activity to fall as: (1) the exchange system is less efficient; (2) price signals are less useful; and (3) borrowing at a nominal interest rate is more of a gamble causing investment to fall.

MULTIPLE CHOICE QUESTIONS

1. D 2. D 3. A 4. C 5. A 6. A 7. D 8. B 9. B 10. D 11. B 12. D 13. D 14. A 15. A 16. C 17. C 18. E 19. C 20. D 21. E

CHAPTER 24

REVIEW PROBLEMS

1. A change in the money supply will have uncertain effects on output because we do not know: (1) how much short-term and long-term interest rates will change; (2) how much stock prices will change; (3) how long it will take for changes in the above variables to affect investment and consumption; and (4) how long it will take for the J-curve effects to disappear (i.e., for NX to increase in response to a depreciation).

2. Unemployment equals the natural rate of unemployment and the rate of growth of output equals the normal growth rate (i.e., 3%).

3. a. VAR b. Liverpool c. EEC d. tie: DRI and Taylor

4. Self restraint by policy makers represents policy makers who recognize the limitations of macro policy and, therefore, use less active policies. They do this recognizing that more active policies may be harmful to the economy. Restraints on policy makers represent restrictions imposed on policy makers. An example would be a constant-money-growth rule.

5. It is not clear if there are any advantages to such a policy. Because of the uncertainties presented here, it would be virtually impossible for a central bank to achieve this objective. Attempts to achieve this objective would require active monetary policy. Such fine tuning could easily cause greater fluctuations in output and employment.

6. a. This policy reflects the time inconsistency problem. Despite the stated policy, hijackings will likely continue.
b. This is the best of the policies. It would most likely result in the fewest of hijackings.
c. Not a great policy! Actually, such a policy might increase the frequency of hijackings.
d. The stated policy invites hijackings. Once they occur, the government does not negotiate which would increase the costs of the hijackings.

7. a. Recall that Okun's coefficient indicates how much the unemployment rate will change given a growth rate of 1% in excess of normal growth. If Okun's coefficient can take on values from .3 to .9, more growth (caused by the Fed's increase in the rate of growth of money) can have significantly different effects on the change in the unemployment rate.
b. Recall that α captures the effect of unemployment on inflation. Suppose this increase in money growth causes the unemployment rate to fall by 1% with certainty. Since α can take on a range of values, the effects of the money growth on inflation are unknown. For example, if $\alpha = 2$, the inflation rate rises by 2%. If α is .5, inflation increases by only .5%.
c. If both α and Okun's coefficient can take on a range of values, the final effects on inflation will be even more dispersed (i.e., uncertain).

8. a. Once firms and workers have adjusted their expectations based on this stated policy of the Fed (zero inflation), the Phillips relation becomes: $\pi = -\alpha(u - u_n)$ since $\pi^e = 0$. Now that wages are set, the Fed can reduce u 1% below the natural rate by accepting just 1% of inflation.
b. The actions described in (a) would not be consistent with its policy. The Fed, via expansionary monetary policy, has caused inflation of 1%, a result that is inconsistent with its stated policy of zero inflation.
c. Fed credibility would be lost (or at least reduced).
d. Here is a case where there is an incentive, once the policy has been announced and firms and workers have adjusted their expectations to it, to deviate from the policy.

9. While such a policy/rule would clearly impose restraints on policy makers, it would also prevent monetary policy from being used as a policy instrument. For example, the presence of such a rule would prevent the Fed from responding to a negative shock that causes a severe recession.

10. The table in the chapter indicates that there is a negative relation between central bank independence and average inflation. Since there is a positive relation between money growth and inflation, you should expect a negative relation between central bank independence and average money growth.

11. a. The presence of political business cycles would indicate that policy makers are attempting to (and succeeding!) increase the growth rate prior to an election. This suggests that we should observe the following during the periods prior to an election: (1) higher G; (2) lower T; (3) lower unemployment; and (4) higher growth rate of output.
b. No. The average rate of growth is lower in the fourth year of the Democratic administrations. This result is the exact opposite of what we would expect if political business cycles existed.

12. Since Republicans tend to care more about inflation than unemployment, we would expect relatively lower money growth during their administrations. Since Democrats tend to care more about unemployment, we would expect relatively faster money growth during their administrations.

13. a. The drop in consumer confidence causes a drop in consumption. The lower C causes a leftward shift in the IS curve, a reduction in the demand for goods and a leftward shift in the AD curve. The drop in AD causes a reduction in output and a reduction in tax revenues. The decline in tax revenues causes a budget deficit to occur.
b. To eliminate this budget deficit, policy makers will have to cut G and/or raise T. Note: either of these policies will cause a further reduction in AD.
c. The balanced-budget amendment requires that policy makers pursue contractionary fiscal policy while output is already dropping. This amendment, therefore, worsens the effects of the negative shock to AD. The output effects are greater, the recession worse.
d. This is partly answered in (c). Such an amendment would cause fluctuations in output caused by AD shocks to be greater.

MULTIPLE CHOICE QUESTIONS

1. D 2. B 3. C 4. B 5. B 6. C 7. A, B 8. C 9. B 10. D 11. B 12. B 13. A 14. D

CHAPTER 25

REVIEW PROBLEMS

1. a. Plug the numbers in the equation in the text. When inflation is 3%: .25(.13739) = .0343 = 3.43%. When inflation is 6%: .25(.2527) = .063 = 6.3%. When inflation is 0%: .25(0) = 0%.
b. The real value of the house does not change because the nominal value is assumed to increase at the same rate as inflation.
c. When inflation is 0, no tax is owed. Why? Because the value of the house did not change; she sold the house for the same price for which it was bought.
d. The effective tax rate increases as inflation rises.

2. Shoe-leather costs, tax distortions, money illusion and inflation variability.

3. a. Seignorage (and, therefore, lower borrowing or lower taxes), the option of a negative real interest rate, and money illusion which facilitates the adjustment of real wages.
b. The optimal rate of inflation will depend on one's views of the costs and benefits of inflation.

4. No. If i were negative, individuals would not hold any bonds; they would hold only money.

5. a. r = i - the rate of inflation. So, r is: 3%, 2%, 1%, 0%, -1%, -2% and -4%.
b. As inflation increases, the real interest rate falls (given i).
c. As r falls, investment will increase (so will consumption).
d. A negative real interest rate, especially in a recession, will stimulate investment and cause an increase in aggregate demand and output.

6. M1 is smaller than M2. Why? M1 is a component of M2. M2 also includes assets not included in M1.

7. a. currency, travelers checks, and checkable deposits
b. same as in M1 PLUS money market mutual fund shares, money market and savings deposits, and time deposits
c. time deposits

8. a. The demand for M1 decreases:

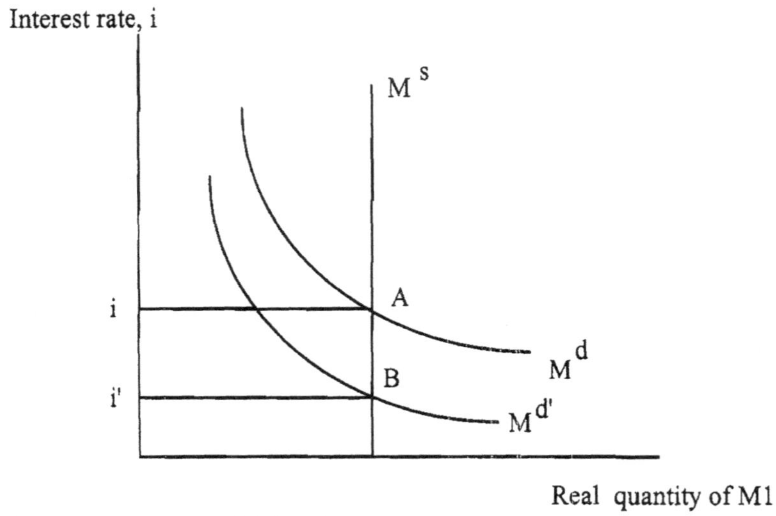

b. The interest rate will fall from i to i'.

9. a. The reduction in the demand for M1 causes a lower interest rate and a shift down in the LM curve. i will fall and Y will increase (go from point A to C).

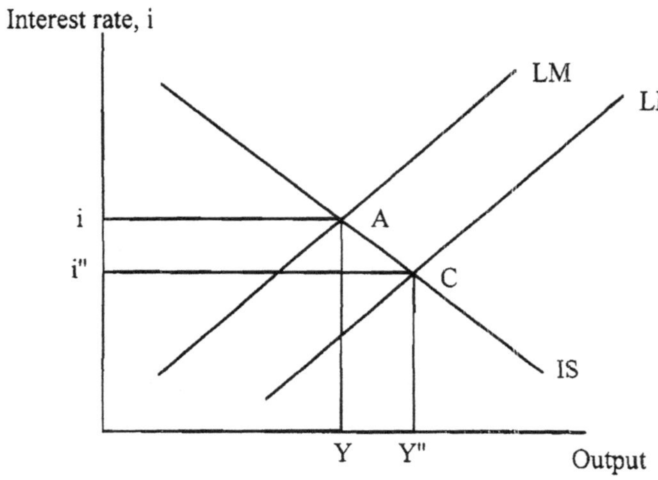

b. Aggregate demand increases, the AD curve will shift to the right and the price level will increase.
c. The supply of M1 did NOT change. The higher price was, therefore, not caused by a change in the money supply.

10. a. The demand for both M1 and M2 will fall.
b. As discussed in #9, aggregate demand and the price level will increase.
c. To prevent the increase in AD, the Fed must prevent i from falling. To keep i constant as the demand for M1 falls, the Fed should reduce the supply of M1. LM' returns to LM and AD does not increase.

11. The analysis suggests that changes in the price level (and inflation) will not always be caused by changes in the money supply. Therefore, the relation between monetary aggregates and inflation will not be perfect.

12. a. If inflation is above target, the central bank will raise the nominal interest rate. If unemployment is above the natural rate, the central bank will reduce the nominal interest rate. When both situations occur simultaneously, the central bank's actions will depend on the relative magnitude of the parameters a and b (in addition to the extent to which inflation and unemployment deviate from target). If a is relatively large, the central bank will raise i. If, however, b is relatively large, the central bank will reduce i.
b. In the extreme, b = 0. Specifically, the central bank will care about only the deviations of inflation from target. Unemployment deviations from target will, in theory, have no effect on the central bank's actions.

13. a. 12 b. 7, 14 years c. 12

14. a. reserve requirements, discount policy, and open market operations
b. (1) lower reserve requirements to increase the money multiplier and, therefore, M; (2) increase lending to banks to increase the monetary base, H, and, therefore, M; and (3) increase the purchase of bonds (open market purchase) which will increase the monetary base and, therefore, M.

15. (1) to send a signal about the Fed's intentions; and (2) to serve as a benchmark for judging the Fed's behavior.

MULTIPLE CHOICE QUESTIONS

1. D 2. D 3. A 4. D 5. C 6. A 7. A, B, C 8. C 9. C 10. B 11. D 12. B 13. C 14. E 15. C 16. B 17. B 18. C 19. B 20. C 21. D 22. A 23. B 24. B,C

CHAPTER 26

REVIEW PROBLEMS

1. a. 100 b. 55 c. 10
d. Nothing happens to the primary deficit as i increases. The primary deficit is G - T which is independent of the interest payments (real or nominal).
e. 100 - 55 = 45.
f. $B_t = 955$; it increases by the size of the correct measure of the deficit.

2. a. G = T which implies that T must equal 200.
b. $B_t = 900$ to keep the debt constant. Plug in the numbers in equation (29.3): 900 = 945 + 200 - T. T must equal 245.
c. $B_t = 0$ if the debt is to be repaid in full. Plug in the numbers in equation (29.3): 0 = 945 + 200 - T. T must equal 1145!

3. a. The official measure of the deficit (iB + G - T) does not change as inflation increases. It remains constant at 100.
b. As inflation increases, the real interest rate will drop (since i is fixed). The correct measure (rB + G - T) will be: 72, 64, 46 and 10.
c. Subtract the correct measure from 100: 28, 36, 54 and 90.
d. As inflation increases, the official measure becomes more inaccurate. As inflation increases, the real interest rate falls and the real interest payments decreases. The official measure does not capture this.

4. a. Plug in the numbers into equation (29.3): $B_t = 1.05(0) + 400 - 350 = 50$.
b. The debt at the end of t+1 will be 0 since the government repaid it! 0 = 1.05(50) + 400 - T implies that T must increase to 452.5 -- an increase of 52.5.

5. Plug the numbers into equation (29.3) to obtain the debt levels for the end of each period: (1) at the end of period t+1 we have 52.5; (2) at the end of t+2 we have 55.125; and (3) at the end of t+3, the debt will be zero since the government pays it off. Use the same approach to solve for T in t+3. 0 = 1.05(55.125) + 400 - T. T must equal 457.9 in period t+3, an increase of 57.9.

6. a. The size of the future tax increases gets larger. Why? The longer the government waits, the more interest payments have been accumulating on the debt issued when the taxes were cut.
b. The higher interest rate means higher interest payments and larger increases in the debt over time. Again, the tax increase will have to increase.

7. To keep the debt constant, the primary surplus must be equal to the real interest payments. If the primary surplus equals the real interest payments, the inflation-adjusted deficit must be zero to keep the debt from increasing.

8. a. The debt ratio in year t-1 is 1000/2000 = .50. The level of debt in year t is 1150; the debt ratio in year t is 1150/2000 = .575.
b. The debt ratio increased between these two years for two reasons: (1) there were interest payments on the previous level of the debt; and (2) there was a primary deficit in t.

9. The debt ratio increases when $r > g$ (when $g = 0$). The debt ratio remains constant when $r = g$ (when $g = .02$). The debt ratio falls when $r < g$ (when g is .04 and .06).

10. See answer to #9. The ratio increases when r is .03 and .04; the ratio is constant when r is .02; and the ratio falls when r is .01.

11. The debt ratio will fall if: (1) g increases; (2) r falls; and (3) primary deficits become primary surpluses.

12. a. Taxes will have to increase by 100(1 + r).
b. Recognizing that future taxes will increase and that human wealth is unaffected by this tax cut, individuals will not increase consumption. Private saving will rise by 100. Total saving does not change. The IS curve does not shift out since consumption has not changed. The interest rate and, therefore, investment does not change. Output does not change since consumption does not increase.
c. It has no effect.

13. a. No effect. b. It increases. c. It will fall. d. No effect.

14. (1) To pass on the burden of the debt; and (2) to reduce tax distortions (smooth taxes).

15. a. A higher r will increase the debt ratio since interest payments will be higher.
b. A lower g will also increase the debt ratio since output is not growing as fast.
c. The primary deficit would have to become a primary surplus. To do this, either G must be cut or T increased. Either of these actions will likely cause output growth to slow (g falls).

16. A country could cancel its debt. This would, however, make it very difficult to borrow in future. Who would want to buy bonds from a government that recently canceled its debt? Investors would require a very high risk premium which would cause the interest rate to be high as well.

MULTIPLE CHOICE QUESTIONS

1. B 2. C 3. C 4. D 5. A 6. A, D 7. D 8. C 9. C 10. D 11. A 12. B 13. C 14. D 15. B 16. E 17. A 18. D 19. E 20. E 21. D 22. D

CHAPTER 27

REVIEW PROBLEMS

1. The building blocks introduced by Keynes: (1) the multiplier; (2) the notion of liquidity preference (demand for money); (3) the importance of expectations in affecting consumption and investment; and (4) the idea that expectations can cause changes in demand and output.

2. a. Hicks and Hansen. b. Modigliani and Friedman. c. Tobin and Jorgensen. d. Tobin. e. Solow. f. Lucas, Sargent and Barro. g. Prescott. h. Romer and Lucas.

3. As the IS curve becomes steeper, a given reduction in the interest rate has a smaller effect on demand and, therefore, output. An increase in the money supply causes the LM curve to shift down and the interest rate to fall. The steeper IS curve, therefore, reduces the output effects of a given change in the money supply.

4. Yes, the Fed should announce it. Why? Under rational expectations, anticipated changes in the money supply do not affect output. If the Fed announces the reduction in the money supply and it is, therefore, anticipated, the lower money supply will not cause output to fall. The price will fall without a recession.

5. a. Here, the money supply increases 2% above expected. With the price level above expected, output will increase above the natural level.
b. Here, all of the 4% increase in the money supply is expected/anticipated. Output, therefore, will not change; it will remain at the natural level of output.
c. Here, the increase in the money supply is 2% less than expected. With the price level below expected, output will fall below the natural level of output.

6. Yes. The work of Fischer and Taylor about the staggering of wage and price decisions explains how output can adjust slowly even in the presence of rational expectations.

7. (1) competitive; and (2) fully flexible wages and prices

8. Output will increase when the state of technology improves (i.e., the economy experiences technological progress). Output will fall if there is technological regress.

9. (1) efficiency wages; (2) nominal rigidities; (3) imperfections in credit markets; (4) menu costs.

10. (1) aggregate demand affects output in the short run; (2) expectations play an important role in determining behavior in the economy; (3) Y returns to the natural level in the long run; (4) Y is determined by the size of the labor force, capital stock and technology in the long run; (5) monetary policy affects output in the short and medium run and affects inflation only in the long run; (6) fiscal policy affects output in both the short and long run.

MULTIPLE CHOICE QUESTIONS

1. A, B 2. C 3. B 4. C 5. B, C 6. D 7. D 8. F 9. C 10. B 11. B 12. A 13. A 14. C 15. B 16. D 17. C 18. A, B, D 19. C 20. A

APPENDIX. THE GOODS MARKET: DYNAMICS [OPTIONAL]

REVIEW PROBLEMS

1. a. 2000. They set production in t equal to demand in the previous period. This is the demand they expect to occur in period t.
b. Y does not change. Sales increase by 75. Inventory investment is -75. Consumption does not change.
c. Production will increase by 75. Consumption will increase by .8(75) = 60.

2. Firms expect demand in t+1 to be equal to demand in t. Firms, therefore, set production in t+1 equal to demand in production in t. Since demand in t is a function of Y in t (C increases as Y increases), production in t+1 will depend on Y in t.

3. a. See the graph.

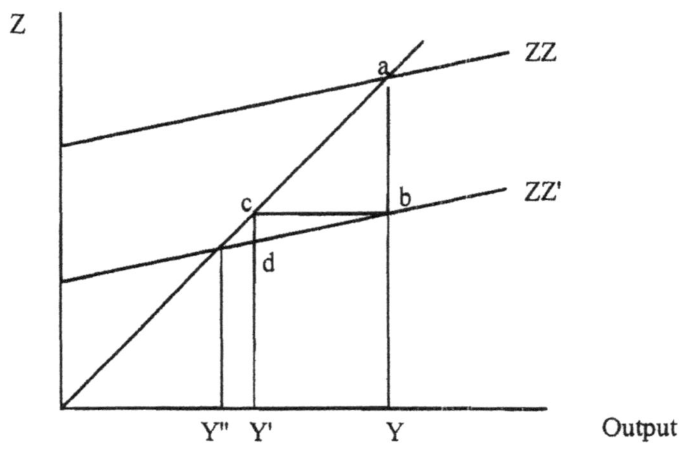

b. Output in t is Y. Sales in t equal the distance Yb. Inventory investment in t equal the distance ab.
c. Output in t+1 will drop by the drop in demand to Y' (the distance cb equals the distance ab). Demand in t+1 equals the distance Y'd. Inventory investment in t+1 equals the distance dc.
d. It will drop to Y''.
e. The size of the multiplier will determine the size of the drop in Y. This is determined by the slope of ZZ.

4. a. When $c_1 = .5$, we get: 1.9937. When $c_1 = .9$, we get 6.86.
b. The multiplier.
c. 2 and 10.
d. When the marginal propensity to consume (mpc) is .5, it does. When the mpc is .9, the number is still getting larger. If you were to continue the analysis, it would confirm your calculations in c.

5. a. $C_t = c_0 + c_1 Y_{Dt}$, and $Y_{t+1} = Z_t$

b. $I_t = \overline{I}$, $T_t = T$, $Y_{Dt} = Y_t - T$, $Z_t = C_t + I_t + G_t$,and $G_t = G$

c. None.

6. a. See the table.
b. See the table.
c. The multiplier is 1/(1 - .6) = 2.5. So, Y will increase by 125.

Quarter	Production	Government Spending	Consumption	Sales
		Quarter-to-quarter increases		
1997:1	0	50	0	50
1997:2	50	0	30	30
1997:3	30	0	18	18
1997:4	18	0	10.8	10.8
		Cumulative increases		
1997:1	0	50	0	50
1997:2	50	50	30	80
1997:3	80	50	48	98
1997:4	98	50	58.8	108.8

7. a. See the table
b. See the table.
c. The multiplier is 1/(1 - .75) = 4. So, Y will decrease by 400.

Quarter	Production	Government Spending	Consumption	Sales
		Quarter-to-quarter changes		
1997:1	0	-100	0	-100
1997:2	-100	0	-75	-75
1997:3	-75	0	-56.25	-56.25
1997:4	-56.25	0	-42.19	-42.19
		Cumulative changes		
1997:1	0	-100	0	-100
1997:2	-100	-100	-75	-175
1997:3	-175	-100	-131.25	-231.25
1997:4	-231.25	-100	-173.44	-273.44

8. a. $Y = Y_{t+1} = Y_t$ in equilibrium.
So, Y = 100 + .5(Y - 400) + 200 + 600. Y = 700 + .5Y; .5Y = 700. Y = 1400.
b. 0. Demand equals production.
c. See the graph.

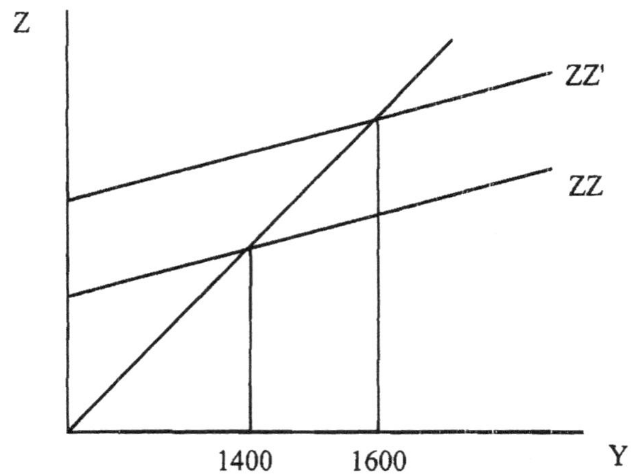

d. Production in t does not change. Demand increases by 100 in t. Consumption does not change in t.
e. -100.
f. The multiplier is 2 (1/.5) so the final level of output will be 1400 + 2(100) = 1600.

9. a. Y = 200 + .5(Y - 800) + 200 + 1000; Y = 1000 + .5Y; Y = 2000.
b. Production does not change in t. Demand increases in t as consumption increases in t. The tax cut causes an increase in disposable income in t which causes an increase in C. Y does not change since it depends on last period's level of demand.
c. Be careful!! Demand/Consumption increases in t by: .5(-100) = +50. So, inventory investment is -50.
d. The multiplier is 2; so, the change in output will be +100. The new level of Y is 2100.

10. a. .60.
b. Y = 100 + .6(Y - 400) + 200 + 600; Y = 660 + .6Y; Y = 660/.4 = 1650.
c. Y does not change in t. Sales increase by 100. Consumption does not change in t. Inventory investment is -100 in t.
d. The multiplier is 2.5; so, Y will increase by 250 to 1900. Or, Y = 760 + .6Y; Y = 760/.4 = 1900.

11. a. The mpc in A is .5. The mpc in B is .5.
b. The multiplier is the same in A and B: 2.
c. With the exception of the lagged nature of the consumption function in economy A, the economies are identical. Since autonomous expenditures and the multipliers are the same, the equilibrium level of output is the same in A and B.
d. Production will not change in either country since production in t+1 is set equal to demand in t.
e. In A, production will increase by 100 and consumption will increase by 28 in t+2. In B, production will increase by 100 and consumption will increase by 50 in t+2.
f. The effects will be felt more rapidly in B since consumption depends only on current disposable income. In A, it takes more time for the effects to occur since C is a function of lagged disposable income.
g. Y will eventually increase by the same amount (200) in A and B. The multiplier is the same and the change in G is the same. It just takes more time for Y to change in A.

MULTIPLE CHOICE QUESTIONS

1. A 2. A 3. B 4. C 5. A 6. D 7. D 8. D 9. B 10. D 11. E 12. D 13. D 14. C 15. A